THOMIST TRADITION SERIES

While his birth and death and everything in between remain confined to the thirteenth century, the intellectual legacy of St. Thomas Aquinas perdures to the present day. The Catholic Church continues to recognize the sapiential fecundity of this Doctor whom she invokes as "Common" and "Universal." God gave to the world through the wisdom of his Thomas a gift that does not expire.

There was only one Thomas. However, there have been many Thomists—philosophers and theologians who have assimilated the principles of his instruction and found the freedom that only the truth can provide.

The THOMIST TRADITION book series from Cluny Media arises from a dual conviction: (1) the thought of St. Thomas Aquinas contains an incomparable fullness of wisdom, and (2) the writings of the Thomists who followed him play a necessary role in mediating his wisdom to subsequent generations. Admittedly, those figures who constitute the Thomist tradition were by no means equals in regard to talent, influence, and renown. Moreover, their individual and collective contributions to the Thomist tradition elude facile comprehension or easy summary. Nonetheless, this series attempts to make available the key texts of figures—both classic and contemporary, major and minor— who rightly claim membership in the living tradition which bears the intellectual imprint of their master, Thomas.

The THOMIST TRADITION series makes these books available not merely as static works of antiquated value or anachronistic interest. Rather, the series is the fruit of our conviction that each Thomist has participated in a legacy perennially alive and perpetually relevant. Under this inspiration, each carefully selected volume in the series includes a new introduction that explains the book's original historical and speculative context. These introductions also outline their volume's enduring relevance to contemporary questions and disputes. Finally, the texts themselves have undergone extensive editorial review and certain footnotes have been added in order to highlight, explain, and clarify themes and passages of particular significance.

It is our sincere hope that this endeavor from Cluny Media will contribute to the renewed interest in the Thomist tradition among contemporary philosophers and theologians. For 800 years, Thomas and the Thomists have demonstrated unparalleled service in the defense and exposition of the saving truth Christ confided to his bride, the Catholic Church. The THOMIST TRADITION book series is designed both to honor that service and to provide the Thomists of today and tomorrow with resources for their own service to the Truth who sets us free.

Cajetan Cuddy, O.P.
General Editor

THOMIST TⓉT TRADITION

PHILOSOPHIZING IN FAITH

Philosophizing in Faith

Essays on the Beginning and End of Wisdom

Réginald Garrigou-Lagrange, O.P.

Collected and translated by
Matthew K. Minerd

THOMIST TRADITION
SERIES

CLUNY MEDIA

"*Among all human pursuits, the pursuit of wisdom
is more perfect, more noble, more useful,
and more full of joy.*"

~Saint Thomas Aquinas,
Summa contra Gentiles

THOMIST TRADITION SERIES

TITLES

* * *　　* * *

Metaphysics and the Existence of God
by THOMAS C. O'BRIEN, O.P.

What Is Sacred Theology?
by JOSEPH CLIFFORD FENTON

The Natural Law According to Aquinas and Suárez
by WALTER FARRELL, O.P.

Mary, Full of Grace
by ÉDOUARD HUGON, O.P.

Philosophizing in Faith: Essays on the Beginning and End of Wisdom
by RÉGINALD GARRIGOU-LAGRANGE, O.P.

Cluny Media edition, 2019

ACKNOWLEDGMENTS:
*For permission to translate the essays contained in this volume,
grateful acknowledgment is made to the publishers of the sources noted under
"Original Texts for This Section" at the conclusion of the Translator's Introductions
to Parts I–V, and to Thomas DePauw and Edward M. Macierowski.*

For more information regarding this title
or any other Cluny Media publication,
please write to info@clunymedia.com, or to
Cluny Media, P.O. Box 1664, Providence, RI 02901

VISIT US ONLINE AT WWW.CLUNYMEDIA.COM

ISBN: 978-1950970506

Library of Congress Control Number: 2019954102

Cover design by Clarke & Clarke
Cover image: Master of Imola, *The Nativity with Six Dominican Monks,*
1265/1274, miniature on vellum
Courtesy of The National Gallery of Art, Washington, DC

Contents

* * *

TRANSLATOR'S INTRODUCTION

O nce known as the "Sacred Monster of Thomism" and as "Réginald the Rigid,"[1] Fr. Réginald Garrigou-Lagrange, O.P., has experienced something of a renaissance of interest in recent years. Many people know Fr. Garrigou-Lagrange for his spiritual works, especially his two-volume masterpiece, *The Three Ages of the Interior Life*, as well as *Christian Perfection and Contemplation* and *Mother of the Saviour and Our Interior Life*. Those who are more familiar with his oeuvre have likely consulted his various commentaries on St. Thomas's *Summa*, and experts are likely well aware of his erudite fundamental theology text, *De revelatione per ecclesiam catholicam proposita*, as well as his tome of philosophical theology, *God: His Existence and His Nature*. In more recent history, the heretofore untranslated *Le sens du mystère* was published by Emmaus Academic as *The Sense of Mystery: Clarity and Obscurity in the Intellectual Life*.[2] Studies by Frs. Aidan Nichols, O.P.,[3] and Richard Peddicord, O.P.,[4] have also helped to provide context for this once well-known Thomist. While joy does not abound universally over some of these developments,[5] it is fair to say that the time is ripe for listening to the tradition of which Fr. Garrigou-Lagrange was a leading exponent.[6]

This present volume was born of my work on a variety of forthcoming translations to be published by Emmaus Academic (as well as personal work on sections of *De beatitudine*, which itself stands in need of a retranslation because of the abbreviated nature of the current

English translation). Every translator of a Frenchman must experience something similar to what I did. On many occasions, Fr. Garrigou-Lagrange's citations were so incomplete that I had to cast about to find complete details regarding the texts being referenced. Some translators (including those who have translated Garrigou-Lagrange's own works) seem to be so daunted by this task that they merely reproduce the partial citations that Maritain once described as being composed in "the rather off-hand manner which is customary among French authors."[7] As Maritain says in the context of the same remark, the details provided are clear enough to track down the source. On the whole, this was true for Fr. Garrigou-Lagrange—on both counts. His citations were "off-hand" in style but generally sufficient for research. However, I decided early on that I would attempt to rectify these citation shortcomings and provide full details for all content, so far as that was reasonably possible.

In the course of my translating and research into the sources cited by our Dominican theologian, I happened upon a surprising number of untranslated articles written by him, often of a philosophical character. I began to keep a list of these articles in hope that I may someday publish a

1.   These titles have been most recently reported in Tracey Rowland, *Catholic Theology* (London: Bloomsbury T&T Clark, 2017), p. 58.

2.   See Réginald Garrigou-Lagrange, *The Sense of Mystery: Clarity and Obscurity in the Intellectual Life*, trans. Matthew K. Minerd (Steubenville, OH: Emmaus Academic Press, 2017).

3.   Aidan Nichols, *Reason with Piety: Garrigou-Lagrange in the Service of Catholic Thought* (Naples, FL: Sapientia Press, 2008).

4.   Richard Peddicord, *The Sacred Monster of Thomism: An Introduction to the Life and Legacy of Réginald Garrigou-Lagrange, O.P.* (South Bend, IN: St. Augustine's Press, 2005).

5.   For example, see the recent remarks in Daniel Rober, "Engaging the Neo-Thomist Revival," *Horizons*, Vol. 42 (2015): pp. 262–94.

6.   This sentiment is echoed, to various degrees, in Brian T. Mullady, "Rehabilitation of Garrigou-Lagrange," *Homiletic and Pastoral Review* (April 1, 2009); http://www.hprweb.com/2009/04/rehabilitation-of-garrigou-lagrange; R. R. Reno, "Defending Truth," *First Things* (July 7, 2009), https://www.firstthings.com/web-exclusives/2009/07/defending-truth. Positively but less so in Robert Royal, *A Deeper Vision: The Catholic Intellectual Tradition in the Twentieth Century* (San Francisco, CA: Ignatius Press, 2015), pp. 133–35. More overtly positive is Romanus Cessario and Cajetan Cuddy, *Thomas and the Thomists: The Achievement of Thomas Aquinas and His Interpreters* (Minneapolis, MN: Fortress Press, 2017), pp. 130–32.

7.   Jacques Maritain, *Distinguish to Unite or The Degrees of Knowledge*, trans. Gerald B. Phelan et al., ed. Ralph McInerny (Notre Dame, IN: University of Notre Dame Press, 1995), p. xviii.

translated volume containing a selection of them. Later, when I decided to compile a full volume of these essays, I consulted the bibliography of Fr. Garrigou-Lagrange's works with the intention of compiling a series of themes that would bring to light new aspects of the theologian's work.[8] One difficulty encountered in compiling this volume was the fact that Fr. Garrigou-Lagrange often republished his materials. As I note in the preface to my forthcoming translation of *The Realism of the Principle of Finality*, this fact greatly vexed the young Yves Simon, who in a letter to Jacques Maritain exclaimed that the book was only a *per accidens* unity stitched together from journal articles by means of verbal artifices.[9] On several occasions while compiling the text you have in hand now, I discovered that I had produced a translation for a text that already existed in English. Thus, in my initial overview of his corpus, I somehow overlooked the fact that his paper, "The Physical and Metaphysical Applications of the Doctrine Concerning Act and Potency according to St. Thomas," was substantially included in *Le synthèse Thomiste* (known in English as *Reality: A Synthesis of Thomistic Thought*).[10] Likewise, the article "On the Universality of the Principle, 'Acts are Specified by their Formal Objects,'" was included in his commentary on the *Summa theologiae*'s treatise on grace.[11] Additionally, after noting his treatments of personality in relation to the Incarnation,[12]

8.   See B. Zorcolo, "Bibliografia del P. Garrigou-Lagrange," *Angelicum*, Vol. 42 (1965): pp. 200–272.

9.   See Jacques Maritain and Yves Simon, *Correspondance*, vol. 1: *Les années françaises* (*1927–1940*), ed. Florian Michel (Tours: CLD, 2008), p. 105 (July 30, 1932). Later in their correspondence, Maritain upbraids Simon for what Maritain diagnoses to be youthful ingratitude that does not take into account Garrigou-Lagrange's duties as a teacher at the Angelicum.

10. See Réginald Garrigou-Lagrange, *Reality: A Synthesis of Thomistic Thought*, trans. Patrick Cummins (St. Louis: Herder, 1950), pp. 32–49. Originally, Réginald Garrigou-Lagrange, "Applicationes tum physicae tum metaphysicae doctrinae de actu et potentiae secundum S. Thomam," *Acta primi Congr. Thomistici. Intern. Romae, 1925 habiti in: Acad. Rom. S. Thom. Aq.* (1925): pp. 33–52.

11. *Grace*, trans. Dominican Sisters of Corpus Christi Monastery (St. Louis: Herder, 1952), pp. 467–80. Originally, Réginald Garrigou-Lagrange, "Actus specificantur ab obiecto formali. De universalitate huiusce principii" in *Acta Pont. Acad. Rom. S. Thom. Aq. Et Rel. Cath*, Vol. 1 (New Series) (1934): pp. 139–53.

12. See Réginald Garrigou-Lagrange, *Our Savior and His Love for Us*, trans. A. Bouchard (St. Louis: Herder, 1951), pp. 92–100. Réginald Garrigou-Lagrange, *Christ the Savior*, trans. Bede Rose (St. Louis: Herder, 1950), pp. 119–72.

I later had the thought of double-checking his commentary *The Trinity and God the Creator*, wherein I did indeed find his "Concerning the True Notion of Personality" substantially reproduced.[13] Finally, he had tucked away "Universal Attraction—St. Thomas and Newton" in his discussion of the problem of pure love in *The Love of God and the Cross of Jesus*.[14] Alas, however, I had already drafted translations of several of these texts. Such is life!

Furthermore, there were a number of articles from the 1940s and 1950s that were quite tempting for inclusion in this volume. Often, they pertained to something surrounding the controversies over the "Nouvelle Théologie."[15] Upon reflection, I thought it better to leave these articles untouched for a possible future volume. The difficulties and ambiguities surrounding these controversies require a different sort of translational study. It is too easy for adversarial camps to form in these matters, and a level-headed assessment of Fr. Garrigou-Lagrange's involvement in the controversies leading up to the Second Vatican Council requires a very careful historical hand, and a lengthy, fair contextual exposition. Such an account calls for a separate treatment which includes the various voices in that debate, one which the French ecclesiastical historian, Étienne Fouilloux, has referred to as "the only theological debate of any importance at least in France, between the condemnation of modernism and the Second Vatican Council."[16]

---

13. Réginald Garrigou-Lagrange, *The Trinity and God the* Creator, trans. Frederic C. Eckhoff (St. Louis: Herder, 1952), pp. 147–56. The original was Réginald Garrigou-Lagrange, "De vera notione personalitatis" in *Acta. Pont. Acad. Rom. S. Thom. Aq.*, Vol. 5 (Rome: Marietti, 1938), pp. 78–92.

14. Réginald Garrigou-Lagrange, *The Love of God and the Cross of Jesus*, vol. 1, trans. Jeanne Marie (St. Louis: Herder, 1947), pp. 126–35. Originally, Réginald Garrigou-Lagrange, "L'attraction universelle (saint Thomas et Newton)" in *Philosophia Perennis. Abhandlungen zu ihrer Vergangenheit und Gegenwart. Festgabe Joseph Geyser zum 60. Geburtstag*, ed. F.-J. von Rintelen (Regensburg: Habbel, 1930), pp. 67–79.

15. For an honest history, although sympathetic to the "New Theologians," see Jurgen Mettepenningen, *Nouvelle théologie—New Theology: Inheritor of Modernism, Precursor of Vatican II* (New York: T & T Clark International, 2010). Also see Jon Kirwan, *An Avant-garde Theological Generation: The Nouvelle Théologie and the French Crisis of Modernity* (Oxford: Oxford University Press, 2018).

16. See E. Fouilloux, "Dialogue théologique? (1946–1948)," in *Saint Thomas au XXe siècle: Actes du colloque Centenaire de la "Revue thomiste," Toulouse,25–28 mars 1993*, ed. S.-T. Bonino, O.P., (Paris: Saint-Paul, 1994), p. 153. Cited in Aidan Nichols, "Thomism and the Nouvelle Théologie," *The Thomist*, Vol. 64 (2000): pp. 1–19 (see p. 2).

The present volume includes five main sections of content. The first contains two chapters on topics pertaining to logic. I have broadly called a second section, "Certain Questions Concerning Knowledge." Although current parlance might call this "epistemology," I hesitate to use a term that finds no parallel in traditional Thomism. This decision will be discussed more in the introduction to this second section. A lengthy collection of texts is found in the third section pertaining to moral and political philosophy. Following these selections, the fourth section presents what we might call "Garrigou the Critic," gathering five essays in which he directly defends aspects of Aristotelianism and Thomism against various modern philosophers and currents in early-twentieth-century thought. Finally, this volume closes by going to the edges of philosophy, presenting four texts containing reflections by Fr. Garrigou-Lagrange on the nature and relations between philosophy, theology, and the life of faith.

I will speak more below about the contents included in each section in the introductions I have included to each of these sections. These introductions are meant both to provide an overview for the reader and also to help situate the contents in a broader philosophical outlook.

In the context of contemporary ecclesiastical balkanization, I think it important to explain the reason for bringing this volume to press. The goal of the present volume is not only to present a past thinker but also to help in adding his voice to the Thomistic debates of today. During the iconoclasm of recent decades, the Dominican school of Thomism has been shunned as an accretion on the pure thought of St. Thomas. Today, there is growing interest in revivifying that school's thought, not as a kind of "Baroque answer book" but as a living tradition of philosophical and theological debate.[17] This volume intends to help in this process by presenting some hitherto unavailable texts of a master pedagogue in that tradition. It is not an ideological salvo but, rather, an invitation to give a fair consideration to one of the great exponents of the august Thomist school that for centuries defended the thought of St. Thomas in the midst of lively (and often contentious) debates. Indeed, if for no other reason, my canonical ascription as a Ruthenian

---

17. See especially the work of Frs. Cessario and Cuddy.

Catholic should prevent the reader from interpreting this volume as a kind of salvo in some of the broader, quite fraught contemporary battles being waged within the Catholic world. There is no small irony—I ever find such irony to be divine—in the fact that a Byzantine Catholic is translating a Thomist such as Fr. Garrigou-Lagrange. Nonetheless, I owe no small intellectual debt to him in my own intellectual and spiritual formation, much of which was passed in former days as a Roman Catholic, and I wished to help others benefit from so great a master. It is an act of filial piety—one not always encouraged by contemporary academia, ever ready to pressure intellectuals to present their thought as "something new" to tenure committees—to recognize one's intellectual forebears:

> And so too, it seems, should one make a return to those with whom one has studied philosophy; for their worth cannot be measured against money, and they can get no honour which will balance their services, but still it is perhaps enough, as it is with the gods and with one's parents, to give them what one can.[18]

Intellectuals—and philosophers and theologians in a particular way, given the great abstraction of their disciplines—owe their forebears an incalculable debt, part of which should be paid by recognizing these forebears' own thought instead of leaving it pass in silence under our own pens and, as it were, in our own names. Even if Fr. Garrigou-Lagrange's language is quintessentially Roman, much of his thought is of universal value and deserving of a broader reception. I have spent many hours with his work and am aware of its warts, weaknesses, and repetitions. And yet, I remain ever grateful for those many pivotal insights I owe to this great soul of a past era.

Unlike other writings by Fr. Garrigou-Lagrange, there is less in the way of scriptural citations in these essays. My procedure has been mixed in this regard. At times, I translate the citation by drawing from the Revised Standard Version, parenthetically noting that I have done so.

---

18. Aristotle, *Nicomachean Ethics*, trans. W. D. Ross, ed. Jonathan Barnes, in *The Complete Works of Aristotle* (Princeton: Princeton University Press, 1995), bk. 9, ch. 1 (1164b3–6).

On other occasions, it made sense to translate directly from the text at hand. In these cases, I do not include any RSV indicator in the parenthetical citation. Sometimes, Latin citations of scriptural texts are drawn from the Douay-Rheims translation. All citations from Denzinger are taken from Ignatius Press's forty-third edition of the text. At times, Fr. Garrigou-Lagrange includes Latin citations in his French works and French citations in his Latin works. These have all been translated into English. Also, on a number of occasions, I have filled out the details of Fr. Garrigou-Lagrange's citations, which as noted above, are regularly partial. Also, where available, I provide citations of the English translations of Fr. Garriou-Lagrange's works when he cites himself. As in other work that I have done on Garrigou-Lagrange, I have included occasional pedagogical footnotes to aid the reader in understanding this or that subtle point made by the Dominican thinker.

No work comes about without the involvement of many hands. Special thanks go to Fr. Cajetan Cuddy, O.P., who encouraged me to bring this volume to press when I had for long left dust gather on an earlier edition of this work, devoting no small energy in his review of the volume, even in the midst of his quite busy schedule. Similar gratitude is owed to the editorial staff at Cluny Media, especially editor-in-chief John Emmet Clarke. Further editorial thanks go to Mr. David Capan, whose editorial eye was, as ever, a great help for several of the essays included in here. Moreover, I express particular thanks to Matthew Levering for his kind personal support during so much of the lonely work of translating. I pray that many scholars in the Catholic world learn from his kind soul, ever ready to offer a kind word, even to an inconsequential "scholar" such as myself.

Thanks are owed to Thomas DePauw and E. M. Macierowski for allowing me to use their own work for an essay in this volume. I greatly desired to include this text in the present volume but did not wish to insult them by retranslating a text that they themselves had worked so diligently to bring to press in *Studia Gilsoniana*.

And finally, together, give thanks to God Almighty for the grace to begin this project and bring it to completion.

This volume is dedicated to my wife, Courtney, who suffers through so many financially unprofitable projects that I undertake, doing so with great grace and understanding. Without her example of holiness, I would perhaps get lost in all too many machinations!

Matthew K. Minerd
Feast of the Protection of the
Most Holy Mother of God, 2019

* * *

PART I

Logic

* * *

INTRODUCTION TO PART I

When I first reviewed Fr. Garrigou-Lagrange's bibliography, I was surprised to find the two articles that have been included in this chapter, especially the one concerning the method of pursuing definitions. Further acquaintance with his untranslated works (especially *Le sens commun*) removed this surprise, as he often returns to this theme throughout his works. Nonetheless, these two forays into topics of logic should be of some interest to any Thomist, for such discussions are not a frequent topic among most writers on Thomism, as a review of secondary literature well attests.[1]

According to the position generally accepted in the Thomist School, logic is a science of second intentions.[2] That is, it studies the particular kinds of *relations* that the human knower forms among *things insofar as they are known by us*. In our experience of the physical world, there are neither *syllogisms*, nor *judgments*, nor *definitions*, but all of these play a vital role in the way that we navigate the world of our thought.[3] Indeed, there is a vast domain of such relationships involved in all three acts of our intellect: the simple insight attained in reaching a definition, the complex relationship we form between two notions when we judge that one objective concept *is* united to another objective concept in some *thing* that is known,[4] and how we pass from the known to the unknown in our reasoning.

Because these relations are dependent upon our reasoning, they are called by St. Thomas and his school *relationes rationis*—a term that is difficult, given that "relations of reason" is a clunky literal translation at best. The same goes for the broader domain into which these relations fall—*entia rationis* is quite awkward when translated as "beings of reason."[5] As John Deely showed throughout his life-long devotion to the topic of *relationes secundum esse* and semiotics, *entia rationis* can be easily overlooked by what he called a "cyclopean" Thomism that focuses solely on predicamental being (e.g., substance, quantity, quality, etc.).[6]

1. See the comments in Robert W. Schmidt, *The Domain of Logic According to Saint Thomas Aquinas* (The Hague: Martinus Nijhoff, 1966), p. vii, n. 7. One sees the same dynamic in *Thomistic Bibliography, 1904–1978*, ed. Terry L. Miethe and Vernon J. Bourke (Westport, CT: Greenwood Press, 1980). The subsection "Logic, Grammar, and Epistemology" includes some logical topics among a mixture of topics that properly speaking fall into the disciplines of metaphysics (i.e., its critique of knowledge), philosophical psychology (i.e., the "metaphysics" or ontology of knowledge), and logic proper.

2. One can consult, of course, Schmidt's work *The Domain of Logic According to Saint Thomas*. This work makes about as good of a claim as is possible that this is the doctrine of St. Thomas, although Schmidt's work perhaps gives *more* clarity to Thomas than the Angelic Doctor himself expressed. In the Thomist School, for instance, see John of St. Thomas, *The Material Logic of John of St. Thomas*, trans. Yves R. Simon, John J. Glanville, and G. Donald Holenhorst (Chicago: University of Chicago Press, 1955), q. 1, a. 3 (p. 17–32); Jacques-Casimir Guerinois, *Clypeus philosophiae thomisticae contra veteres et novos eius impugnatores*, vol. 1: *Logica* (Venice: Balleoniana, 1729), *Logica Major, Quaestio praeambula (De natura logicae)*, a. 1 (p. 123–49); Antoine Goudin, *Philosophia iuxta inconcussa tutissimaque Divi Thomae dogmata*, vol. 1, ed. Roux-Lavergne (Paris: La Nouvelle Bibliothèque, 1851), *Logica major, quaestio praeambula*, a. 1 (pp. 76–85). A good overview is also provided by Angelo M. Pirotta in *Summa philosophiae aristotelica-thomisticae*, vol. 1: *Philosophia rationalis* (Turin: Marietti, 1931), p. 145–51. For a summary, see Matthew K. Minerd, "Thomism and the Formal Object of Logic," *American Catholic Philosophical Quarterly*, Vol. 93, No. 3 (2019): pp. 411–44.

3. Merely to note some: the five predicables (species, genus, etc.), extension (of terms), division (of terms), universality (of terms), opposition (of propositions), subalternation (of propositions), subjects and predicates (of propositions), form (of syllogisms), middle term (of a syllogism), conclusions (of syllogisms), etc.

4. On this topic, Fr. Garrigou-Lagrange was the source for important elaborations undertaken by Maritain and Simon. For the nucleus of their reflections, see Réginald Garrigou-Lagrange, *Le sens commun: La philosophie de l'être et les formules dogmatiques*, 4th ed. (Paris: Desclée de Brouwer, 1936), pp. 41–42. Also see John C. Cahalan, "The Problem of Thing and Object in Maritain," *The Thomist*, Vol. 59, No. 1: pp. 21–46. Also, see Maritain, *Degrees of Knowledge*, pp. 96–107. Yves R. Simon, *Introduction to Metaphysics of Knowledge*, trans. Vukan Kuic and Richard J. Thompson (New York: Fordham University Press, 1990), pp. 136–49.

5. See Robert W Schmidt, "The Translation of Terms Like *Ens rationis*," *Modern Schoolman*, Vol. 41 (1963): pp. 73–75.

6. See John N. Deely, "Quid sit postmodernismus?" in *Postmodernism and Christian Philosophy*, ed. Roman T. Ciapalo (Washington, DC: The Catholic University of America Press, 1997), pp. 68–96.

For the Thomist school, the unique thing about *relation*, precisely as a relation, is that it straddles the domains of *ens reale* and *ens rationis*. Relation is quite unique in the Thomist metaphysic, I assure the reader.[7] The character of human reason, making progress through history and in culture, is revealed in the domain of intentional or objective existence, and it is a vaster domain than many often suspect, though some Thomists have noted this vast *terra non considerata*—the domain of human thought and culture.[8] Fr. Garrigou-Lagrange was not fascinated with these vitally important topics, which are centrally important today, for we seem to live in an intellectual climate that would reduce all reality to socially constructed thought and culture. We are more worried about thought and method than with content and reality, and this needs sapiential adjudication. While detailed discussions of method are not the ken of Fr. Garrigou-Lagrange, these two chapters do bear witness to his concern with the fringes of such problems, in his own, very traditional way.[9]

In the chapter entitled, "On the Twofold *Via inventionis* and the Twofold *Via iudicii* According to St. Thomas," Fr. Garrigou-Lagrange reflects on how our thought progresses in reasoning from the known to the unknown. Although brief, this essay is pregnant with consequences

---

7. See Charles Journet, *The Wisdom of Faith: An Introduction to Theology*, trans. R. F. Smith (Westminster, MD: The Newman Press, 1952), pp. 203–204, n. 24: "The notion of relation can be found realized in its place among the other categories of being… But the notion of relation has exceptional privileges and properties. First of all, the notion of relation continues to exist even when it is deprived of all reality and thus passes into the purely logical world. These are logical relations or relations of reason… Secondly, the notion of relation continues to exist when the process is reversed by intensifying its reality until its reality is made to coincide with that of the Absolute."

8. See John Deely, *Four Ages of Understanding: The First Postmodern Survey of Philosophy from Ancient Times to the Turn of the Twenty-first Century* (Toronto: University of Toronto Press, 2001), pp. 350–58, 468–79. I chronicle a small bit of this in Matthew K. Minerd, "Beyond Non-Being: Thomistic Metaphysics on Second Intentions, *Ens morale*, and *Ens artificiale*," *American Catholic Philosophical Quarterly*, Vol. 91, No. 3 (Summer 2017): pp. 353–80.

9. One could also well argue that certain aspects of his lengthy *De revelatione* text also articulate many pertinent points in questions of theological methodology in the line of Fr. Garrigou-Lagrange's teacher, Fr. Ambroise Gardeil, whose various works on theological methodology bear witness to this stamp, a point noted in the introduction written by his nephew H.-D. Gardeil in "De la méthode dans le problème du réel," *Revue des Sciences philosophiques et théologiques*, Vol. 28, No. 2 (1939): pp. 173–203.

for one's approach to scientific knowledge (taking "science" in the Aristotelian sense). On the one hand, we can consider an architectonic pair of intellectual *viae*: first, the intellectual path to knowledge of God and, second, its correlative return pathway when all reality is judged in light of Him who has been discovered as the Source and Ultimate End of all reality. This theme is perhaps better known because of popular accounts of Thomistic thought. These metaphysically-oriented writers are always ready to note this sapiential journey undertaken by the metaphysician (and, in a higher order, by the theologian).

However, a second pair of *viae* are equally as important in the constituting of human knowledge in its scientific and sapiential forms. According to this second way of speaking, we can consider the investigation of a science's conclusions as representing a kind of *via inventionis*. However, in the midst of this journey of discovery, the scientific knower must also turn around, so to speak, and reevaluate these conclusions in light of the principles from which he or she set out in the *via inventionis*. This is the critical evaluation of a science's value, whether that science be established on *per se nota* first principles or upon postulates that function in place of such first principles. Today, discussion of this critical, reflective judgment of the whole of a scientific body would likely give Thomists a robust, yet traditional, vocabulary for discussing the development of the sciences and the phenomenon of scientific revolutions and paradigm shifts.[10]

The second chapter in this section has a rather direct title: "On the Search for Definitions According to Aristotle and St. Thomas." The text ostensibly is a commentary on a commentary: Fr. Garrigou-Lagrange's observations based upon Thomas's treatment of definition found in the second book of Aristotle's *Posterior Analytics*. The work of defining is incredibly important in any discourse. Without correct and clear terms, no amount of reasoning is of much worth: cheap flour makes wretched

---

10. This latter topic was quite popular in the second half of the twentieth century often in terms set by Thomas Kuhn (whether for or against him). See Thomas Kuhn, *The Structure of Scientific Revolutions*, 50th Anniversary Edition (Chicago: University of Chicago Press, 2012). I take up this topic in an essay forthcoming in *Nova et Vetera* (English edition) under the title, "Wisdom be Attentive: The Noetic Structure of Sapiential Knowledge," especially at its closing.

bread. In this essay, Fr. Garrigou-Lagrange only provides the scantiest outline regarding the methodology used in defining. Nevertheless, he makes some quite illuminating observations, and an outline is always needed before we get down into the details. What is most unique in this chapter is Fr. Garrigou-Lagrange's insistence that defining is an activity of the first operation of the intellect, of νοῦς (*nous*). On this topic, he cites with approval the Jesuit Fathers Charles Boyer and Joseph de Tonquedec, and because of his interest on this point, he includes in this chapter a bibliography by the famed Dominican logician, Fr. Józef Maria Bocheński, on the topic of Aristotelian methods of definition.[11]

This essay is of great importance. The discursive work of syllogistic logic usually gets the most attention when logic is taught in a traditional, Aristotelian manner (especially by Thomists, who lean heavily on St. Thomas's treatment of the *Posterior Analytics*). However, logic is the art of defining, dividing, and arguing. The most valid syllogism is worth nothing if one's terms are not defined. One ought to return to the *ars definiendi et dividendi* today to give it a much more robust form within the tradition of the metaphysics of logic of the Thomist School. Second intentions are formed even by the first operation of the intellect.[12] Without this definitional activity, we would not have the famed predicables of Porphyry: species, genus, property, accident, and, indeed, *definition*. Here, Fr. Garrigou-Lagrange provides the skeleton for future work.

What is more, we see a point articulated here that will be taken up again and again in Fr. Garrigou-Lagrange's theological works, namely, that the working model to be used when discussing doctrinal

---

11. Although I am primarily concerned here to note the implications in logic, this topic could be fruitfully related to the reflections undertaken in Robert Sokolowski, "Making Distinctions," in *Pictures, Quotations, and Distinctions: Fourteen Essays in Phenomenology* (Notre Dame, IN: University of Notre Dame Press, 1992), pp. 55–91.

12. It is a point admitted commonly by the Thomist school, as one can garner from any number of such exponents, including (but not limited to) John of St. Thomas, Jacques Casimir Guérinois, Antoine Goudin, as well as Hervaeus Natalis, a thinker of more dubious "Thomistic" credentials but on this point at home in the claims of the Thomist school regarding second intentions. On this, see my "Thomism and the Formal Object of Logic," cited above.

development should be the passage from *vague* to *distinct* in definitions. Though not the only possible model for understanding the nature of doctrinal development,[13] it is a rather understandable one to deploy, for doctrinal development finds its perfection in the form of *definitions*. One recognizes *in the Dormition / Assumption* the *same* idea as in older liturgical practices and statements concerning the Theotokos, she who is the Mother of God; however, *whereas it* was *vague* before, now *it* is now *more distinct*.[14] The *same* idea passes from a more vaguely grasped state to another, more distinct state of expression.[15]

Of course, all of this is but a mere initial foray into philosophical (and theological) issues of much greater difficulty. What is the "texture" of the intentional being, the *esse intentionale*, of sciences and definitions in a culture and in history? That question passes beyond what we get from Fr. Garrigou-Lagrange. Nonetheless, his insightful remarks do

---

13. See Fr. Garrigou-Lagrange's placement among the authors considered in Reginald-Marie Schultes, *Introductio in Historiam Dogmatum* (Paris: Lethielleux, 1922), pp. 287–96; also, see the work of Fr. Marín-Sola (who, holding that objectively inferential conclusions can be defined as dogmas, expresses a quite different position from that taken by Fr. Garrigou-Lagrange), in *The Homogeneous Evolution of Catholic Dogma* (Manila: Santo Tomas University Press, 1988).

14. To meditate on this particular example, one may consider reading Matthew Levering, *Mary's Bodily Assumption* (Notre Dame, IN: University of Notre Dame Press, 2015). Also, see Réginald Garrigou-Lagrange, *The Mother of the Savior*, trans. Bernard J. Kelly (London: Catholic Way Publishing, 2013), pp. 133–43. Charles Journet, "La définition solennelle de l'assomption de la vierge" in *Oeuvres completes*, vol. 12 (Paris: Lethielleux, 2011), pp. 233–56. In the late 1950s / early 1960s, there was some controversy over a supposed private comment made by Pope Pius XII to the effect that Mary's assumption was a transferral into heaven, not an anticipated resurrection involving her dormition as well. Cardinal Ottaviani forcefully responded to this, defending the tradition of the Dormition of the Theotokos. Details of this topic were treated in several very lengthy footnotes in the Pre-Conciliar Schema on the Blessed Virgin Mary written in preparation for the Second Vatican Council. See *Schema De Beata Maria Virgine, Matre Dei et Matre Hominum*, trans. Joseph Komonchak, available at https://jakomonchak.files.wordpress. com/2012/09/draft-on-the-blessed-virgin-1962.pdf (accessed October 15, 2019), nos. 26–27. The closing of the latter note states: "Of course, the fact of the Blessed Virgin's death must be admitted as certain, not because of these or similar reasons alone, but above all because of the constant and quite common consensus of the teaching and learning Church." For a gathering of testimonies related to the Theotokos's death, see the analytic index entries in C. Balić, *Testimonia de assumptione Beatae Virginis Mariae ex omnibus saeculis*, vol. 2 (Rome: Accademia Mariana, 1950), pp. 496–99.

15. In *Sens commun*, Fr. Garrigou-Lagrange discusses this theme at length with regard to dogmatic development. It will also be taken up in the final chapter of this volume, "Theology and the Life of Faith."

provide us with a vague idea to which a rigorous Thomism, interested in the problems of culture, history, and methodology, can add great precision.

ORIGINAL TEXTS FOR THIS SECTION

"De duplici via inventionis et de duplici via judicii secundum Sanctum Thomam." *Doctor Communis*, Vol. 7 (1954): pp. 189–96.

"De Investigatione definitionum secundum Aristotelem et S. Thomam. Ex posteriorum Analyt. l. II, c. 12–14; lect. 13–19 Commentarii S. Thomae." *Acta Pont. Academiae Romanae S. Thomae Aq. et Religionis Catholicae*, Vol. 2 (1935), pp. 193–201.

* * *

CHAPTER I

On the Twofold *Via inventionis* and the Twofold *Via iudicii* According to St. Thomas

I n this chapter [*relatio*], I intend to show how, according to St. Thomas, the classic *via inventionis* ("way of discovery") differs from classic *via iudicii* ("way of judgment") in our knowledge of God, a knowledge that first ascends to God and then descends from Him to the things of the universe. And after this, I intend to show how St. Thomas holds that there is another *via inventionis* and another *via iudicii*, which, in the constitution of the sciences, are, as it were: (*a*) direct knowledge that discovers various conclusions and, then, (*b*) reflexive or critical knowledge concerning the value of the principles from which the conclusions that have already been discovered are drawn.

CONCERNING THE CLASSICAL *VIA INVENTIONIS*

The classic distinction between the *via inventionis* and the *via iudicii* of wisdom is expressed by St. Thomas when he says in *ST* I, q. 79, a. 9:

> *According to the via inventionis, we arrive at knowledge of eternal things by way of temporal things,* as St. Paul says in Rom. 1:20 (DR): "The invisible things of him from the creation of the world are clearly seen, being understood by the things that are made." *However, in the via iudicii we judge concerning temporal things by*

means of eternal things that are already known (namely, the judgment of wisdom through the highest cause), *and we dispose of temporal things according to eternal reasons* (as in Christian ethics, which is part of sacred doctrine).

Thus, St. Thomas first ascends to God by the five ways in order to prove that God exists. Indeed, these five ways arrive at their terminus in reaching this summit: the First Mover of bodies and spirits, the Supreme Cause, the Necessary Being, the Supreme Truth and Good, the and Orderer of the Universe is *Self-Subsistent Existence* and *He Alone is His Own Existence*, for no limited being *is its own existence* but, rather, only *has existence by participation.*[1] This is the summit of these five ways, a summit found in *ST* I, q. 3, a. 4. In this way does the fivefold *via inventionis* leading to God arrive at its terminus.[2]

Then, in wisdom's *via iudicii*, St. Thomas deduces from Self-Subsistent Existence the Divine Attributes and relations of God with the universe (or, rather, the relations of the universe with God), and then, according to this *via iudicii* descending from God to creatures, he explains expressly that *creatures*, whether the highest or the lowest, *only have existence through participation.* In this way, the truth contained in the Platonic theory of "participation" finds its rightful place. St. Thomas asks in *ST* I, q. 44, a. 1, "Whether it is necessary that every being be created by God," and responds:

We must say that every being existing in any manner holds its existence from God. For, if something is found in a thing by way of participation, it must be caused in it by that to which it belongs essentially: just as iron becomes fiery [*ignitum*] from fire. Now,

---

1. *Before our mind's consideration,* created substance *is not* its existence (i.e., it is really distinguished from its existence). Only God is His own Existence, as we will see clearly *in Patria.*

2. Therefore, Fr. Norbert del Prado said in the introduction to *De veritate fundamentali philosophiae christianae* (Fribourg, 1911): "This proposition, 'In God Alone are essence and existence identical' is *fundamental* not in the *via inventionis* but in the *via iudicii.* For, in the *via inventionis,* the fundamental truths are the first principles of reason (the principle of [non-]contradiction and the principle of causality), as well as general and primary facts, for example, the fact that motion exists all throughout the world."

it was shown above (*ST* I, q. 3, a. 4), in treating of the Divine Simplicity, that God is *Existence Itself Essentially [per se] Subsisting*. And also, it was shown above (*ST* I, q. 11, a. 4) that *Subsistent Existence* must be *only one*, just as if whiteness were subsistent it would have to be one, since whitenesses are multiplied by what receives them. Therefore, it remains that all things other than God *are not their own existence but, rather, participate in existence...* Whence, Plato said that we must posit unity before multiplicity [*multitudinem*]."

Thus, existence through participation cannot be understood aright unless we first know, at least abstractly, Being *per essentiam*.

* * *

Now, as the history of philosophy shows, some philosophers confuse universal being according to predication [*ens universali in praedicando*] with *universal being in essendo et causando* (i.e., with the Supreme Being, God Himself). This confusion was committed in antiquity by Parmenides and, in another way, by Plato, who supposed that he had a vague [*confusam*] intellectual intuition of the Supreme Being and Good. Later on, we find the same confusion in the Neo-Platonists and, among the moderns, in Spinoza's pantheistic ontologism, as well as in the thought of the ontologists, who thought that we see the necessity of the first principles of reason in the Divine Being, confusedly known. This doctrine represents an immoderate form of intellectual realism, according to which the universal formally exists from the perspective of reality itself [*a parte rei*] (i.e., outside the soul). However, this leads to the confusion of universal being according to predication (or, in common) with universal being *in essendo et causando*, thus leading to pantheism.

Whence, these philosophers confuse the ascending *via inventionis* with the *via iudicii* of descending wisdom. Therefore, if we say, "St. Thomas's fourth way for knowing God's existence is founded on the Platonic theory of participation," we must proceed cautiously, for the Platonic theory of "participation" is true in some way, but it must be attentively purified from the deviation of immoderate realism in which the ascending *via inventionis* is not distinguished well enough from the *via iudicii* of descending wisdom. St. Thomas corrects this deviation when he asks in *ST* I, q. 88, a. 3: "Whether God is something that is first known by us," responding:

> In Jn. 1:18 it is said that "nobody has ever seen God." I respond that it must be said that since the human intellect, in the state of the present life, cannot understand the substances of created immaterial things, as we said (in the preceding articles), much less can it understand the essence of the Uncreated Substance. Whence, it must be said without qualification that God is not the first thing that is known by us; but, rather, by way of creatures we arrive at knowledge of God according to that expression of the Apostle in Rom. 1:20 (DR): "The invisible things of Him from the creation of the world are clearly seen, being understood by the things that are made." Now, the first thing that is understood by us in the state of the present life is the quiddity of material things, which is the object of our intellect, as we have said many times above (cf. *ST* I, q. 84, a. 7, q. 85, a. 1; q. 87, a. 2, ad 2).[3]

As St. Thomas shows elsewhere, in *ST* I, q. 76, a. 5: "According to the order of nature, *the intellective soul holds the lowest degree among intellectual substances*...and it must gather the notion of truth from sensible things by way of the senses." The proper (or, proportionate) object of *the lowest intellect* is the *lowest sort of intelligible*, namely, the intelligible being of sensible things, in which our intellect knows itself and God, as though in a mirror.

Whence, the ascending *via inventionis* leading us to knowledge of God must be attentively distinguished from the descending *via iudicii*. And in this ascending *via inventionis*, St. Thomas rightly uses *the Aristotelian distinction between potency and act*, which Aristotle discovered in the first book of his *Physics* by following the *via inventionis*, while resolving the arguments of Parmenides against the existence of motion. Parmenides said, "Being cannot come from being, for being

---

3.   See also the response to the objections to *ST* I, q. 88, a. 3.

already is, just as a statue is not made from a statue, for the statue already exists. And nothing comes from nothing. Therefore, becoming is itself impossible." Aristotle responded by saying that being does not come into being from being in act, but, instead, the generated being comes into being *from being in potency*, as the plant comes into being from the seed, and an animal from germ cells. And, *nothing is reduced from potency to act except through some being in act*; passive generation requires active generation, and on account of the superiority of act over potency (i.e., over the real capacity either for receiving or producing a perfection), we of necessity arrive at Pure Act, as is shown in the eighth book of the *Physics* and in the twelfth book of the *Metaphysics*.

The principle, "*Nothing is reduced from potency to act except through some being in act, and in the final analysis, through some uncaused being, which is Pure Act*," is the best formulation of the principle of efficient causality.[4] Therefore, the distinction between potency and act found in the *via inventionis* can be applied to God in this *via inventionis*. By contrast, the Platonic theory of participation is not understood correctly and fully unless it is purified of every deviation arising from Plato's immoderate realism, which runs the risk of committing the pantheistic confusion of universal being according to predication with universal being *in essendo et causando*.

This deviation must be completely avoided. Equally, Thomists cannot admit that the first thing known by our intellect is the "*cogito*" itself (or, the very activity of the knowing subject) as Descartes said.

Nor can we hold that the distinction between potency and act would be exposed as a kind of appendix to metaphysics. Indeed, this is completely impossible, for this distinction pertains to the essential structure of the metaphysics of St. Thomas and Aristotle.[5]

---

4. The principle of causality is expressed in a simpler manner: everything that comes into being demands a cause and, in the final analysis, a supreme actually existing and uncaused Cause, as, for example, the center of attraction of all bodies and as, in a higher order, there is a Supreme Intelligence and a Highest Good, as Aristotle says in treating of Pure Act in the twelfth book of the *Metaphysics*.

5. We had to note these two points because of the recent publication of an otherwise excellent book which does not sufficiently preserve the traditional methods of metaphysics.

CONCERNING ANOTHER *VIA INVENTIONIS* TO WHICH THERE IS ANOTHER, CORRESPONDING *VIA IUDICII*

St. Thomas speaks about another *via inventionis* and another *via iudicii* when he says (in *ST* I, q. 79, a. 8): "According to the *via acquisitionis* (or, *via inventionis*), human reasoning proceeds from certain things that are simply known, which are first principles. And then reflexively turning back [*rursus*], the *via iudicii*, by way of resolution, returns to the first principles in light of which it examines what it has discovered."[6]

In pursuing this *via acquisitionis* or *inventionis*, our intellect proceeds from first principles to proximate conclusions and, then, progressively all the way to remote conclusions. In this way, the sciences come to be constituted. Thus, for example, arithmetic and geometry were constituted as sciences, with reason gradually deducing proximate and remote conclusions (e.g., concerning circumference, concerning the nature of circles, concerning that of spheres, etc.). And then "reflexively, the *via iudicii*, by way of resolution, returns to the first principles in light of which it examines what it has found." In like manner was physics constituted, as well as its parts, hydrostatics, acoustics, optics, and thermodynamics. So too was the Philosophy of Nature constituted, concerning motion, the species of motion, action, passion, the continuum that is infinitely divisible, and the subordination of movers. And in this way, many conclusions have been deduced in the various sciences. Then, by way of reflection upon the sciences thus constituted, reason renders its judgment in a critical manner concerning the value of these sciences, especially about the value of their principles— whether the principles are self-evident [*per se nota evidentia*] or are only postulates freely granted by the intellect. In particular, this is the way the philosophy of the sciences [*philosophia scientiarum*] proceeds in its investigations.

Such investigations consider, for example, Euclid's indemonstrable geometric postulate [*sic*]. They examine the value of the principle of inertia which seemingly all the theories or hypotheses of modern physics depend on. In such reflection, one seeks to know the value of the

---

6.   See also *De veritate*, q. 15, a. 1.

second part of the principle of inertia, namely, "every body in motion, no longer being influenced by another body's motion, *will always remain in rectilinear and uniform motion*," considering whether this is evident (either *a priori* or *a posteriori*)[7] or *is freely admitted* by our intellect as a postulate in accord with what is suggested by experience.

This question is of great importance, for in it, modern physics is opposed to ancient physics.[8]

This is a crucial example of the aforementioned affirmation by St. Thomas: "Reflexively, the *via iudicii* by way of resolution returns to the first principles *in light of which it examines what it has discovered*." Thus, one asks: Can inertia in perpetual motion, without any actual influx from a mover, be reconciled with the first principles of contradiction, causality, and finality; is it true that *motion endures forever* [*in infinitum*] *without an actual mover so long as there is no obstacle?*

It seems true to say with Henri Poincaré and Pierre Duhem (and many others) that the principle of inertia, for its part, is not evident,

---

7. TRANSLATOR'S NOTE: The senses of *a posteriori* and *a priori* here are not the same as what is received from Kant's *Critique of Pure Reason*. Although Kant is the inheritor of much medieval, renaissance, and baroque Scholasticism, his sense of the terms is quite different from the developed Scholastic position within the Thomist school. Although Fr. Garrigou-Lagrange may be using the terms a little bit loosely, he was well aware of how these terms were used by Thomist logicians in his day. Indeed, he approved of Éduoard Hugon's *Cursus Philosophicus Thomisticae*, vol. 1: *Logica* (Paris: Lethielleux, 1927). In this text, see p. 384: "Demonstration *a priori* does not coincide with demonstration *propter quid*, nor does demonstration *a posteriori* coincide with demonstration *quia*. For demonstration *a priori* proceeds through causes of any sort, whether proximate or remote; however, demonstration *propter quid*...through proper, immediate, and adequate causes. Hence, every demonstration *propter quid* is *a priori*; however, not every demonstration *a priori* is *propter quid*. Demonstration *a posteriori* is only through an effect; however, demonstration *quia* is through an effect or [lit. *et*] through remote causes. Therefore, every *a posteriori* demonstration is *quia*, while it is not the case that every *quia* demonstration is *a posteriori*." Although the immediate context justifies reading "et" as "or," see also his remarks from p. 383: "Demonstration *quia*, taking the word 'quia' not as causal [i.e., meaning "because"] but meaning 'that the thing is,' proceeds either through a sign and effect or through remote, common, and inadequate causes."

8. TRANSLATOR'S NOTE: There are interesting parallels here between Garrigou-Lagrange's development of thought and that of Maritain. Compare the text here to Garrigou-Lagrange, *Sense of Mystery*, p. 88, n. 30. Regarding Maritain's view (and that of his close friend and student, Yves Simon), see "The Science and Philosophy of Inertia," in *The Great Dialogue of Nature and Space*, ed. Gerald J. Dalcourt (Albany, NY: Magi Books, 1970), pp. 37–58.

either *a priori* or *a posteriori* but, rather, under the suggestion of experience, is freely admitted by the intellect as a hypothesis and *an indemonstrable postulate*, useful for classifying phenomena, until the phenomena no longer can be reconciled with it.[9]

On the other hand, the traditional principles for the demonstration of God's existence by way of causality are not postulates freely admitted by our intellect but, instead, are *per se nota* (i.e., self-evident) principles.[10] The same is true for the distinction between potency and act, as well as the principle "nothing is reduced from potency to act except by some being in act and, in the final analysis, by Pure Uncaused Act."

---

9.   This is more clearly explained as follows. *The principle of inertia* is formulated: "A body at rest will remain eternally at rest if no external cause comes to act upon it; a body in motion, if no external cause acts upon it, indefinitely preserves its rectilinear and uniform motion."

The first part of this principle is obvious. The second part is not. See Henri Poincaré, *La science et l'hypothèse* (Paris: Ernest Flammarion, 1902), pp. 112–19. On p. 113, he notes: "Has there ever been an experiment performed upon bodies that were utterly removed from any force's activity, and if this has been done, *how can one know that these bodies were not submitted to any force?*"

Without a doubt, resistance, the friction that a mobile thing encounters, contributes to stopping its movement, but is it scientifically demonstrated that this resistance is *the sole cause* of the stopping? Is it demonstrated that the given movement is not slowed down also of itself? On this point, see our work *God: His Existence and His Nature*, vol. 1, trans. Bede Rose (St. Louis: Herder, 1949), pp. 258–60, 270–78, 274–75.

How could a small impulse given thousands of centuries ago produce in the void *a movement that would last forever*, a movement in which there would be something ever new, the translation from one place to another. Now, this non-evident postulate lies at the basis of all the theories or hypotheses of modern physics, from which arises the necessity for the philosophy of sciences to examine it again. It seems confirmed to a degree by this other principle: "a constant force acting alone upon an entirely free material point impresses a *uniformly accelerated* movement upon it." Despite this confirmation, the principle of inertia is only a *postulate*, for the reason given by H. Poincaré. According to this postulate, what would require a cause is not movement but the passage from rest to what one wishes to call "the state of movement."

TRANSLATOR'S NOTE: With the exception of the introductory clause to the note, the text is written in French, not Latin. He does not cite the publisher of Poincaré's text and cites its year as 1905. The pagination appears to match the 1902 edition cited above. The aforementioned citations are from the 11th edition of *Dieu, son existence et sa nature* (Paris: Beauchesne, 1951), pp. 239, 249, 256, 260, 774–79. The English translation was taken from the 5th edition of the text. The final section is a later addition, not currently in the English translation.

10.   TRANSLATOR'S NOTE: I.e., Non-mediate evidence grasped by the *habitus* of understanding of first principles, as opposed to the manner that one grasps conclusions through objective syllogistic illation.

As we said above, the distinction between potency and act, in fact, provides the only solution to Parmenides's objection against the existence of motion. It provides the only way to reconcile reason's first principles of identity, contradiction, and causality with the existence of motion, which is experientially certain.

Thus, there is a twofold *via inventionis*: the first discovers the Supreme Cause, before one undertakes a deduction of the Divine Attributes through the *via iudicii*. However, the second *via inventionis* arrives at the various conclusions of the sciences before the intellect by reflection returns, by way of resolution, to the principles [themselves] and judges the value of the more or less constituted science in question.

COMPARISON OF THESE *VIAE* WITH ANALYSIS AND SYNTHESIS

It should be noted that the *via inventionis* of the sciences is partly inductive and partly deductive. In mathematics it is more deductive, and in experimental physics it is more inductive.[11] Then, the *via iudicii*, through resolution to the first principles of the sciences is at once analytic (or resolutive) and synthetic, for it judges concerning the value of the various conclusions of a particular science through a resolution to its principles, through which the synthesis of this science is gradually constituted.

Thus, there is a *twofold via inventionis*, namely, (1) the *via inventionis* to the Supreme Cause or to the Existence of God, and (2) the *via inventionis* of the sciences (or, that which they follow in coming to their conclusions).

Equally, there is a *twofold via iudicii*, namely, (1) the *via* that *judges* concerning all finite things in light of their Supreme Cause, and (2) the *via* that *judges* concerning the values of the various conclusions of a given science through resolution to its first, certain principles or to its hypothetical postulates, in order to arrive at the synthesis of this science.

---

11. Likewise, the hunt or search for definitions is undertaken in a twofold manner: (1) *through comparative ascending induction*, by comparing the thing to be defined with similar and dissimilar things, and (2) *through descending division* of the genus of the thing to be defined; thus, we arrive at the definition of man: rational animal. See *Posterior analytics*, bk. 2, lect. 2, 5, 8, 14–16.

TRANSLATOR'S NOTE: See the next chapter in this volume.

Thus, *analysis* arriving at God *precedes the universal synthesis* that judges concerning all beings through the Highest Cause, and *analysis* of the facts of experience *precedes the synthesis* that judges concerning the value of the conclusions of a given science through its principles or through its hypothetical postulates in order to gradually arrive at the synthesis of this science.

CONCLUSION

As we draw this chapter [*relatio*] to a close, we must note that the distinction *between the classic via inventionis* first exposited by us and the correlative *via iudicii* through the Highest Cause must be preserved in its entirety.

However, this classic *via inventionis* is connected with a fundamental thesis in Thomistic metaphysics, namely, that *the first object* of our intellect is *the intelligible being of sensible things* (or, universal being, by way of predication). This first object known by our intellect in direct intellection (before reflexive cognition) is not the *cogito* itself as Descartes thought, nor is it universal being *in essendo et causando*, as the ontologists thought, thereby exposing themselves to the danger of pantheistic ontologism.

For this reason, St. Pius X said in his Encyclical *Pascendi* (September 8, 1907), and in his *motu proprio, Sacrorum antistitum* (September 1, 1910): "Moreover, let professors remember that they cannot set St. Thomas aside, especially in metaphysical questions, without grave detriment. Just as is said in the words of St. Thomas himself: '*A small error in the beginning is great by the end.*'"

* * *

CHAPTER 2

On the Search for Definitions
According to Aristotle and St. Thomas

In this chapter [*relatio*], I would like to briefly set forth what Aristotle says in *Posterior Analytics*, bk. 2, ch. 12–14, concerning the investigation (or, as he calls it, the hunt) for definitions, likewise recalling the principles that are discussed concerning this matter in St. Thomas's Commentary on this text (bk. 2, lect. 13 to 19). This topic is insufficiently well-known, even though it is of great importance.

* * *

The importance of inquiring into the nature of definition itself is clear *in relation to demonstration*, for in *a priori* demonstrations, the demonstrative middle term is the very definition of the subject from which its first property is deduced; and from a correct definition of its first property, we deduce the second, the third, and so forth. Thus, from the definition of man as a *rational animal*, we demonstrate that he is free inasmuch as reason is the root of freedom. From freedom, we demonstrate man's [moral] responsibility, etc. However, in *a posteriori* demonstrations, as St. Thomas notes, the middle term is the nominal definition of the thing whose existence is to be demonstrated, e.g., the nominal definition of God considering Him [in a general and nominal fashion] as the First Cause or the First Orderer.[1]

These observations make clear the importance of nominal definitions in *a posteriori* demonstration, as well as the importance of real definitions in *a priori* demonstrations. Without a good definition, the syllogism is akin to an excellent gristmill that lacks good grain. Without grain that is itself good, we cannot mill out good flour, no matter how excellent our gristmill. If we do not carefully take note of this fact, we risk falling into formalism. Therefore, definitions are of great importance—and, indeed, both nominal and real definitions.

Now, nominal definitions express the vague [*confusum*] concept of the thing without which we would not know what a given name signifies in its common use among men and as indicated in ordinary language. For this reason, Socrates was highly praised by Aristotle for the fact that, in opposition to the Sophists, he inquired into the exact signification of various terms (e.g., of wisdom or virtue) and thus forced the Sophists into silence.

* * *

However, the principal problem in the current question facing us is as follows: *How are we to pass methodically from the nominal definition to the real, exact definition* expressed through a proximate genus and specific difference? Aristotle often says that the *nominal definition* [*quid nominis*] *vaguely contains the real definition* [*quid rei*], just as a kind of elementary ontology is contained in the vague concepts of common sense (or, natural reason).[2] Leibniz will also come to say this. However, how are we to pass methodically from a vague concept to a distinct one? For example, how do we arrive methodically at the true definition of man, the soul, nature, person, freedom, virtue, wisdom, prudence, justice, etc.? Nominalists deny that we can arrive at real definitions that

---

1. *ST* I, q. 2, a. 2, ad 2: "When the cause is demonstrated through an effect, the effect must be used in place of the definition of the cause for the sake of proving that the cause exists... We must take as the middle term what the name signifies... Whence in demonstrating through an effect that God exists, we can take for the middle term what this name 'God' signifies (namely, First Mover, First Cause, First Orderer, etc.)."

2. TRANSLATOR'S NOTE: On this, the reader should consult Garrigou-Lagrange, *Sense of Mystery*, pp. 47–55. Also, see Réginald Garrigou-Lagrange, *Le sens commun: La philosophie de l'être et les formules dogmatiques*, 4th ed. (Paris: Desclée de Brouwer, 1936), pp. 79–153.

express the nature of things. According to them, nominal and descriptive definitions are all that we can form. Indeed, something true is said here concerning the case of sensible things that have forms immersed in matter, as is the case for the specific forms of an oak, a rose, a dog, or a lion, all of which can be only descriptively defined. However, this does not hold for the case of defining man, whose specific form emerges above matter and is more intelligible in itself and with respect to us than are the specific forms of the aforementioned material beings. Moreover, this limitation does not hold for the case of the soul, along with its properties and virtues.

Therefore, how are we to methodically make the passage from the nominal definition to the real definition?

* * *

Aristotle responds: *Sometimes the essential definition through genus and specific difference can be* demonstrated, namely, if we already have another definition through the efficient or final cause of the thing to be defined. Thus, he says, the eclipse of the moon is first nominally defined, "A darkening of the moon," or a privation of light in it. Then, we come to know the cause of this privation, thus enabling us to define the moon's eclipse causally as, "The obscuring of the moon by the earth coming to be set between the sun and the moon." Thus, we come to know *what* an eclipse *is* and *why it is such* [*propter quid*]. Again, an echo is defined through its efficient cause as the reverberation of sound in some different region than from where it initially sounded. In this way, we come to know what an echo is and why it is such. So too for the case of a hallucination, which is related to a true sensation as an echo is to an original sound, for the hallucination primarily [*prius*] is said to exist when someone believes himself to sense something that other people present in the same place do not sense. Then, one discovers the cause of a hallucination just like the cause of an eclipse or an echo, namely: *a hallucination* (whether visual, auditory, or tactile, e.g., after an amputation) *is a false sensation arising from past sensations, now happening on the occasion of some perturbation or lesion of the organism.*[3] In this way,

---

3. See the index of Aristotle's works for "eclipse," "echo," and "hallucination."

one comes to have the "what" and the "why it is such" of hallucination, likewise coming to understand why a hallucination *exists without a real sensed thing*, whereas a genuine sensation cannot exist without the existence of a real sensed thing to which it is essentially relative. Note well that the true definition of hallucination is today of great importance against idealism for showing that there cannot be a genuine sensation without a real sensed thing.[4]

In the aforementioned cases, the essential definition expressing *what something is* is demonstrated from the causal definition, which assigns the *reason for* the thing. However, note also that the term *circle* (or, rather, *circumference*) is defined causally (or, genetically) as *a figure generated by the revolution of a line around one of its extremes*, and from this definition we can apodictically demonstrate that the circumference essentially must be *a figure with all of its points equally distant from its center*. A sphere is defined in the same manner. Leibniz and Spinoza insisted on this in discussing matters pertaining to genetic definitions; Aristotle substantially said the same thing when he spoke of causal definitions, e.g., of the eclipse through the positioning of the earth between the sun and the moon.

Whence, when the essential definition can be *demonstrated* from the causal definition, we have the best explanation for the *legitimate passage* from the nominal (or, vague and common) definition to the distinct one. And again, Aristotle explains that this very *reason why it is such* [*propter quid*] can be assigned in various manners on the basis of the four causes (e.g., corruptibility arises from the material cause).[5]

Now, *the reason for which* [*the propter quid*] is the *reason for being* [*ratio essendi*], as the principle of *raison d'être*[6] alludes to the four causes and proportionally (or, analogically) is verified in them.

---

4.   TRANSLATOR'S NOTE: See the chapter in this section below, entitled, "There Cannot Be Genuine Sensation Without a Real Sensed Thing," pp. 101–119.

5.   It is to be noted that theologians deduce the essential definition of grace from the fact that *grace* is *the seed of glory: grace is a formal participation in the Divine Nature*, in other words, the root principle of strictly Divine activities), such that grace disposes us radically [i.e., as a root source] to see God immediately as He sees Himself, and to love Him as He loves Himself.

6.   TRANSLATOR'S NOTE: After long meditation on Fr. Garrigou-Lagrange's language, this has been my manner of translating his *principe de raison d'être*. Sometimes, it

* * *

However, we find ourselves faced with a special difficulty when the essential definition cannot be demonstrated, that is, when we do not have another definition for the thing to be defined, namely a causal definition through the final or efficient cause. *How, therefore, are we to discover the real definition when it cannot be demonstrated through another?* Thus, the question set before us is: how are we to arrive methodically, that is, legitimately, at the true definition, e.g., of man, the soul, intelligence, freedom, person, personality, virtue, wisdom, prudence, justice, etc.?

To this, Aristotle responds that, in such a case, the hunt for the real definition will be performed in two ways: on the one hand, through a progressive and methodical division of the ultimate genus of the thing to be defined, and, on the other, through a philosophical, comparative and ascending induction in which the thing to be defined is compared with things that are similar and dissimilar.

Many modern historians [of philosophy] have written about the Aristotelian methodology for undertaking this twofold hunt. Some of them have observed only what in this twofold hunt is, as it were, an *instrument* of understanding, in the end saying: Aristotle was not able to establish a rigorous method for discovering definitions, and without this, the value of demonstrations (or, of the demonstrative middle term) is destroyed.[7]

However, here standing aside St. Thomas, the majority of historians [of philosophy] today hold that, according to Aristotle, this twofold hunt or investigation (namely, *descending* through the division of the genus and *ascending* through comparative induction) *is directed by the intellect itself,* νοῦς, *under the light of the vague notion* (or, nominal

---

is translated as the principle of "sufficient reason," which can be misleading. A text such as the current chapter confirms the choice to render it in English in a way that maintains the sense of "reason for being" expressed by the French *raison d'être,* for Fr. Garrigou-Lagrange writes in the original Latin "*principium rationis essendi.*" Moreover, see his own remarks in *De revelatione,* 5th edition (Rome: Desclée et Socii, 1950), pp. 238–39, n. 2. Note, however, the fact that Fr. Rose, in his admirable translations, renders "principe de raison d'être" as "the principle of sufficient reason."

7.   See M.-D. Roland-Gosselin, "Les methods de la définition d'après Aristote," *Revue des sciences philosophiques et theologiques,* Vol. 6 (1912): pp. 235–52 and pp. 661–75.

definition of the thing to be defined).[8] Accordingly, from the perspective of the principal cause, this investigation pertains more to understanding [*intellectus ipsum*] (to the progress of the first intellectual apprehension which comes to increasingly penetrate what it knows, *intus legentis*—reading into the depths of that which is known) than to discursive reason, although in the end it can be expressed in a kind of syllogism, namely an explicative one, not an illative one.[9]

---

8.   Carl Prantl, *Geschichte der Logik im Abenlande*, vol. 1 (Leipzig: Hirzel, 1855), pp. 263 and 265, explains well this part of Aristotle's logic. Also, Heinrich Maier, *Die Syllogistik des Aristoteles*, (Tübingen, 1896–1900). Also, see C. Kuhn, *De notionis definitione qualem Aristoteles constituerit* (Halle, 1844). Also, see the bibliographical note at the end of this chapter.

9.   This is observed with clarity by Fr. Carolus Boyer in his *Cursus philosophiae ad usum seminariorum*, vol. 1 (Paris: Desclée de Brouwer, 1935), p. 258, and also in Fr. Tonquédec cited in the same work.

TRANSLATOR'S NOTE: Properly speaking, a syllogism is objectively illative, inferring a given truth (i.e., the conclusion) from two premises. As regards the distinction between an explicative and an illative syllogism, see the remarks of Fr. Garrigou-Lagrange's student, Fr. Austin Woodbury, S.M., in Austin Woodbury, *Logic* (St. Vincent College, Latrobe, PA: The John N. Deely and Anthony Russell Collection), pp. 239–41 (nn. 299–300):

In every syllogism properly so-called, from one truth is inferred ANOTHER TRUTH. Therefore, whenever by a syllogism there is not inferred a NEW TRUTH, this is a syllogism improperly so-called. The syllogism improperly so-called is twofold, to wit: the expository syllogism and the explicative syllogism… From the expository syllogism must be distinguished the explicative syllogism; whereof, this is an example: 'Man is mortal. But a rational animal is a man. Therefore, a rational animal is mortal.'

Here, [the middle term] is universal, and therefore there is a true illation. Nevertheless, it is not a syllogism properly so-called, because it does NOT infer in the conclusion another truth, i.e. a judgment other than in the premises. For here, the conclusion expresses the same truth but explicates it BY OTHER CONCEPTS. For these two propositions, 'man is mortal,' and, 'rational animal is mortal,' express the same truth, but the latter expresses it by more distinct concepts than the former. Wherefore, to this is rightly given the name of EXPLICATIVE syllogism.

In the explicative syllogism, the conclusion is IDENTICAL AS REGARDS ITSELF (*quoad se*) with the major but NOT AS REGARDS US (*non quoad nos*); and therefore, there is a formal illation, but not an objective illation. [He cites here R.-M. Schultes, *Introductio ad historiam dogmatum* (Paris: Lethielleux, 1922).] OBSERVE that the major [premise] and the conclusion of an explicative syllogism are in THE SAME MODE OF SAYING 'PER SE'; otherwise, there would be had, not an explicative syllogism but a syllogism PROPERLY SO-CALLED. In the example given above, both these propositions are IN THE SECOND MODE of saying 'per se.' But the case is otherwise with this syllogism: 'A rational animal is capable of science. But man is a rational animal. Therefore, man is capable of science.' Here, the major [premise] is in the FOURTH mode of saying 'per se'; otherwise, the syllogism would be employed to no purpose. But the conclusion is in the SECOND manner of saying 'per se.' Wherefore this is a syllogism properly so-called.

* * *

Here, we cannot set forth all of the details of this twofold ascending and descending process. We will only note the principal points in this matter. It will be readily apparent that in this twofold process, *the vague concept* gradually passes to the state of being *distinct*, just as one and the same man, first half-asleep but then fully awake, comes to be distinctly aware of himself or of his own identity. In this way, we have an explanation for how the intellect, already possessing a vague concept, arrives at *certitude concerning the value of the real definition* at the end of this twofold investigation, when the descending division and comparative induction truly arrive at the same point, namely at the specific difference of the thing to be defined or at the *distinct concept* that at first was only vaguely grasped.

Above all, we must observe that Aristotle, in explaining the right method for the progressive division of the ultimate genus of the thing to be defined, most excellently formulated (though, in the *via inventionis*) the *rules of division* that now are set forth in scholastic manuals as an already settled affair [*in facto esse*] (or, in a static manner). In Aristotle's own text, these rules captivate the intellect, in short, as we see him in the process of searching out the truth.

* * *

With regard to the progressive division of an ultimate genus (or, at least, of a general notion[10] which is a kind of quasi-genus, although such a notion can be more universal than a genus), Aristotle most excellently shows that this division of the ultimate genus of the thing to be divided must be performed *step by step through immediate differences, immediately* taken *according to the formal notion of the whole being divided* and *contradictorily opposed* to one another, so that the division may be *immediate, per se* (not *per accidens*), and *adequate*.

---

10. Thus, being is divided into the categories (or, the ultimate genera).
   Translator's Note: Fr. Garrigou-Lagrange's view on analogy favors proper proportionality, as is obvious from his many works. Here, he is noting that the analogical term is related in a quasi-generic fashion to the subordinate analogates to which it is applied, though it only imperfectly abstracts from the analogates, unlike the case of univocal genera.

In this way, *substance* is divided into corporeal and incorporeal. *Corporeal* substance is divided into living and non-living. *Living* corporeal substance is divided into sensing and non-sensing. Then, *sensing* (or, animal) is divided into rational and non-rational. Porphyry's tree is merely a recapitulation of those things that already were most excellently explained and established by Aristotle.

Consequently, we can clearly see that in order to define man *with certitude* (i.e., for the right and adequate division of *animal*), we do not need to know all the species of animals that existed once upon a time and that even now exist in exotic regions of the world. It suffices that we have a good definition for animal itself in general (namely, *a bodily substance living by a sensitive life*) and, according to the formal notion of animal, discover the immediate differences dividing this *genus* through contradictory opposition (taking care not to overlook some third member that might exist between them), namely: *the sensitive life of animals either is or is not subservient to superior intellective knowledge.* Thus, animal is immediately, *per se*, and adequately divided into *rational* and *non-rational.* Therefore, in order to rightly define man, we need not know in specific detail all the species of irrational animals. Now, these species of brute animals must themselves be distinguished formally and *per se*, to the degree this is possible, *according to the formal notion of sense life*, in as much as they do or do not have all five external senses and all the internal senses. However, if we cannot determine the members of a division so explicitly (given the fact the specific forms of brute animals are immersed in matter and are barely intelligible for our abstractive manner of knowing), then we must have recourse to descriptive definitions, as the lion is descriptively defined, as well as the dog, the wolf, etc. Thus, brute animals are divided inasmuch as they do or do not have vertebrae, inasmuch as they are quadrupeds or bipeds, inasmuch as their feet are cloven or not, etc.

And the value of the correct division of the categories is defended by means of these same principles.

In this way, the descending division [of a given genus or quasi-genus] is perfected step by step.[11]

---

11.   In other words, for the right division of the categories of being, it is not of great importance to know whether there are six, eight, or ten categories, provided that *the first*

* * *

Finally, how must *ascending philosophical induction* be established? In the same text, Aristotle responds: *It is to be established methodically by comparing the thing to be defined with things that are similar and dissimilar.* However, this inductive comparison is directed by the intellect under the light of the vague notion (or, the nominal definition) of the thing to be defined. Otherwise, it would never reach the real definition through genus and species. Whence it is, as it were, *the same concept*, that seeks after itself, beginning in a vague state and tending toward its own distinction. It is as though the concept were to say to us in the natural order what God says in the order of grace: "You would not seek me if you did not already know me in some way."

According to Aristotle, the following steps are necessary in this comparison of the thing to be defined with things that are similar and dissimilar to it. First, *we must examine those things that answer to the directive nominal definition.* For example, in order to define man, we must ask *what* is found to be the *same* in all, and there are many such things (namely, reasoning, speaking more or less rationally, intelligent laughter, free choice on the basis of a judgment which can be changed, etc.). Second, *this class* (namely, man) *must be compared to others that are more or less similar* (e.g., apes, which appear to have a certain kind of intelligence) and the common characteristics of this second class, the ape which imitates human characteristics [*simii imitatoris*] are sought out.[12] Third, then, we must compare *the dominant characteristic of the first class* (i.e., man) with the *dominant characteristic of the second class* (i.e., apes) so that it may be clear whether they have the same formal notion or diverse ones. Then, for example, it is made manifest that the ape imitating human characteristics does not speak like man. Likewise, we come to see that he *is not an inventor* like man, inventing neither mechanical nor liberal arts, neither

---

divisions and subdivisions are *necessary*. In fact, the categories of being are not immediately divided *into ten* but first into two, namely *substance* and *accident*, and then *accident* is subdivided as is explained in *In V Meta.*, c. 7, lect. 9, inasmuch as *it is in the subject* (either according to matter, thus being quantity, or according to form, thus being quality, or in respect to something else, thus being relation) *or whether it is taken from something outside the subject*, as a measure, thus being time and place, etc.

12. See in the index of Aristotle's works: apes hold a middle place between man and quadrupeds, make use of their front feet as though they were hands, etc.

eloquence nor logic. It does not know how to order means in various ways to an end but, rather, reproduces what it sees, ever doing so in the same manner and not by perfecting its work according to the requirements of the circumstances, as we see happening in the case of man. That is, it sensibly knows *the thing that is the end* but not the *notion of end as such*, i.e. the *reason for the being of the means*. This makes clear the fact that it does not have an intellect,[13] by which we ourselves are able to know intelligible being and the reasons for the being of things, both *what* things are and *that on account of which* things and their actions are what they are.

Likewise, in the same place, Aristotle gives another example of the hunt for definitions by inquiring into the definition of *magnanimity*. First, he considers what is shared by all who are called magnanimous, such as Alcibiades, Achilles, and Ajax. They share the fact that they do not tolerate insult. Second, he compares these with others who are also called magnanimous, in a higher way, such as Socrates and Lysander, and these share the fact that they are not changed by the prosperity coming from fortune or by adversity coming from lack thereof but, instead, indifferently have the same bearing in either set of circumstances. Third, he explains the character of the first class and that of the second inasmuch as all these men *judge themselves to be worthy of great things.* Finally, magnanimity is defined: *the virtue by which man tends, in accord with right reason, to great things, ones that are worthy of great honors, though not on account of honors.* (Thus, we see how magnanimity differs from ambition.[14])

Aristotle searched in like manner for the definitions of the soul, life, virtue, prudence, art, wisdom, and justice, as well as for the definition of nature, on the basis of which theologians come to define that

---

13. **Translator's Note:** Literally "*intelligentiam*," or, intelligence. To render this as saying the animal has no "intelligence" may lead the reader to underestimate the place that Fr. Garrigou-Lagrange accords to the estimative sense. His Latin is written in a style that calls to mind his French, wherein he often uses "intelligence" for "intellect." Hence, the latter has been chosen. Moreover, in other Latin texts, he can be found occasionally using "*intelligentia*" in a sense like the French "intelligence," which often should be translated in his works as "intellect," not "intelligence." Concerning the question of animal intelligence, see John Deely, "Animal Intelligence and Concept-Formation," *The Thomist*, Vol. 35, No. 1 (January 1971): pp. 43–93. This text can also be found in John Deely, *Realism for the 21st Century: A John Deely Reader*, ed. Paul Cobley (Scranton, PA: University of Scranton Press, 2009), pp. 91–139.

14. See in the index of Aristotle's works: *magnanimous* and *ambitious*.

which is above nature[15] as well as how the term "supernatural" is said in different ways,[16] etc.

* * *

The methodology that we have been discussing casts light on many of the questions considered among theologians. For example, *concerning the definition of person* and personality, we can see easily enough that the definition taken from Boethius and perfected by St. Thomas optimally corresponds to the aforementioned rules for the definitional hunt, preserving the meaning that we first form for the nominal definition of *person* or of the personal pronouns, I, you, and he. By contrast, the definition of *person* given by Scotus and certain other thinkers preserves neither the first-formed meaning of the nominal definition nor the laws holding for the investigation of the real definition. Cajetan notes this fact most excellently.[17]

Finally, the aforementioned doctrine of Aristotle and St. Thomas concerning the legitimate transition from the vague concept to the same distinct concept provides great illumination for the question concerning *how dogmas develop while nonetheless preserving the same meaning and sense.* This is obvious for the notions of nature and person in the

---

15. **TRANSLATOR'S NOTE:** This is a central point of contention in the text of "On Evolutionism and the Distinction between the Natural and Supernatural Orders" in Part IV below.

16. **TRANSLATOR'S NOTE:** For a summary of this point, see Garrigou-Lagrange, *Sense of Mystery*, pp. 206–216.

17. Scotus says that a person is an individuated human nature not taken up by a superior person and not united to it. He defines person through something *negative*: through the absence of the Hypostatic Union. Quite clearly, personality, which pertains to the natural order, cannot be defined through the absence of an altogether extraordinary supernatural grace. Cajetan says in *In ST* III, q. 4, a. 2, no. 8, following the exposition of the nominal definition of person and of the personal pronouns, *I, you, he*: "If we all admit all this, why is that we turn away from the common opinion [*confessione*] while carefully investigating the meaning of the thing signified [*quid rei significatae*]?" That is: why do we arrive at an explicit definition that no longer preserves the general meaning of the commonly accepted nominal definition? We have explained this opinion of Cajetan in Réginald Garrigou-Lagrange "De personalitate iuxta Caietanum," *Angelicum*, Vol. 11 (1934): pp. 407–24.

TRANSLATOR'S NOTE: A later discussion of this topic, still defending Cajetan, though not solely focused on his position, can be found in Réginald Garrigou-Lagrange, *Christ: The Savior*, pp. 144–73. Likewise, see T. U. Mullaney, "Created Personality: The Unity of the Thomistic Tradition," *New Scholasticism*, Vol. 29 (1955): pp. 369–402.

mysteries of the Holy Trinity and the Incarnation, as well as for the notions of will, merit, demerit, grace, reward, punishment, and, again, for
the notion of a sacrament in general. Likewise, we see this process in the
elaboration of the notion of each given sacrament, in particular for the
notion of the conversion applied to the case of the Eucharist, a notion
which gradually passed from a vague state to the entirely distinct state
as enunciated in the doctrine of transubstantiation as it is found in the
texts of the Council of Trent.[18] Likewise, in considering the beginnings
to the various treatises in St. Thomas's *Summa theologiae*, what we have
discussed here helps us to distinguish the articles where we are faced with
only *explicative discourse* from those in which we find *discourse, properly
speaking* (*i.e., objectively illative discourse*). Thus, in the introduction of
dogmatic treatises, the first articles, nay even the first questions, explain
revealed truths through metaphysical analysis,[19] prior to any concern
with deducing theological conclusions, properly speaking, conclusions
that express new truths that are virtually contained in revelation.

Therefore, the aforementioned doctrine of Aristotle and St. Thomas
concerning the method of investigating definitions in the philosophical
order provides great assistance for understanding dogmatic definitions.
Following upon the explanatory labor of theology, such definitions propose revealed truths in an increasingly explicit form, truths that are to
be believed formally on the authority of God who reveals.

BIBLIOGRAPHICAL NOTE

As a complement to what we said above, we here include a bibliographical note provided by Fr. I. M. Bochenski, O.P., professor of
logic at the Angelicum.[20]

---

18.   We develop this in the work Réginald Garrigou-Lagrange, *Le sens commun, la philoso-
      phie de l'être et les formules dogmatiques*, 4th edition (Paris: Desclée de Brouwer, 1936),
      pp. 263–374. Also in *De revelatione*, vol. 1, c. 5, a. 2, and more recently in Réginald
      Garrigou-Lagrange, "La théologie et la vie de foi," *Revue thomiste*, Vol. 40 (New Series,
      18) (1935): pp. 492–514.

      Translator's Note: The final article is included in this volume in the chapter below,
      entitled "Theology and the Life of Faith," pp. 421–43.

19.   Translator's Note: By this, Fr. Garrigou-Lagrange means *an analysis concerning the
      being of the given revealed truths in question*, and not *a metaphysics of revelation* which
      would consider revealed truths in a merely created, rational light.

20.   Translator's Note: Everything after this line was written in French.

The Aristotelian methods of definition. Nowhere have I found a critique as negative as that registered by Fr. Roland-Gosselin, "Les methods de la définition d'après Aristote," *Revue des sciences philosophiques et theologiques*, Vol. 6 (1912): pp. 235–252 and 661–675.

1. The traditional explanation, based on Posterior Analytics B (2).19 (νοῦς), is vigorously supported by Carl Prantl in *Geschichte der Logik im Abenlande*, vol. 1 (Leipzig: Hirzel, 1855; reimp. 1927), pp. 106ff, 135, and 338ff. Also, despite his predilection for "dianoetic" logic, see Heinrich Maier in *Die Syllogistik des Aristoteles*, vol. 1 (Tübingen, 1900), pp. 405ff, especially pp. 411 and 422. Likewise, though more superficial, see Herman Rassow, *Aristotelis de notionis definitione doctrina* (Berolini, 1843), pp. 27ff. Also, C. Kuhn, *De notionis definition qualem Aristoteles constituerit* (Halle: 1844), pp. 31ff.

2. Guido Calogero, *I fondamenti della logica aristotelica* (F. Le Monnier, 1927), pp. 128–145. The author at length discusses definition in Aristotle and everywhere finds contradictions between his "noetic" notion (concept) and his "dianoetic" [one] (judgment). He logically should apply the same procedure to methods [of definition] but does not do so.

3. Friedrich Solmsen, *Die Entwicklung der Aristotelischen Logik und Rhetorik* (Berlin: Weidmann, 1929), pp. 53ff. Solmsen asserts that, given the *Posterior Analytics'* status as a work of Aristotle's youth (when he was still a Platonist), his methods explained in B.13 do not represent the Aristotelian doctrine of his mature age. On the contrary, Aristotle rejects expressly διαίρεσις in *Prior Analytics* A.31. The mature Aristotle is a formalist. In the *Posterior Analytics*, he bases himself exclusively on Platonic metaphysics and does not yet know his own.

4. Paul Gohlke, *Die Entstehung der aristotelischen Lehrschriften* (1931), pp. 11ff. He combats Solmsen's thesis. The *Posterior*

Analytics had a second redaction after the *Prior Analytics*. Therefore, the methods of B.13 would be authentically Aristotelian.

5. Julius Stenzel, *Studien zur Entwicklung der Platonischen Dialektik von Sokrates zu Aristoteles* (Leipzig: 1931). This is an important work. Stenzel shows that διαίρεσις in Plato is not an induction but, rather, a deduction in the proper sense of the word, one that as such is valid, on the condition of being material, that is to say, on the condition of following the joints [*articulations*] of the thing [being investigated]. He critiques Aristotle (in *Prior Analytics* A.31), saying this formalism is unwarranted.

6. Dubislav, *Die Definition*, 3rd ed. (Leipzig: Felix Meiner, 1931). Among the monographs concerning definition, this is without historical importance. From the systematic perspective, the author, a radical nominalist, denies the possibility of attaining essences. Similarly, the recent work by Moser does not touch upon our question. See Simon Moser, *Zur Lehre von der der Definition bei Aristoteles* (Innsbruck, 1935).

In sum, all serious Aristotelians agree that νοῦς is what forms definitions. However, I believe it necessary to add with Solmsen and Gohlke that the *Posterior Analytics* had at least one redaction prior to the writing of *Prior Analytics* and that, in particular, the thirteenth chapter of Book B comes from the Philosopher's youth. After writing *Prior Analytics* A.31, he could no longer write *Posterior Analytics* B.13 in the same manner. However, to say, like Solmsen, that Aristotle became a formalist in his old age is an unfounded assertion that can be argued against on the basis of very efficacious arguments.

* * *

PART II

Certain Questions Concerning Knowledge

* * *

INTRODUCTION TO PART II

As I noted in the general introduction to this volume, the contents of this section likely bring to mind a title like "Thomistic Epistemology" to the contemporary reader. However, "epistemology" has never had its place in the traditional Thomistic distinction of disciplines. For the Thomistic school, the topics often falling to epistemology mostly are divided between the natural philosophy treating human knowledge along the lines found in Aristotle's *On the Soul* and in an expanded metaphysical critique of the value of human knowledge, which Fr. Garrigou-Lagrange sees as being in continuity with what Aristotle does in *Metaphysics* IV (Γ) in his discussion of the principle of non-contradiction. The essays in this second section are concerned with both of these general domains of investigation, the first chapter covering them both, whereas the latter three primarily focus on issues more generally falling to the first sort of outlook on "epistemological" matters (i.e., "philosophical psychology").

The first chapter in this section serves as a kind of summary of "Thomist Realism," as it was exposited in the first half of the twentieth century. Granted, there was far from universal agreement on what it meant to be a "Thomistic Realist" during that period (or today). For some, such as Étienne Gilson, there were grave risks involved in articulating a Thomist "realism," especially if one styled it as being a kind of "critical realism," for such a "critique" often led one, he thought, by a kind of methodological bias, down the byways of modern philosophy in one of its solipsistic and idealistic forms. For Gilson, a methodical realism must not fall prey to an idealistic problematic which would close the door to mind-independent reality even before it could be opened.[2] In *Le réalisme du principe de finalité*, Fr. Garrigou-Lagrange responded with great charity to Gilson,[3] but in the end, the Dominican theologian's position (one shared with thinkers like Joseph Gredt, Angelo Pirotta, Francois-Xavier Maquart, Maritain, and Fr. Garrigou's disciple Austin Woodbury—to name a few)[4] was different from that of the famed medievalist. For the tradition of thought to which Fr. Garrigou-Lagrange belonged, the "critical" character of Thomist metaphysics is based on the simple fact that metaphysics, precisely as a form of wisdom, is "critical" through its concern with defending its principles, something of no small importance for "epistemological" questions.

In "The Threefold Foundation of Thomist Realism," Fr. Garrigou offers an excellent overview of a line of thought that can be found

---

1.   More broadly, this would include topics such as those found in the portion of John of St. Thomas's *Cursus philosophicus* dealing with the soul. See Ioannis a Sancto Thoma, *Cursus philosophicus,* vol. 3 (p. 4) (Turin: Marietti, 1937). Likewise, consider the excellent work of Simon on this topic, praised elsewhere by Fr. Garrigou-Lagrange. See Yves R. Simon, *An Introduction to the Metaphysics of Knowledge,* trans. Vukan Kuic and Richard J. Thompson (New York: Fordham University Press, 1990). Concerning the placement of the study of the rational soul according to Thomistic principles, see Yves R. Simon, "Knowledge of the Soul" in *Foresight and Knowledge*, ed. Ralph Nelson and Anthony O. Simon (New York: Fordham University Press, 1996), pp. 121, 129, n. 5. Also, from a different perspective, see Charles de Koninck, *Introduction to the Study of the Soul: Being the Preface to Précis de Psychologie Thomiste by Stanislas Cantin,* ed. Vincent M. Martin, trans. Bruno M. Mondor (Somerset, OH: Dominican House of Philosophy, 1951).

2.   See Étienne Gilson, *Methodical Realism: A Handbook for Beginners,* trans. Philip Trower (San Francisco, CA: Ignatius Press, 2011), and *Thomist Realism and the Critique of Knowledge,* trans. Mark A. Wauck (San Francisco, CA: Ignatius Press, 2012).

3.   See Réginald Garrigou-Lagrange, *Le réalisme du principe du finalité* (Paris: Desclée de Brouwer, 1932), pp. 148–75.

4.   See the discussion on this in Austin Woodbury, S.M., *Defensive Metaphysics* (St. Vincent College, Latrobe, PA: The John N. Deely and Anthony F. Russell Collection, Latimer Family Library), nos. 5–10. Woodbury also seems to owe much to the lecture notes of Fr. Angelo Pirotta, whose *Metaphysica Defensiva seu Critica* was never published. Moreover, as in much of his work, Maquart's *Elementa Philosophia* remains the textual backbone of Woodbury's own text, which then builds upon it in important and significant ways. Also see F.-X. Maquart, *Elementa philosophia*, vol. 3, pt. 1: *Metaphysica defensiva seu Critica* (Paris: Andreas Blot, 1938); Maritain, *The Degrees of Knowledge,* pp. 75–144.

throughout a number of his works. Certainly, the text is only a brief pedagogical presentation, but its clarity provides the reader with a direct and clear articulation of principles of supreme luminosity: First, *the fact that knowledge involves becoming the other precisely as other (and this goes "all the way down" to the order of sense knowledge)*; second, *the notion of being is the luminous objective center of all of our intellection in the order of nature*, along with *the principle of non-contradiction as the very first principle, upon which all others depend, indeed with an extra-mental value and not merely as a logical law of thought*; third, *and finally, we can reflect on our knowledge and thereby know the nature of our intellect as a faculty that is essentially relative to being.*[5] As he concludes this essay, we also feel the influence of his life-long battles with the proponents of the "philosophy of action" (for him, almost always implying Maurice Blondel and those under his influence),[6] which he believed gave too much credence to Kantianism's declarations concerning the limitations of human intellection. Fr. Garrigou-Lagrange's convictions are quite clear, in any case: Traditional realism can defend itself, at least through arguments in the form of *reductiones ad absurdum*, defending of our mind's ability to reflect on reality and not solely on the mere projections of our own subjective making.

I decided to leave the title of the second chapter in its original form, as the Latin expression served as a maxim in the Thomist school.

---

5. As Fr. Garrigou-Lagrange is clear in other texts, it is far from the case that all other principles would be inferentially deduced from the principle of non-contradiction. For example, the principle of finality (every agent acts for an end) is a *per se nota* ("self-evident") proposition. However, the denial of it will lead to a denial of the principle of non-contradiction (and vice-versa), precisely because we are here dealing with extra-mental laws of being as such. Nonetheless, there is an ordering among principles, something stated by St. Thomas and defended by Fr. Garrigou in texts found in our current volume, as well as at length in *Sens Commun: La philosphie de l'être et les formules dogmatiques*, 4th ed. (Paris: Desclée de Brouwer, 1936), pp. 159–92.

6. It should be noted, however, that Fr. Garrigou-Lagrange took care not to vilify Blondel personally, for whom he attempted to express personal kindness, as one can see even in the midst of heated battles such as those witnessed in Réginald Garrigou-Lagrange, "Verité et immutabilité du dogme," *Angelicum*, Vol. 24 (1947): pp. 124–39 (esp. pp. 124–25, n. 1). Various correspondence between the two men is publicly found in journals from during their lifetime. A recent work in Croatian gathers the correspondence and merits consideration for details concerning the relationship between the two men. See *U potrazi za istinom: korespondencija Blondel - Garrigou-Lagrange*, ed. Hrvoje Lasic (Zagreb: Demetra, 2016).

It is at the heart of Fr. Garrigou-Lagrange's position in this article: "Cognoscens quodammodo fit vel est aliud a se. [The Knower in Some Manner Becomes or is What is Other Than Itself.]" This essay was written in response to a criticism registered against remarks that he made in his work *God: His Existence and His Nature*. The text presented here provides an utterly lucid exposition of a theme that was taken for granted in the Thomist school once upon a time: knowledge is *a way of being the other precisely as other*. The most important thing to heed in this article is that this difficult topic applies to created knowers in the broadest sense, even to the utterly basic knowledge we have through our external senses. As Fr. Garrigou-Lagrange will explain, knowledge *as such* is a unique kind of becoming. It involves becoming the other *precisely as other*, the reception of a form while retaining the alterity of what is known. Thus, the actual sensation of being burned differs from all the various physical changes involved in being burned, though all of those are required so that sense knowledge can be achieved.[7] This chapter constitutes one of the clearest explanations of the Thomist school on this topic and serves as an entrée into these important topics of intentional / objective existence in sensation and intellection.[8]

---

7.   On this topic, the aforementioned text by Simon is perhaps the best exposition of the Thomist school on these matters. Also, see Garrigou-Lagrange, *Sense of Mystery*, pp. 80–85. One should also consult Simon's masterful *An Introduction to the Metaphysics of Knowledge*, cited above. Also see Yves R. Simon, "An Essay on Sensation," in *Philosopher at Work: Essays by Yves R. Simon*, ed. Anthony O. Simon (Lanham, MD: Rowman and Littlefield, 1999), pp. 57–111.

8.   See also Yves R. Simon, "To Be and to Know" in *Philosopher at Work*, pp. 173–93. Also, Austin Woodbury, S.M., *Natural Philosophy* (St. Vincent College, Latrobe, PA: The John N. Deely and Anthony F. Russell Collection, Latimer Family Library), pp. 472–578. John N. Deely, "The Immateriality of the Intentional as Such," *The New Scholasticism*, Vol. 42 (1968): pp. 293–306. In addition, there are perceptive remarks in a personal essay by Deely presented to Mortimer Adler in the midst of a dispute between the two of them in 1971. The text is in the process of being considered for publication by Peter Redpath, who is compiling Deely's correspondence with Adler from this period. See John N. Deely, "Towards an Ontology of the Intersubjective" (St. Vincent College, Latrobe, PA: The John N. Deely and Anthony F. Russell Collection, St. Vincent College Library).

      Recently, this topic has been treated with much insight, albeit not in a manner completely isomorphic with the traditional Thomist school, in Therese Scarpelli Cory, "Knowing as Being? A Metaphysical Reading of the Identity of Intellect and Intelligibles in Aquinas," *American Catholic Philosophical Quarterly*, Vol. 91, No. 3 (Summer 2017): pp. 333–51.

The third chapter, "Whether the Mind Knows Itself Through its Essence or Through Some *Species*," likewise introduces some very important topics in the context of questions that have recently received detailed scholarly treatment in Therese Cory's *Aquinas on Human Self-Knowledge*.[9] In that text, she only lists this article in a lengthy footnote detailing a debate that erupted in French scholarly literature in the 1920s and 1930s.[10] Her monograph does not focus on the Dominican commentatorial tradition concerning these topics, so a lengthy discussion of Fr. Garrigou-Lagrange's article would likely have been outside of her chosen hermeneutic. However, given that the article was written quite explicitly within said tradition, it is an important voice concerning these matters, especially as regards the requirement for the production of an internal word in all created cognition.[11]

Many contemporary authors arguably minimize the distinction between subjective and objective reception, especially when it comes to reception of forms by sense powers. Error on this point is not a small matter. It ultimately involves the destruction of the rational explanation of the very phenomenon of knowledge in all its forms. As regards the current state of the discussions on the nature of the reception of forms, see Eleonore Stump, *Aquinas* (London: Routledge, 2003), pp. 253–54. See Robert Pasnau, *Theories of Cognition in the Later Middle Ages* (Cambridge: Cambridge University Press, 1997), pp. 1–60. For a survey of the discussion on these matters, see S. M. Cohen, "St. Thomas Aquinas on the Immaterial Reception of Sensible Forms," *The Philosophical Review*, Vol. 91 (1982): pp. 193–209. John J. Haldane, "Aquinas on Sense-Perception," *The Philosophical Review*, Vol. 92 (1983): pp. 233–39. Paul Hoffman, "St. Thomas Aquinas on the Halfway State of Sensible Being," *The Philosophical Review*, Vol. 99 (1990): pp. 73–92. Gabriele De Anna, "Aquinas on Sensible Forms and Semimaterialism," *The Review of Metaphysics*, Vol. 54 (2000): pp. 43–63. A more recent article of interest, although ultimately not in line with the interpretation advanced by Fr. Garrigou-Lagrange, can be found in James D. Madden, "Is a Thomistic Theory of Intentionality Consistent with Physicalism?" *American Catholic Philosophical Quarterly*, Vol. 91, No. 1 (Winter 2017): pp. 1–28.

9. Therese Scarpelli Cory, *Aquinas on Human Self-Knowledge* (Cambridge: University of Cambridge Press, 2015).

10. See ibid., pp. 92–93, n. 2.

11. The doctrine of the internal word has been questioned as being only theological by John P. O'Callaghan in "*Verbum Mentis*: Philosophical or Theological Doctrine in Aquinas," *Proceedings of the American Catholic Philosophical Association*, Vol. 74 (2000): pp. 103–119. This topic, taken up in later work by O'Callaghan was vigorously critiqued in John Deely, "How to Go Nowhere with Language: Remarks on John O'Callaghan, Thomist Realism and the Linguistic Turn," *American Catholic Philosophical Quarterly*, Vol. 82, No. 2 (2008): pp. 337–59. O'Callaghan's response can be found in "Concepts, Mirrors, and Signification: Response to Deely," *American Catholic Philosophical Quarterly*, Vol. 84, No. 1 (2010): 133–62. [CONT. NEXT PAGE]

In the text, Fr. Garrigou-Lagrange interprets St. Thomas's later writings on this matter as being generally consistent with earlier writings in his corpus.[12] At first, the article reads as though it is making a set of ordinary "Thomistic" claims: in a state of union with the body, the soul can know itself only by reflection on its acts of knowledge; in the state of separation from the body, the soul can know itself directly through its essence, since its essence will then be actually immaterial, as is also the case with the angels. However, the reader will do well to heed the third section of this chapter in which Fr. Garrigou-Lagrange discusses how the separated soul (and also the angels) must produce an internal word (i.e., a *species expressa*) so as to *actually understand* what they know, *even in their self-knowledge*.[13] This is the nature of all creaturely

---

The developed Thomist school (especially following on John of St. Thomas) held it to be a necessary part of the human knowing process. Simon penetratingly studies this in *An Introduction to the Metaphysics of Knowledge*, pp. 127–136. One can also profitably consult John Frederick Peifer, *The Concept in Thomism* (New York: Bookman Associates, 1952), pp. 132–212. Jacques Maritain, "Appendix I: The Concept" in *The Degrees of Knowledge*, pp. 411–41. From outside the traditional Thomist school, see also Bernard Lonergan, *Verbum: Word and Idea in Aquinas*, ed. David B. Burrell (Notre Dame, IN: University of Notre Dame Press, 1967).

12. Thus, since he is particularly interested in showing that *De veritate* and the *Summa theologiae* are in agreement on these matters, Fr. Garrigou-Lagrange substantially agrees with what Cory concludes, although she notes an initial development between the Commentary on the *Sentences* and the *De veritate* as well as a general maturing *within* the position reached by Aquinas in the *De veritate*. See Cory, *Aquinas on Human Self-Knowledge*, pp. 40–65.

13. This is also discussed with great insight in Simon, *An Introduction to the Metaphysics of Knowledge*, pp. 19–20, n. 28, p. 130, n. 49. In the former footnote, he states: "As far as the angel's knowledge of himself is concerned, the natural presence of the object (the substance of the angel) in the subject (the angelic intelligence) makes unnecessary any initial representative form (*species impressa*), but not the terminal representative form or concept (*species expressa*). The role of the initial representative form is to make the object present to the knower with the degree of immateriality proportionate to his knowing power; but the substance of the angel is by its very nature present to the angelic intellect and by its very nature endowed with intelligibility. The union of the understanding and the object is far better assured here than it can be by any idea... And yet a terminal representative form (*species expressa*) remains necessary because... our thinking has to have a concept for its term and because no created being enjoys by its own nature the immateriality of what is thought in act."
As is clear in the essay itself, this topic set Fr. Garrigou-Lagrange in disagreement with Fr. Ambroise Gardeil, whom he held in great esteem. See Ambroise Gardeil, "Examen de Conscience," *Revue thomiste*, Vol. 34 (New Series, 12) (1929): pp. 70–84. On this topic, and the discussions related thereto that were undergoing until the time of Fr. Gardeil's death, see Maritain, "On a Work of Father Gardeil," in *Degrees of Knowledge*, pp. 469–74.

knowledge (i.e., all knowledge other than God's self-knowledge and the divinized knowledge that the blessed have of Him in the Beatific Vision). Fr. Garrigou-Lagrange then goes on to defend the claim that experiential knowledge is possible even when a word (or, *species expressa*) is produced as a prerequisite for an act of self-knowledge.[14] Based on this conclusion he returns to the point with which the essay opens, hinting that parallel claims that can be made regarding the quasi-experiential knowledge belonging to mystical knowledge one can have of God. However, one must turn elsewhere in his works to see a fuller discussion of this topic.[15]

The final essay in this section is concerned with the question of the nature of sensation, understood precisely as the initial knowledge we have prior to any further articulation by our "internal" senses of imagination, memory, and estimation / cogitation: "There Cannot Be Genuine Sensation Without a Real Sensed Thing." I have drawn this chapter from a translation published by Thomas DePauw and E. M. Macierowski in *Studia Gilsoniana*. On the whole, I have left their text in its original state in order to respect their own translational style, which is slightly more literal than my own, which retains the literal content while trying to be slightly more adaptive to the English ear. However, I did feel the need to adjust some points of punctuation and citation style in order to bring the essay in line with the remainder of the text. This essay presents a wonderful meeting of minds as Fr. Garrigou-Lagrange reflects on the nature of our external sense knowledge in a paper dedicated to the work of the great Benedictine Fr. Joseph Gredt, whose *Elementa Philosophiae* presented a pedagogically clear introduction to philosophy to many pre-Conciliar Thomists, attempting to follow the order and doctrine of the Thomist school (in particular John of St. Thomas in matters falling to natural philosophy).

Discussions of "realism" too often get lost in the weeds with questions like: "How can we know that our senses are to be trusted?" There is a great temptation to try to answer this kind of question "up

---

14. As will be noted in the chapter itself, this involves some very important points of doctrine concerning the so-called intuitive cognition enabled through the external senses.

15. See Réginald Garrigou-Lagrange, "Love of God and the Indwelling of the Blessed Trinity," in *The Love of God and the Cross of Jesus*, vol. 1, pp. 136–73.

front," but in fact, it is a question that actually should come quite late in one's epistemological reflection, for it is a matter of great difficulty. At the very borders of our knowledge, sensation (*precisely considered as external sensation*) includes the experiential awareness that what we know is existentially present to us. To remember something is quite different experientially than is the immediate experience of that same reality as actually present. There is much more (namely, existence) in a friend present than in a friend imagined. Moreover, the basic knowledge of sensation is very difficult to articulate in its own right. We normally formulate our knowledge in already-articulated wholes, grasped through "higher" sense powers traditionally known as the "internal senses." Rarely do we experience *pure sensation*, as Yves Simon insightfully remarks at the opening of his excellent "An Essay on Sensation":

> The worst difficulties of the present subject originate in our inability to achieve the experience of a sensation free from association with images, instinctive judgments, memories, and thoughts. If it were possible for us to suspend, no matter how briefly, all such associated representations and processes, if it were possible to elicit pure sensations and yet to watch ourselves sensing, the understanding of sensation would, no doubt be greatly facilitated. But sensation is the center of a complex, and from this complex it cannot be extracted, except by rational analysis.[16]

We think of many abstract things that cannot exist *in their abstraction* in reality. (We will never encounter *justice-as-such* or *gorilla-as-such* in our day-to-day life.) Moreover, we can actively imagine or remember many particular cases of realities without those realities actually being present (*the just action of a friend who may indeed come to repay a particular debt* or *a gorilla that we remember seeing at the zoo*). External sensation includes the existential presence of the sensed as part of its very nature, but it is also a very basic knowledge immersed in a great

---

16. See Yves R. Simon, "An Essay on Sensation," in *Philosopher at Work*, pp. 57–111. Moreover, see Yves R. Simon, *Introduction to Metaphysics of Knowledge*, pp. 85–112.

apparatus of interpretation and insight.[17] Moreover, the nature of sensation is not something that we have to argue on behalf of in light of some other principle. It is self-evident. We either grasp it or do not. As Aristotle stated in a related matter, likely with tongue in cheek:

> But to attend equally to the opinions and the fancies of disputing parties is foolish; for clearly one of them must be mistaken. And this is evident from what happens in sensation; for the same thing never appears sweet to some and bitter to others, unless in the one case the sense-organ which discriminates the aforesaid flavours has been perverted and injured. And if this is so the one party must be taken to be the measure, and the other must not. And say the same of good and bad, and beautiful and ugly, and all other such qualities. For to maintain the view we are opposing is just like maintaining the truth of what appears to people who put their finger under their eye and make the object appear two instead of one must be two (because they appear to be of that number) and again one (for to those who do not interfere with their eye the one object appears one).[18]

Obviously, there are limitations in each of the essays presented in this chapter, and a full "realism" requires many further things to be

---

17. Thus, we see the importance of articulating the nature of the so-called "internal" senses in the Thomistic theory of knowledge, in particular, the "cogitative power" which is so significantly influenced by our intellectual knowledge. This topic has received excellent treatment in the works of Daniel D. De Haan, "Perception and the *Vis cogitativa*: A Thomistic Analysis of Aspectual, Actional, and Affectional Percepts," *American Catholic Philosophical Society*, Vol. 88, No. 3 (2014): pp. 397–437; "Moral Perception and the Function of the *Vis Cogitativa* in Thomas Aquinas's Doctrine of Antecedent and Consequent Passions," *Documenti e studi sulla traditione filosofica medievale*, Vol. 25 (2014): pp. 289–330.

18. See Aristotle, *Metaphysics*, in *The Complete Works of Aristotle*, bk. 11, ch. 6 (1062b33 –1063a10).

    Obviously, the problem of sensation *does* require a *detailed* discussion of hallucinations and the problem of false sense-stimulation, as one will find in many modern works of epistemology. This is all part of the critical reflection on sensation that comes *very late* in one's philosophical reflection, presupposing a great deal concerning one's metaphysical presuppositions—including, among other things, the fact that sense knowledge includes this existential component, as well as the fact that knowledge's very nature is *to exist as relative to the other precisely as other.*

articulated. Nonetheless, the basic principles and distinctions offered by Fr. Garrigou-Lagrange here are rich with implications. Indeed, that is the very nature of true principles: they are white-hot illuminative centers around which we can organize further articulations of our knowledge. Progress in Thomist metaphysics cannot come at the cost of rejecting these certain principles merely because they are not "the whole story." Rather, they should be accepted for their self-evident value and rejoiced in as a kind of gift: the gift of knowing, in some small way, the lofty reality that is knowledge.

ORIGINAL TEXTS FOR THIS SECTION

"Le réalisme thomiste: Son triple fondement." In *Actas del Primer Congreso Nacional de Filosofía* (Mendoza: 1949): pp. 1147–59.

"'Cognoscens quodammodo fit vel est aliud a se.'" *Revue néo-scolastique de philosophie*, Vol. 25 (1923): pp. 420–30.

"Utrum mens seipsam per essentiam cognoscat, an per aliquam speciem." *Angelicum*, Vol. 5 (1928): pp. 37–54.

"Non potest esse genuina sensatio sine reali sensato." *Studia Anselmiana*, Vol. 7–8 (1938): pp. 189–201. [Originally translated as: "There Cannot Be Genuine Sensation Without a Real Sensed Thing." Translated by Thomas DePauw. Edited by Edward M. Macierowski. *Studia Gilsoniana*, Vol. 4, No. 2 (April–June 2015): pp. 165–79.

* * *

CHAPTER I

The Threefold Foundation of Thomist Realism

I.

The fundamental thesis of traditional realism, at least as it was conceived of by St. Thomas, following Aristotle, is that our intellect can, by its natural powers, come to have metaphysical certitude concerning extra-mental being and its immutable laws.

Above all, this realism maintains the traditional definition of truth: *adaequatio rei et intellectus.* The truth is not merely the conformity of our judgment with the subjective laws of our mind but, rather, is its conformity with *extra-mental reality* and its *immutable laws of non-contradiction or identity* (that which is, is; that which is not, is not; being is not non-being), *of efficient causality* (that which becomes does not exist by itself and, therefore, requires a cause), and *of finality* (every agent acts for an end, whether or not it knows it).

From this perspective, this traditional realism maintains that our intellect can arrive at metaphysical certitude concerning the existence of God, the First Cause and man's Last End. Why? Because given that *that which comes into being* does not exist by itself, it requires a cause, and in the final analysis requires an *Uncaused Cause* who acts through Itself and exists through Itself, a Cause who is related to being as A is related to A, through the principle of identity, such as it is verified in the Supreme Reality.[1]

Thus, there needs to be a Cause which would be *Being Itself*, ever in act, Eternally Subsistent *Pure Act, Truth, Wisdom*, and *Perfect Goodness*, a Cause that is sovereignly *simple* and *immutable* and, consequently, really and essentially *distinct* from the imperfect, composite, and changing world.

Therefore, there needs to be a Cause that is really distinct from humanity, which is ever capable of progress as well as of tremendous backsliding, a Cause who alone can say, "*Ego sum qui sum*" (Ex. 3:14), whereas we can only *have* truth and life, without however *being* truth and life. Here, we can see the immeasurable distance separating the verb *to be* and the verb *to have*.[2] This is self-evidently true.

Nonetheless, this traditional doctrine is rejected by subjectivism, which holds that *the truth* is not the conformity of our judgment with extra-mental reality and its ontological laws but, rather, *the conformity of our judgment with our thought's own subjective laws* or, again, *with human life*, which is ever-evolving and (as the philosophy of action puts it) the conformity of our judgment *with the requirements of human action* as they manifest themselves throughout time. Thus, according to Kant, we can therefore only arrive at a *subjectively sufficient*, though *objectively insufficient*, certitude concerning God's existence. A number of people even draw the following conclusion, thus joining the intellectual élan of absolute evolutionism: "In response to the relative and provisional truth of given thesis, there forever follows the provisional truth of an antithesis, followed by that of a superior synthesis, etc. Immutable, absolute truth no longer exists but, rather, only an ever-changing and mutable truth."

The point of departure for this relativism appeared before Aristotle in Heraclitus and in the Sophists (in particular in Protagoras) and then

---

1.   The *primacy of being over becoming* must be admitted, for there is more in *that which is* than in *that which comes into being* and does not yet exist, *more* in the begotten adult than in the embryo in the midst of its development. Likewise, there is *more* in *act* than in *potency*, more in the oak than in the seed contained in the acorn. And *it is wholly necessary* that, in an actually subordinated series of movers, we must come to a halt at a First Mover, Pure Act, ἀνάγκη στῆναι.

2.   TRANSLATOR'S NOTE: This is a theme that recurs in Fr. Garrigou-Lagrange. See Garrigou-Lagrange, *Sense of Mystery*, pp. 47–55.

later on was found in the Greek skeptics. It can be found once more in various forms[3] in modern subjectivism.

According to such modern subjectivism, if the truth consists in the agreement of knowledge with the extra-mental object, my knowledge can be regarded as being true only on the condition that it is in accord with it. Now, this agreement is unverifiable. To compare knowledge with the extra-mental object is to compare knowledge with itself, *since everything I know is known only through knowledge*. Given that the object is always outside of me and my knowledge inside of me, I can make only one kind of judgment concerning a thing, namely, whether my knowledge of the object is in agreement with my knowledge of the object. Therefore, man is enclosed within himself and cannot escape from this self-enclosed state. He knows only the phenomena, all in accord with the subjective laws of his mind.

Even before Aristotle's own day, we can find the sophist Protagoras making this same point. What was the Stagirite's response to this problem, and how was this response understood by St. Thomas and by his best disciples? This is the question we would like to respond to here. We will do so by pointing out the threefold foundation of Thomist realism: the sense foundation of our knowledge, its objective-intelligible foundation, and its reflexive-intellectual foundation.

Aristotle had already responded to the sophists by showing:

1. That *the knower* in a certain manner becomes *something other* than itself, *aliud a se*;
2. That the first object known by our intellect is not the phenomenon or phenomena but, rather, *the intelligible being* of sensible things;
3. That our intellect immediately grasps in intelligible being its contradictory opposition to non-being, as well as *the real value* of the principle of non-contradiction, a real value which no amount of argumentation can destroy;
4. That our intellect, by reflecting back on its act, knows not only the fact of this act but, likewise, *the nature* of this act,

---

3.   TRANSLATOR'S NOTE: Reading "formes" for "fermes."

as well as *the intellect's own nature*, which is (in all three of its operations) *essentially relative* to intelligible being as sight to the colored and hearing to sound.

Aristotle's teaching on this matter was deepened by St. Thomas, and here we would like to recall the principal landmarks [étapes principales] in this traditional realism.

II. *COGNOSCENS FIT QUODAMMODO ALIUD A SE*[4]

First of all, according to Aristotle, the knower, by *its nature* and its more or less perfect *immateriality*, differs from the non-knower precisely because, without ceasing to be what it is, it can in some manner *become something other* than itself, through the representation which is *essentially relative* to the object represented, without implying a vicious circle or a *petitio principii*.

This is what we find already occurring in animals, precisely because they are endowed with sense knowledge. Whereas plants remain *enclosed within themselves*, animals *are opened up*, through sense knowledge, to the external world. For example, when the sun arises, the animal is not only illuminated and heated, as is the plant, but beyond this, *it sees the sun*, which the plant does not see in any way. The animal's eye is a mirror which contains the impression and image of the sun, but it is an animated *mirror which sees*. In seeing the sun, through the impression and representation that it has of it, the animal in a certain manner becomes *something other* than itself, *quodammodo fit aliud a se—anima quodammodo fit omnia*. On this, see Aristotle's *De anima*, bk. 3, ch. 8 and bk. 2, ch. 12. Moreover, in *ST* I, q. 14, a. 1, St. Thomas says:

> Knowers are distinguished from non-knowers in the fact that non-knowers have nothing except their own forms, whereas it is of the nature of knowers to have even the form of another thing, for the species of the known exists in the knower... On account of

---

4.   TRANSLATOR'S NOTE: For a more complete discussion of this topic, see the chapter in this volume having this same title. Likewise, see "There Cannot be Genuine Sensation Without a Real Sensed Thing."

their materiality, plants do not know. However, a sense power is a knowing power, for it receives the species without matter…and the intellect is even more so a knowing power, for it is more separate from matter and unmixed, as is said in *De anima*, bk. 3, ch. 8.

The reader should here consult the profound commentary provided for this article by Cajetan, as well as that which can be found in John of St. Thomas. Doubtless, it will be objected: However, sensation does not essentially differ from a subjective hallucination.

In treating of hallucination,[5] Aristotle notes that it always presupposes a prior sensation, just as an *echo* always presupposes a true sound. Indeed, we must consider not only the fact of sensation, but moreover, *its nature*. Now, for our intellect, *the sense of sight is, by its very nature, essentially relative to the extra-mental colored* [thing] and cannot exist without it: *non potest esse genuine sensation sine reali sensato*. By contrast, hallucinations are, by their very nature, not relative to a really-present exterior object but, rather, necessarily presuppose a true sensation, just as an echo presupposes a real sound. This is why those who are born blind never experience visual hallucinations. A sensation without a real sensed thing, an external object without a really-experienced external object, cannot be conceived of, for such notions are meaningless, forms of absurdity, contrary at once to the principles of contradiction, causality (a causeless sensation), and finality. The sensation of resistance presupposes that which resists.[6]

Now, if the animal endowed with sense knowledge is already *opened up on the entire sensible world* of colors and sounds, man who is endowed with intellectual knowledge is *opened up on the intelligible world* and will be able *to become*, in some way, everything that is

---

5.   See *Index operum Aristotelis: hallucinatio* and *echo*.

6.   TRANSLATOR'S NOTE: Granted, a much longer critique of sensation is necessary for a full philosophical account to be provided. On this topic, the reader would benefit significantly from consulting Yves R. Simon, "An Essay on Sensation," in *Philosopher at Work*, pp. 57–111. Moreover, independent insights from within the same Thomist tradition (heavily influenced, in particular, by Maritain, Simon, and Deely) can be found in John C. Cahalan, *Causal Realism: An Essay on Philosophical Method and the Foundations of Knowledge* (Lanham, MD: University Press of America, 1985), pp. 387–417.

intelligible. "*Anima humana fit quodammodo omnia per cognitionem.*" In order to provide a better account of how this is so, we must ask what is the first object known by the human intellect. This first-known object is not the same as the first object of the divine intellect, nor that of the angelic intellect.

III. THE FIRST OBJECT KNOWN BY OUR INTELLECT

According to Aristotle and St. Thomas, the first object known by our intellect is the *intelligible being of sensible things.* In *Summa contra gentiles* (*SCG*) II, ch. 83, §32, St. Thomas says: "Just as sight naturally knows color and hearing sound, so too the intellect naturally knows being and those things that *per se* belong to being as such, and our notions of the first principles are founded on such knowledge." Likewise, in *ST* I, q. 5, a. 2: "Being is the first thing that is intelligible, just as sound is the first hearable thing." In *De veritate*, q. 1, a. 1: "That which the intellect first conceives, as that which is most known and that into which it resolves all of its conceptions, is being." So too see *ST* I-II, q. 94, a. 2 and *In IV Meta.*, ch. 3, lect. 5.

Whereas the sense of sight attains the colored reality as colored and not as being, and the sense of hearing attains the sounding reality *as sounding*, and whereas the sense of taste attains, for example, milk *as sweet*, the intellect attains the sweet being precisely as being, "*dum gustus attinget ens dulce, non ut ens, sed ut dulce, intellectus attingit ens dulce, ut ens.*"[7] The human intellect immediately attains its proper object: the intelligible being of sensible, colored, sonorous (etc.) things. As sight grasps the colored under the light of the sun, our intellect directly and immediately attains *the intelligible being* of sensible things under its own natural light, which Aristotle calls the light of the agent intellect. Here, we find ourselves entering into a new order, one that is

---

7. St. Thomas says that the sheep knows its lamb not as *a being* that is distinct from it but, rather, as something to be given milk, *ut lactabilem*. He also says that the lamb itself, through its instinct [i.e., through its estimative sense], knows that the wolf is an enemy to be fled from, *ut inimicum naturalem*. By contrast, from quite early on in its life, the small child knows the verb *to be* in the present and past tenses ([e.g.,] the presence and absence of its mother), as well as the verb *to have*. If one comes to ask this child questions, one will see that he makes use of these verbs very soon after having begun to speak, long before coming to distinguish moral (or fitting) good from moral evil.

immensely superior to the sensible order. Here we see what Pascal will come to say in *Les Pensées*: "All bodies, the firmament and the stars, the earth and its kingdoms, do not have the same value as the least of minds, for the latter knows all of this, as well as itself, whereas bodies know nothing." Man differs from animals first of all because the object of his intellect is not limited to the mere sensible phenomenon but, rather, is intelligible being, because he knows the meaning of this little word, "is," and quickly grasps that *the verb to be* is the root of all the others ("Socrates acts," means, "Socrates is acting"), and he distinguishes the three grammatical persons, the subjects of the verb to be in the singular and the plural, likewise grasping all the tenses and various moods of this verb and those of others as well. He first learns them grammatically, then gradually discovers the *ontological riches virtually contained in the verb to be* and the verb *to have*. Aristotle speaks about this in a profound manner at the beginning of the *Perihermeneias*, bk. 1, ch. 1, where he studies judgment, the subject, the verb, the predicate, the substantive, the adjective, and the adverb. However, what is the first principle founded on the notion of being?

IV. THE ONTOLOGICAL VALUE
OF THE PRINCIPLE OF NON-CONTRADICTION

Under its natural light, our intellect, in attaining the intelligible being of sensible things, immediately sees within that very being its contradictory opposition to non-being. Concerning this point, see what Aristotle says in *Metaphysics*, bk. 4 (3), ch. 3 (lect. 5 in St. Thomas's commentary), as well as *ST* I-II, q. 94, a. 2, where St. Thomas says:

> That which first falls into [our intellect's] apprehension is being, the understanding of which is included in everything that someone grasps. And therefore, the first indemonstrable principle is that we cannot simultaneously affirm and deny [the same thing of the same subject in the same respect], which is founded on the notion of being and non-being, and all the other principles are founded on this principle, as the Philosopher says in *Metaphysics*, bk. 4, ch. 3.

The principle of identity affirms, "That which is, is; that which is not, is not." The principle of non-contradiction expresses the same truth in a negative fashion: "Being is not non-being," or more explicitly, "It is impossible that one thing, one reality (the smallest or the most supreme) at one and the same time would exist and not exist, that it would have a given nature and not have it." This is not only *unimaginable*, not only subjectively *inconceivable*, but beyond this is *really impossible, something that cannot be realized* outside of our mind, whatever any [Cartesian] evil genius may say about it.

However, the sophists, then the Greek skeptics, along with modern subjectivists, all denied the real or ontological value of principle of identity (or, of non-contradiction), basing their claim upon the perpetual alteration undergone by sensible phenomena or that of our own internal [psychological] phenomena.

How do Aristotle and St. Thomas respond to their denial? They carefully and extensively examined all of the arguments invoked by the sophists (themselves following along the path paved by Heraclitus) against the real value of the principle of identity (or, of non-contradiction). This is the object considered in *Metaphysics*, bk. 4 (3), from ch. 3 (lect. 5 in St. Thomas's commentary) to the end of that book.

Aristotle and St. Thomas respond *redarguitive* [by way of refutation] by showing that the sophists' arguments do not at all prove what they claim to establish against the very first natural evidence of our intellect's natural knowledge. These arguments, like those of Heraclitus, base themselves on the perpetual mobility of sensible phenomena, claiming to conclude from this fact that *nothing identical* or *stable* exists, no immutable truth, not even that of the principle of non-contradiction, which would be only a grammatical law of our discourse and, at the very most, of discursive and abstract thought, though not of reality.

Aristotle first of all comments that the perpetual mobility of sensible phenomena does not preclude the stability of the nature of bodies, that of gold and silver, of plants and animals. The oak always begets the oak, the horse always begets the horse, the cow always begets the cow, and man always begets man. One and the same *natural cause*, being determined *ad unum* by its very nature, always produces, in the same circumstances, the same effect. Otherwise, the change of the effect would lack a *raison d'être*. This is the principle of induction, which passes from the particular to the general, ultimately to *stable* natural laws.[8] Moreover, as Aristotle comments in the same text, if one comes to deny the real value of the principle of non-contradiction or to doubt it, one ultimately ends up not only in universal becoming but, moreover, *at absolute nihilism* in the order of being, thought, desire, and action. Indeed, to doubt the ontological value of this principle leads to the suppression of:

1. *All language*, every determinate signifying value for words, the substantive, verb, adjective, and adverb;

2. *Every essence and substance*, for all predicates thus will be accidental, since one will be able to affirm them and deny them of any given subject;

3. *The diversity of things*, for there no longer is a contrary and contradictory opposition between a stone, a plant, and a man, between a wall, a trireme, and Callias; this represents a state of universal confusion, for no distinction exists any longer between matter and spirit, between necessity and freedom, between God and the world;

4. *All truth*, for one can attribute any predicate whatsoever to any subject whatsoever;

5. *All opinion and probability*, for opinion inclines more so toward one side of a contradiction than toward the opposed side, inclining toward affirmation more than to denial;

---

8. If the mule is sterile, this is because it no longer has within itself either the species of the horse nor that of the donkey. *If it were either, it would transmit it.* (It has generative organs, but it no longer has the either the sense soul of the donkey nor that of a horse.) This is a sign that the *species* of the horse and that of the mule are truly distinct. Cf. *Opera Aristotelis, index, mulus*, and *sterilitas*.

The problem of the universals, which was so debated in antiquity and in the Middle Ages between the nominalists, the conceptualists, and the realists, today reappears in the problem concerning the evolution of animal species: are these species only common names (empirical nominalism), provisional concepts (subjectivist conceptualism), or rather, do they have a stable foundation in reality (the moderate realism of Aristotle and St. Thomas). In virtue of the principle of causality, a natural cause cannot produce *by its own power* an effect which is superior to itself.

however, on this supposition, there would no longer be any opposition between the two sides;

6. *Every form of desire, aversion, and action*, for we desire an object only because it is suitable for us and detest only that which is harmful to us; however, on this supposition, there would no longer be anything that is suitable for us and nothing that could be harmful to us; thus, one would find oneself in a state of absolute *indifferentism* and utter *inaction*;

7. *Even the degrees of error*, for if one is in doubt concerning the real value of the principle of non-contradiction, it is no falser to say, "2 + 2 = 1,000," than to say, "2 + 2 = 5";

8. Finally, against Heraclitus and the foundation for his absolute form of evolutionism, the denial of the principle of non-contradiction *makes all motion impossible*, for there would no longer be a contradictory opposition between the point of departure and the point of arrival; thus, one would arrive before setting out toward one's destination.

Thus, by denying the principle of non-contradiction, one does not merely end up at universal becoming but, moreover, at complete nihilism in the order of being, as well as in the order of becoming and in the orders of thought, truth, error, opinion, desire, and action.

At the very least, Protagoras, even in his great deviousness, must admit *that he cannot at one and the same time be Protagoras and not be him*. Otherwise, he would completely vanish and become "similar to a plant," incapable of every form of knowledge, even sense knowledge.

Thus, we see now how Aristotle responded *redarguitive* to the sophists by showing that their arguments completely fail to reach a conclusion against *the utterly first natural and necessitating evidence of our intellect*. They deny it as a consequence of their prejudices and through their sophistical arguments. However, they simultaneously preserve it, for otherwise, they would no longer be able to say anything, nor to think anything, nor even to exist. The skeptic's proper demeanor is to remain silent.

In the same place, Aristotle said, "Heraclitus seems to have denied the value of the principle of non-contradiction, but one need not think everything that one happens to say," for in the end, Heraclitus himself, whether he wishes to or not, finds himself compelled to obey the principle of non-contradiction.

An old Thomist, Fr. Norbert del Prado, once said to a Kantian, "Can Kant simultaneously be Kant and not be him?" In other words: Can he seriously doubt the real value of the principle of non-contradiction, the first law of thought and of reality, a law whose *self-evidence is necessitating?*

If he is in doubt concerning this matter, he no longer is merely afflicted with an incurable form of spiritual consumption but, rather, suffers from *the very death of the intellect*. Such a denial represents an unpardonable sin against the natural light of our mind [*esprit*], representing in the philosophical order a fault similar to that which the sin against the Holy Spirit is in the spiritual order, "*impugnatio veritatis agnitae*," [resistance to truth that is recognized]. One thus fights against the very principle which alone can deliver us from error.[9]

V. OUR INTELLECT KNOWS ITS OWN NATURE, ITS ESSENTIAL AND VITAL RELATION TO BEING

We have seen what are the first two foundations of Thomist realism in the sensible and intelligible orders: the metaphysical certitude of the ontological value of the principle of non-contradiction, as well as of the other first principles, is founded *materially* on its prerequisite sensation and *formally* on the necessitating evidence of these principles as the first laws of being. As St. Thomas says in *In Boetium de Trinitate*, q. 3, a. 1, ad 4; "Just as knowledge of principles is taken from the senses, even though the light by which the principles are known is innate, so too faith comes from hearing, even though the *habitus* of faith is infused." Our metaphysical certitude concerning the ontological value of the first principles is materially founded on the prerequisite sensation and formally upon *the necessitating evidence* of these principles, an evidence of an order that is immensely superior to sensation, namely, evidence of the intelligible order, not merely that of the sensible order.

However, Thomist realism has a third foundation, one in the reflexive-intellectual order. In short, it is: By reflecting on itself, our intellect

---

9. See *ST* II-II, q. 14, aa. 2–3 (on the sin against the Holy Spirit).

knows not only the existence of its act but also knows *the nature* of its
act, as well as *its own nature* as a faculty that is essentially relative to
being and conformed to it.

As St. Thomas says quite clearly in *De veritate*, q. 1, a. 9:

> The intellect reflects upon its own act, not only inasmuch as it
> knows its own act, but also inasmuch as it knows its proportion to
> the reality that is known [*ad rem*]. Now, it cannot know this unless
> it knows the nature of its act, which cannot be known unless the
> nature of its active principle is known, namely, the intellect whose
> nature is to be conformed to reality [*rebus*]. Whence, the intellect
> comes to know the truth by reflecting on itself.

Through reflection, our intellect knows *its own nature*, knowing
that it is immensely superior to the external and internal senses (e.g.,
to the imagination). It knows that it is *essentially relative to intelligible
being*, as sight to the colored. In this way, no matter what subjectivism
may say, the intellect *is not enclosed* within itself but, instead, is *opened*
up on the whole of intelligible reality. It *sees* that there is no vicious
circle here, whatever Kant may say. On the contrary, it is a natural
affirmation made by our mind, an affirmation which should be more
precious to us than the apple of our eye, and if we do not maintain it,
we will suffer intellectual death, as we see in positivism (which represents the denial of the possibility of philosophy) and in Kantianism
(which represents the denial of the real value of every form of speculative knowledge).

This essential and vital relation of our intellect to intelligible being
manifests itself through its three operations: conception, judgment, and
reasoning.

First of all, every act of intellectual conception immeasurably exceeds our acts of imagination because the former do not merely juxta-
pose sensible phenomena to each other but, rather, contain the *raison
d'être* which makes them *intelligible*. For example, the concept of a
clock immensely surpasses the averaged-out or composite image of the
clock, for the concept of a clock indicates the efficient and final *raison
d'etre* for its movement. The clock is conceived as being a self-moving

machine which has uniform movement *in order to indicate the solar hour*, which is a fraction of time. *Time is conceived as being the measure of movement according to before and after.* And *movement is conceived as being the passage from potency to act*, which expresses the primordial division of intelligible being: being in act and being in potency.

Likewise, every notion presupposes the very first notion, *being*, which is like the intellect's sun. Being has as its properties, unity, truth, and goodness, which dominate the categories of being, substance, quantity, quality, action, passion, relation, etc. *The production of beings* is explained by the four causes which render this production intelligible, and these four cases are themselves reduced to potency and act.

Thus, everything is conceived in function of being, the first intelligible, just as sight attains nothing except in function of that which is colored.

Likewise, *the soul of every judgment is the verb to be, the root of all other verbs*: "Socrates acts," means, "Socrates is acting."

Finally, *a priori*[10] reasoning expresses the *raison d'être* of the properties of a nature (for example, of the nature of circles). It renders them intelligible, and *a posteriori* reasoning expresses the *raison d'être* for our affirmation of the existence of a cause manifested by its effects, for example, the reason why we affirm the existence of God, the First Being, First Living One, the First Thought, and Supreme Goodness who draws all things to Himself.

The three operations of our intellect [*esprit*] (conception, judgment, and reasoning) are thus—in an order which is far superior to the imagination—essentially ordered to knowledge of intelligible being, of that which is, to the knowledge of its causes and of the subordination of efficient causes, as well as of the subordination of ends.

Thus, our intellect looks upon itself and sees that it is a *vital relation to intelligible being*. The intellect sees that it is *conformed to being* in order that it may know it. "Thus, our intellect in some way (namely, immaterially and representatively) becomes something other than itself."

---

10. TRANSLATOR'S NOTE: To understand Fr. Garrigou-Lagrange's use of the terms *a priori* and *a posteriori*, see note 7 in "On the Twofold *Via inventionis* and the Twofold *Via iudicii* According to St. Thomas," in the first section above.

Or, as we said at the beginning, with Aristotle, "The intellectual soul in some way becomes all things."[11]

VI. CONCLUSION

Through its threefold (sensible, objective-intelligible, and reflexive-intelligible) foundation, Thomistic realism thus maintains the traditional definition of truth: *Adaequatio rei et intellectus*, the conformity of our judgment with extra-mental being and its immutable laws of identity (or, of non-contradiction), causality, and finality.

As we said at the beginning of this essay, this realism (or, philosophy of being) refuses to give in to the demands of the philosophy of action (or, [what we may call] a superior form of pragmatism), namely, the demand that we must declare that the traditional definition of truth is "chimerical" and thus "substitute" another (subjective and practical) one for it: *conformitas mentis cum vita et exigentiis subjectivis humanae actionis* [conformity of the mind with life and the subjective requirements of human action].

Thus, one would come to have only a "subjectively sufficient and *objectively insufficient*" certitude concerning the real value of the first

---

11.   This moderate realism of Aristotle and St. Thomas thus avoids falling into the extreme errors which are opposed to each other, whether that of Heraclitus's *radical nominalism* (taken up by Hume and then, in a very different fashion, by Hegelian evolutionism), or of the *excessive realism* of Parmenides, taken up anew by Spinoza.

These extremes touch each other in the sense that nominalistic phenomenalism, which suppresses every substance and every cause, leads to "universal becoming," which is nothing other than *the realization of an abstraction*, just like the immoderate realism of the "universal and unique substance" admitted by Parmenides and Spinoza.

On the other hand, for its own part, this immoderate realism of the universal and unique substance leads to nominalism in the case of particular substances, [as well as] for genera and species, which no longer are anything more than a *flatus vocis*, a name and nothing more.

The extremes touch each other in their fluctuations. Why? Because they ultimately agree in the fact that they equally misunderstand a *summit* which is found between both of them. Stability is reached only at this culminating point, whereas at the base of the triangle one finds oneself tossed from one extreme to the other. Thus, in the domain of morality, when undisciplined curiosity is satisfied, it then leads to laziness, which equally misunderstands the nature of the virtuous application of oneself to work. Thus, to take another example, one will remain fluctuating between presumption and discouragement for however long one does not have the virtue of Christian hope.

principles of reason, as well as of the proofs for God's existence, as Kant himself said once upon a time.

Let us repeat what we have already said: This would represent the death of the speculative intellect, in place of which one would like to substitute a practical reason which is unable to prove the value of its foundations.

Indeed, it does not suffice to say: Truth is the conformity of our judgment with the requirements of moral action or with the right intention of the man of good will. This definition only holds for prudence's practical truth, *per conformitatem ad appetitum rectum, ad intentionem rectam*, as Aristotle says in *Ethics*, bk. 6, ch. 2, and St. Thomas in *ST* I-II, q. 57, a. 5, ad 3.

This practical truth of prudence can be accompanied with an absolutely involuntary error when we find ourselves deceived without being able to discover the deception. And even then, it presupposes that *our intention is truly right* in relation to man's true ultimate end. Now, our judgment concerning man's end should be true not only *secundum conformitatem ad intentionem rectam* (for this would represent a vicious circle), but *secundum conformitatem nostri iudicii ad realitatem extra-mentalem, immo ad realitatem supremam* [according to the conformity of our judgment to extra-mental reality, nay, to the supreme reality].

This is what St. Thomas says in *ST* I-II, q. 19, a. 3, ad 2: "In those things that are directed to the end [i.e., the means], the rectitude of reason (in prudence) consists in conformity to right appetition of a due end. However, appetition of a due end itself presupposes right apprehension of the end, which is had through reason." This is what Émile Boutroux also said in his critique of the philosophy of action, which in the end is only a superior form of pragmatism.[12]

If the philosophy of action wishes to rejoin traditional philosophy, it must first become a philosophy of being and recognize the intrinsic value of ontology, as well as *the necessitating self-evidence of the*

---

12. See Émile Boutroux, *Science et religion* (Paris: Flammarion, 1908), p. 296: "Therefore, does one intend to speak of a special action by the will? However, *the will requires an end.*" And this true end of the will can only be known through the intellect, indeed, through a judgment that is conformed to reality itself and not only to right intention.

first principles as laws of being (or, of extra-mental reality) and not only of thought. Elevated above positivistic nominalism and Kantian subjectivism, this is the primordial assertion of traditional realism, which defends itself *redarguitive*, by showing the inefficacy of the objections raised against these primordial and necessitating forms of evidential knowledge, which are indispensable for the life of the mind [*esprit*].

CHAPTER 2

Cognoscens quodammodo fit vel est aliud a se
(On the Nature of Knowledge as
Union with the Other as Other)

In August of 1923, the *Revue néo-scholastique de philosophie* published an article[1] on this question in which Nicolas Balthasar declared himself in agreement with us as regards our doctrine, but not as regards our formulation of it. He reproached us for proposing a new formula as an expression of Thomist thought—*cognoscens fit aliud in quantum aliud* [the knower becomes the other inasmuch as it is other]—a formula that supposedly would not be even found in substance in St. Thomas, nor in the works of his commentators whom we cited (Cajetan and John of St. Thomas).[2] In his critique, Balthasar likewise added that this formula could not be applied to the Divine knowledge (since there is no *fieri* [becoming] in God) nor to the knowledge that we have of ourselves.

Finally, it seems that it "is vulnerable to metaphysical agnosticism," for "the *other* that knowledge reaches is other inasmuch as it is *a given* being. It is not *absolutely* other, other inasmuch as it is being."[3]

In order to respond to these difficulties, we merely need to place the critiqued formula in its context. We employed it in order to resolve a well-known objection raised by subjectivists and idealists in relation to human knowledge of external (or, extra-mental) objects. The concern here is not with the question of Divine Knowledge.

This idealist objection runs: "Something outside of thought or beyond it is by definition something absolutely unthinkable." Moreover, the idealist adds: One could never verify the value of the representation [in thought] by comparing it with an extra-mental thing in itself, which cannot be attained immediately.

Elsewhere,[4] we responded to this objection that in the act of direct knowledge, the representation is not that which is known (*id quod cognoscitur*) but, rather, is that by which (*id quo*)[5] the extra-mental object is known, and we recalled the Aristotelian doctrine as St. Thomas explains it in *ST* I, q. 14, a. 1 where he shows that on account of its immateriality, *the knower can* precisely *become* and *be other beings* in some way.

All Thomists know the text of this fundamental article: "Knowers are distinguished from non-knowers in the fact that non-knowers have nothing but their own form, whereas the knower is of such a nature to have even the form of another thing, for the *species* of the known is in the knower…"

In order to summarize this entire article, as well as the profound commentaries given for it by Cajetan and John of St. Thomas, we said:

If we wish to understand the very foundation of this doctrine, we must understand that the principle of the representation's representative capacity is found in the very *immateriality* of the representation itself. In substance, St. Thomas says in *ST* I, q. 14, a. 1, "The knower, precisely as a knower, differs from non-knowers in that the knower becomes the other inasmuch it is other, and

---

1.   Nicolas Balthasar, "'Cognoscens fit aliud in quantum aliud,'" *Revue néo-scolastique de philosophie*, Vol. 25 (1923): pp. 294–310.

2.   See ibid., pp. 306–310.

3.   ibid., pp. 296 and 301.

4.   See Garrigou-Lagrange, *God: His Existence and His Nature*, vol. 1, pp. 142–43.

      TRANSLATOR'S NOTE: Throughout, I will cite the English translation, which was taken from the fifth edition. The French original is one volume. Fr. Garrigou-Lagrange cites from the 3rd French edition.

5.   TRANSLATOR'S NOTE: Elsewhere, Fr. Garrigou-Lagrange more carefully notes the role of the *species intellecta expressa* as *id in quo* the known is grasped, as opposed to the *species intellecta impressa*, which properly speaking plays the role of an *id quo*. See Garrigou-Lagrange, *Le réalisme du principe de finalité*, p. 204, n. 1: "Properly speaking, the *verbum mentis* is not *id quod intelligitur*, but *id in quo res concepta intelligitur*." Cf. John N. Deely, *Intentionality and Semiotics* (Scranton, PA: University of Scranton Press, 2007), pp. 56–71.

this presupposes IMMATERIALITY." For him, as for Aristotle (cf. *De Anima*, bk. 2, ch. 12; bk. 3, ch. 8), it is a fact that, by means of sensation, the animal in a certain manner *becomes other beings* when it sees them and hears them, whereas the plant is enclosed in itself. And far from denying this fact on the pretext that something outside of and beyond thought is impossible, St. Thomas explains the fact by the immateriality of the faculty of knowing.[6]

The following objection has been registered against us:

Cognoscens natum est habere formam etiam rei alterius: a formula that is found many times under St. Thomas's quill, did not need to be supplanted by this non-Thomist formula, "*cognoscens fit aliud in quantum aliud*," which Fr. Garrigou-Lagrange would like to offer to us as expressing the substance of the Aristotelico-Thomist noetic doctrine.[7]

The formula "*cognoscens fit aliud in quantum aliud*" cannot be found in St. Thomas and, as such, can be found neither in Cajetan nor in John of St. Thomas.[8]

* * *

We have neither the desire nor the time to prolong the discussion of this matter. We will limit ourselves to several remarks.

In no way is it the case that we here present a new formula that would come to "supplant" that of St. Thomas. Rather, in following his thought and that of his best commentators, we have summarized *two well-known formulas* of the Angelic Doctor here in one single formula.

The first of these two formulas is: the knower is of such a nature to have even the form of another thing.

---

6. See Garrigou-Lagrange, *God: His Existence and His Nature*, vol. 1, p. 142.
    TRANSLATOR'S NOTE: This is my translation of the text.
7. Balthasar, "'Cognoscens fit aliud in quantum aliud,'" p. 306.
8. Ibid., p. 310.

The second, which is found already in Aristotle in *De anima*, bk. 3, ch. 8, is: the soul in a certain manner is all things. This second formula is cited in the same article as the first (*ST* I, q. 14, a. 1) and in *ST* I, q. 80, a. 1. Likewise see *De veritate*, q. 2, a. 2 where this doctrine is developed at length. The soul in a certain manner *is* all things, all those that it knows, and in a certain manner it *becomes* them from the moment it is determined to know them. With the exception of God, *fieri precedes esse*, at least when there is not a creation, properly speaking, *ex nihilo*.

Therefore, in substance, these two formulas, which are frequently found in St. Thomas's works, can be joined together into one, single formula for the sake of succinctness: *cognoscens fit vel est aliud a se*.

This last formula (as was recognized[9]) is dear to John of St. Thomas and (here we have something our opponent has not seen), he explains it with great profundity:

> Now, *knowers* are elevated above non-knowers in the fact that they can receive into themselves THAT WHICH IS OTHER, AS OTHER [*ID QUOD EST ALTERIUS, UT ALTERIUS*] (that is, inasmuch as it remains distinct in the other) so that they [i.e., knowers] exist in themselves [i.e., as substances] but also *can become other things [alia a se]*.[10]

Commenting on *ST* I, q. 14, a. 1, Cajetan likewise remarked: "The soul *is made into* [*efficitur*] the knowable thing." Moreover, he had added, "In no nature can matter and form or subject and accident be elevated to such a degree *that one thing would be the same as the other, while maintaining their own natures*, as is the case for the knower and the known."

Making allusion to these texts, on which we have meditated for some time, we summarized the formula in these terms, "*cognoscens fit aliud in quantum aliud*," or, "*potest fieri et esse aliud in quantum aliud*."

---

9. See ibid., p. 309.

10. Ioannis a Sancto Thoma, *Cursus philosophicus Thomisticus*, vol. 2, *IV Pars: De ente mobile animato*, ed. Beatus Reiser (Turin: Marietti, 1937), q. 4, a. 1 (104a1–8).
TRANSLATOR'S NOTE: Given the date of this article, Fr. Garrigou-Lagrange almost certainly has before him the Vivès edition of 1883. The text matches in the citations given from the Reiser edition.

This reduplication is not something that we have invented; it is absolutely equivalent to John of St. Thomas's words cited above: *id quod est alterius, ut alterius*. All of this comes down to saying: The knower can become, in some manner, *something other* than itself, an extra-mental object (or, an object *outside the mind* [*l'esprit*]). Quite surely, this does not mean that the knower becomes an object *outside of being* in general, for then this object would be pure non-being, leading not merely to agnosticism, but in the end, to a kind of nihilism. Obviously, we always presuppose the analogy of all beings with each other. Without this, they would not exist and could not act upon one another, nor have any inter-relations.

By means of this formula, thus placed back in its context, we can see that we are not here speaking about God's knowledge but, rather, are concerned with human knowledge (whether sense knowledge or intellectual knowledge), indeed human knowledge that reaches an extra-mental being, no matter what subjectivism may say about the matter.

* * *

However, why should we join John of St. Thomas in employing the reduplication for which we have been reproached? The wise commentator very well explained why by showing how St. Thomas (in *ST* I, q. 14, a. 1) passes from the first formula to the second, which is found already in Aristotle.

At the beginning of this article, St. Thomas writes, "Non-knowers have nothing but their own form, but the knower is of such a nature to have even the form of another thing." We must note well, as does John of St. Thomas,[11] that the holy Doctor does not say, "Knowing beings can have another form," but rather, says, "the form of another thing." Indeed, it is already the case that inferior beings that are in no way capable of knowledge can receive *another form* (*formam alteram*). For example, the stone, from being cold and dark, becomes warm and illuminated under the influence of the sun. It does not see the sun as does the dog or some other animal capable of sight. This stone, which becomes warm and illuminated, receives from outside of itself an

---

11. See ibid., 103b30–33.

accidental *form that is other* than that which it already had; however, it does not receive *the form of another being (formam rei alterius)*, for precisely because the stone receives heat and light, it makes them *its own*. It *appropriates* them to itself, thus meaning that this heat and light no longer belong to the sun. They only derive from it but are *accidents* of the stone, *individuated* by this subject.

The knower surpasses the non-knower inasmuch as it can receive into itself *the form of another being*, inasmuch as it is other or distinct from the knower:

> Now, *knowers* are elevated above non-knowers in the fact that they can receive into themselves that which is *other, as other* (that is, inasmuch as it remains distinct in the other) so that they [i.e., knowers] exist in themselves [i.e., as substances] but also *can become other than themselves*.[12]

By this, the knower not only *becomes other* (like the stone, which passes from being cold to being warm) but, instead, in a certain manner *becomes the other*, the other distinct from it, the extra-mental object.

In this way, we thus pass from St. Thomas's first formula to the second one already stated by Aristotle: "The soul (becomes or) is, in a certain manner, all things."

One must reread and meditate on the pages where John of St. Thomas shows the significant difference separating this Thomist notion of knowledge from that proposed by Duns Scotus and Francisco Suárez. For these latter thinkers, the object contributes to knowledge *ex aequo* with the faculty of knowledge; it does not inform this faculty but, rather, aids it, *quasi illi assistens*, through a simultaneous concurrence which calls to mind the expression, "like two people dragging a ship," as though there were *two partial coordinated causes* and not *two subordinated total causes*, subordinated not only in their being but also *in their causality*.[13] The problem at hand is analogous to that of the Divine

---

12. Ibid., 104a1–8.
13. See J. M. A. Vacant, Études comparées sur la philosophie de S. Thomas d'Aquin et sur celle de Duns Scot, vol. 1 (Paris: Delhomme et Briguet, 1891), pp. 88–107.

concurrence and our free will, and to the problem of the relations between our intellect and our will in choice.[14]

For St. Thomas, the union of the subject and the object is much more intimate: by informing the faculty, the object constitutes with it a single proximate principle of the act of knowing, *cognoscens fit cognitum*, *in actu primo*, when the faculty is determined by the representation, and *in actu secondo* in the very act of knowing. And what is marvelous here in the creature endowed with knowledge is the fact that alterity is safeguarded despite the intimacy of this union.

Here is one of the principal texts of John of St. Thomas on this matter:

Now, however, St. Thomas, having more profoundly probed the nature of knowing beings, distinguished a twofold notion of passive reception, for there is immaterial passivity [*passiva*] and material passivity...

[Now, there is] *immaterial passivity*, which not only receives forms that are appropriated to the receiver [*formas proprias*] and belonging to the receiver (as already is the case in material reception [of forms]) but also can receive *the form of the other* or can *become other than oneself.* And therefore, in *ST* I, q. 14, a. 1, St. Thomas insightfully places the difference between knowers and non-knowers in the fact that non-knowers *have nothing but their own form,* whereas knowers can also have the form of another thing. Hence, note that St. Thomas did not say that knowers can have *another form* but,

---

14. TRANSLATOR'S NOTE: Concerning the Divine causality involved in the will's exercise, see Réginald Garrigou-Lagrange, *De beatitudine, de actibus humanis, et de habitibus* (Rome: Berutti, 1951), pp. 219–88. The current English translation of this volume, published by Herder, is a paraphrastic translation and should not be taken as a definitive expression of Fr. Garrigou-Lagrange concerning these matters.

On the question concerning the relationship between the intellect and the will in free choice, see Garrigou-Lagrange, *God: His Existence and His Nature: A Thomistic Solution of Certain Agnostic Antinomies*, vol. 2, trans. Bede Rose (St. Louis: Herder, 1949), pp. 306–38 and 370–72. Maritain provides something of a *précis* of Garrigou-Lagrange's thought on this matter in the sixth chapter of the first part of *Bergsonian Philosophy and Thomism*, ed. Ralph McInerny, trans. Mabelle L. Andison and J. Gordon Andison (Notre Dame, IN: University of Notre Dame Press, 2007). Also, see Jacques Maritain, *Existence and the Existent*, trans. Gerald B. Phelan and Lewis Galantiere (New York: Pantheon, 1948), pp. 47–61.

rather, *the form of another thing*, for anything that receives into itself a given perfection or form coming forth from something extrinsic can have another form, for that form is *other*—i.e., distinct from itself and coming forth from something extrinsic. However, *it is not [the form] of another thing* because this very form that is received into itself becomes *its own* so that it does not belong to the other but, rather, to itself, for it neither inheres or is subjected in the other. Indeed, although it is subjected, it nonetheless informs inasmuch as it is in itself as *appropriated* to it and is its own.

Now, *knowers* are elevated above non-knowers in the very fact that they can receive into themselves THAT WHICH IS OTHER, AS OTHER, or *inasmuch as it remains distinct in the other*, so that they [i.e., knowers] exist in themselves [as substances] but also *can become other than themselves*—just as when I see color the eye does not become colored in itself but, rather, the color, which is really in the other, is placed intentionally and visually in the eye.

And, for this to occur, immateriality is required in the very power thus receiving the form, as St. Thomas proves in the same *ST* I, q. 14, a. 1 and in *De veritate*, q. 2, a. 2, because one thing cannot *become the other or draw to itself the form of the other as other* in its own material and entitative existence in which it exists, for thus it would not be able to become the other and to draw it to itself, except through some immutation or *conversion* of one into the other. And if such were to happen, it would not be said *to become that which is other than itself, remaining other* but, rather, would be said *to transmute it* [*i.e., the other*] *into itself*, and to make [the other] its own.

Therefore, this reception must occur in an *immaterial manner*, for it cannot occur according to the condition *of matter, whose character is to restrict and draw fast the form*, rendering it incommunicable to another subject and entering into composition with the other according to transmutation in existence [*esse*]. Thus, in order for *something to become other than itself and receive that thing, not by communicating in existence with it but as something other than itself*, it must lack that restrictive condition of materiality, and must have the condition of amplitude that is called *immateriality*. All of this can be seen in St. Thomas where he explains this reason for knowability found in immateriality in *ST* I, q. 14, a. 1, in *De veritate*, q. 2, a. 2, which we will discuss below in q. 4, a. 2 [of the *De Anima* portion of the *Cursus Philosophicus*].[15]

As we will see more clearly by what follows, all this is St. Thomas's own doctrine. His commentator only underlines the important words and places the accent where it is necessary.

* * *

How can this quite special form of becoming be produced? It does not suffice to say that external object acts first upon the animated organ, that the action of the agent is received in the patient, and that this latter, "becoming aware" of this modification received in it, "knows the object." Rather, we are concerned with explaining precisely in what the knower differs from the non-knower, which also can receive the action of other bodies, and likewise are here concerned with direct knowledge, prior to consciousness, properly speaking or reflexive.

St. Thomas explains this in this same article by appealing to the *immateriality* of the knower; indeed, already, the sense [power] has a kind of immateriality.[16]

The holy Doctor says in *ST* I, q. 14, a. 1:

The nature of the non-knowing being is more restricted and limited (*magis coarctata et limitata*); however, the nature of knowing beings has a greater amplitude and extension. For this reason, in the third book of the *De anima*, Aristotle says that the soul is, in a certain sense, all things. Now, the restriction of form occurs through matter (*coarctatio autem formae est per materiam*)... Therefore, it is obvious that the immateriality of a given thing is the reason that it is able to know; and the mode of knowledge is in accord with the mode of immateriality.[17]

---

15. Ioannis a Sancto Thoma, *Cursus philosophicus*, p. 4, q. 4, a. 1 (103b1–104a45).

16. See *ST* I, q. 78, a. 3.

17. TRANSLATOR'S NOTE: The parentheses are found in the original, as Fr. Garrigou-Lagrange is emphasizing similarities with John of St. Thomas. The passage was only rendered in French, but I have taken it from the Latin original. The two agree without any significant differences.

Material reception appropriates the received form, which is thereby individualized by the subject that receives it. By contrast, immaterial reception, by which we know another being, does not appropriate or individualize the received form. The received form remains the form of this other being; alterity is safeguarded and, with it, so too is *objectivity*. When I see the color of an object, my eye does not become *colored* but, instead, in a certain manner (*repraesentive* or *intentionaliter*) becomes the color of this object.

However, at the same time as *alterity and objectivity*, this knowledge involves an utterly profound *union* of the knower and the known, by which the immanence of knowledge is affirmed. Far from misconceiving this unity, we express it quite strongly in the aforementioned formula by the word *fit* or *est*. Although matter receives the form but never becomes the form (i.e., it never is the form), the knower in a certain manner (*repraesentive*) *becomes* and *is* the known object. Cajetan profoundly noted this fact in *In ST* I, q. 14, a. 1, no. 4:

> The knower *is* the very known [thing] in act or in potency; however, matter never is its own form. From this difference with regard to *esse* there follows a difference with regard to *unity*, namely that *the knower and the known are more one than are matter and form*, as Averroes excellently said his Commentary on *De anima* 3 (comm. 5). And he explains how this is so by noting that *a third thing* is not made from the knower and the known [*ex intellectu et intellecto*], as is the case for matter and form. Now, by assigning *the exclusion of a third thing* as the reason for [this] greater unity, he manifestly taught that the unity [of knowledge] consists in the fact that one *is* the other. Whence, in *De anima*, bk. 3, ch. 8, Aristotle already taught this same point, saying that the soul *is* all sensible and intelligible things.

The unity of the knower and the known cannot be more affirmed than by this word *is* or *becomes*.

The knower and the known do not constitute a composite (*non faciunt tertium*). Rather, the one becomes the other, and the other maintains its alterity on account of the immaterial reception involved here, a reception which does not appropriate and does not individualize but, rather, remains turned outward, toward "the other." This alterity is *real* from the physical perspective when I know another being that is distinct from myself and it is also *known* by me. It goes without saying that all of this presupposes the analogical community of beings, without which they would not exist and could not enter into relations with each other.

We find ourselves faced with a natural mystery in the union of this *alterity* with this *unity*, for here it is formally a question of an immaterial or *spiritual* reception, and we know the spiritual only by analogy with material things, *ex communibus*. If we wish to determine what is proper to it, *ex propriis*, we can reach it only *negatively* by defining spirituality in terms of immateriality, or *relatively*, by saying, for example, that the spiritual union of the knower and the known is much more intimate than that of the matter and form that constitute, nonetheless, one and the same substance: "The knower and the known are *more one* than matter and form...because one *is* the other."

This unity is confirmed by another analogy [*comparaison*]: The substance receiving an accident does not become this accident. The quantity or extension receiving a quality, like color, does not become this quality, whereas, the faculty of knowing becomes the known object.

Perhaps it will be countered that this object is in it in a representative manner and that the faculty of knowing remains really distinct from this new and transitory *accident* that is the representation itself. Thomists have always responded to such an objection by saying that, *precisely as an accident* in the thinking subject, the representation contributes to knowledge only *in a material manner*, and here, we are concerned with its *formal contribution*, which it provides not as an accident but, instead, precisely *as a representation* of the object, a pure *quo* [that by which] and not *what is known*. The representation as an accident is here something negligible, like a completely material preparation which is not spoken of, something akin to the necessary utensils [*cuisine*] not in question when one is concerned with the formal [nature] of knowledge. This is what Cajetan likewise noted very well in *In ST* I, q. 14, a. 1, no. 6: "Nor is it a problem that the visible, as received in sight, is an *accident* and [the power of] sight the subject, for this is *per accidens*, that is, *from the necessity of matter*, and not strictly *per se primo*. For the form, intention, or visible *species* specifies not inasmuch as it is an accident but inasmuch as the visible passes over [*transiens*] into sight."[18]

* * *

This Aristotelian and Thomist notion of knowledge is simultaneously elevated above materialism and subjective idealism. Materialists conceive only of a material reception by which a body becomes *other* (e.g., the cold thing becomes warm) without becoming *the other*. Likewise, they wish to reduce knowledge to a material, physical impression received in the organism—which, in fact, represents the destruction of [the very notion of] knowledge.

On the other hand, subjective idealists, seeing only the immanence of knowledge, conceive of the representation as something purely interior and closed in upon itself, not as something essentially relative to the extra-mental object. They conceive of the representation *as WHAT is known, not as that BY WHICH something extra-mental is known*. Thus, they fall into a kind of materialism, for their outlook ultimately conceives of the representation as being a kind of *painting*, a kind of a *picture*, which is itself *seen*, whereas the representation in a direct act of knowledge makes one see without itself being seen. This is also to halt at the *material side* of the representation (*esse entitativum*), at that by which it is an accident in our mind [*esprit*] like many other accidents found there, instead of considering the representation formally as such (*esse intentionale*), in its essential relation to the represented. Under the pretense of a critical science, this is to stop at the wholly material preparation for the act of knowing, like someone who would like to perform a chemical analysis of a dish of food so that he or she might appreciate its taste.

Neither materialism, nor idealism have understood precisely that in which the knower exceeds the non-knower. They have not grasped the meaning of the Aristotelian formula: "*Anima est quodammodo omnia*."

---

18.   TRANSLATOR'S NOTE: On the dual entitative and intentional role of *species* in cognition, see Jacques Maritain, *Degrees of Knowledge*, pp. 127–36, 411–41; John Frederick Peifer, *The Concept in Thomism*, pp. 63–96, 162–64. On the further distinction (in the internal senses other than the common sense, as well as in intellectual knowledge) between the *species impressa* as *quo* and the *species expressa* as an *in quo*, see the texts cited above in note 5.

* * *

Let us add that, according to St. Thomas, our direct knowledge of sensible beings precedes the reflexive knowledge that we have of ourselves. By contrast, God knows Himself before knowing creatures, since He knows them only in knowing His own creative power. We have insisted too emphatically upon the immanence of the Divine Knowledge[19] for us to need to return to this question. However, the formula "*cognoscens quodammodo fit vel est aliud a se*" indeed does analogically hold even in God, on the condition that one no longer says *fit* but *est*, since there is no *fieri* [becoming] in God.

By writing this formula, we did not leave out the Divine Knowledge, nor "knowledge in the pure state," which as such exists only in God, *ipsum intellegere subsistens* [Self-Subsistent Thought], without admixture of potentiality and imperfection. This uncreated, absolutely transcendent knowledge can only be known by us analogically, and in such attributions, we must always recall what the Fourth Lateran Council states: "Between Creator and creature no similitude can be expressed without implying a greater dissimilitude."[20]

In speaking of knowledge in general, the metaphysician must take care not to fall into an exclusively *a priori*[21] method, which would lead him to confuse (in a Hegelian manner) knowledge in general with knowledge in its pure state, which is only found in God. By falling into such a method, one would come to give certain formulas in St. Thomas a meaning that is wholly different the meaning he himself gave them, leading to a merely verbal agreement with St. Thomas and no longer a doctrinal one, agreeing in letter and no longer in spirit. Thus, one would be led to identify the analogue with the superior analogate, as the ontologists and Rosmini[22] confused being in general with the Divine Being and the good in general with the Divine Good.

---

19. See Garrigou-Lagrange, *God: His Existence and His Nature*, pp. 59ff.
20. Lateran IV, ch. 2, The False Doctrine of Joachim of Fiore (Denzinger, no. 806).
21. TRANSLATOR'S NOTE: To understand Fr. Garrigou-Lagrange's use of the terms *a priori* and *a posteriori*, see the chapter above, entitled "On the Twofold *Via inventionis* and the Twofold *Via iudicii* According to St. Thomas," p. 17, note 7.
22. TRANSLATOR'S NOTE: Blessed Antonio Rosmini-Serbati (1797–1855) had his work *Delle Cinque Piaghe della Santa Chiesa* placed on the index during his lifetime. After his death, forty propositions taken from his works were condemned. He was later

From this perspective, our intellect would no longer be *the faculty of being*, specified by being, but rather, would be *a faculty of the Divine*. Consequently, like infused faith and the Spirit's gift of wisdom, it would be *of the same order* as the light of glory, thus representing a confusion of the natural and supernatural orders.[23] And just as infused faith cannot err—*nothing false comes under faith*[24]—our natural understanding would be infallible.

So too, one would be led to confuse the will in general with the will in its pure state, which is nothing other than the very *ipsum velle subsistens*. The object of our will would no longer be the universal good, *not restricted to such or such good*,[25] an object which doubtlessly in its own universality and all its perfection exists only in God. Instead, the object of our will would *immediately* be *the Divine, God Himself*. Now, if God specified our will *immediately*, it could only love and will *from the formal perspective of God* [*sub ratione Dei*], *from the formal perspective of the Divine Goodness* and not merely *from the formal perspective of the good*. The specifying object of the will would then be identical with that of infused charity, and just as infused charity cannot be the principle of sin, our will would be incapable of sinning. Thus, to the point of confusing the natural and the supernatural, and even to the point of pantheism, one would come to exaggerate St. Thomas's principle: "Because every creature, according to what it is by its very nature, is of God [or, from God; or, belongs to God], it follows that by a natural love the angels and man also love God before themselves and more greatly than themselves."[26]

Such are the reasons why, in distinguishing the human intellect precisely as human from the intellect precisely as intellect (i.e., in

---

rehabilitated and beatified for his heroic virtue in 2007. Details on his rehabilitation should be interpreted in light of the 2001 decree by then-Cardinal Ratzinger, "Note on the Force of the Doctrinal Decrees concerning the Thought and Work of Fr. Antonio Rosmini Serbati," promulgated July 1, 2001. *Rosmini* was rehabilitated, not the conclusions that might be drawn from his works by those who are not careful.

23.   See the condemned propositions of Rosmini, especially the first sixteen, the thirty-sixth, and the thirty-eighth.

24.   See *ST* II-II, q. 1, a. 3.

25.   See Cajetan, *In ST* I-II, q. 2, a. 7.

26.   *ST* I, q. 60, a. 5.

distinguishing the inferior analogate from the analogue itself), we have always noted the difference between the intellect as intellect and the Divine Intellect, which alone is intellect in the pure state, without any mixture of potentiality. Fr. Ambroise Gardeil has himself written a profound article on this topic.[27]

These fundamental truths have not always been noted well enough in the history of the problem of understanding [*l'intelligence*] and that of the problem of love.

---

27. See Ambroise Gardeil, "Faculté du divin ou faculté de l'être? Observations sur une note de l'article de M. P. Rousselot: 'métaphysique thomiste et critique de la connaissance,'" *Revue néo-scholastique de philosophie*, Vol. 18 (1911): pp. 90–100. TRANSLATOR'S NOTE: Fr. Garrigou-Lagrange cites this as being from 1910.

* * *

CHAPTER 3

Whether the Mind Knows Itself Through Its Essence or Through Some *Species*

I n recent days, many have asked[1] how, according to St. Thomas, the mind experientially knows itself. In other words, it is asked whether, according to him, this experience is utterly *immediate*, as Dom Butler wishes, or whether it comes about through the mediation of a *species impressa* or at least through a *species expressa* (or [intellectual] word). Considered in itself, this question is not of small importance from two perspectives, namely, that of philosophical psychology and that of the critique of knowledge. Moreover, the resolution of this question can help one to analogically explain how the righteous *in via* on earth can have, as St. Thomas says, "a quasi-experiential knowledge" of God dwelling and acting in their souls.[2] Indeed, in order to explain the words of St. Paul in Romans 8:16 (RSV), "the Spirit Himself bearing witness with our spirit that we are children of God," St. Thomas says, "The Spirit renders testimony through the effect of filial love, which he makes exist in us."[3] And among many of his disciples, John of St. Thomas observes:

> Just as *the contact of the soul by which it is experientially perceived*, even though it is not seen in its substance, is an information and animation by which it renders the body living and animated, so too *the contact of God by which He is perceived experientially and as a conjoined object*, even before He is seen intuitively in Himself, is a

contact of the intimate operation by which He acts within the heart such that He is perceived and experientially manifested because "His anointing teaches us concerning all things" as is said in Jn. 2:27[4]. This experiential knowledge is given *even if the reality in question is not intuitively seen in itself*, for it suffices that it be perceived *through its proper effects*, as though through touch and vivification, *just as we know our soul experientially* even though we do not see its substance intuitively.[5]

Stated more briefly: just as how, in the natural order, we perceive our soul experientially in its acts, so too, analogically in the supernatural order, we know God dwelling and acting in us in a quasi-experiential, although obscure, manner.

---

1.   As, for example, in Dom Cuthbert Butler, *Western Mysticism*, 2nd ed. (New York: Harper, 1966), pp. xlix–li.
       TRANSLATOR'S NOTE: Fr. Garrigou-Lagrange cites pp. lxvff. of an unnamed edition. The pages cited in the note appear to be the location to which he is referring.

2.   Aquinas, *In I Sent.*, dist. 14, q. 2, a. 2, ad 8.

3.   Aquinas, *Comm. In Epist ad Rom.* 8:16. Also, *ST* I-II, q. 112, a. 5; II-II, q. 97, a. 2, ad 2.

4.   TRANSLATOR'S NOTE: The text incorrectly reads 1 Jn. 4.

5.   John of St. Thomas, *Cursus theologicus, In ST* I, q. 43, disp. 17, a. 3, no. 13 and 17.
       TRANSLATOR'S NOTE: The distinction between intuitive and abstractive cognition was at best inchoate in the works of St. Thomas. By the time of Blessed Duns Scotus, it begins to play a pivotal role, one that would have significant outcomes in all of the *scholae* of the later middle ages and beyond, especially in nominalism. According to the position accepted by Fr. Garrigou-Lagrange, the distinction between abstractive and intuitive cognition can be simply understood as pertaining to the distinction between knowing something without or with the physical presence of that which is known. It is one thing to know intellectually a tree's essence; it is another for a tree to be present *here and now*. Intuitive cognition adds no quidditative note to what is known, only attention to the existential presence of what is known. For the Thomist position on these matters, one can consult John of St. Thomas's *Material Logic*, trans. Yves R. Simon, John J. Glanville, and G. Donald Hollenhorst (Chicago: University of Chicago, 1955), q. 23, a. 1 (pp. 405–21). Also, see John of St. Thomas, *Cursus Philosophicus*, vol. 1 (Turin: Marietti, 1930), q. 23, a. 2 (732a1–741b3): "Utrum possit dari cognitio intuitiva de re absenti, sive in intellectu sive in sensu exteriori."
       In the state of union with the body, the human person has such intuitive cognition only through the mediation of the external senses and the common sense; also, through reflex knowledge, man has intuitive knowledge of the soul, the intellect, and the *habitus* therein. On the last point, see Austin Woodbury, *Natural Philosophy: Psychology* (St. Vincent College, Latrobe, PA: The John N. Deely and Anthony F. Russell Collection, Latimer Family Library), no. 1107. Also, see Régis Jolivet, *L'Intuition intellectuelle et le problème de la métaphysique* (Paris: Beauchesne, 1943).

Thomas de Vallgornera[6] speaks the same way about this matter, and Fr. Ambroise Gardeil, O.P., greatly insists on this point in his recent work, *La structure de l'âme et l'expérience mystique.*[7]

Hence, it is very useful to carefully determine how, according to St. Thomas, the mind naturally knows itself, so that it we may more clearly understand how the mind, elevated to the order of grace, could "quasi-experientially" know God dwelling in oneself. If the first form of experience is not entirely immediate, *a fortiori* the second cannot be absolutely immediate.

Therefore, let us see whether, according to St. Thomas, the soul knows itself *through its own essence*, first, in the state of union with the body, as well as, second, in the state of separation [i.e. from the body], and, third, whether even the separated soul requires an [intellectual] word for knowing itself through its essence.

I. DOES THE SOUL, WHEN IT IS UNITED TO THE BODY, KNOW ITSELF THROUGH ITS ESSENCE?

St. Thomas treated this question expressly in *De veritate*, q. 10, a. 8 ("Whether the mind knows itself through its essence or through some *species*") and in *ST* I, q. 87, a. 1 ("Whether the intellective soul knows itself through its essence"). And he posed a similar question concerning the separated soul in *ST* I, q. 89, aa. 1 and 2 and concerning the angels in *ST* I, q. 54, aa. 1–3; q. 58, a. 1.

In *De veritate*, q. 10, a. 8, the Holy Doctor expresses the state of the question quite excellently by developing sixteen arguments against the doctrine holding that the mind knows itself *through its essence* and eleven arguments for this doctrine.

Let us see the principal arguments considered against it. If the soul were to know itself *through its essence*, first, all men would be most certain concerning the spirituality of their minds, and materialists would not exist (cf. obj. 2 and 3). Second, likewise, this knowledge would exist

---

6.   TRANSLATOR'S NOTE: Thomas de Vallgornera (1595–1665), a Catalonian Dominican theologian. See Thomas de Vallgornera, *Theologia mystica D. Thomae*, 3rd ed., ed. J. J. Berthier (Turin: Marietti, 1911).

7.   Ambroise Gardeil, *La structure de l'âme et l'expérience mystique*, 2 vols. (Paris: Gabalda, 1927).

without needing to turn toward the phantasms; however, in his present state, man knows nothing without turning toward the phantasms (cf. obj. 1). Third, moreover, the soul would always see itself, given the that it is always present to itself (cf. obj. 11). Quite clearly, these arguments, especially the second one, are in accord with Aristotle's own outlook concerning these matters.

However, for the opposite side of the issue, St. Thomas offers arguments drawn from St. Augustine, who teaches in *De trinitate*, bk. 9, ch.3: "The mind knows itself through itself because it is incorporeal." In addition, everything that is present to the intellect as intelligible in act is understood by it; however, the essence of the soul is present to the intellect as something intelligible in act; [therefore, the essence of the soul must be understood by the intellect]. Finally, Aristotle himself says in *De anima*, bk. 3, ch. 4: "In those things that exist without matter, the intellect and what is understood are the same"; however, the mind exists without matter [therefore, the intellect and the mind itself are related as knower and known and hence are the same].

Having thus expressed the state of the question, in the body of the article, St. Thomas provides two preliminary observations and responds in three conclusions.

First, he notes that to ask whether the soul understands itself *through its essence* is not to ask whether it knows its essence in some manner but, instead, whether its essence is *"that by which* it is known," or whether it is known through a superadded (impressed) *species*.

Second, he likewise notes that the fact that a given man *experientially knows* (either actually or habitually) that he has a soul and the fact that he knows the nature of the soul in general, abstractly and scientifically (as is occurs in psychology) are two different issues. In fact, this second kind of knowledge requires study, whereas the first does not.

Now, this article's three conclusions can be expressed schematically as follows:

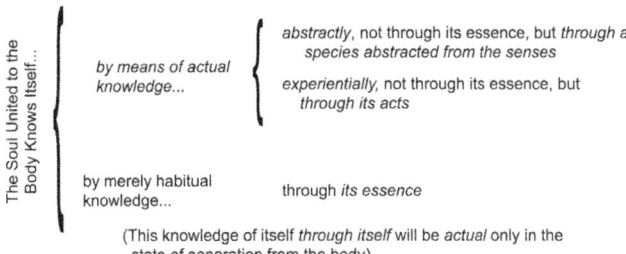

The **first conclusion** of the aforementioned articles from *De veritate* is *concerned with actual experiential knowledge.* It is formulated as follows: "*As regards **actual knowledge**, by which someone considers himself in act to have a soul, in this case, I say that the soul is known **through its acts***." St. Thomas proves this by saying:

> For in this [kind of knowledge] he who *perceives that he senses and understands* (and exercises other such acts of life, cf. Aristotle, *Nicomachean Ethics*, bk. 9, ch. 9) perceives that he has a soul, lives, and exists... However, nobody perceives himself to understand except because he *understands something,* for we understand something (e.g., a stone or wood) prior to understanding that we understand. Therefore, the soul comes to actually perceive that it exists through what it understands or senses.

Now, if the soul were immediately to know itself through its essence, its spirituality would be entirely evident to it, and no materialists would be numbered among men, just as there no angels who are materialists.

Again, in *ST* I, q. 87, a. 1: "Because, as was said in *ST* I, q. 84, a. 7, it is connatural to our intellect in our present state of life to consider material and sensible beings, it follows that our intellect understands itself inasmuch as it is in act through *species* abstracted from sensible beings..."

The **second conclusion** in *De veritate*, q. 10, a. 8, is concerned with *habitual knowledge.* It is expressed thus:

*As regards **habitual knowledge**, I say that the soul sees itself **through its essence**.* That is, precisely because its essence is *present to itself,* it *can pass* into an act of knowledge of itself—just as a person can perceive those things that fall under a *habitus* of a given science precisely because that *habitus* is present in his soul.

Thus, the essence of the soul is living, though only *in first act,* living indeed a life that is not only vegetative and sensitive, but also intellective.

This habitual knowledge is in no way actual. It is akin to the *habitus* of geometry in the sleeping geometer.

This second conclusion receives a better explanation at the end of the response to the first objection to this article: "Before it abstracts [its *species impressa*] from the phantasms, the mind has a *habitual* notion of itself, by which *it could* perceive that it exists." St. Thomas does not say, "by which it vaguely perceives that it exists," but, rather, "by which *it could* perceive that it exists."

Again, in the response to the first objection in the contrary sequence of arguments, he writes:

> It must be said that Augustine's expression, "the mind knows itself through itself because it is incorporeal," must be understood as meaning that, of itself, the mind has the ability by which **it could** pass into *act, by which* it would actually know itself, by perceiving itself that it exists, akin to how the mind *could* actually consider something on the basis of a *species* habitually received in the mind.

Again, later on in ad 4: "The soul is present to itself as intelligible, that is, as something that *could* be understood, *though not as something understood through itself but, rather, from its object,* as we have said." Therefore, even when it *actually* knows itself through its acts, the soul does not know itself through its essence "but, rather, from its object."

However, in the state of union with the body, why is the knowledge that the soul has of itself actual only following upon our knowledge of sensible things and based on that knowledge? Because, as is said in the final paragraph in the current article, our intellect is *the least of intellects,* and the proper object corresponding to it is *the least kind of intelligible,* which exists in potency in the shadow of sensible things. And for this reason, our intellect is united to the senses, which are useful for it *per se* and not only *per accidens,* as *ST* I, q. 76, a. 5, teaches:

> Of its nature, the intellective soul stands at the lowest degree among intellectual substances inasmuch as it does not have the notion of truth naturally placed in it as do the angels. Rather, it must collect truth from individual things [*divisibilibus*] by way of the senses... Whence, the intellective soul must not only have the power of understanding but also the power of sensing.[8]

Whence, the meaning of the second conclusion of the current article from *De veritate* is that knowledge of our soul **through its essence** remains *habitual* in the state of union with the body and will be simultaneously *through its essence* and *actual* only in the state of separation from the body. Hence, a little later on, St. Thomas writes: "*Whence, our mind cannot understand itself in such a way that it would immediately know itself.*" Likewise, in *ST* I, q. 89, a. 2:

> So long as the soul is united to the body, it understands by turning itself to the phantasms. And therefore, it can understand itself only inasmuch as it becomes intellective in act through a *species* abstracted from the phantasms, for thus it understands itself through its act, as was said above in *ST* I, q. 87, a. 1. *However, when it is separated from the body,* it will understand by turning itself to those things that of themselves are intelligible and not by turning itself to the phantasms. Whence, *it will understand itself through itself.*

That is, it will understand itself just as the angel does, without any superadded impressed *species,* not, however, without an [intellectual] word (as we will discuss below).

---

8. See *ST* I, q. 84, a. 7 and q. 87, a. 1.

The third conclusion in *De veritate*, q. 10, a. 8, is *concerned with actual, abstract knowledge.* It is formulated thus: "*The nature of the soul is known by us through species that we abstract from the senses.*" It is proven as follows:

> For, our soul holds the last place in the class of intellectual beings, as is obvious from what is said by Averroes in *De anima*, bk. 3. For just as prime matter is in potency to all sensible forms, so too is our possible intellect in potency to all intelligible forms. Whence, *in the order of intelligibles it is like unto pure potency*, as matter is in the sensible order. Therefore, just as matter is not sensible except through a supervening form, so too the possible intellect is not intelligible except through a *species* introduced into it. *Whence, our mind cannot understand itself in such a way that it would **immediately** grasp itself*; rather, on the basis of its grasp of other things, it arrives at knowledge of itself...
>
> For on the basis of its knowledge of *the universal natures of things*, the human soul perceives that the *species* by means of which we understand is *immaterial*; otherwise, it would be individuated and thus would not lead to knowledge of the universal. However, through knowing that the intelligible *species* is immaterial, philosophers have come to understand that the intellect is a thing that is independent from matter, and on the basis of this knowledge, they have gone on to know other properties of the intellective power... (And concerning these matters, *we judge* with certitude) inasmuch as we know some things naturally *as being self-evident*, in light of which we examine all other things, judging all things according to those self-evident notions.

In this way, "we contemplate the inviolable truth" as Augustine said in *De trinitate*, bk. 1, ch. 6. Thus, St. Thomas reconciled the dicta of Augustine with the principles of Aristotle by determining more explicitly what St. Augustine was affirming when he said, "Our mind knows itself *through itself.*" According to St. Thomas, this is true concerning merely habitual knowledge, and will be experienced in the actual cognition had by the soul that is separated from its body, when it will see its essence *immediately*, having no possible doubt about its spirituality. It will have such knowledge already at the very instant of its separation from the body.[9] In *ST* I, q. 87, a. 1, St. Thomas raises the same question ("whether the intellective soul knows itself through its essence"). In this question, his concern is with the soul united to the body, and here he no longer speaks expressly about merely habitual knowledge. Instead, he merely speaks about actual knowledge, expressing his conclusion as follows:

> *Therefore, our intellect knows itself through its act and not through its essence.* This occurs in two ways. In one way, it knows itself *singularly*, inasmuch as Socrates or Plato perceives himself to have an intellective soul from the fact that he perceives that he himself understands. In another way, we can have such knowledge *in a universal manner*, inasmuch as we consider the nature of the human mind on the basis of the knowledge that we have of the act of the intellect... [Self-]presence alone does not suffice for having the second kind of knowledge concerning the mind. In addition, it requires diligent and subtle inquiry. Whence, many people are unaware of the nature of the soul and, likewise, many err concerning its nature.

The proof of this conclusion in the *Summa theologiae* is reduced to the same principle and argumentation of *De veritate*, q. 10, namely:

> Each thing is knowable inasmuch as it is in act and not inasmuch as it is in potency, as is said in *Metaphysics*, bk. 9, ch. 9... However, the human intellect is related to the [various] kinds of intellects as

---

9.   Now, however, we *positively* know our soul with regard to that which is common in it and in substances inferior to it. Thus, we know it is a *substance*, is *living* in first act, and has *powers* or faculties. However, we know that which is proper to it *negatively* and *relatively*. *Negatively*: by defining its spirituality by the denial of matter and independent from matter; thus, for us, spirituality is immateriality. *In relation to* bodies: by speaking of the height, depth, and extension of knowledge or by saying, for example, that the knower and the known make up something *more* one than what is made from matter and form (for the knower intentionally becomes the known reality itself, becomes that which is other than itself, while matter does not become form). However, at the first instant of separation from the body, the soul will positively see its spirituality, and it will be completely impossible that it will be in doubt concerning this fact.

a being that is only in potency... whence it is called the *possible* [intellect]. Therefore, considered in its essence, it is only potentially understanding. Whence, of itself, it is in potency to understanding but is *understood* only insofar as it is *in act*... Because it is connatural to our intellect according to our present state of life, that it look upon material and sensible beings, as was said above (cf. *ST* I, q. 76, a. 5 and q. 84, a. 7), it follows that our intellect understands itself inasmuch as it is in act through *species* abstracted from sensible beings...

Therefore, St. Thomas's principal conclusion concerning the state of union with the body, both in the *Summa theologiae* and in the *Disputed Questions on Truth*, is in accord with the words cited from *De veritate*, q. 10, a. 8: "*Whence, our mind cannot understand itself in such a way that it would immediately know itself.*"

II. DOES THE SEPARATED SOUL KNOW ITSELF THROUGH ITS ESSENCE?

When it is a question of the soul that is separated from the body, then, St. Thomas's teaching in this matter is just like what he says concerning angelic self-knowledge: "Since (the soul) will have been separated from the body, it will understand by turning itself toward those things that are intelligible of themselves and not by turning itself toward the phantasms. Whence, it will understand itself *through itself.*"[10] In this case, such self-knowledge through its essence will be actual and not merely habitual (that is, in the mode of a kind of *habitus*, as was said in *De veritate*, q. 10, a. 8). It will exist *without any superadded impressed species*, for given the spiritual nature of the spiritual soul, it is already, of itself, *intelligible in act* and not only in potency (like the nature of wood), although, it is not, of itself, understood in act. Moreover, in the state of separation from the body, the human soul does not understand by turning itself to the phantasms.

St. Thomas's conclusion here, one that is similar to what he teaches in various places concerning angelic self-knowledge,[11] is utterly sure.

---

10.   *ST* I, q. 89, a. 2.
11.   See *ST* I, q. 56, a. 1; *SCG* II, ch. 98; *De veritate*, q. 8, a. 6; *De causis*, lect. 13.

Indeed, the impressed species, which is the object's vicar, is only necessary in order for the object, which exists outside the intellect, to become intimately *present* to it, and in order for what is material to become *immaterial* with an immateriality of the same order as the knowing intellect. "If, therefore," says St. Thomas, "A given intellectual being is a subsistent intelligible form, he will understand himself. Now, since the angels are immaterial, they are kinds of subsistent forms and for this reason are intelligible in act. (However, St. Thomas does not say understood in act.[12]) Whence it follows that the angels understand themselves *through their own forms,* which are their substances."[13] Therefore, this holds true for the separated soul, inasmuch as it is intelligible in act of itself, meaning that it does need to turn itself to the phantasms in this state. Hence, it will understand itself, *through itself, without need for any impressed species.*

St. Thomas's firm conclusion in this matter is of great importance for responding to philosophers who doubt the value of the demonstration of the soul's immortality, for the separate soul, as they say, cannot understand without superadded *infused species,* the existence of which are problematic. For it is impossible, they say, to prove apodictically through reason alone that the separated soul will receive these infused *species* from God akin to how the angels receive such *species* from Him. Whence, doubt concerning the way that the separated soul has knowledge leads these philosophers to doubt its immortality, although this could be demonstrated in a different way by arguing from its simplicity and intrinsic independence from the body.

To this, we must respond that the separated soul certainly will know itself *through itself without infused species,* as St. Thomas says, and thus, it will know its spirituality, as well as the resolution of all the philosophical problems pertaining to itself and to God the Author of its nature, knowing all of this in a much better way than it does in the state of union with the body. "When it comes to be separated from the body...the soul will understand itself *through itself.* However, every separate substance

---

12. TRANSLATOR'S NOTE: Yves Simon undertakes profound reflections on this point in two lengthy footnotes in *Introduction to the Metaphysics of Knowledge,* pp. 19–20, n. 28 and 128–30, n. 49.

13. *ST* I, q. 56, a. 1.

understands that which is above itself and that which is below itself according to the mode of the knower."[14] Thus, in knowing itself through itself, it will see most clearly that its essence is not *its existence*, nor *its understanding*, and hence, will naturally know much better than we do that *God alone*, the Author of its soul, *is His existence* and *His understanding*. Thus, for other necessary kinds of knowledge and without infused impressed *species*, it will know the resolution of the principal philosophical problems much more clearly than it now knows them.

III. DOES EVEN THE SEPARATED SOUL REQUIRE AN [INTELLECTUAL] WORD (OR, A *SPECIES EXPRESSA*) IN ORDER TO KNOW ITSELF?

Touching on this question in passing, Cajetan wrote on *ST* I, q. 27, a. 1: "Given that the angel already is objectively present through himself, he would in vain form an [intellectual] word of himself for himself,"[15] and certain contemporary authors today agree with him on this.[16] Thus the soul, at least when it is separated from its body, would have *an entirely immediate* experiential knowledge of its essence, that is, without an impressed *species* and without an expressed *species*.

Hence, some hold that, under a special inspiration of the Holy Spirit, the just would similarly *have an immediate experience* of God dwelling and acting in them, although through signs, which would be *that by which* God would thus be experientially and obscurely known. Even John of St. Thomas is cited in favor of this opinion.

In St. Thomas's works, this issue is connected with the loftiest and most beautiful questions concerning the Trinity, especially concerning the Divine Word, as will be clear in what follows.

Is it true, according to St. Thomas, that the soul, at least when separated from the body, as well as the angels, know their essence *in a completely immediate manner*, without needing to form an [intellectual] word (i.e., an expressed *species*)? In fact, John of St. Thomas, the

---

14. See *ST* I, q. 89, a. 2.

15. According to some, Cajetan seems to insinuate the same in his Commentary on *ST* I, q. 56, a. 1, no. 9 and q. 8, a. 2, no. 3.

16. See Ambroise Gardeil, *La structure de l'âme et l'expérience mystique*, vol. 1, pp. 16–21, and vol. 2, p. 115.

Salmanticenses, and Jean Baptiste Gonet, after Sylvester of Ferrara, Domingo Bañez, and many other Thomists, all firmly hold that St. Thomas taught the contrary.

John of St. Thomas says in his *Cursus philosophicus, De anima*, q. 11, a. 2: "*A word is formed in every intellection concerning a created object or concerning God insofar as He is not clearly seen* [i.e., in the Beatific Vision]. That this is most certainly St. Thomas's own opinion can be seen in *ST* I, q. 27, a. 1, *De potentia*, q. 9, a. 5, *De veritate*, q. 4, a. 1, *SCG* IV, ch. 11, and in several other places." John of St. Thomas makes a similar point in his *Cursus theologicus, De Deo* on *ST* I, q. 12, a. 2, as well as *De angelis* on *ST* I, q. 56, a. 1, disp. 21, a. 2, no. 17. The same can be found in Sylvester of Ferrara (on *SCG* IV, ch. 11), Domingo Bañez (on *ST* I, q. 56, a. 1, dubitatur secundo),[17] Jean-Baptiste Gonet, and the Salmanticenses. Let us look at St. Thomas's own texts.

In *ST* I, q. 27, a. 1, in order to have some understanding of the mystery of the divine processions, St. Thomas says:

> *Whoever understands in act, and from the very fact that he understands, has something proceed within himself, which is the conception of the understood thing*, coming forth from his intellective power and proceeding from his knowledge of it. And, indeed, the spoken word signifies this conception, which is called the *word of the heart*, signified by the spoken word.

Thus, the image of the Trinity exists in the angels and in the human soul not only when they know God *in via* by forming a word concerning Him but also when they know their own essence.[18]

Again, in *De potentia*, q. 9, a. 5 (*in medio*), St. Thomas says:

> That which is first and essentially understood is what the intellect conceives in itself concerning the understood thing... However,

---

17.   In this same text, Bañez says, "To us, the opinion of Sylvester of Ferrara is more probable, and I judge it to be that of St. Thomas. And this is proven in *SCG* IV, ch. 11... Wherefore, Cajetan's opinion, though it may be probable, cannot however be supported in line with St. Thomas's own doctrine."

18.   Cf. *ST* I, q. 93.

what the intellect conceives is called the interior word... And in this respect, it does not matter whether the intellect knows itself or understands that which is other than itself. For just as when it understands what is other than itself it forms a concept of that thing, which concept is signified by a spoken word, *so too when it understands itself, it forms a concept of itself,* which also can be expressed by a spoken word.

Therefore, since there is understanding in God and by understanding Himself He understands all other things, it is necessary that there be an intellectual conception in Him... However, God understands both Himself and all other things by one act. And therefore...the word conceived by God is only one (not multiple as in us).... Again...the Divine Word is perfect, perfectly representing all things... Likewise, in our intellect *it is one thing to understand* and *another to exist*; and therefore, *the word conceived in our intellect,* since it proceeds from the intellect, inasmuch as it is an intellect, *is not united to it in nature* but *only in understanding.* Now, God's act of understanding is His existence. Whence the word that proceeds from God inasmuch as He is understanding proceeds from Him *inasmuch as He is existing,* and for this reason, in His case, the conceived Word *has the same essence and nature* as the conceiving intellect. And because what receives a nature in living things is called "begotten" and a son, the Divine Word is called begotten and the Son.

This is even more explicitly set forth by St. Thomas in the sublimely beautiful pages of *SCG* IV, ch. 11. Nowhere, perhaps, does the Angelic Doctor speak so admirably about the Trinity and, in particular, about the Word than he does here. The opening discussion is concerned with understanding how generation can be admitted in divine things:

To the degree that a given nature is loftier, so too is that which emanates from it more intimate...(as is obvious from the vegetative life of plants and even more so from the sensitive life of animals, both of which surpass the activity of inanimate bodies).

Therefore, the supreme and perfect degree of life is that which is according to the intellect, for *the intellect reflects on itself and can know itself*. However, there are various degrees found even in intellectual life, for even though the *human intellect* can know itself, it nevertheless takes the first beginning of its knowledge from outside of itself, given that it does not understand without a phantasm, as is obvious from what was discussed earlier (*SCG* II, ch. 60).

Therefore, intellectual life is more perfect *in the angels* in whom the intellect does not proceed for its knowledge from something external. Rather, the angel *knows himself through himself*. However, their life does not reach the ultimate perfection of life, for although *the understood intention* is entirely intrinsic to them, *the very understood intention, nevertheless, is not their substance, for understanding and existence are not the same in them*, as is obvious from what was said above. Therefore, the ultimate perfection of life belongs to God, in whom understanding and existence are not distinct, as was shown above. Thus, it is necessary that *in God the understood intention be the Divine Essence itself*. However, I call the understood intention that which the intellect conceives *in itself* concerning the understood thing… This very intention is called the internal word…

However, this point can be made even clearer if we consider what is said in the same article, §3: "Now, *the being* [*esse*] *of the* interiorly conceived *word* or the understood intention is *its own act of being understood*."[19] What does this mean, considering that God alone is His understanding and, hence, His own act of being understood [*suum intelligi*]? In short, we can see what this means merely by looking at what St. Thomas says in §4 of the same article:

When our intellect understands itself, the *being* [*esse*] *of the intellect* is one thing and *its very understanding* is another, for the substance of the intellect was in potency to understanding before it came to

---

19. Thus, only in this manner is the axiom formulated by Berkeley, "*esse est percipi*," true: namely, the existence [*esse*] of the word (or, the conception) is its own existence as understood [*est ipsum suum intelligi*].

be understanding in act. Therefore, it follows that *the being [esse] of the understood intention* is one thing and (the being) *of the intellect itself* is another, since the *being [esse] of the understood intention* is *the very act of being understood.* Whence, it is necessary that in a man understanding himself, *the interiorly conceived word* not be **a true man** [*homo verus*], having the natural being [*esse*] of man, but, rather, must be *an understood man only*, as it were, a kind of likeness of the true man grasped by the intellect. However, the very *Word of God*, from the very fact that He is *God Understood*, is **True God** naturally having the divine existence because in God it is not the case that the natural being of God is one thing and His understanding another, as has been said. This is what is said in Jn. 1:2: "*God was the Word.*"

In no way can we say that St. Thomas said something different in *De veritate*, q. 4, a. 2, when he showed that the Divine Word [*Verbum in divinis*], if properly taken, is not said essentially but personally. There, we find him saying:

To understand this point, it must be noted that *our intellect's word*, which can serve as a likeness for our discussion of the Divine Word, *is that at which the operation of our intellect is terminated*, which is the understood thing itself, which is called *the conception of the intellect*, whether it is the conception that is able to be signified through a non-complex expression as happens when the intellect forms the quiddities of things or whether it is able to be signified through a complex expression, which occurs when the intellect composes and divides. *Now, every understood thing* in us is *something really proceeding from something else*, either as when conceptions of conclusions[20] proceed from principles…or at least as *actual conception proceeds from habitual knowledge*: and **this is universally true concerning all that is known by us, whether it be understood through its essence or through a likeness,** for the conception itself is an effect of the act of understanding. Thus, *it is also the case that when the mind knows*

---

20. **Translator's Note:** Reading *conclusionum* for *conclusionem.*

itself, its conception is not the mind itself but, rather, something expressed by the mind's knowledge.

Based on this fact, St. Thomas shows that the word, properly considered, has two aspects in its meaning, namely the fact that it is understood and the fact that it is *expressed by another*. Hence, in God, it is only said personally such that the Divine Word is True God from True God, whereas the word of our mind is not the mind itself but, instead, only its likeness.

Whence, according to St. Thomas, as John of St. Thomas[21] and nearly all the Thomists say: "A[n internal] word is formed in every intellection concerning a created object or God not clearly seen,"[22] even when the soul or the angel knows its essence, for even though the essence of the soul or the essence of the angel is *intelligible* not only in potency but, indeed, *in act*, nevertheless they are not, of themselves, *understood in act*. That is, they are not their own understanding, nor, hence, *their own act of being understood*. Therefore, in order for them to be not only intelligible in act but, moreover, understood in act, they must be expressed in some mental word. Otherwise, they would ultimaly be identical to the essence of God, who alone is Pure Act in the order of understanding, just as He is Pure Act in the order of being.

Whence, according to St. Thomas, the created intellect always forms some mental word. There is no exception to this requirement except in the case of the Beatific Vision because the Divine Essence, clearly seen, is not only intelligible of itself in act but is *understood in act*, pure act in the very order of intelligibility, just as it is in the order of being, since it is its existence, its *understanding*, and *its act of being understood*. Moreover, the Divine Essence cannot be represented *precisely as it is* by any created *species*, for a created *species* is intelligible only through participation. Hence, even if it were indefinitely perfected, it would always remain inadequate. It would never be equal (not only in the order of being, but also in the order of being) to Self-Subsistent Understanding, which is, as it were, an infinitely intense light and an

---

21. See *Cursus philosophicus*, vol. 2, p. 4 (*De anima*), q. 11, a. 2.
22. **Translator's Note:** That is, God so long as He is not known in the Beatific Vision.

eternally subsisting intellectual refulgence. For this reason, St. Thomas states in *ST* I, q. 12, a. 2, ad 3: "The Divine Essence is *existence itself.* Whence, just as other intelligible forms, which are not their own *existence,* are united to the intellect according to *some existence* by which they inform the intellect itself and make it to be in act, so too, the Divine Essence is united to the created intellect *as what is understood in act,* making the intellect be in act *through its very self* (and not through a likeness)." God alone is His *existence,* His understanding, and His act of being understood. Hence, God alone can be seen without a mental word. Nay, were God seen through a created word, which would be always and essentially inadequate, He would not be seen *just as He is.*

However, this does not mean, in contradiction to faith, that philosophical reason could assert that there could not be an uncreated and infinite Word in God Himself. The only things that follow from what we have said are as follows. First, the possibility and existence of the Divine Word can be known only through supernatural revelation. Second, God the Father does *not* speak the Word *on account of indigence* as we do but, rather, does so *on account of the superabundance* of His infinite fecundity, which according to Revelation belongs necessarily to God. Third, the Son and the Holy Spirit know the Divine Essence by the same understanding as the Father and nevertheless do not speak the Word. Fourth, the Word spoken of in divine revelation is not merely God understood or represented but True God from True God. Fifth, and finally, in this eternal generation of the Word, we have the loftiest of verifications for the principle thus enunciated above by St. Thomas: "To the degree that a given nature is loftier, so too is that which emanates from it more intimate." In other words, what is generated in this Divine generation is not an individual separate from Him who generates, thus involving a multiplication of the Divine nature, nor is He only a particular accidental word, like ours, but instead, is True God from True God, so that to Him may be communicated not only an intelligible truth concerning God (as occurs in divine revelation) nor only a participation in the Divine Nature (as occurs in the infusion of grace) but rather, the complete, indivisible Deity, which is numerically identical in the Three Divine Persons. Thus, even if God would have created none of those finite things that He created in utter freedom, the principle, "The good is essentially diffusive of itself," would still find a confirmation in God Himself, namely, on account of this infinite and necessary fecundity *ad intra*, wherein the Good cannot diffuse itself to any greater or more intimate degree.

Having surveyed all these testimonies in St. Thomas's own texts concerning the [intellectual] word, whether created or uncreated, it is quite clear that *even the soul separated from the body cannot actually know itself except in some word*, and when it thus knows itself, an image of the Trinity is found quite explicitly within it, although it will be found in it even more perfectly when it knows and loves God Himself. Likewise, let us say that the mystical and quasi-experiential knowledge of God dwelling and acting in the soul cannot be so *immediate* that it would take place entirely without a word, for as we have said, this absolute immediacy exists only in the Beatific Vision.

However, there is one difficulty that we still must examine. In various places, St. Thomas states that a word is not formed in sensation. Indeed, he says in *Quodlibet* V, q. 5, a. 2, ad 2: "An external sense's knowledge is perfected solely through a change of the sense by the sensible. Whence, it senses through the form that is impressed upon it by the sensible thing. *Now, the external sense itself does not form a given sensible form for itself.* However, the imaginative power does do this..." He says the same in *Quodlibet* VIII, q. 2, a. 1 and *ST* I q. 85, a. 2, ad 3. Nay, it seems to some that knowledge would not be truly experiential unless it would reach the existing thing *in an entirely immediate manner* without a word.

Therefore, how are these two points of St. Thomas's doctrine reconciled: An expressed word is not found in sensation, thus meaning it is truly experiential cognition, and nevertheless, the knowledge that the separated soul and the angel have of themselves is experiential, notwithstanding the word that is formed in it?

These two points are firmly defended in separate places by John of St. Thomas.[23] Although some may think that they contradict each other, nevertheless, they can be reconciled for at least three reasons.

---

23.   See John of St. Thomas, *Cursus philosophicus*, vol. 2, pt. 4 (*De anima*), q. 6, a. 4; q. 10, a. 2.

First, precisely because the external object of sight is illuminated by the sun and is united with the sensing being, it is not only *visible* in act but, moreover, is *seen in act*. Here, as Aristotle noted, the act in question is held in common by the sensing being and the object of sensation. By contrast, in the order of spirits, only the Divine Essence is of Itself understood in act. The essence of the soul or of the angel of itself is only intelligible in act [and not *understood* in act]. Otherwise, it would be pure act, at least in the order of intelligibility.

Second, if a *word* were formed in sensation, the word would be expressed by the mediation of some first likeness, namely by the mediation of an impressed *species*. Then, there would be two likenesses, the second of which (namely, the expressed *species*) would proceed from the first. By contrast, when the angel or the separated soul sees its essence, *the word of the mind* does not proceed from any superadded likeness but, rather, proceeds immediately from the very essence of the angel or of the soul. Hence, there cannot be an organic deformation in this production of the word [as could happen in sensation]. Nay, there are no organs in this merely spiritual order. There is no matter that could escape the domination of form and become the cause of error.

Third, in the visual perception of a given external object, *distance* properly speaking (namely, local distance) exists between the animated organ and the external object. Therefore, if a *word* were found to be immanent in it, there would be distance properly speaking between this word (i.e., the *medium in which* [knowledge is terminated]) and the external object. However, this seems to be contrary to the immediacy of experiential knowledge. Nonetheless, nothing akin to this holds for the self-knowledge had by the angel or the soul. Therefore, this knowledge can be experiential, notwithstanding the presence *of the mental word* needed for the essence of the angel or the soul to be *understood* in act, for this word is in no way distant from that essence in its entitative existence [*physice sumpta*] and is immediately derived from it in the order of intelligibility along with the intellection itself.

Thus, these two points of St. Thomas's doctrine can be reconciled: Sensitive experiential knowledge takes place without a word, and intellective experiential knowledge does not exclude a word.

Therefore, our conclusions remain in force, namely: *The mind united with the body does not know itself actually through its essence* but, rather, does so in its acts and by turning to the phantasms through *species* abstracted from sensible things; *however, the mind separated from the body* knows itself actually *through its essence, though not without a word.* Such knowledge is truly experiential.

We will see hereafter [*sic*] that the mystical knowledge of God dwelling and acting in the soul is called "quasi-experiential" by St. Thomas inasmuch as it takes place through certain effects of God who is life-giving and who moves us to love of Him. These effects not only are *that which* is known but, moreover, are *that by which* we *non-discursively* and obscurely know, under the inspiration of the Holy Spirit, God Himself, dwelling and acting in us, knowing Him, as it were, as the soul of our soul and the life of our life.

* * *

CHAPTER 4

There Cannot Be Genuine Sensation Without a Real Sensed Thing

The[1] most eminent Fr. Joseph Gredt in all his works always defends the real value of external experience and most firmly holds, that there cannot be genuine sensation without a real sensed thing, just as each properly experimental cognition is distinguished from a cognition that is not experimental insofar as it terminates in an existing or actually present thing. In other words, there cannot be experience without a thing having been experienced. Fr. Joseph Gredt says in the latest edition of his work, *Elements of Aristotelian-Thomistic Philosophy*[2]: "The truth of the cognition of the external senses demands that the external senses immediately attain transsubjective objects both according to matter and form, and *according to presence*; therefore, we know transsubjective objects by means of all of our senses. The truth of abstract cognition demands that the intellect immediately know transsubjective objects with respect to their matter." In the same place this doctrine is explained and defended at great length and seems to be the traditional thought [of Thomists].

Recently, however, the opposite position was proposed in a presentation at the most recent Thomistic Congress under the title: "On Sensation in St. Thomas."[3] In this presentation it is said:

Translated by Thomas DePauw * Edited by E. M. Macierowski, Ph.D.

And sensation is commonly explained by many Neo-Scholastics in
this way: since the determination of a faculty is supposed to be by
dint of the *species*, that which is sensed is the object in its physical *material* being, and indeed that which immediately touches
the sensitive power [*nervum sensitivum*]…that afterwards, through
repeated experiences and successive approximations, it is localized
outside, where it is commonly believed to be present. They add that
the nature of sensation is such that this would be utterly repugnant
without a real sensed thing as [its] material term. For the sensation
would be without an object, i.e., no sensation [at all].

I say that I could never understand sensation as explained in
that fashion for the following reasons, which if I have not misunderstood, utterly exclude the notion of sensation just described.

(1) … To know, according to the Angelic Doctor, is to *possess
something immaterially*. Hence to see a tree or to hear a sound is
nothing other than to possess the *species* of the tree or the sound in
act. Hence, he who is still seeking knowledge when the *species* is in
his possession is seeking what he already possesses.

(2) Like all cognition, sensation is an *immanent act*, which is, as
a whole, achieved within the one sensing. Therefore, the term that
it involves has to be an intrinsically immanent term…And so sensation does not terminate at the object in its material, physical being,
but at the object in being known, i.e., at the object in a *species*, in
[its] representation; for to step out from the *species* is to step out
from immateriality and therefore from cognition itself…

But here a rather delicate question arises: just what is the
species at which sensation is said to terminate? Among Thomists it

---

1.   TRANSLATOR'S NOTE (MINERD): As was mentioned above, in reflecting on this topic,
     the reader would benefit significantly from consulting Yves R. Simon, "An Essay on
     Sensation," in *Philosopher at Work*, pp. 57–111. Also, see Cahalan, *Causal Realism*,
     pp. 387–417.

2.   Josephus Gredt, *Elementa Philosophiae Aristotelico-Thomisticae*, 7th ed. (Herder, 1937),
     vol. 2, p. 70.

3.   "De Sensatione apud S. Thomam," *Acta Secundi Congressus Thomistici Internationalis*,
     Romae (November 23–28, 1936), p. 145–48.

     TRANSLATOR'S NOTE (DEPAUW): Following Scholastic etiquette, Fr. Garrigou-Lagrange
     does not mention the name of the individual he is citing, namely H. degl'Innocenti.

is a firmly held belief that the Angelic Doctor excludes the *expressed species* from the external senses, at least as a preliminary to sensation. Therefore this is not possible unless the sense be said actually to attain its object in the *impressed* species, and this is called by Cajetan: "an intermediate image in which the object is seen" (Commentary on the *De Anima*, bk. 2, ch. 10)...

Nevertheless, the physical presence of an object is required *to determine* or cause the sensation through the emission of the species by which the sense is changed. But if the thing should perish after the species has been emitted, a sensation will nevertheless follow. For the sense cannot help knowing once the determination for knowing has been received. Hence neither does a contradiction follow concerning a sensation without a real sensed thing.

The author of this presentation does not seem to remember the many texts of St. Thomas about to be cited now, nor to recognize sufficiently that *there are many degrees of immanence*, from divine intellection all the way to the vital acts of vegetative life, as the Angelic Doctor often observes in speaking of "sensing."[4] Nor in the same place is it shown sufficiently in what manner *experimental cognition* differs from cognition that is not experimental, and *external experience* from internal [experience]. If furthermore "sense actually attains its object in the impressed species," it reflects upon itself just as the intellect [does]. If, on the contrary, in sensation the impressed species replaces [*gerit vices*] the expressed *species*, why would it not be so *a fortiori* in intellection, since those things which exist separately in inferior things, exist in a united manner in superior things? There would be also many other difficulties that are to be considered below.[5]

---

4. ["sentire"]. Cf. *ST* I, q. 27, a. 5: "Sensing is not totally removed from the genus of actions that are related to the outside, for sensing is perfected through the action of the sensible thing upon the sense" (translation ours). Immanence is not predicated univocally, but rather analogously, of divine operations, of our understanding, of sensation, and of the acts of vegetative life. [All translations of the *Summa* used in this chapter, unless otherwise noted, will be taken from the translation of the Dominican Fathers of the English Province.]

5. See Fr. Édouard Hugon, *Cursus Philosophiae Thomisticae*, vol. 3: *Philosophia Naturalis, Psychologia* (Paris: Lethielleux, 1927), p. 270–73, which rightly says: "The impressed species is related as the principle of sensing. But the principle of an action cannot be its end. Therefore...if a sense were to know its act and its species directly, then it would be

* * *

Recently, too, some others in favor of the opinion according to which sensation can obtain without a real sensed thing have cited this text of St. Thomas, in *ST* III, q. 76, a. 8: "Such apparition comes about in two ways (in the Eucharist), when occasionally in this sacrament flesh, or blood, or a child, is seen. Sometimes it happens on the part of the beholders, whose eyes are so affected as if they outwardly saw flesh, or blood, or a child, while no change takes place in the sacrament." Those who cite this text do not explain, while those extraordinary visions are going on, in what respect *bodily vision* properly so called differs from *imaginary vision*, which exists along with an overflow in the exterior senses but without a real sensed thing. Yet this classical division, which is found in all the treatises of mystical theology, must be explained philosophically.

THE IMPORT OF THIS QUESTION

The present problem is of no less significance. For contrary to the thesis according to which sensation without a real sensed thing can obtain, many difficulties immediately come to mind. (1) In that case genuine sensation would not be distinguished in its proper nature from hallucination, but the latter, as Aristotle says, is related to true sensation as an echo is to a sound. (2) In the same way among the extraordinary visions, bodily visions would not be essentially distinguished from imaginary vision. (3) The metaphysical certitude of the real value of the first principles of contradiction, efficient causality, finality, etc., which is formally resolved in their intellectually evident [character], could not be further *resolved materially* within the real thing sensed, since there could be a genuine sensation without a real sensed thing. In that case the way would be opened to rational phenomenalism, as in the doctrine of Descartes, as Monsignor Francesco Olgiati[6] has recently shown in a

---

reflecting upon itself; in fact, it is blocked by the [sense] organ. The opposite position paves the way to skepticism.

Moreover, if the object be present (such that sensation be a truly experimental cognition), sensation terminates at the object itself and the expressed species is superfluous."

6.   See Francesco Olgiati, *La Filosofia di Descartes* (Milan: Vita e pensiero, 1937), pp. v, 26, 66, 175, 176, 241, 323.

particularly fine way. Whence St. Thomas not infrequently insists on this material resolution, for example when he says in *De veritate*, q. 12, a. 3, ad 2: "since the first principle of our cognition is sense, it is necessary in some way to resolve everything about which we judge to a sense. Whence the Philosopher says...in bk. 6, ch. 8 of the *Ethics* that *the senses are of that which is ultimate [or particular] as the intellect is of principles*. He calls ultimate those things at which the resolution of the one who judges comes about" (cf. ibid, ad 3).

Therefore, the true thought of Aristotle and St. Thomas is to be sought; namely whether for them sensation (inasmuch as it is a *properly experimental cognition* and experience, not internal but external) implies a *transcendental* or essential *relation* to a *real sensed thing*,[7] namely to a really present object (or at least to its real influx into an animated organ, as in the case of stars which are no longer present where they seem to be). The sensation of vision does not indeed leave from the eye of the one seeing in the fashion of the breath of air from the mouth of the speaker, but has a transcendental relation to the real sensed thing. For if the impressed *species* (which would miraculously replace [*gereret vices*] the expressed species) has this relation, why should sensation itself not have it?

THE TRUE POSITION OF ARISTOTLE
AS EXPLAINED BY ST. THOMAS

Now Aristotle talks about this matter in the *De anima*, the *De sensu et senato*, and the *De memoria et reminiscentia*.

De anima, bk. 2, ch. 5, lect. 10, of St. Thomas (ed. Pirotta), no. 350: "*Sensing is a sort of being affected*." St. Thomas explains it thus: "For sense is a certain alteration in act, and what is altered is affected and moved." In this way sensing is a sort of being affected in a causal sense, although it is a vital cognitive act formally speaking.

Ibid., lect. 12, no. 375: "*The sense is not cognizant except of things present.*" St. Thomas: "For a person cannot sense when he wants, since he does not have sensible things in himself, but it is necessary for them

---

7.   TRANSLATOR'S NOTE (MINERD): On the notion of transcendental relation, see the added "Translator's Appendix" at the end of this chapter.

to be present to him outside." In this respect sensing differs from understanding and from imagining. Ibid., ch. 11, lect. 23, no. 547. That sensing is a sort of being affected is explained specifically through the relation to touch and to the tangible qualities of external bodies. Ibid., bk. 3, ch. 2, lect. 2, nos. 590–94, as to these words of Aristotle: "*If then motion is both an action and a passion in that in which it is performed,* it is necessary that *sound* and *what is heard,* as actual, be in that which is according to potency. *For the act of what is active and motive comes about within the patient... The act of the sensible thing and of the sensitive power is one.*" St. Thomas explains this passage in this way, nn. 590ff: "The act of any sense is one and the same in subject with the act of the sensible thing, but is not one in formal aspect... Since that which is able to hear has its operation and what is able to sound has [its] sounding, then *sound according to act,* which is called *sounding,* and *hearing according to act,* which is called *hearing,* will come into being at the same time...[8] And as has been said in *Physics,* bk. 3, ch. 3, that *action and passion are one act in subject,* but differ in formal aspect, inasmuch as action is signified as [performed] *by the agent,* passion however as *in the patient,* he spoke in such fashion that the act of the sensible thing and the sensing [power] is the same in subject, but not in formal aspect. Therefore, the act of that which produces the sound or [that] of the sound is *sounding,* whereas the act of the hearer is *hearing...*but in some sensible things and sensing [powers] each of the two acts has a [distinct] name, both that of the sensible thing, e.g., sounding, and that of the sensitive [power], e.g., hearing. In some cases, however, only one gets a name, i.e., the act of the sensitive [power]: for the act of sight is called vision, but the act of the color is not named."

Hence just as there cannot be hearing without sounding, neither can there be in the other external senses a genuine sensation (distinct from hallucination) without a real sensed thing.

The same doctrine is found in *De sensu et sensato,* ch. 1, lect. 1, no. 11: "Sense according to its proper formal aspect is not cognitive of

---

8.   TRANSLATOR'S NOTE (DEPAUW): *Sonus* is to *sonatio* as *auditus* is to *auditio.* The English word "hearing" is used here for both *auditus* and *auditio.*

anything except things present." Ibid., lect. 2, no. 19: "The action of the sense comes into being in being affected."

Again, in *De memoria et reminiscentia*, ch. 1, lect. 1, no. 306: "The Philosopher shows that memory is not of something present; but this pertains to sense, through which neither the future nor the past is known, but only the present."

Therefore, the transitive action of the external thing is in that which is affected, that is to say it exists as a term in the animate organ of the sensing [agent]. And the sensation itself terminates at the thing sensed which flows into the organ, or at the real influx of this external thing.

THE POSITION OF ST. THOMAS IN HIS OWN WORKS

St. Thomas in his own works always holds that *there is no sensation except of that which is present*, namely of the present thing which is sensed, and although it is an immanent act, it apprehends the external thing to the extent that it flows into the sense organ.

In *III Sent.*, dist. 14, a. 1, q. 2: Sight "comes to be in act by being affected by colors and it is assimilated to them…but since sense senses only in the presence of a sensible thing, the impression of its active [power] in the manner of a passion alone is sufficient for its perfect operation." In this way, an expressed *species* is not required in sensation, though it is indeed required in imagination and in intellection, since their object is not present or has not been proportioned to them.

Again, in *IV Sent.*, dist. 49, q. 3, a. 1, qa. 2: "For a sense can only be of things present; although glorified bodies can sense at a greater distance than non-glorified bodies."

Again, in *IV Sent.*, dist. 49, q. 3, a. 1, qa. 4: "We experience delight only in things present, and so also since the exterior sense apprehends only a present thing, we are not said to rejoice with respect to it, but to be delighted. The interior sense, however, apprehends a thing whether present or absent."

Similarly, in *De veritate*, q. 25, a. 3: "Since the object of sense is a body, which is naturally able to move a sense organ, the [sensitive] powers must be diversified according to the diverse formal aspects under which movement is induced."

In the *Summa theologiae* the same doctrine is expressed in many ways; in *ST* I, q. 18, a. 3, diverse levels of immanence are laid out, [starting] from the vital action of a plant, in which one part moves another, up to the divine operations. In this way, the immanence of sensation differs from that of intellection. *ST* I, q. 75, a. 3: "Sensing... evidently accompanies some change in the body." Cf. *ST* I, q. 78, a. 3. Again, *ST* I, q. 78, a. 4: "The internal senses are distinguished from the external senses insofar as they apprehend a thing "even in its absence." *ST* I, q. 81, a. 3, ad 3: "The exterior senses require exterior sensible things for their actions, whereby they are affected, [things] whose presence is not in the power of reason."[9]

ST I-II, q. 15, a. 1: "It is proper to sense to take cognizance of things present," [and] in this respect it differs from the imagination and from the intellect. *ST* I-II, q. 35, a. 2, ad 2: "the external sense perceives only what is present." *ST* I-II, q. 17, a. 7, ad 3: "Since the external sensible is necessary for the apprehension of the senses, it is not in our power to apprehend anything by the senses unless the sensible be present, which presence of the sensible is not always in our power."

Finally, St. Thomas has spoken on several occasions concerning the *material resolution* of our intellectual awareness to a *real sensed thing*. For example, in *IV Sent.*, dist. 9, q. 1, a. 4, sol. 1: "Since, therefore, each cognition of our intellect arises from the sense, there cannot be right judgment unless it be traced back to the sense."

De veritate, q. 12, a. 3, ad 2: "Since the first principle of our cognition is the sense, it is necessary to resolve all the things about which we judge to the sense in some fashion...therefore, since in a dream the senses are bound, there cannot be a perfect judgment..." Again in ad 3.

Ibid., q. 28, a. 3, ad 6: "In sleeping, the intellect is not kept from perceiving something either on the basis of the features which it has previously considered, or from the illumination of some superior substance... But perfect judgment of the intellect cannot exist in sleeping, because in that case the sense, which is the principle of our cognition, is bound."

He says the same thing in *ST* II-II, q. 154 a. 5, ad 3.

---

9.   [Translation ours.]

Hence there cannot be genuine sensation, distinct from a hallucination that has arisen from preceding sensations, without a real sensed thing present.

The principal commentators on St. Thomas have understood the matter in this way. Cajetan, *In Post. Anal.*, c. 13, explains it in an excellent way as follows: The intellectual certitude of the real value of the first principles of reason is indeed formally resolved in their intellectual evidence, but is resolved materially in the real sensed thing. Similarly, Cajetan says on *ST* I, q. 51, a. 2, no. 3: "Now the purely imaginary vision terminates at an object within, *whereas the vision of the eyes terminates at an extrinsic object.* And from this another difference follows: that what is seen by way of imagination, as such, exists only in the one imagining, and consequently appears to him alone. *But what is seen by the eyes, since it exists outside the one seeing,* can commonly be seen by all." Again, Cajetan on *ST* III, q. 57, a. 6, ad 3. Cf. below.

Again, John of St. Thomas, in the *Cursus Philosophicus Thomisticus*, *Logica*, q. 22, a. 4, says, "The external sense has to be borne to a thing placed outside [it]." And q. 23, a. 2: "It implies that a thing is known *by sensing* and *by experiencing with external sensation*, which differs from the imaginative [power], *only by attaining something external* in itself and not as formed within itself." Ibid, *Philosophia Naturalis*, on the three books of the *De Anima*, q. 6, aa. 1 and 4.

Generally, the commentators of St. Thomas hold the same doctrine, for example, cf. the commentary on *ST* I, q. 51, a. 2, of Bañez, the Salmanticenses, Gonet, etc.

Most modern Thomists understand this in the same way, among whom it is possible to cite Monsignor Albert Farges,[10] Édouard

---

10. See Albert Farges, *Theorie fondamentale de l'acte et de la puissance ou du mouvement: le devenir, sa causalité, sa finalité: avec la critique de la philosophie 'nouvelle' de M. M. Bergson et Le roy on du modernisme philosophique* (Paris: Berche et Tralin, 1909), pp. 375–401. Objections drawn from the so-called specific energy of nerves and those that arise from hallucination. "Hallucination presupposes true external perception and would not be produced without it." It is also necessary to speak of the facts mentioned by the partisans of the hypothesis of the specific energy of the nerves. The author cites and fully approves these words of Henri Bergson (*Matière et Mémoire*, pp. 227, 244): "In our perception we grasp at once both a state of consciousness and a reality independent of us." "For if action and passion are only one and the same act with two aspects, like front and back; and if the action of the agent is really in the patient, I ought immediately to grasp within

Hugon,[11] Francis-Xavier Maquart,[12] Jacques Maritain,[13] Paul Geny,[14] Joseph de Tonquédec,[15] Joseph Gredt,[16] etc.

According to this doctrine immanence is not predicated univocally but analogically of sensation and of intellection. Thus, it is understood why St. Thomas would have written in *ST* I, q. 27, a. 5: "Sensing is not totally removed from the genus of actions that are related to the outside, for sensing is perfected through the action of the sensible thing upon the sense."[17]

Confirmation is found in the various articles of the Angelic Doctor concerning preternatural visions and apparitions.

CONCERNING EXTRAORDINARY VISIONS

On many occasions St. Thomas treated of these visions, very nicely distinguishing bodily vision from imaginary vision and from intellectual vision. Cf. the *Tabula Aurea* of his works under the word "visio", nos. 5–16, 21.

Only the principal texts are to be referred to. At the beginning of this article, we cited the passage in *ST* III, q. 76, a. 8, in which there is a

---

the ego the action of the non-ego when it strikes me. It is therefore perfectly useless to look for the famous 'suspended bridge,' as it is impossible to find the philosopher's stone. It is enough no longer to separate what nature has united: the action of the mover and the passion of the mobile thing. Thus is explained the invincible evidence that while perceiving the exterior world through the senses we perceive something other than the sensible modifications of the ego…it is reality itself which is grasped."

11.   See Hugon, *Cursus Philosophiae Thomisticae*, vol. 3, p. 270: "That which the sense directly perceives is not the impressed species, nor a modification of the sense, but the external sensible thing."

12.   F.-X. Maquart, *Elementa Philosophiae* (Paris: Andreas Blot, 1937), vol. 2, p. 260: "It must be said that sensation terminates at the physical object or the physical quality inasmuch as it acts upon the sense. For action is in what is affected, and in this way sensation terminates at the physical quality inasmuch as it is in the sense organ by its action."

13.   Maritain, *Les degrés du Savoir*, p. 229.
      Translator's Note (Minerd): Edition not cited.

14.   *Critica*, where the value of sensation is discussed.
      Translator's Note (Minerd): Edition not cited. See Paul Geny, *Critica de cognitionis humanae valore disquisito* (Romae: Apud aedes Universitatis Gregorianae, 1927).

15.   Joseph de Tonquédec, *La Critique de la connaissance* (Paris: Beauchesne, 1929), p. 59ff.

16.   Gredt, *Elementa Philosophiae Aristotelico-Thomisticae*, 7th ed., vol. 2, p. 70.

17.   [Translation by DePauw].

discussion of an apparition of flesh or blood or of a boy in the Eucharist: "Sometimes it happens on the part of the beholders, whose eyes are so affected as if they outwardly saw flesh, or blood, or a child, while no change takes place in the sacrament." This is so when among the witnesses [of the sacrament, there is] only one who enjoys the apparition. It is to be immediately noted that St. Thomas does not say that the witness [in question] properly sees the apparition, but rather that "his eyes are changed in such fashion *as if he were seeing*."

Whence John of St. Thomas[18] explains this [passage], saying: "Those external apparitions can only come about in two ways, either through eliciting an *external vision*, or through eliciting an *imaginative vision*, which thinks or judges that it sees externally inasmuch as the internally existing *species* descend near the sense organs, whether of the common sense or of the exterior senses, and the imagination moved by them thinks that it sees by external vision," as in a hallucination.

In fact, in order for there to be a *genuine bodily vision*, there would have to be at least an exterior influx into a sense organ, such as the actual luminous influx of a light ray of a star no longer present. Otherwise, there is an imaginary vision with a certain overflow in the external senses, as in a hallucination, which presupposes preceding sensations, as an echo presupposes a sound. This is confirmed from many passages of the Angelic Doctor.[19]

For when St. Thomas speaks of bodily vision properly speaking, inasmuch as it is distinguished from imaginary vision, he always says that it terminates at an exterior body, or at least at its action upon a sense organ. Cf. *ST* I, q. 51, a. 2, "whether the angels assume bodies": "Some have maintained that the angels never assume bodies, but that all that we read in Scripture of apparitions of angels happened in prophetic vision, that is, according to imagination. But this is contrary to the intent of Scripture; for whatever is beheld in imaginary vision is only in the beholder's imagination, and consequently is not seen by everybody... From all this it is clearly shown that such apparitions were beheld by

---

18. John of St. Thomas, *Cursus Philos. Logica*, q. 23, a. 2 (at the end).
19. See Tonquédec, *La Critique de la connaissance*, p. 485–90 (Appendice V. Hallucination, rêves et visions d'après Aristote et S. Thomas).

bodily vision, whereby *the object seen exists outside the person beholding it*, and can accordingly be seen by all. Now by such a vision only a body can be beheld." The commentators of St. Thomas generally speak in this way [when commenting] upon this article.

In the same way the Angelic Doctor in *ST* III, q. 57, a. 6, ad 3, regarding the vision which St. Paul had about the resurrected Christ on the way to Damascus after the Ascension in Acts 9, says, "Christ by once ascending into heaven acquired for Himself and for us in perpetuity the right and worthiness of a heavenly dwelling-place; which worthiness suffers in no way, if, from some special dispensation, He sometimes comes down in body to earth; either in order to show Himself to the whole world, as at the judgment; or else to show Himself particularly to some individual, e.g., in Paul's case, as we read in Acts 9. And lest any man may think that Christ was not bodily present when this occurred, the contrary is shown from what the Apostle says in 1 Cor. 15:8, to confirm faith in the Resurrection: 'Last of all He was seen also by me, as by one born out of due time.'" Now, this vision would not indeed prove the truth of the Resurrection, "unless he had beheld Christ's very body." Cf. the commentary of Cajetan on this article, and the commentary of St. Thomas on 1 Cor. 15:8.

From these texts and many others like them it follows that for St. Thomas bodily vision is distinguished from imaginary vision insofar as it terminates at the very external thing which is being sensed, or at least at its real influx into a sense organ.

CONCERNING SENSATION AND HALLUCINATION

Now to understand better the significance of this question, it is necessary to note attentively that there is an immense difference between genuine sensation and hallucination, as between *properly seeing* something real actually present and *not seeing it*, for example between seeing Christ really brought back to life and bodily present, as the Apostles and even St. Paul on the road to Damascus saw Him, and not properly seeing Him, but vividly imagining Him while He is absent. The first proves the resurrection of Christ, but not the second.

Even when not speaking about extraordinary facts, it is a question not only of the conditions of *sensation*, nor only of what is material in it, but [also] of that which is formal in its *proper essence*, which is unchangeable. It is a question of the true *nature* of genuine, normal sensation, which results from the union of an external object with a sense organ as [that object] has been created by God, and is known by [that sense organ] without any fallacy or confusion with an image produced in a hallucination. We can say to the idealist philosopher: "There are more things in heaven and earth than in all your philosophy." For genuine sensation is much richer if it immediately touches upon a real sensed thing than if it does not immediately touch on it. No, rather it is exactly this question which is at stake: *Is it possible* or contradictory *properly to see that which really is not*, for example, properly to see a non-existent ray of a star and properly to hear a non-existent sound? Not even God can bring it about *that I see that which is not* and that *I touch what is not tangible*, since it does not exist. Would not the immense distance between seeing and hallucinating be destroyed, between properly seeing the brother whom many kept saying was dead and to have a hallucination about him? It is amazing that we should have to defend at such length a truth which in French is called a "vérité de La Palisse" [i.e., a kind of obvious truism].

With respect to this great difference which ought to be attentively noted, there are [still more] texts of St. Thomas on this matter that ought to be read which are duly cited by Fr. J. de Tonquédec.[20]

The Angelic Doctor says in *IV Sent.*, dist. 44, q. 2, a. 1, sol. 3: "Others say that (in heaven) *sensing in act* will come about through a receiving, *not indeed from exterior sensibles*, but through an outflowing from higher powers, just as the higher powers now draw from the lower powers. So [in heaven], conversely, the lower [powers] will draw from the higher ones. *But that mode of reception does not make for truly sensing*, since every passive potency is determined *according to the formal character of its species* to a specific active [principle], since potency as such has an ordering to that in respect of which it is predicated. *Hence, since the active property in the exterior sense is a thing existing outside the soul, and not its intention existing in the imagination or in reason, if a sense organ should not be moved by things outside, but from the imagination or from other higher*

---

20. See ibid., pp. 488–90.

powers, it will not truly be sensing. Hence, we do not say that the insane and other mentally handicapped [people], in whom *an influx of such species to the sense organs comes about* because of the dominance of the imaginative power, *truly sense*, but rather that *it seems to them that they sense.* And so, with the others, it must be said that the sense of glorified bodies will exist through a reception from things that are outside the soul."

Again St. Thomas in *De potentia*, q. 3, a. 7, corp., says against the occasionalists of the Middle Ages: "They used to say that God arranged things in such a way that the present course of things would be preserved, i.e., that He would never cause heat except on contact with fire, [*but*] *not because the fire that was brought into such contact would make anything* [*actually*] *hot.* This position, however, is *manifestly repugnant to sense*: for *since one does not perceive a sensed thing unless one is affected by a sensible thing*, it follows that *a man does not sense the heat of a fire if the likeness of the heat of the fire in a sense organ does not exist through the fire acting* [*on it*]. For if that species of heat in the organ were brought about by some other agent, then even though [the sense of] touch might sense heat,[21] *nevertheless it would not be sensing the heat of a fire, nor would it sense that the fire is hot*, even though the sense, whose judgment does not err in the [case of its] proper sensible [object], judges this [to be so]."

The same doctrine is found in the *De malo*[22] and in the *Summa theologiae.*[23]

---

21. For God can produce an exterior influx similar to fire, at which point heat would be sensed. If, however, there were no external influx, then there would not be a true sensation, but an apparent sensation, as was said in the text of *IV Sent.* cited immediately before.

22. *De Malo*, q. 3 a. 3, ad 9: "That the *species or likenesses of things* are not distinguished from the *things themselves*, comes about because the higher power, which is capable of judging and distinguishing [them], is bound…as in the case of the mentally ill."
   De Malo, q. 16 a. 11, corp.: "In chapter 3 of *On Sleeping and Waking*, the Philosopher, assigning the cause of the appearance of dreams, says that whenever an animal is sleeping, when a lot of blood descends to the sensitive principle, *there descend at the same time motions or left over impressions* from the motions of sensible things that are preserved in the sensible spirits and move the apprehensive principle in such fashion that *some things appear as if at that point the sensitive principle were being changed by the exterior things themselves.* And this is how demons are able to change the imagination and sense, not only of those sleeping, but even of those who are awake."

23. *ST* I, q. 111, a. 3, is completely the same text as in *De Malo*, q. 16, a. 11, and it is added: "The disturbance of humors and spirits can be so great, that apparitions of this sort come about even in those who are awake, as is clear in the case of those who are mentally ill and the like."

* * *

Therefore, it must be concluded: Just as intelligence is essentially relative to an intelligible being, knowledge [*scientia*] to a knowable being by abstracting from its existence, and imaginary vision to an imagined object, so proportionally *sensation is essentially relative to a real sensed object* or at least *to its real influx* into a sense organ, in such a manner that there cannot be genuine sensation distinct from hallucination and from imaginary vision without a real sensed thing.

Just as a transitive action of an external thing upon a sense organ cannot occur without the one sensing being affected, so too sensing and being sensed cannot be separated, anymore than perceiving and being perceived. And although, whatever Berkeley might say, something can be without being perceived, for example things that are in the bosom of the earth or of the sea, nevertheless *it is not possible for anything to be sensed or perceived unless it exists*, at least unless there be a real influx of it into a sense organ. "*For the act of the sensible thing and of the sensitive* [*power*] *is one* [*and the same*], to the extent that the action of the sensible thing is ultimately in the affected sensing [power],"[24] as Aristotle says in *De anima*, bk. 3, ch. 2 (426a16). In this way the metaphysical certitude of the real value of first principles, [i.e.,] of contradiction, of causality, [and] of finality, which is *formally* resolved in their intellectually evident [character], is *materially* resolved without any danger of subjectivism in

---

Cf. also the index of Aristotle's works under the words: *hallucinatio, echo, eclipsis*.

For Aristotle, the definition of sensation is totally different from the definition of hallucination, and in each of the two cases we ought to proceed methodically from the nominal definition, investigating according to the laws for tracking down a definition, *the true, real definition* both of *sensation* and of *hallucination*. Hallucination, however, is related to a sensation as an echo is to a sound: for hallucination is primarily said to exist when someone thinks that he is sensing something, which others present in the same place do not sense; and then the cause of the hallucination is found, [in the same way] as the cause of an eclipse or an echo [is found], i.e., *hallucination*, be it visual, auditory, or tactile (e.g., after the amputation of a foot), *is a false sensation that has arisen from past sensations on the occasion of some disturbance or trauma of the organism*. In this way, one obtains [both] the *what* and the *why* of hallucination, and one [can] explain why hallucination *exists without a real sensed thing*, while there cannot be a genuine sensation without a real, existing, sensed thing, to which it is essentially relative. This is of great importance today against idealism.

24. TRANSLATOR'S NOTE (DEPAUW): Only the italicized portion of the quotation is to be found in the actual text of Aristotle's *De Anima*. It is likely that the quotation mark was extended beyond the original quotation by a typographical error.

the real sensed thing, which is the proper object of experience. As St. Thomas says in *De veritate*, q. 12, a. 3, ad 3: "The judgment of the intellect does not depend on sense in such a way that the act of the intellect [in question] is performed by a sense organ. *However, it does need the [sense] as the ultimate endpoint at which [the act of judgment] is resolved.*" In this way skepticism and idealism are avoided. Therefore, as Fr. Joseph Gredt[25] says very well, "it is superfluous and impossible to build a bridge to cross over from the subjective to the transsubjective… Many critical realists strive to infer a transsubjective world thanks to the *principle of causality*… But this reasoning is *impossible* owing to the manifest logical fallacy on which it is based." For doubt remains concerning the real or ontological value of the principle of causality itself, if its certitude is not materially resolved in a *real sensed thing*, existing not only apparently but [also] really.

This is surely the traditional thought [of Thomists], and this alone is fully coherent with the words of Aristotle and St. Thomas regarding sensation and human certitude.

TRANSLATOR'S APPENDIX (MINERD)

Following Antoin Goudin, we could briefly define a transcendental relation as: "The very entity of the thing, inasmuch as it is ordered to something, as the eye is ordered to colors and a science to its object."[26] The classic text contesting the later Thomistic notion of transcendental relationality is A. Krempel, *La doctrine de la relation chez saint Thomas: Exposé historique et systématique* (Paris: Vrin, 1952). For important corrective responses to certain points in Krempel, see John Deely's remarks in John Poinsot, *Tractatus de Signis: The Semiotic of John Poinsot*, 2nd ed., ed. and trans. John Deely and Ralph Austin Powell (South Bend, IN: St. Augustine's Press, 2013), pp. 462, 473, n. 114, 477–78, n. 119, 499, and 500, n. 139.

---

25.   Gredt, *Elementa Philosophiae Aristotelico-Thomisticae*, vol. 2, p. 76.

26.   See Antoine Goudin, *Philosophia iuxta inconcussa tutissimaque Divi Thomae dogmata*, vol. 1, *Logica*, ed. Roux-Lavergne, 2nd ed. (Paris: V. Sarlit, 1857), praem., a. 1 (p. 84). Techincally, Goudin here refers to an "ordo transcendentalis."

An excellent summary of the doctrine can be found in the following text drawn from the work of Austin Woodbury, the brilliant Australian student of Fr. Garrigou-Lagrange, whose works have been cited elsewhere in this edition concerning other such technical matters from within the Thomist tradition:

But *real* relation itself is *twofold*, according as it is either a pure relation, i.e. nought except a relation, such as sonship, or is together some absolute being, [e.g.,] a quality, such as sight, which besides being a relation to vision and to color, is also a quality. A *pure* real relation is called a *predicamental relation*, which is *a pure order towards other*, so that it is not together some absolute being; wherefore it is named *"predicamental,"* since it constitutes a *special mode* of being really distinct from every absolute mode of being. This predicamental relation is a real purely relative accident superadded to its subject, this subject being constituted related to another: not formally through itself, but formally through this accident really distinct from itself. *Examples* are fatherhood, sonship, equality, similarity.

But a *real relation which is together some absolute being* is called a *transcendental relation*: because it extends itself beyond the special predicament of relation and is found in all the predicaments or modes of being ([e.g.,] in substance, quality, etc.). A transcendental relation accordingly is the *very entity of some absolute being from its very essence ordered towards another*, or proportioned or adapted or adjusted to another, as matter from its very essence is ordered towards form, or essence towards being [i.e., existence], or act towards object. Therefore, a transcendental relation is nothing else than the very *essence* of a being, which is not only a relation, *as it is adapted or ordered towards another*—as the essence of sight (which is not merely a relation, but is a quality) is adapted or ordered towards vision and color; wherefore, it is nothing else than an *essential adaptation* of a thing that is not a mere or pure relation. Accordingly, that which is related through a transcendental relation is constituted related: *formally through its own entity*, so that it *is* its own relation, not formally through a relation really distinct from its entity—in

this case, its order or adaptation to another would be only accidental, not essential.

It is manifest from what has just been said that: whereas, as will
be explained later (cf. n. 1206), in predicamental relation there is
real distinction between these *four*: the *relation* itself, its *subject*, its
foundation, and its *term*; when it is a question of transcendental relation, there is real identity between the relation itself and its subject,
and its foundation, the *only* real distinction lying between that one
reality which is together these three and the term.

From what has just been said follow *two further distinctions*
between predicamental and transcendental relation. *First* indeed,
whereas *predicamental* relation respects its term as a *pure* term;
transcendental relation, on the contrary, respects its term, not as a
pure term, but as that whereunto the subject is essentially adapted,
to wit, as specificative, or perfective, or complement, or proper
subject. But *secondly*, whereas *predicamental* relation perishes if its
term does not *really actually exist*, since its sole office is to refer
the subject to that term *as to a term*—which it cannot do if that
which is the term does not exist; *transcendental* relation, on the
contrary, does not require that its term really exist actually, since
something can be essentially adapted to another without the real
actual existence of that other; thus, for example, [the] human soul
is transcendentally related to the human body, but can exist after
the body has ceased to exist; also, there can be science of an object
which does not exist really ([e.g.,] logic, whose object is mental
being [*entia rationis,* namely *relationes rationis* that are second
intentions].

It is to be noted that the distinction of *real* relation into predicamental relation and transcendental relation does not fully coincide
with the distinction, commonly made by *St. Thomas* and the ancient
scholastics, of relation into "relation according to [existence] (*secundum esse*)" and "relation according to be-spoken (*secundum dici*)."
See *ST* I, q. 13 a. 7, ad 1. For, they called by the name of "*relation
according to [existence]*" every pure relation or relation whose whole
[existence] is [*to*]-[*exist*]-*towards-other*, whether such relation be real
(and then it is predicamental) or mental; for also of mental relation

is it true that its whole [existence] is towards other. See *De potentia*, q. 7, a. 10, ad 11. While, they called by the name "*relation according to be-spoken*," the relation that is together some absolute being (and this is transcendental relation): inasmuch as such absolute beings are understood and are defined and therefore are-spoken through reference to another; as potency is understood and is defined and is-spoken through reference towards act, and similarly matter through reference to form, and similarly sight through reference to vision and color, and similarly habit through reference to its operation and object.[27]

---

27. Austin M. Woodbury, S.M., *Ostensive Metaphysics* (St. Vincent College, Latrobe, PA: The John N. Deely and Anthony Russell Collection), n. 1201 (pp. 930–32).

* * *

PART III

Moral and Political Philosophy

* * *

INTRODUCTION TO PART III

The articles gathered together in this section fall into two major categories. In the first subsection, there are two articles that treat general issues of moral philosophy: First, an overview concerning the Thomistic doctrine on the virtue of prudence and, second, a defense of the claim that when one lacks the theological virtue of charity the acquired moral virtues exist only in weakened state (i.e., as virtues in the state of disposition, *in statu facile mobilis*). In the second subsection, there are four articles concerning topics related to the political order and the human person's place therein.

These latter four selections have been included to allow Fr. Garrigou-Lagrange to speak in his own words concerning political matters, about which he has received much condemnation because of his sympathy for the movement *L'Action Française* and for the Vichy regime.[1] This volume cannot attempt to adjudicate these matters in detail. Such an undertaking would require a full historical study, something beyond my own competence and calling for the steady hand of someone capable of writing both an intellectual history and a political one. Nonetheless, these four articles are included so as to make clear that although his political positions are highly conservative, emphasizing the positive duties of the natural political order vis-à-vis the order of revealed supernatural truth, it would be utterly unjust to associate his political thought with European fascism of the first half of the twentieth century.[2] More will be said below about the contents of these political essays. First, however, a few summary remarks regarding this section's first two chapters are in order.

Fr. Garrigou-Lagrange had intended the chapter entitled, "Prudence in the Organism of the Moral Virtues," to be one in a series providing an introduction to the dominating principles of various positions taken by Thomistic philosophy and theology. Alas, this venture was never accomplished. In this article, however, he sets forth the central place of prudence in the moral life, a point of great importance. That he chose this cardinal virtue as an illuminating principle for Thomistic moral philosophy in general might give the reader pause. It is certainly the case that the governing principle of all human felicity, whether natural or supernatural, is the topic of human beatitude,[3] and all of our moral

---

1.   See André Laudouze, *Dominicains français et Action française, 1899–1940: Maurras au couvent* (Paris: Éditions Ouvrières, 1989). This text was recommended to me as this volume was close to publication, so I cannot vouch for the content. Nonetheless, for the purposes of reference, I felt it advisable to include it, given that it came from a trusted collaborator. For an example of a Thomist opposed to *L'Action Française* (and Vichy), see Yves R. Simon, *The Road to Vichy: 1918–1938*, rev. ed., trans. James A. Corbett and George J. McMorrow (Lanham, MD: University Press of America, 1988). In particular, regarding Fr. Garrigou-Lagrange, one can see Simon's strong and negative opinions on pp. xx–xxiii. Simon's words are quite forceful, and one wonders if there is not some (understandable, given the circumstances) unkindness in his intensely vexed judgment rendered against Fr. Garrigou-Lagrange. To be quite clear: My sympathies are *not at all Pétainist!* Yet, my heart grieves when I read the words of those brethren in Christ who came to be separated during this sad era. So much unnecessary division was caused by hardening over these matters, divisions that still sadly separate Catholics. The separation here, however, pierces me most deeply, given the debt I owe to Simon and Fr. Garrigou-Lagrange alike.

2.   This should be of no surprise to the reader, given the honest, if contentious, debates surrounding the Second Vatican Council Declaration *Dignitatis humanae*. Fr. Garrigou-Lagrange's position was the common position of the time, one that receives too little attention, despite the fact that Vatican II's *Dignitatis humanae* states at its very beginning: "Therefore it leaves untouched traditional Catholic doctrine on the moral duty of men and societies toward the true religion and toward the one Church of Christ." For a recent appraisal of this issue, see the study by David L. Schindler and Nicholas J. Healy, *Freedom, Truth, and Human Dignity: The Second Vatican Council's Declaration on Religious Freedom. A New Translation, Redaction History, and Interpretation of* Dignitatis Humanae (Grand Rapids, MI: Eerdmans, 2015). Also, see Thomas Joseph White, "The Right to Religious Freedom: Thomistic Principles of Nature and Grace," *Nova et Vetera* (English Edition), Vol. 13, No. 4 (2015): pp. 1149–84.

3.   A point stressed of late by Fr. Servais Pinckaers, although certainly not unknown to Fr. Garrigou-Lagrange, as any reader of his *De beatitudine* will note. See Réginald Garrigou-Lagrange, *De beatitudine, de habitibus, et de passionibus* (Rome: Berutti, 1951), pp. 6–7 and 29–166. Note that the currently available English translation of *De beatitudine* is a paraphrase that often truncates and at times alters Fr. Garrigou-Lagrange's thought. A new translation of this text is in the process of being produced.

activity must be ruled by the "immobile axis" of the ends of the virtues, above all charity.[4] Nonetheless, it is also the case that *every* morally good act is, by the same stroke, a prudent act. Prudence is not mere precautious activity. It is the full, dominating rectitude of practical reason, enabling one to command oneself to perform (or, we might say, actualize) the moral good that surges up from the virtues in the will's intention of a virtuous end to be pursued.

Despite the fact that prudence has such a central place in the organism of the moral virtues, this topic has not always been given the central role it deserves. In another article, our Dominican theologian noted this fact, commenting:

It is truly astonishing, as has been well noted recently by Fr. Merkelbach, a professor at the Dominican College in Louvain, that *the principal cardinal virtue holds such a small place in moral science today.*[5] Prudence, which directs all of the moral virtues and is called the conductor of the virtues, is so fundamental that no human act is good without, at the same time, being prudent; and despite this fact, numerous modern manuals of moral theology pass over this virtue in near silence. This quasi-suppression of the treatise on prudence would have been a kind of scandal in the eyes of the ancient Thomists.[6]

---

4. See Ambroise Gardeil, *La vraie vie chrétienne* (Paris: Desclée de Brouwer, 1935), pp. 118–25. Indeed, this entire chapter (pp. 101–189) is an excellent reflection on supernatural prudence. The publication of a translation of this volume is expected in the relatively near future.

5. See Benedict Henry Merkelbach, "Quelle place assigner au traité de la conscience?" *Revue des sciences philosophiques et théologiques*, Vol. 12 (1923): pp. 170–83.

    TRANSLATOR'S NOTE: Josef Pieper notes this same point, indeed citing this very page in Garrigou-Lagrange. See Josef Pieper, *The Four Cardinal Virtues*, trans. Richard and Clara Winston, et al. (Notre Dame, IN: University of Notre Dame Press, 1966), p. 6.

6. Réginald Garrigou-Lagrange, "Du caractère métaphysique de la Théologie morale de saint Thomas, en particulier dans ses rapports avec la prudence et la conscience," *Revue thomiste*, Vol. 30 (1925): p. 345.

    TRANSLATOR'S NOTE: This article appears in translation as "Remarks Concerning the Metaphysical Character of St. Thomas's Moral Theology, in Particular as It Is Related to Prudence and Conscience, in *Nova et Vetera*, Vol. 17, No. 1 (2019): pp. 245–70.

In the discussion of prudence, one brings to bear the virtues and vices, the specification of acts by their chosen objects and circumstances (especially the end intended by the agent), man's freedom of choice in view of the will's dominating indifference to all finite goods, etc. In the decree *Optatum totius*, the Second Vatican Council called for a renewal of moral theology.[7] Anyone who honestly apprises the Church's history during the decades immediately following the Council knows that it would be, at best, naïve to claim that this renewal was brought about in full.[8] It is not without reason that Pope St. John Paul II published

---

7.   Vatican II, *Optatum totius*, no. 16: "Special care must be given to the perfecting of moral theology. Its scientific exposition, nourished more on the teaching of the Bible, should shed light on the loftiness of the calling of the faithful in Christ and the obligation that is theirs of bearing fruit in charity for the life of the world."

8.   See the comments of Joseph Ratzinger, who as a theologian and as the head of the Congregation for the Doctrine of the Faith (CDF) was well aware of the developments and devolutions of this period of history, in "The Renewal of Moral Theology: Perspectives of Vatican II and *Veritatis Splendor*," *Communio*, Vol. 32, No. 2 (2005): pp. 357–68.

And yet, in my opinion, Ratzinger's own appraisal does not match up to the status of *all* moral theology during this preconciliar era. Above all, his comments seem generally out of touch with the flourishing veins of spiritual theology which bequeathed not only Garrigou-Lagrange's works but, merely to name two other great lights of the era, Frs. Juan Arintero and Ambroise Gardeil. Likewise, hidden under the somewhat hardened scholastic format of Merkelbach's *Summa theologiae moralis*, we find the outlines for a rigorously scientific moral theology that is apprised of the place of beatitude and the virtues in the moral life, written with great rigor drawn from six hundred years of scholastic disputation among the *scholae*. And what of the five large volumes written on beatitude by Fr. Santiago Ramírez, let alone his other commentaries on the moral parts of the *Summa theologiae*? And who could deny the thought of Fr. Michel Labourdette a place here, mostly restricted to his teaching and the *Revue thomiste* during the preconciliar era, although his course notes would be copied for some time and finally brought to print posthumously? These veins of thought could have benefitted from further engagement with the Fathers and Scripture (though, it would be wholly unfair to act as though they were disengaged from these *loci theologici*). To this degree, Ratzinger's observations are disappointing for their grim broad-brush depiction of preconciliar moral theology, painting a vista that is also sketched out by more "progressive" theologians with whom the great German theologian would most certainly have parted ways.

The point remains: Who would legitimately say that the profound sense of the essentially supernatural vocation of the life of grace has benefitted much in the exposition of moral theology, broadly speaking, especially during the immediate tumult after the Council? One need only read Charles E. Curran, *Catholic Moral Theology in the United States: A History* (Washington, DC: Georgetown University Press, 2008), to see a panoply of discussions quite remote from the central issue of divinization or *theosis* so dear to the Thomist school (although mention is made in relation to Fr. Cessario's work). For all of the problems with Curran's thought and work, he does lay out the terrain of the reigning exponents of moral theology in America. It gives one no small grief,

Veritatis Splendor to stress the *true* nature of the needed renewal of moral theology. There are many elements to such a renewal, which certainly must include a deepened appreciation of the supernatural nature of moral theology.[9] However, a mature articulation of the theology's philosophical instruments is also necessary. A metaphysical analysis of prudence should have a preeminent place in such an articulation.

Thus, the first chapter in this section provides an excellent pedagogical summary of the nature of prudence, its place in the organism of the natural virtues, and the main themes involved in considering the nature of choice and command. Fr. Garrigou-Lagrange stresses the role of right intention of the end (which arises from the moral virtues) in guiding prudence in its choice concerning the means to that intended end. (Again, this is its "immobile axis.") He takes for granted here, as in other works, the interpretation of practical truth that has Thomas de Vio Cajetan as its principal exponent, stressing that practical-moral truth is *a truth of direction.*[10]

----

despite whatever gains there may have been. Without the central illuminating principle of the Uncreated Life given to us participatively through grace, all the rest of moral theology is nothing more than gold plated moral philosophy.

Alas, many more "conservative" Catholic theological approaches to these issues emphasize the natural law (which should be retained most certainly, of course) to the point of forgetting the immense domain of the theological and infused moral virtues (or, at least for the Scotists, the reverberations of the theological virtues on the acquired moral virtues). It is precisely in this very domain that the *loci theologici* of Scripture, Tradition, the Fathers, ascetic writers, and faithful theologians should come to bear in filling out the "phenomenology" of the divine life in the infused virtues and the gifts of the Holy Spirit. No doubt, *this* sort of lacuna is what Ratzinger himself experienced in his own formation before the Council (along with the legalism that accompanied much of casuistry during that era). Yet, his presentation sadly does not redeem the veins of encouraging work being done prior to the Council.

9. A point certainly *not* missed by Fr. Garrigou-Lagrange, who held the common position of the Thomist School, namely, that moral theology is an integrating part of the single science of theology, which has as its *obiectum formale quod* the supernatural depths of the Deity and as its *obiectum formale quo* (or, objective light under which it considers its data) so-called virtual revelation, which, by the extensive labor of reason, draws conclusions from what has been formally revealed (and, a form of wisdom, it defends its principles as well). This point is evident in all of his spiritual writings. As regards the nature of theology and of moral theology, see the translation of "Du caractère métaphysique de la Théologie morale de saint Thomas, en particulier dans ses rapports avec la prudence et la conscience," noted above, and also Garrigou-Lagrange, *De beatitudine,* pp. 1–12.

10. This point will be discussed below, along with several applicable texts. The classic formulation of this position is found in *ST* I-II, q. 57, a. 5, ad 3.

Thus, speculative and practical truth are not quite the same. As Yves Simon has justly noted, they share in the notion of truth only through the analogy of proper proportionality.[11] Speculative truth is concerned with conformity to the reality known: Does the judgment combine or separate two objective concepts in a way that holds for their unity or disparity in the reality known? In our basic moral knowledge, elicited through the *habitus* of synderesis, practical truth indeed does start out with the reality of the human agent. Conformity with reality is at the basis of our speculatively-practical grasp of moral truths.[12] Nonetheless, practical knowledge is brought to its full, *practically-practical*[13] perfection in right and efficacious command. Thus, after due and virtuous consideration of the options involved, the parents in a family decide that driving on Interstate 95 is the safest way to travel to vacation. However, while traveling on this way, they suffer a horrific, though accidental, wreck, thus ending the lives of the whole family. Purely

---

11.   Yves R. Simon, *Practical Knowledge*, ed. Robert J. Mulvaney (New York: Fordham University Press, 1991), pp. 39, n. 11, 103. In p. 39, n. 11, he insightfully writes: "It goes without saying that the unity of the meaning of the word truth, as predicated of (1) the conformity of a judgment to a real state of affairs and (2) the conformity of a judgment to a right intention is but one of analogy. The analogy of truth, as divided into theoretical and practical, is one of proper proportionality. It is in intrinsic fashion that both the theoretical and the practical judgment are true."

12.   See Garrigou-Lagrange, *De beatitudine*, p. 349. Arguably, this point is at the heart of the recent debates regarding the importance of human teleology in the formation of moral knowledge. Although it is not always explicitly stated in such discussions, such authors seem to be searching to explain how the first speculatively-practical moment of practical intellection (i.e., synderesis's grasp of a universal moral principle) comes to birth. On this discussion, see, for example, Steven J. Jensen, "The Role of Teleology in the Moral Species," *The Review of Metaphysics*, Vol. 63, No. 1 (September 2009): pp. 3–27; *Knowing the Natural Law* (Washington, DC: Catholic University of America Press, 2015); and Steven A. Long, "*Veritatis Splendor* §78 and the Teleological Grammar of the Moral Act," *Nova et Vetera*, Vol. 6, No. 1 (2008): pp. 139–56; *The Teleological Grammar of the Moral Act* (Naples, FL: Sapientia Press, 2007). As Martin Rhonheimer has well noted, however, important points of qualification would be made by heeding the work of Fr. Leonard Lehu, whose careful articulation of the distinction between the physical rule of objects and their moral rule helps to avoid a naïve physicalism. See Leonard Lehu, *La Raison: Règle de la Moralité d'après Saint Thomas* (Paris: Lecoffre, 1930).

13.   On this somewhat scholastic seeming expression, see my summary comments in "Remarks Concerning the Metaphysical Character of St. Thomas's Moral Theology," pp. 266–70: "Appendix 2: On the Speculative, the Speculatively-Practical, and the Practically-Practical."

"according to reality," this was a *physically* unsafe choice. Nonetheless, "according to rectified, virtuous intention," this truly was a *morally* upright choice. It was not merely a correct opinion. Prudence infallibly attains its truth—but it is a truth of direction.[14]

This account of practical truth was a standard piece of the Thomist school, especially where it took Cajetan as an important commentator.[15] In the twentieth century, some of the most profound philosophical accounts of these topics can be found in Jacques Maritain[16] and, especially, Yves Simon.[17] While Fr. Garrigou-Lagrange's words in the article will lay out this topic with great lucidity, it is also helpful to keep in mind the sage comments offered by Simon precisely on the nature of practical truth, which is such an important topic at the heart of the Thomistic "moral psychology":

> Who and what we are matters greatly in choosing the course of action that is right for us. Our choice, therefore, will not necessarily be everybody's choice. But if we are trained in virtue, the choice we make will be objectively right, for our judgment guided by inclination will be the right judgment under our circumstances. Consciously looking for the best choice, we shall attain our object if our reason agrees with our heart, so to speak, or if, as some Scholastics used to put it, we join right reason to good will… Understanding human nature, we can train ourselves in virtues according to objective standards. And whoever succeeds in acquiring virtues will be easily recognized, as we suggested at the start of our discussion, by his or her unshakable dependability in human affairs.[18]

---

14. As regards the various elements involved in the morality of the human act, see Garrigou-Lagrange, *De beatitudine*, pp. 309–71.

15. For a recent account, see José Luis Galán Muñoz, "Razón práctica y virtudes en el Comentario del Cardenal Cayetano al Tratado de Virtudes de la *Summa theologiae* (I-II, qq. 55–67)" (Ph.D. diss., Pontifical University of the Holy Cross, 2011).

16. Also, see Jacques Maritain, *Existence and the Existent*, pp. 47–61.

17. See Yves R. Simon, *The Definition of Moral Virtue*, ed. Vukan Kuic (New York: University of Fordham Press, 1999), pp. 96–98, 111–9; *The Critique of Moral Knowledge*, trans. Ralph McInerny (New York: Fordham University Press, 2002), pp. 1–40; and Simon, *Practical Knowledge*, pp. 1–40.

18. Simon, *The Definition of Moral Virtue*, pp. 118–19.

Prudential reasoning unfolds through three acts: counseling, judging and choosing what is to be done, and commanding oneself to do this act.[19] One can take advice very well and nonetheless not have the strength of character even to choose the right thing to do. Likewise, one can decide to courageously defend the truth but ultimately fail when the time comes to command oneself to do so in front of a crowd of people. Full moral perfection leads to virtuosity in the chief act of prudence: command. Indeed, this last point serves as a good transition to the second chapter in this section, "The Instability of the Acquired Moral Virtues in the State of Mortal Sin," for as Fr. Garrigou-Lagrange notes, deprived of the theological virtue of charity, even acquired, "natural" prudence "begins to decline and barely leads one to its third act, namely, right and efficacious *command*."

How are the "natural" / "acquired" moral virtues found in a person who is in a state of mortal sin? This question has been the subject of debate recently,[20] and the second chapter is presented here as a monument to Fr. Garrigou-Lagrange's position on this matter. It was written as a defense of a remarks made by Jacques Maritain in his *Essay on Christian Philosophy* and *Science and Wisdom*, wherein the latter made the claim that, lacking the theological virtue of charity, the natural, acquired moral virtues are only virtues *in a state of disposition*.[21] It seems that Maritain was misinterpreted (e.g., by Fr. Santiago Ramírez[22]) as claiming that in the state of mortal sin such virtues no longer exist but, instead, are replaced by subjective dispositions. In *Science and Wisdom*, Maritain brusquely dismisses this critique, stating that Ramírez should know better as regards the vocabulary: "He makes me say that without charity the acquired moral virtues *are only* simple dispositions. I said that they remain *in the state* of a disposition; and there is no need to point out to so experienced a Thomist as Fr. Ramírez the difference

---

19. See *ST* II-II, q. 47, a. 8.

20. The debate is well summarized and adjudicated in Thomas M. Osborne, "Perfect and Imperfect Virtues in Aquinas," *The Thomist*, Vol. 71 (2007): pp. 49–64.

21. See Jacques Maritain, *An Essay on Christian Philosophy*, trans. Edward H. Flannery (New York: Philosophical Library, 1995), pp. 100–101, n. 5.

22. See Santiago (Iacobus) María Ramírez, "Sur l'organization du savoir moral," *Bulletin Thomiste*, Vol. 12 (April–June 1935): pp. 423–32.

between the two formulae."[23] For those of us in need of a good Thomist teacher to explain the difference between a virtue, a disposition, and a virtue in a state of disposition, we luckily have the clear text of Fr. Garrigou-Lagrange on this controversial topic.

As Fr. Garrigou-Lagrange remarks in another article in this volume ("On the Relationship Between Philosophy and Religion"), it makes a great deal of difference what *state* a given *habitus* is in. An intelligent high school student can truly possess the *habitus* of Euclidean geometrical knowledge, though the state of this qualitative perfection is not the same as someone holding a doctorate in mathematics. Both have the same objective, qualitative perfection, but the person with the doctoral education has this same perfection in a deeper and more penetrating state. Indeed, the young geometrician is at risk of being quite deceived when someone poses some difficult question that she could not have even remotely conceived on her own.

Another interesting comparison could also be made with regard to the various intellectual *habitus* that are called "sciences," that is, intellectual virtues inclining the knower to know, by way of objectively illative reasoning, the conclusions that can be drawn from the first principles of the particular science. It has been argued in the Thomist school, that such scientific *habitus* are found in their perfect state only when the knower has also mastered logic.[24] Between the physicist who has been trained in logic and the person who has not received any such training, there is *not* a difference of formal object. Both are physicists and both have the intellectual perfections with the same formal objects.[25] Nevertheless, there *is* a difference of state: one imperfect, the other perfected. In his well-known *Elementa philosophiae Aristotelico-Thomisticae*, Fr. Joseph Gredt, O.S.B., not only uses the language of a

23. See Jacques Maritain, *Science and Wisdom*, trans. Bernard Wall (London: Geoffrey Bles, 1944), pp. 224–25.

24. John of St. Thomas, *Material Logic*, q. 1 a. 1 (p. 3–11). Jacques Casimir Guerinois, *Clypeus Philosophiae Thomisticae*, vol. 1: *Logica* (Venice: Balleoniana, 1729), *Logica maior*, quaestio praeambula, a. 6 (pp. 184–97). Antoine Goudin, *Clypeus philosophia iuxta inconcussa tutissimaque Divi Thomae dogmata*, vol. 1: *Logic*, ed. Roux-Lavergne, *Logica maior*, quaestio praeambula, a. 5 (p. 92–100).

25. Thus, the natural light of the intellect and its "natural logic" enables the scientist to have his or her subject in an imperfect state.

habitus existing *in statu imperfecto* (*per modum dispositionis facile mobi-lis seu defectibilis*) and one existing *in statu perfecto* (*difficulter mobilis, seu difficulter defectibilis*),[26] he also makes a bold and relevant remark: "Therefore, just as all the moral virtues are connected among them-selves and with the final end, so too the speculative virtues (or, sciences) are all connected with logic."[27]

Fr. Gredt's remark is an analogy at best, but it helps us see the point that Fr. Garrigou-Lagrange makes in this chapter: Just as the acquired moral virtues are connected in prudence and perfected by their ordi-nation to man's ultimate moral end, so too are they lacking something when either of these two aspects fall short in some way. Thus, as nature inclines man to naturally good acts, including the obediential non-op-position to the supernatural order to which nature may be gratuitously raised, natural rectitude will fail to achieve its full perfection if it is not ordered to the final end to which the human person has been, in reality, ordered.[28] Fr. Garrigou-Lagrange here presents a version of this thesis and, in so doing, also provides the definitive defense for the aforemen-tioned comments by Maritain.

As mentioned above, the second portion of this section is re-lated to political matters. Thus, the third chapter of this section is "The Subordination of the State to the Perfection of Human Person According to St. Thomas." A key tool for Fr. Garrigou-Lagrange's expo-sition is the distinction he makes between personality and individua-tion. He sees this doctrine as being a continuation of a theory deployed by his teacher, Marie-Benoît Schwalm. The doctrine has sources deep in Fr. Garrigou-Lagrange's own treatment of the metaphysics of indi-viduation and subsistence. Interestingly, he cites not only Marie-Benoît Schwalm but also Jacques Maritain, with whom he was, for the most part, estranged by the time of the original publication of this article

---

26. See Joseph Gredt, *Elementa philosophiae Aristotelico-Thomisticae*, vol. 1, ed. Eucharius Zenzen (Friburg: Herder, 1961), *Logica pars II (Logica materialis)*, ch. 1, no. 86–90 (pp. 89–92). Also, see Angelo M. Pirotta in *Summa philosophiae aristotelica-thomisticae*, vol. 1: *Philosophia rationalis* (Turin: Marietti, 1931), pp. 139–45.

27. Gredt, *Elementa philosophiae Aristotelico-Thomisticae*, no. 88 (p. 91).

28. On this, one should also consult Réginald Garrigou-Lagrange, "Whether Aversion from the Supernatural End Cannot Exist Without Aversion from the Natural End," in *Grace*, pp. 504–506.

(1949). As noted in the article itself, Fr. Garrigou-Lagrange deploys this distinction in a number of works, including *Le sens commun, The Trinity and God the Creator,* and *Christ: The Savior.* One will again find our Dominican theologian deploying it in his 1951 commentary *De beatitudine, de habitibus, et de passionibus.*[29] It is fascinating to see this theme repeated by him without hesitation from his work *Le sens commun* all the way to works relatively late in his life. Thus, at least on this point of metaphysical articulation, he remains significantly in line with Maritain's own language (even if they diverge in other respects).[30]

One thus understands why it is reportedly the case that Charles De Koninck of Laval insisted strongly that Garrigou-Lagrange was a so-called "personalist."[31] The contentious argument that involved Eschmann, Simon, De Koninck, and Maritain is well known, though it had the unfortunate consequences of setting up significant barriers between Thomist thinkers.[32] Indeed, the way in which some dismiss the distinction between personality and individuality (understood as metaphysical principles), immediately proclaiming anyone drawing this distinction is a "personalist" calls, in fact, for slightly more nuance. For Fr. Garrigou-Lagrange, the distinction between personality and individuality is vitally important for him because of theological concerns regarding the Hypostatic Union and the Three Divine Persons

---

29. See Garrigou-Lagrange, *De beatitudine,* pp. 85–86.

30. One of the somewhat well-known testimonies to their conflict (and Fr. Garrigou-Lagrange's care not to be pulled into the more whole cloth claims of some critics) is found in Julio Meinvielle, *Correspondance avec le R. P. Garrigou-Lagrange à propos de Lamennais et Maritain* (Buenos Aires: Editions Nuestro Tiempo, 1947). This volume has recently been republished in Paris by Éditions Saint-Remi.

31. Edmund Waldstein, "Was Garrigou-Lagrange a 'Personalist'?" *Sancrucensis,* July 10, 2015, available at https://sancrucensis.wordpress.com/2015/07/10/was-garrigou-la-grange-a-personalist (accessed October 25, 2019). An important citation provided by Waldstein is taken from Cummins' translation of *De beatitudine,* which on this point (as on many others) is an abridgment of the original Latin. Cf. Réginald Garrigou-Lagrange, *Beatitude,* trans. Patrick Cummins (St. Louis: Herder, 1955), 74–75 and Garrigou-Lagrange, *De beatitudine,* pp. 85–86. Indeed, in the Latin (but not in the English edition), Fr. Garrigou-Lagrange cites the article that forms the third chapter of this section.

32. See *The Writings of Charles De Koninck,* vol. 2, ed. and trans. Ralph McInerny (Notre Dame, IN: University of Notre Dame Press, 2009), pp. 63–363. Also, see the subsection entitled "L'affaire du bien commun: une controverse philosophique?" in Florian Michel, *La pensée catholique en Amérique du Nord* (Paris: Desclée de Brouwer, 2010).

in the Trinity: Christ's divine personality is distinct from His human nature's individuality, thus calling for different metaphysical principles. Alas, at times, Fr. Garrigou-Lagrange's style leaves one wanting more philosophical reflection on such difficult matters. Even in philosophical problems, he proceeds with a kind of rapidity that likely comes from the fact that he is often a theologian reflecting upon his philosophical instrument. Nonetheless, there is an internal coherence that should be discussed. If one wishes to dismiss his so-called "personalism," one should also prepare an argument against his theory of subsistence.

Indeed, Fr. Garrigou-Lagrange believes his position is distinct from a false "personalism" that would be a cover for individualistic liberalism. In fact, the only sentence in which he uses the word reads, "Kant obviously falls into an excessive individualism, even if the term 'personalism' is used in defense of it." For Fr. Garrigou-Lagrange, individuation (or individuality), as such, arises from the side of our material nature; it merely particularizes what is formal in a given being. On the other hand, personality, which is the particular kind of subsistence pertaining to intellectual beings, designates the substantial mode that renders an essence incommunicable and capable of receiving or "facing" its existence to be received. According to Fr. Garrigou-Lagrange's exposition, which he based on Cajetan and those who followed him in the Thomist school,[33] personality and individuality answer to two different metaphysical principles, not only in human persons, but also in the Incarnate Son of God.[34]

Because of the amplitude of the spiritual will, the person (inasmuch as he is a person exercising freedom) is an agent outside the whole order of the universe. This is a striking claim, but Fr. Garrigou-Lagrange makes it his own in reflecting upon the so-called "secrets of the heart" or the free acts of thought and willing. By its dominating formal object, the will—even the weak human will—is not necessitated by any

---

33. Granted, there are weaknesses to this way of proceeding. As is shown well in De Koninck's texts, St. Thomas holds that the *person* is the substantial whole and not a part of the whole. Fr. Garrigou-Lagrange is more concerned, though, with distinguishing the abstract principles *personality* and *individuality*.

34. On these topics, see also Mullaney, "Created Personality: The Unity of the Thomistic Tradition."

finite, created good whatsoever. Fr. Garrigou-Lagrange has treated this briefly elsewhere, clearly developing a theme drawn from John of St. Thomas,[35] namely, the fact that such secrets of man's heart, arising from human freedom, are not, properly speaking, parts of the universe and, hence, are known by God alone. Even the angels cannot know our thoughts and our free acts.[36]

Fr. Garrigou-Lagrange's claim regarding the subordination of the state to the man's own moral and divinized perfection can be summarized in saying that, as free human agents, we are subordinate to the Supreme Common Good to be loved above all things. In his own words:

> We have a strict obligation to obey God, whose supreme rights found our first duties and every moral obligation properly speaking. *What we demand above all else* is not freedom for its own sake, as liberalism does but, rather, *the inalienable right to do our duty*—or, *the right of truth*, above all the ultimate truth to be known and loved. We can freely renounce some of our rights but not the right of doing our duty…
>
> A better affirmation cannot be spoken concerning the dignity of the human person whose superior duties are founded on God's imprescriptible rights, far above all the legitimate demands of the temporal common good that is end of the State. In this way, the State is quite clearly subordinated to the intellectual, moral, and spiritual perfection of the human person, whose destiny immensely exceeds the end and temporal duration of political society. All the Papal Encyclicals on this subject have stongly affirmed this fact.

In a later chapter of this section ("On Royal Government"), Fr. Garrigou-Lagrange will acknowledge that the temporal common good is indeed a true and fitting good (a *bonum honestum*), that is, something

---

35. See John of St. Thomas, *Cursus theologicus* (Vives, vol. 4), *In ST* I, qq. 56–58, disp. 22, a. 3. Also, see Maritain, *The Person and the Common Good*, p. 20.

36. See *De veritate*, q. 8, a. 13; *SCG* I, ch. 68 and III, ch. 154; *ST* I, q. 57, a. 4; *De malo*, q. 16, a. 8. Also, regarding God's action on the will, see *ST* I, q. 105 and I-II, q. 9, a. 6. Also, see Garrigou-Lagrange, *Sense of Mystery*, pp. 283–84.

good for its own sake and not as a mere means. However, this fitting good is founded upon this first orientation that persons have to God precisely because persons have wills of so great an amplitude as to be greater than all of creation.[37] As regard to the vexed issue of "the person and the common good," Fr. Garrigou-Lagrange's immediate concern is with the temporal common good (as a particular, finite *bonum honestum*) in distinction from the *perfection* of the human person, who by the infinite depths of the will—indeed, the "doubly infinite" will that is divinized through grace—is ordered directly to God in a unique way, establishing a hierarchy between the temporal common good and the ultimate Good of the life of beatitude. Thus, nothing the Dominican theologian says can lead one to believe that he subordinates the love of God (as the separate common good) to the human person's individual good in some sort of "personalistic" manner, whatever this nebulous term might mean.[38]

In the fourth chapter, this theme is continued in "The Divine Requirements of the Final End in Political Matters." This text brings

---

37. Needless to say, for Fr. Garrigou-Lagrange, this amplitude is only a negative obediential potency to a direct and beatifying knowledge and love of God. Nonetheless, in the natural order, man would still be bound to love God above all others, as the common good of all created nature.

38. Indeed, the opposite is the case. See Garrigou-Lagrange, *Grace*, pp. 160–61: "First objection. The common good of the Church is better than the good of one man. But sanctifying grace is ordained only to the good of one, whereas grace *gratis data* is ordered to the common good of the Church. Therefore, [grace *gratis data* is better than sanctifying grace.]

Reply. The major is to be distinguished: the common good which is in the Church is below the separated common good, that is God, granted; otherwise, denied.

I distinguish the minor: sanctifying grace is ordained to the good of the individual and also to the separate common good, that is to God to whom it unites us immediately: granted; otherwise, denied.

Hence, above the common good of the Church, which is the ecclesiastical order, there is the separate common good, which is God Himself, to whom sanctifying grace unites us immediately. Similarly, above the common good of an army, which is its order, there is the common good considered separately, namely, the good of the country.

On account of this, St. Thomas says later (*ST* II-II, q. 182, aa. 1–4) that contemplative life, which is immediately ordained to the love and praise of God, is, in an absolute sense, better, higher, and more meritorious than the active life, which is ordained toward the love of neighbor and to the common good of the Church not considered apart. Therefore did Christ say (Luke 10:42): 'Mary hath chosen the best part, which shall not be taken away from her.' Many moderns would do well to read this response to the first objection.

us to a central point in a current controversy surrounding Fr. Garrigou-Lagrange.[39] He wrote the article in the midst of the controversies surrounding the papal condemnations of *L'Action français*.[40] In contrast to the multi-authored volumes *Porquoi Rome a parlé*[41] and *Clairvoyance de Rome*,[42] as well as Maritain's *Primauté du spirituel* (translated into English as *The Things That Are Not Caesar's*),[43] Fr. Garrigou-Lagrange's article likely will appear tepid. Indeed, if one were not aware of the controversy and were to read the article, one would not be certain what event occasioned its writing.

The text opens with a summary of the classic doctrine of the Church's direct and indirect power. Fr. Garrigou-Lagrange basically echoes the positions of Bellarmine, Suárez, and Juan de Torquemanda (not to be confused with the infamous inquisitor Tomás de Torquemada). According to this explanation, the Church's power is "indirectly" concerned with

---

Again, St. Thomas declares (*ST* II-II, q. 182, a. 1, ad 1): 'It not only pertains to prelates to lead the active life, but they should also excel in the contemplative life'; which St. Gregory had already expressed in the words: 'Let the leaders be eminent in action, and sustained in contemplation above all others.'"

Also, Réginald Garrigou-Lagrange, *The Love of God and the Cross of Jesus*, vol. 1, p. 116: "In the natural order, every creature is naturally inclined to love its own good for the common good of the universe and, in a more or less obscure fashion, to manifest the goodness of the Creator whose might is the source and support of the universe." Also, ibid., p. 347: "Some, following Luther, unreasonably object that the common good of humanity, the perpetuation of the human race assured by marriage, is higher than the individual good sought by the preservation of virginity. Through St. Thomas, wisdom answers that God, the sovereign good, is above the common good of the human race; the divine good comes before any human good, the good of the soul comes before the good of the body, the good of the contemplative life before that of the active life. Now, holy virginity is immediately ordered to the good of the soul, to the contemplative life and union with God, whereas marriage is ordered to the conservation of the human species and to the active life."

39. Another such point of contemporary distaste for him is, of course, his critique of the *"nouvelle théologie."*

40. For an overview of Fr. Garrigou-Lagrange's place in this affair, with some documentation, see Nichols, *Reason with Piety*, pp. 123–27. Also, see the brief observations in Peddicord, *The Sacred Monster of Thomism*, pp. 88–100.

41. V. Bernadot, P. Doncoeur, E. Lajeunie, D. Lallement, F. X. Maquart, and J. Maritain, *Porquoi Rome a parlé* (Paris: Éditions spes, 1927).

42. V. Bernadot, P. Doncoeur, E. Lajeunie, D. Lallement, F. X. Maquart, and J. Maritain, *Clairvoyance de Rome* (Paris: Éditions spes, 1929).

43. Jacques Maritain, *The Things That Are Not Caesar's*, trans. J. F. Scanlan (New York: Scribner's, 1931).

temporal matters only from the perspective of their relation to man's supernatural end. As his exposition develops, Fr. Garrigou-Lagrange explains the condemnation of *L'Action Française* (without explicitly stating the movement's name) in terms of this indirect power, especially with regard to *L'Action Française*'s subordination of religion to politics (although it seems that the French Dominican wants to give the charitable interpretation that the movement only embraces such a subordination in an unconscious manner).

When this hierarchy of ends is disoriented, the entire outlook one has about government will be wrong-headed. It distorts the entire scale of values. Thus, if one follows Maurras's tendency to find Catholicism useful *for the sake of* assuring order to the political body, one's very allegiance to the Church and the entire supernatural order would be a means subordinated to a temporal, political end: one would be Catholic so as to be a virtuous French citizen. This would represent the enslavement of eternity to time. In the end, one would merely replace a naïve naturalistic "democratism" with a naturalistic monarchism. In either case, the temporal common good would be supreme. Fr. Garrigou-Lagrange was well aware of this danger, about which he states:

> Obviously, neither can anyone claim that the formal motive for a Frenchman to be Christian and Catholic is because France can find the tranquility of order only by returning to the regime that gave her greatness, to Christian and Catholic monarchy. Such considerations could perhaps put one back upon the paths of faith, as has often enough happened, but it is important not to lose sight of the distance separating these two orders, as well as the subordination of one to the other.

Yet, it is quite obvious, as the chapter comes to its close, that Fr. Garrigou-Lagrange is struggling with the obedience thus required by Pius XI. He affirms that he must ultimately conform even his speculative judgments concerning the matter to the judgment rendered by the pontiff when it is clear that the latter has considered the matter fully and has taken note of objections made in private concerning the matter. This is clearly, however, a cross for Fr. Garrigou-Lagrange, albeit one that is meant to purify French Catholics so that a truly just and patriotic politics may be constituted. This chapter makes it obvious that this cross did not strip the Dominican theologian of his own political inclinations. He is quick to note that the Church is ready to take what is good from the conservative reaction to the dogmas of the Revolution. One does not sense that he is quite as ready to concede that perhaps the revolutionary zeal of the eighteenth century also sprang from some positive, albeit gravely distorted, sources.

I have sometimes encountered insinuations that Fr. Garrigou-Lagrange harbored secret disobedience to this necessary submission to the pontiff. For my part, I would be hesitant to judge a man's heart so quickly. As mentioned above, even the angels have enough difficulty in these matters. Instead, I think it is useful to start, at least, by considering how he publicly wrote about the events that transpired in 1926 and 1927. Political positions are always such heated affairs, and nobody is likely free from some dubious *opinions* in such touchy and difficult matters. Let us be thankful that, at the deepest level of history, it is not man but Providence that guides all things. This chapter is presented only as a marker of sorts, an indicator of Fr. Garrigou-Lagrange's mind at that time, in the hopes of humanizing him, which is not the same as endorsing his overall outlook on political matters (although much in this chapter, indeed most of it, is uncontroversial if read charitably).

The fifth chapter, "Truth and Indifferentism," comes from a later period in his life, being published in 1952. In the background, one senses a deep concern on the part of the Dominican for what he diagnoses as a creeping relativism in the culture of his times. As is obvious in his comments, Fr. Garrigou-Lagrange sees all of this in continuity with the modernism of the first half of the twentieth century.[44] No doubt, the battles of his youth left a deep impression upon his thought, so we should not be surprised that the debates from the era of *Pascendi* remained his continued framework for approaching the theological

44. See Michael Kerlin, "Réginald Garrigou-Lagrange: Defending the Faith from 'Pascendi dominici gregis' to 'Humani generis,'" *U.S. Catholic Historian*, Vol. 25, No. 1 (Winter 2007): pp. 97–113. Also, although in a vein slightly more sympathetic to Gilson, see Heather Erb, "Modernism and the Growing Catholic Identity Problem: Thomistic Reflections and Solutions," *Studia Gilsoniana*, Vol. 4, No. 3 (2015): pp. 251–83.

debates arising in France late in his life. Indeed, he is most notorious in some circles for looking upon the "New Theology" (a term that applies to more than one post-Conciliar camp and, therefore, should be used with some care today) and seeing a perilous danger: the resurgence of modernism.[45] He was not wrong to see connections from the theological reformers of the era of *Pascendi* and that of *Humani generis*. That, however, is a history better told by abler scholars.[46]

During the debates of the 1940s and 1950s, the great weight of Fr. Garrigou-Lagrange's own concern came down on the topic of the nature of speculative truth itself (i.e., as the "adequation" of mind to reality in our judgments).[47] In the present essay, concerned with a creeping indifference in political life, Fr. Garrigou-Lagrange puts his pen to paper in defense of the rights that belong to truth itself. This sort of vocabulary, granting rights to a somewhat-disembodied truth, was standard among those who protested most vigorously against the Vatican II declaration *Dignitatis Humanae*.[48] Although there are limitations involved in such expressions, we should listen carefully to Fr. Garrigou-Lagrange's concerns, which provide keen insight into a perspective that echoes the concerns of a number at the Council and even today does not remain without cogency for those who wonder if the project of modern liberal politics has come to its end (not without benefits but, ultimately, run upon the shoals because of its inability to articulate a true common good in any meaningful and significant way).[49]

---

45. See Réginald Garrigou-Lagrange, "La nouvelle théologie où va-t-elle?," *Angelicum*, Vol. 23 (1946): pp. 126–47; the text is available in translation as "Where Is the New Theology Leading Us?" *Josephinum Journal of Theology*, Vol. 18, No. 1 (2011): 63–78. This salvo then gave way to a number of articles by Fr. Garrigou-Lagrange in *Angelicum*, as well as a dialogue / debate in *Revue thomiste* including work written by the Dominicans Michel Labourdette, R.-L. Bruckberger, and M.-J. Nicolas in response to Jesuit (or Jesuit-friendly) authors Henri Bouillard, Bruno de Solages, Jean Daniélou, and others.

46. See Mettepenningen, *Nouvelle Théologie—New Theology*, and Kirwan, *An Avant-garde Theological Generation*.

47. See Garrigou-Lagrange, "Verité et immutabilité du dogme," pp. 124–39; "Notions consacrées par les Concile," *Angelicum*, Vol. 24 (1947): pp. 217–31; "Nécessité de revenir à la conception traditionnelle de la vérité," *Angelicum*, Vol. 25 (1948): pp. 185–98.

48. See Schindler and Healy, *Freedom, Truth and Human Dignity*, pp. 211–42. Also, see Ralph M. Wiltgen, *The Inside Story of Vatican II, Formerly Titled the Rhine Flows into the Tiber* (Charlotte, NC: TAN Books, 2014), pp. 362–80.

49. See Patrick Deneen, *Why Liberalism Failed* (New Haven, CT: Yale University Press, 2018).

This is not an insignificant concern in an era that is, in the sage words of then-Cardinal Joseph Ratzinger, "building a dictatorship of relativism that does not recognize anything as definitive and whose ultimate goal consists solely of one's own ego and desires."[50] Indeed, if we are to truly take the Vatican II declaration at its word, it *must* be read in continuity with these older concerns which were repeatedly stated by the popes prior to the 1960s. Such a reading is all too rare.

The current global-political situation calls out for a sober assessment for this problem, and while much can (and should) be gained from studies like that of Schindler and Healy cited above, we should not fear engaging even more deeply with the "Pre-Conciliar" magisterial outlook on these matters as well. Without such engagement, the language of "religious liberty," so vaunted in all quarters of the Church today as a kind of fragile saber to rattle at an increasingly pugilistic secular state, will ultimately retain the overtones of Enlightenment rationalism—something that seems contrary to the Council's aim, even if the subsequent articulation of these matters did little to stress the paths for continuity.[51] For fear of being called "traditionalist" or even "fascist," many may avoid being honest about this difficulty; however, without falling into sectarianism, we must at least face the fact that while being specified by its own political end, the secular order nonetheless has as its first duty the recognition that man is created, dependent upon on an order of truth that man does not create,[52] and ultimately upon God, from whom, with the exception of sin, man receives all that he is and all that he does. How this should work out in its details in contemporary politics is something beyond my abilities. However, the standing critique offered by Catholicism (and, one might argue, by Orthodoxy as well) remains: Politics is never indifferent. If the civic order does not serve God, it will serve man, indeed man understood as a kind of absolute without any

---

50. Joseph Ratzinger, Homily for *Mass pro eligendo romano pontifice*, April 18, 2005, http://www.vatican.va/gpII/documents/homily-pro-eligendo-pontifice_20050418_en.html (accessed October 25, 2019).

51. This is, however, part of Schindler and Healy's project, for which they should be commended greatly, even if I differ from them in emphasis and perspective.

52. Even though, *of course*, he does create many realities in the orders of *ens morale* and *ens artificiale*. Still, there is a pre-given horizon of human activity, which sets forth on the basis of the primordial gift of nature and of grace.

superior, autonomously self-legislating, at best through the dictates of his own pure practical reason, at worst through the dictates of his pure passionate subconscious. The choice is of immense gravity and must be recognized squarely for what it is. Therefore, we should listen well to Fr. Garrigou-Lagrange's discussion of these problems of great importance.[53] In stressing the rights of truth (especially the rights of the true faith), Fr. Garrigou-Lagrange echoes the sentiment one can find in the social doctrine of the Church enunciated by Leo XIII in *Libertas*, namely:

> Justice therefore forbids, and reason itself forbids, the State to be godless; or to adopt a line of action which would end in godlessness—namely, to treat the various religions (as they call them) alike, and to bestow upon them promiscuously equal rights and privileges. Since, then, the profession of one religion is necessary in the State, that religion must be professed which alone is true, and which can be recognized without difficulty, especially in Catholic States, because the marks of truth are, as it were, engravers upon it.[54]

One will not find much in Fr. Garrigou-Lagrange's writing granting a positive value to religious freedom as such. It is also important, however, to note the primary concern he is addressing. His focus is not on the freedom necessary to a true act of faith. Instead, his direct concern is that the neutrality of the state is unacceptable. In focusing on this issue, he is articulating a position that is amply supported by the social magisterium articulated up to his time—a portion of the social magisterium that we are, today, a little too embarrassed to pronounce in polite circles and to incorporate into our thought.[55]

---

53. Likewise, see Réginald Garrigou-Lagrange, "De officio suscipiendi divinam revelationem ab ecclesia Catholica propositam," *De revelatione*, vol. 2, 5th ed. (Rome: Desclée, 1950), pp. 389–425.

54. Leo XIII, *Libertas*, no. 21.

55. For example, see Gregory XVI, *Mirari vos*; Pius IX, *Quanta cura*; Leo XIII, *Immortale dei*, *Sapientiae christianae*, and *Annum sacrum*; Pius X, *Vehementer nos* and *Iamdudum*; Pius XI, *Quas primas*; Pius XII, *Summi pontificatus*. The current *Compendium of the Social Doctrine of the Church* noticeably emphasizes magisterial documents written following the Second Vatican Council. This is certainly due in no small part to a desire

The Dominican theologian is understandably concerned that indifferentism to both natural religion and supernaturally revealed religion will end in prioritizing freedom over truth. The current age is wearied concerning the possibility of the intellect in attaining even the most basic of truths. Our culture's outlook is not unlike certain aspects of the so-called modernism that lies at the roots of Fr. Garrigou-Lagrange's concerns expressed in this chapter. It would require a willful blindness on our part to deny the fact that the developed West has much more care for freedom of expression than for the duties placed upon us by the truth—whether it be the truth of who we are as created human agents, or the ultimate transcendent truth that is God, who (despite the claims of the contemporary epistemological malaise) can be attained analogically by discursive argumentation and who proposes for belief, through the objective propositional intermediary of the Church, the mysteries of His inner life and of the order of redemption.

The only solution to this situation is a firmness of faith that is warmed by the glow of charity. As Fr. Garrigou-Lagrange comments at the close of this chapter:

> From this traditional perspective, we can avoid two deviations that are contrary to one another: sectarianism and indifferentism. In the middle and above these two contrary deviations, we find a summit where *absolute firmness of faith* is reconciled with *the radiation of charity*. These two theological virtues are like the two arcs of a gothic arch which mutually support each other. *They must be united very intimately* in us *so that the firmness of faith never degenerates into sectarian rigidity* and so that *charity toward* our neighbor *never degenerates into a form of culpable weakness and opportunism. This firmness of faith and this goodness of charity* are united *in the ardor of one and the same zeal,* namely *zeal for the glory of God and the salvation of souls.* All the saints provide us with examples of it. This zeal

---

to exposit the most current formulations of these matters. A concerted integration of the older magisterium, however, into the current articulations would have doubtlessly been desirable. See *Compendium of the Social Doctrine of the Church* (Washington, DC: USCCB, 2005). I would argue that the issue of the relationship between Church and State is *the first* issue (*in ordine iudicii*) to be dealt with in matters of social teaching.

is what attracts and converts those who seek the truth and who are delivered by it. The reign of error can be only transitory; the truth is what will ultimately triumph, indeed, God Himself, the First Truth. *One can do a true good to a sinner only by detesting the sin; one can only heal minds [esprits] from error through an utterly firm and strong love of the Divine Truth,* which alone can unite intellects and hearts.

Although his vocabulary and his emphases differ from that which is employed by the contemporary magisterium, one still finds deep resonances between the Dominican theologian and the words with which Pope Benedict XVI opened his Encyclical *Caritas in veritate*:

> Charity in truth, to which Jesus Christ bore witness by his earthly life and especially by his death and resurrection, is the principal driving force behind the authentic development of every person and of all humanity… To defend the truth, to articulate it with humility and conviction, and to bear witness to it in life are therefore exacting and indispensable forms of charity… The search for love and truth is purified and liberated by Jesus Christ from the impoverishment that our humanity brings to it, and he reveals to us in all its fullness the initiative of love and the plan for true life that God has prepared for us. In Christ, *charity in truth* becomes the Face of his Person, a vocation for us to love our brothers and sisters in the truth of his plan. Indeed, he himself is the Truth (cf. Jn. 14:6).[56]

This section closes by presenting a translation of Fr. Garrigou-Lagrange's preface ("On Royal Government") to Rouget and Poupon's French translation of St. Thomas's *De regimine principium*. This chapter has been included because it provides some counterbalance to a naïve belief that Fr. Garrigou-Lagrange succumbs to a kind of authoritarian monarchism. As has been repeated in various ways above, Fr. Garrigou-Lagrange is somwhat notorious for his political positions. As also noted above, these issues must be adjudicated elsewhere by a concerted historical study of the *L'Action Française* crisis and the clerical support of

---

56. Benedict XVI, *Caritas in veritate*, no. 1.

Vichy. Nonetheless, a work such as this section's final chapter provides an insight into what he thought precisely when he was able to be "as monarchist as possible." Interestingly, this text received a warm reception from none other than Étienne Gilson,[57] who later in life developed a rather negative opinion of Fr. Garrigou-Lagrange.[58] The text attests to the fact that the Dominican theologian's political thought was more than a mere paternalism, royalism, or so-called "ecclesiastical-political integralism." The illuminating principle of the commentary provided by him here is not *royalism* but, instead, *political prudence*. St. Thomas himself notes that there are different kinds of prudence.[59] The unique common good specifying political activity gives a new formal object to political prudence, distinct from the prudence that perfects practical reasoning in personal affairs. Political prudence is not the same as the prudence with which we rule our lives. This theme deserves much consideration by Thomists, who should develop a detailed account of the nature of political prudence *both in rulers and in subjects*.[60]

In countless places throughout his oeuvre, Fr. Garrigou-Lagrange notes the importance of the Thomist school's insistence that the proper object of the human intellect (in the state of union with the body) is the quiddity of sensible beings and that it attains its adequate object

57. See Étienne Gilson, *The Christian Philosophy of St. Thomas Aquinas*, trans. L. K. Shook (Notre Dame, IN: University of Notre Dame Press, 2006), p. 487, n. 90.

58. See Étienne Gilson, *L'être et l'essence*, 3rd ed. (Paris: Vrin, 2000), p. 179, n. 1. Also, see the remarks of Cardinal Henri de Lubac, whose recollections are somewhat seasoned with a tone of scorn in *Letters of Étienne Gilson to Henri de Lubac* (*With Commentary by Henri de Lubac*), trans. Mary Emily Hamilton (San Francisco, CA: Ignatius Press, 1986), pp. 106–110, nn. 8–9.

59. See *ST* II-II, q. 47, a. 11 and q. 50.

60. The same could be said for "economic" (or, "familial") prudence. As Aquinas notes at the start to his Commentary on the *Nicomachean Ethics*, a complete moral philosophy must address personal, familial, and political morality. Arguably, one could go further into the individual domains of particular occupations and groupings, but only after one dealt with the foundational issues pertaining to these three natural orders. It was standard in the Thomist School to include these in overviews on morality such as Chrysostom Javelli, *Philosophi et theologi longe eruditissimi, in universam Moralem Aristotelis, Platonis, et Christianam Philosphiam, epitomes in certas partes distincta* (Lyon: Jerome de la Garde, 1546), pp. 666–768. Also, briefly, in Jacques Casimir Guérinois, *Clypeus philosophiae Thomisticae contra veteres et novos eius impugnatores*, vol. 7: *Ethica* (Venice: Balleoniana, 1729), q. 8 and q. 9 (pp. 576–646). This same tradition can be

through this proper object. The human intellect is the weakest of intellects, and hence it has the most insignificant proper formal object. In a similar way, one could argue that the attempts in the moral order to consider the *doubly* weak human person—by nature bound to the slow path of material progress, and in the order of our supernatural vocation fallen and redeemed yet ever "limping along" due to the so-called *fomes peccati*.

Echoing a historically common theme, Fr. Garrigou-Lagrange notes that a democratic-republican regime requires much virtue in its subjects.[61] For him, such a regime is an imperfect form of regime that must be made up of perfect citizens. By contrast, to his eyes, a more unified regime, with a virtuous king as the chief ruler, is more attuned to our feeble and fallen state. It is the perfect sort of regime (because most unified and historically continuous), the regime that is best adapted to

found with various degrees of detail in manuals including but not limited to Gredt, Grenier, Jolivet, Fagothey, Bourke (although only briefly), et al. Yet this unity of ethics is generally given, at best, minimal treatment in works such as McInerny's *Ethica Thomistica*, Goudin's *Philosophia iuxta inconcussa tutissimaque Divi Thomae dogmata*, Oesterle's *Ethics: The Introduction to Moral Science*, Renard's *The Philosophy of Morality*, and Lehu's *Philosophia moralis et socialis*. The loss of awareness concerning familial or economic moral philosophy has been well noted in Stanley Vodraska, *Philosophical Essays Concerning Human Families* (Lanham, MD: University Press of America, 2014). This is not to say that matters of the family have not been of concerted interest to those favorable to Thomism. For sources to this end, see Jacques Leclerq, *Marriage and the Family: A Study in Social Philosophy*, 4th ed., trans. Thomas R. Hanley (New York: Frederick Pustet, 1949). However, one must bear in mind the weaknesses of Leclerq's own articulation regarding the subordination of ends in natural marriage. See Francis Connell, "The Catholic Doctrine on the Ends of Marriage," *Catholic Theological Society of America Proceedings*, Vol. 1 (1946): pp. 34–45 (esp. p. 38). Fr. Garrigou-Lagrange weighed in on the topic of the ends of marriage briefly in Michael Browne, "Sententia Bernardini Krempel de fine principali matromonii comparata cum illa angelici doctoris," in *Acta Pont. Acad. Rom. S. Thom. Aq.*, Vol. 10 (Rome, 1944), pp. 133–46. However, we cannot trace the issue of the ends of marriage here.

On the nature of political authority, one can benefit much from Simon, both in his well-known studies on the nature of authority and (especially) from his lengthy reflections in *The Philosophy of Democratic Government* (Chicago: University of Chicago Press, 1951). Also, see Marie-Benoît Schwalm's *Leçons de philosophie sociale* (Paris: Bloud et Cie, 1910). Likewise, Grenier's text is of much worth for the pedagogical articulation of these matters. See Henri Grenier, *Thomistic Philosophy*, vol. 3: *Moral Philosophy*, trans. J. P. E. O'Hanley (Charlottetown, Canada, 1941), nos. 1030–71 (pp. 273–481).

61. For a recent summary of this theme as it applies to the American founders, see Thomas G. West, *The Political Theory of the American Founding: Natural Rights, Public Policy, and the Moral Conditions of Freedom* (Cambridge: Cambridge University Press, 2017).

imperfect men. Given the unreflective egalitarianism and democratism of our day, the reader likely will bristle at Fr. Garrigou-Lagrange's description of this state of affairs, yet there is a good deal of level-headed truth in his observations relative to complex societies:

Every regime that favors the ambitions of demagogues who flatter the people in order to come to power, leads to political pharisaism and to ruin, for a durable union exists only in truth and justice. This is why, if it is to last, the republican regime presupposes great virtue and great competence in the subjects who are called to participate, through elections, in the direction of the country. In the case of a canton whose interests are very simple, or a federation of cantons, as in Switzerland, such matters present no great difficulty. However, in the case of a populous nation, with very complex interests, having not only an economic life but also a superior artistic and intellectual life, and who, in the midst of multiple causes of division, must safeguard its unity and the continuity of its traditions—then, the difficulty increases terribly. How are we to find in the subjects, a good number of whom are peasants or workers, the competence and virtue necessary for choosing men capable of responding to the difficult questions that are posed, ones that often baffle jurists, financiers, or diplomats of the first order? The election will most often designate upstarts, ambitious incapable men, who will become ministers when there is need for someone like Colbert, Vauban, or Louvois.

Fr. Garrigou-Lagrange makes concessions that indicate the need for a mixture of elements in a government, thus remaining in line with what St. Thomas says elsewhere about such matters.[62] However, he does not see this merely as mixing in a democratic element, an aristocratic element, and a regal element. Instead, Fr. Garrigou-Lagrange explains such advisors as playing their own important role in the rectification of political prudence so that it can issue practico-moral commands emanating in some way by the primary regal authority. One likely will wish

62. See *ST* I-II, q. 105, a. 1.

that the Dominican theologian would have applied these principles to other forms of government, but such political theory is not to be found in this brief text. Nonetheless, the dominating principles of political life—the common good and political prudence ordering the community in its pursuit of that end—are given insightful and clear exposition in this chapter.

Some may find the outlook expressed in this final chapter to be a bit dour and perhaps paternalistic. Fr. Garrigou-Lagrange does not partake in the lofty rhetoric of human possibility and the politico-social grandeur possible through human liberty. Writing as an American, I cannot help but think of a similar tension in our own political history. Many of the American founders noted the necessity of virtue for the maintenance of republics, and this ancient theme is not unique to them.[63] While American political life is infused with a good dose of French Republicanism through the sundry and quite-varied influences of a broadly "Jeffersonian" outlook,[64] one never can forget the dour old Federalist John Adams, who was never quite ready to expect heroic virtue from his fellow men:

> To expect self-denial from men, when they have a majority in their favor, and consequently power to gratify themselves, is to disbelieve all history and universal experience; it is to disbelieve Revelation and the Word of God, which informs us, the heart is deceitful above all things, and desperately wicked. There have been examples of self-denial, and will be again; but such exalted virtue never yet existed in any large body of men, and lasted long… There is no man so blind as not to see that to talk of founding a government upon a supposition that nations and great bodies of men, left to themselves, will practice a course of self-denial, is either to babble like a newborn infant, or to deceive like an unprincipled imposter.[65]

---

63. See the aforementioned text by Thomas West.
64. For an overview of the topic, see Merrill D. Peterson, *The Jefferson Image in the American Mind* (Charlottesville, VA: University of Virginia Press, 1998).
65. See John Adams, *Defense of the Constitutions of the Government of the United States of America*, vol. 3 (cont.), in *The Works of John Adams*, vol. 6, ed. Charles Francis Adams (Boston: Charles C. Little and James Brown, 1851), pp. 61–62.

These words from the dour and down-to-earth Adams resonate with the general perspective expressed by Fr. Garrigou-Lagrange. They both share a sentiment that can be called broadly "conservative," not in a partisan sense but in the most basic meaning of the word—someone quite unlikely to be taken in by the promises of ideology but, instead, willing to look sanely at the facts of fallen human nature and its limitations. Here, the words of Russell Kirk are similarly appropriate:

[For the conservative, one canon of thought is a] recognition that change may not be salutary reform: hasty innovation may be a devouring conflagration, rather than a torch of progress. Society must alter, for prudent change is the means of social preservation; but a statesman must take Providence into his calculations, and a statesman's chief virtue, according to Plato and Burke, is prudence.[66]

Granting this conservative outlook, it goes without saying that Fr. Garrigou-Lagrange is not a pessimist. His lofty sense for the Christian vocation is amply expressed in his many spiritual masterpieces, including *The Three Ages of the Interior Life, Our Savior and His Love for Us, Christian Perfection and Contemplation, The Love of God and the Cross of Jesus,* and the recently republished *The Last Writings of Réginald Garrigou-Lagrange* (recently republished as *Knowing the Love of God: Lessons from a Spiritual Master*[67]).

In any case, let us heed the central place that Fr. Garrigou-Lagrange gives to political prudence in his overview commentary on political matters. The primacy of prudence is not limited merely to Burkean Conservatives like Kirk. For the Thomist, a clear exposition of political prudence is a golden stone in the overall edifice of political philosophy. The political community's relationship to the common good is "enacted" wherever political prudence allows legitimately authoritative commands to emanate from the body politic through its deputed channels.

---

66. Russell Kirk, *The Conservative Mind: From Burke to Eliot*, 7th ed. (Washington, DC: Regnery, 2001), p. 9.
67. Réginald Garrigou-Lagrange, *Knowing the Love of God: Lessons from a Spiritual Master* (De Kalb, IL: Lighthouse Catholic Media, 2015).

Thus, like a golden chain, the selections in this chapter wrap back around upon each other. Opening with a discussion of prudence and the limits of fallen man, we close with a level-headed account of political prudence that gives context to the general political outlook expressed by Fr. Garrigou-Lagrange, an account that is not unaware of fallen man's weakness. By disposition, he is clearly a political conservative and perhaps too ready to grant authority its place. (It too is *quite* corruptible, and this must be given due emphasis in politics as well.) A Frenchman raised in the midst of an anti-clerical milieu, his reaction is understandable if not suffering from a little naiveté. However, almost all political ideas are a marked by some naiveté, for great personal questions are always on the line when we express our political preferences and outlooks. When matters of such importance are at stake, we understandably can be a bit direct and naïve-seeming in defense of the particular basic truth the utter vitality of which is pellucidly clear to our own eyes. When we consider our Dominican theologian's thought on these matters, fairness requires us to remember that he did not stand outside the pronouncements of the Magisterium on these matters, and perhaps, given the problems we face today, we would do well today to meditate upon those same words that inspired his thought.

ORIGINAL TEXTS FOR THIS SECTION

"La prudence dans l'organisme des vertus." *Revue thomiste*, Vol. 31 (New Series, 9) (1936): pp. 411–26.

"L'instabilité dans l'état de péché mortel des vertus morales acquises." *Revue thomiste*, Vol. 43 (1937): pp. 255–62.

"La subordination de l'état à la perfection de la personne humaine selon S. Thomas." *Doctor communis*, Vol. 2–3 (1949): pp. 146–59.

"Les exigences divines de la fin derniere en matiere politique." *Vie spirituelle*, Vol. 15 (1927): pp. 743–54.

"Verité et indifférentisme." *Doctor communis,* Vol. 5 (1952): pp. 211–28.

"Du gouvernement royal." In *Saint Thomas d'Aquin, Du gouvernement royal. Traduction du De regimine principum.* Translated by Claude Roguet and M. l'abbé Poupon, pp. viii–xxxi. Paris: Éditions de la Gazette Française, 1926; republished ed., Paris: Éditions Saint-Rémi, 2007.

* * *

CHAPTER I

Prudence's Place in the Organism of the Virtues

At first glance, many readers may think that a study concerning prudence is something of little interest. Many think, perhaps, of Mr. Prudhomme.[1] Others think of a virtue that consists above all in not acting whenever some risk might be incurred: "Let us be prudent and not busy ourselves with such affairs." In fact, in many dictionaries, the definition given for prudence calls to mind this kind of wholly negative virtue, one that is scarcely a virtue except in name alone. Is prudence such a negative character quality?[2]

Aristotle had a wholly different idea concerning prudence. According to him, it is a very positive, active virtue. He even speaks about it in terms that are so elevated that certain historians have wished to call Aristotelian prudence "wisdom." In reality, wisdom is much loftier in nature. St. Thomas compares it to a king who directs everything within his kingdom, comparing prudence to the doorkeeper, though indeed, the doorkeeper to the royal palace. Prudence, in fact, ushers one into the residence or kingdom of wisdom.

And if this is true of natural, acquired prudence, what should we say about infused, Christian prudence, above all when it is aided by the special inspirations of the Spirit's gift of counsel?

The importance given to this virtue by St. Thomas astonishes those who think that imprudence is a sin of only the slightest gravity.

It astonishes those who do not even think of accusing themselves of imprudence but, on the contrary, excuse themselves saying, "That was only imprudence on my part." They forget that every sin proceeds from a false direction of reason and, by that very fact, that every sin contains an act of imprudence, even though one may be more aware of the malice or cowardice that is attributable to the will. Imprudence is especially graver when one is more strictly bound to give a sure direction. In the case of a statesman, an imprudent act can be extremely grave and can lead a country to ruin. The same is true for an army's general or, again, for a conductor who directs an express train, as well as for the person who watches over the railway switch, opening up either a good passageway for the train or, perhaps, a disastrous one. Now, in our personal life, we are concerned with steering ourselves in the direction of the final end (i.e., eternal life) by the way of humility and abnegation and not in the opposite direction.

Bearing this mind, we will be a little less astonished to hear St. Thomas tell us (following Aristotle) that prudence is the first of the cardinal virtues, given that it directs all the others. He places it immediately after the three theological virtues, for it directs not only justice, fortitude, and temperance but also directs the virtues that are connected to the aforementioned virtues: religion, humility, penitence, magnanimity, patience, meekness, chastity, virginity [etc.]. Obviously, it is superior to all the moral virtues that it directs: *Auriga virtutum: recta ratio agibilium.*[3] The only thing it is incapable of directing are the theological virtues. By contrast, it is itself directed by faith, which makes us adhere to the mysteries of salvation, to the precepts, and to revealed counsels.[4]

---

1. TRANSLATOR'S NOTE: A mediocre, middle-class character who functioned as a French cultural reference for a kind of agreeable mediocrity.

2. We intend to publish a series of studies aiming to provide an introduction to Thomist philosophy and theology by placing in light the *principles* that dominate each of its great questions. With regard to moral matters, in order to provide a just idea of moral virtue according to St. Thomas, here we will discuss prudence, which directs all of the moral virtues. Likewise, we will discuss the special character of the practical certitude of the prudential judgment.

3. See *ST* I-II, q. 66, a. 3, ad 3; II-II, q. 47, a. 6, ad 3.

4. Prudence, being inferior to faith, hope, and charity, cannot direct them except in a manner that is wholly accidental. It certainly does not fall to it to determine *their wholly Divine objects*. However, for what falls to the *exercise* of these virtues, prudence judges, for example, whether it is opportune or not to speak now or later regarding the truths of faith to an unbeliever for the sake of converting him.

The space devoted to prudence is highly abridged in many modern treatises on moral theology, for at the beginning of these treatises authors devote excessive amounts of space to questions related to conscience. They forget that since *right and certain conscience* is an act of prudence, one can only understand the nature of this act aright by treating of the formal object of prudence, its other acts, and the mutual relations that it has with the moral virtues that it directs.[5] The study of these mutual relations is indispensable for forming a correct idea about how one should *form one's conscience*. From this perspective, St. Thomas's treatise on prudence is a text of great interest. In particular, we recommend the work of Fr. Henri-Dominique Noble wherein he presents a French translation of St. Thomas's treatise on prudence along with explanatory notes joined to the text. In these notes, he summarizes the best remarks that were made by Cajetan, expressing these points in a language that is very accessible to contemporary thinkers and in a way that responds to their own particular preoccupations.[6]

---

5. TRANSLATOR'S NOTE: There is, however, a debate within Thomism whether it is appropriate to conflate the judgment of prudence with the judgment of conscience. To summarize the complex literature, many Thomists (with strong reasons) argue that St. Thomas's use of the term *conscientia* predominantly (and perhaps always) belongs to a kind of quasi-casuisitic judgment of *moral science* (i.e., knowledge belonging to moral philosophical or moral theological reflection on particular act cases, noting therein, however, the fact that such casuistic judgments are not ultimately determined actions specified by a particular agent's situation). This cannot be adjudicated here, but it is important not to be naïve regarding the great difficulties involved herein. For the best summaries of this matter, see the following works: Reginald G. Doherty, *The Judgments of Conscience and Prudence* (River Forest, IL, 1961); P. M. Noonan, "Auriga et Genetrix: Le rôle de la prudence dans le jugement de la conscience," *Revue thomiste*, Vol. 114 (2014): pp. 355–77 and 531–68; Michel Labourdette, *Les Actes Humains* (Paris: Parole et Silence, 2016), pp. 204–245; Cajetan Cuddy, "St. Thomas Aquinas on Conscience," in *Christianity and the Laws of Conscience: An Introduction*, eds. Helen M. Alvaré and Jeffrey B. Hammond (Cambridge: Cambridge University Press, forthcoming).

6. See *Somme théologique de S. Thomas d'Aquin: Texte latin et traduction français; La prudence*, II-II, q. 47–56, trans. H.-D. Noble (Paris: Revue des Jeunes, 1925). The Latin text used for this translation is published following manuscript 15348 of the Bibliothèque Nationale de Paris, fol. 58ʳ. The reasons for the choice of this manuscript are explained in the prologue to the first treatise of *ST* II-II. As regard this translation in particular, it is inspired by the counsel given by St. Thomas himself in the prologue to his opusculum *Contra errores Graecorum*: "While wholly maintaining the meaning of the truths which he translates, a good translator ought to adapt his style to the particular manner of expression used in the language in which the translation is to be expressed." This edition, which is presented at an affordable price in excellent, elegant, and convenient volumes, has already received the best of receptions.

In order to understand aright what prudence, as well as its place in the organism of virtues, let us first consider its three acts: counsel, practical judgment, and command. Second, we will see why prudence necessarily requires the *rectification of "appetite,"* which is assured by the virtues which have their seat in the rational appetite (i.e., the will) and in the sensible appetite (i.e., the sensibility). In this way, we will be led to understand the nature of the practical truth and practical certainty involved in *every* prudential judgment.

* * *

THE THREE ACTS OF PRUDENCE: COUNSEL, PRACTICAL JUDGMENT, AND COMMAND

In order to understand the place of prudence among the virtues, we must first recall what are, according to St. Thomas, the acts of the intellect and those of the will that concur in *deliberation* and in the *execution* of what we decide to do. He distinguishes twelve acts, six on the part of the intellect, six on the part of the will, undertaking a specific study of each of these in *ST* I-II, q. 11–17. The ordering of these twelve acts can be expressed in the following table, which distinguishes (1) the *order of intention* relative to the end, (2) the *order of election* (i.e., that which is relative to the means), and (3) *the order of execution* (i.e., that which pertains to the application of the means chosen in view of obtaining the end). These twelve acts can be considered in relation to any end that we wish to achieve, whether pertaining to the order of salvation (i.e. eternal life) or in relation to some particular subordinate end, for example, obtaining a licentiate or a doctorate.

ORDER OF INTENTION

Acts of Intellect	*Acts of Will*
1. Judgment: "This end is good"	2. Inefficacious *desire* for this end
3. Judgment: This end can and *ought* to be attained	4. *Efficacious intention…*

Order of Election

5. *Counsel* concerning the means

7. *Practical judgment*: "These are the best means"

6. *Consent* to diverse means, envisioned *in globo*

8. *Election* (or, choice) of the means that seem to be the best

Order of Execution

9. *Imperium* or command that directs the execution of chosen means

11. *Usus passivus*: Passive application of other faculties, e.g., attention

10. *Usus activus*: The will applies the other faculties to the execution of the means

12. *Fruitio*, joy in the possession of the achieved end.

The ordering of these twelve acts does not raise any major difficulties. We merely need to take an example like that of finding the means to be employed in order to succeed in an examination. However, note that counsel is not distinct from the practical judgment when one immediately sees what is the best means. In this case, consent is likewise not distinguished from election (or, choice).

Some theologians, like Suárez, did not see the necessity of the *imperium* (or command) as an act of the intellect at the beginning of execution. Indeed, they confused it either with the act of will that precedes it or with that which follows upon it. However, it is quite clear that after the choice of the means (i.e., the election), the *execution* of the chosen means must be *directed* by an act of the intellect at the moment willed, neither too early nor too late (see *ST* I-II, q. 17, a. 1). Deliberating in their tents, some generals see clearly enough what they must command on the following day. They have chosen the means. Nonetheless, they still must execute this choice, and yet they often lack the nerve to *command* at the desired instant the execution of the means chosen the night before. Here, they stand in need of a particular outlook, namely, the glance of execution. It is even more necessary that the subordinate means must be executed *in the opposite order* to how they were intended and chosen. When they were chosen, the agent descended from the willed end to the superior means in close relation with it and from these means to the inferior means that are willed in view of the preceding. Now, in execution, he must begin with the lowliest of means: in the construction of a building, one must begin by digging the foundations, and in following a course of doctoral studies at the university, one must first register for this program. In this sense, the order of execution is the *opposite* of the order of intention and election; therefore, it needs a *special* form of directive activity, that which is indispensable to the executive power. As St. Thomas often stresses, the end, which is first in intention, is last in the order of execution.

From this perspective, in discussing the relations between religion and politics, it would be quietly clearly impious to say, "politics first,"[7] in the order of intention. However, this is not the case in the order of execution, where the lowliest of means ought to be employed first in view of higher ones and be subordinated to them. In order for a city to be inhabitable, it first must be rendered such by the expulsion or incarceration of criminals living therein.

Among these twelve acts, three pertain to prudence: *counsel, practical judgment*, and *command*. The first, counsel, considers the various means that are able to lead to the end. Here, it is important to envision means that are sufficiently different from one another in order later on to judge knowingly which of them is truly the best. One must not forget that the best means is not always the one that first pops into one's mind. That is why the most prudent statesman needs to have at

---

7. TRANSLATOR'S NOTE: The expression is that of Charles Maurras and *L'Action Française*. Note, however, that Fr. Garrigou-Lagrange is qualifying the statement, intending to show that it should not be understood in the sense meaning "politics above all else" in an unqualified sense. It is not clear here how much he wishes to distance himself from Maurras and *L'Action Française*. Nevertheless, to the degree that the movement understood the expression as "politics above all else" to the detriment of spiritual values, it stands in opposition to what Fr. Garrigou-Lagrange is expressing here. His positions on political matters should not be simplified in an attempt to provide a facile apologetic for him on these points. However, this topic exceeds the current volume of essays, which is primarily speculative, not historical, in aim. To see his immediate public reaction to the papal actions regarding *L'Action Français*, see the chapter entitled "The Divine Requirements of the Final End in Political Matters."

his side a council composed of superior men, having very *diverse* forms of competence. He needs to receive sufficiently different opinions, carefully weighing out the reasons for and against each of them. Generally speaking, a consultative vote of many counselors is of great use here. However, he must then elevate this multiplicity of opinions to the unity of a *practical judgment*, which discerns among the various proposed means that which is the best to do *here and now*. Here, it is important not to undertake endless discussions, thus compromising the *unity* and rectitude of judgment, which sometimes requires a great deal of prudence, something which statesmen indeed should have in political matters.[8] Finally, at the opportune moment, he must come to the *imperium* or *command* which directs the execution of the means chosen, rising upward from the last of all the means, passing to the more elevated ones, and finally arriving at the end being pursued.

As is well known, these three acts belong both to *personal prudence* in the conduct of our private lives, as well as to *the political prudence* of statesmen and of all those who must look after the common good of society in some way or another.[9] With these points now in place, we

---

8. See *ST* I, q. 103, a. 3: "It is necessary to say that the world be governed *by one*, for since the end of the world's governance is that which is essentially good and which is the best, it is necessary that the world's governance be the best. *However, the best governance is that which is brought about through one.* The reason for this is because governance is nothing other than the directing of the governed to the end, which is something good. Now, unity pertains to the formal character [*rationem*] of goodness, as Boethius proves in *De consolation*, bk. 3, ch. 11… And, therefore, that to which the intention of him who governs the multitude tends is unity, or peace. Now, *the essential [per se] cause of unity is one,* it is obvious that several things cannot bring unity and concord to many things unless they are united in some manner. Now, that which is *essentially [per se] one* can be the cause of unity more fittingly than many united things. Whence, the multitude is better governed through one than through many."

9. See *ST* II-II, q. 50, a. 2: "Whether politics is rightly placed as being a part of prudence." By this, we can see that the *common good,* which specifies these *virtues* in various ways (i.e., political prudence, as well as legal or social justice), is not only a *useful good,* as the utilitarians say but, instead, is a *fitting good.* Political prudence and military prudence are not only arts specified by the *useful* good but, instead, are virtues specified the *fitting good.* See *ST* II-II, q. 50, aa. 2–4.

TRANSLATOR'S NOTE: The Thomistic tradition also notes that family prudence is a unique kind of prudence, specified by a particular common good, above all related to the raising of the household's children but also to the related tasks that make the household the first point from which all of human culture radiates. On this topic, see the Introduction to Part III, pp. 145–46, note 60.

can easily see the relationship of prudence with the virtues of the will and of the sensibility.

* * *

PRUDENCE NECESSARILY REQUIRES RECTITUDE OF THE WILL AND RECTITUDE OF THE SENSE APPETITE

This point of doctrine, placed in high relief by St. Thomas and Aristotle,[10] admirably makes clear the place of prudence in the organism of virtues, as well as the mutual relations that it has with the moral virtues, which have their seat either in the will (i.e., the rational appetite) or in the sensibility (i.e., the sense appetite).

It is clear that rectitude of the will and of sensibility is required for the third act of prudence, that is, for the *imperium* (or, command) to which the other two are ordered. Indeed, one cannot issue a *right* and *efficacious* command regarding the means unless one first perseveres in having a *right and efficacious intention* of the end. We will see that this rectitude of the rational and sense appetites is likewise required for the practical judgment that must, before the *imperium*, determine the golden mean that is suitable for me *here and now*, given my age, situation, etc., concerning fortitude, patience, magnanimity, humility, chastity, gentleness, etc.

However, we see already that inasmuch as it presupposes rectitude of will, prudence differs from moral science and from art. A wicked man can speculatively know moral science, and his advertence of it is all the greater when he sins. Likewise, a wicked man can be a good artisan, a good mason, and even a good architect. However, a wicked man cannot be prudent. He can be sly, crafty, and cunning, but he cannot have the virtue of prudence, whose principal act is the right and efficacious commanding of the means in view of a *moral end*, previously willed by an intention that is both right and efficacious. Here, we see the distinction between art (*recta ratio factibilium*) and prudence (*recta ratio agibilium*).[11] For example, the art of a shoemaker enables him to make

---

10. See *ST* I-II, q. 57, a. 4 and a. 5, ad 3; q. 58, a. 4 and a. 5. Also, Aristotle, *Nicomachean Ethics*, bk. 6, ch. 2.

11. See *ST* I-II, q. 57, a. 4: "Whether prudence is a virtue distinct from art."

good shoes and that of a sculptor enables him to make beautiful stat-ues, whereas prudence directs the moral conduct of one's life. Unlike art, it does not have for its end the fashioning of some external matter. Instead, its end is the activity of fashioning the good man in ourselves. As is sometimes said, its end is to engrave the character of *man* [*vir*] in the *soil* (*humus*) of the human person (*homo*).

Does prudence require *multiple* forms of *rectification in our ap-petites*? Obviously, this must be the case. This *appetite* itself is either *rational* or *sensitive*, and this latter is divided again into the *concupis-cible appetite* and *irascible appetite*, depending on whether it is directly a question of a sensible good or is a question of the repulsion of the obstacles that oppose the obtaining of this good.[12]

What assures the rectification of the rational appetite? Without speaking here about the theological virtues of hope and charity, which are concerned with the final end, the rational appetite (i.e., the will) is rectified in the order of ends[13] by the moral virtue of *justice*, which renders to each that which is due to him. Likewise, it is rectified by *religion* (i.e., justice in relation to God, rendering to Him the worship that is owed Him), *penitence, filial piety, patriotism, obedience, gratitude, truthfulness, liberality,* etc.[14]

In the sensibility, the irascible appetite is rectified by the virtue of *fortitude,* to which are united the virtues of *magnanimity, patience,* and *perseverance.* The concupiscible appetite is disciplined by the virtues of *temperance, sobriety,* and *chastity,* as well as by the connected virtues of *gentleness* and *humility.*[15] We can see why all of these moral virtues are connected together under the direction of prudence, and what kind of mutual relations they have with it.[16]

---

12. See *ST* I, q. 80, a. 1 and a. 2; q. 81, a. 2.

13. TRANSLATOR'S NOTE: Here, I am reading "fins" for "moyens," given that the moral virtues other than prudence rectify our appetites in line with the *ends* to be intended. The appetites are rectified by *prudence* in the order of means.

14. See *ST* II-II, qq. 81–120. Here, St. Thomas treats of the virtues connected to the virtue of justice.

15. See *ST* II-II, qq. 123–68.

16. See *ST* I-II, q. 65. Here, St. Thomas discusses the interconnection of the virtues.

Infused prudence, which proceeds under the light of faith and directs our life according to revealed truths toward the ultimate, supernatural end, additionally presupposes charity, which rectifies us with regard to the ultimate end. As regards *acquired* prudence, in order for it to be in the state of perfect virtue (*in statu virtutis*), it also presupposes charity without which we would not love God above all things. Nonetheless, a single mortal sin, which deprives us of charity and infused prudence, does not by the same stroke deprive us of acquired prudence. This virtue remains in us, though in an imperfect state. In this state, it begins to decline and barely leads one to its third act, namely, right and efficacious *command*.[17]

Thus, we can see what kind of habitual rectification is required in the will and sensibility for the *virtue* of prudence, as well as what kind of *actual* rectification is required for the *acts* of prudence, above all for its principal act, namely, the *imperium* (or, command).

* * *

Is it the case that the right and efficacious intention of the ends of different moral virtues is also normally required for the other two, anterior acts of prudence, namely, *good counsel* and *good practical judgment*, in particular so that this judgment might determine of the *golden mean* that is individually appropriate for me in view of my age, condition, various circumstances concerning fortitude, magnanimity, patience, sobriety, chastity, meekness, or humility? Why is it that I cannot be led to determine this *golden mean*, this *medium rationis*, neither by moral philosophy nor by the experience that I have of my own temperament?

Here too, rectification of the rational and sense appetites is, as a rule, necessary. Moral philosophy and experience concerning my own temperament cannot supply for this. Why not? Because moral philosophy,

---

17. See *ST* II-II, q. 47, a. 13: "Whether prudence exists in the wicked."
    TRANSLATOR'S NOTE: On this, see the chapter below, entitled "The Instability of the Acquired Moral Virtues in the State of Mortal Sin," pp. 171–82. This topic has occasioned much spilling of ink. Fr. Garrigou-Lagrange's article on the topic already shows that Maritain is misunderstood by those who interpret his words in *Science and Wisdom* as implying that without charity the virtues are *mere* dispositions. An excellent overview of these matters can be found in Osborne, "Perfect and Imperfect Virtues in Aquinas."

which deduces universal and necessary conclusions from principles, does not descend to the *particular* and *concrete* case that is set before me *here and now*. Likewise, this is so because although the experience that I have of my temperament can enable me to know what is fitting for me in the majority of cases (*ut in pluribus*), such experience does not determine with *certitude* the golden mean of humility, magnanimity, or of any other moral virtue, suited to me in a given particular case.[18]

If I do not currently wish to be humble, when I search for the golden mean to observe with regard to this virtue (a golden mean that varies with the abilities of each person, his particular achievements, defects, and circumstances), I will easily find a pretext for self-love, which will provide me with a suitable pretext for action: instead of performing a true act of humility, I will perform a false act of humility (or, of pusillanimity), and all the while, at another time, believing myself to be magnanimous, I will give myself over to arrogance or to presumption. By this, one can see that rectitude of will and sensibility are required not only for the principal act of prudence (i.e., right and efficacious command) but also for its two anterior acts (i.e., good counsel and good judgment). This is above all the case when it is a question of determining the golden mean that is suitable for me *here and now* regarding certain delicate and mysterious virtues that must not be confused with the completely external brilliance of certain defects that resemble them, as glass beads may well resemble a diamond. Nothing is more difficult than avoiding every wrong note upon the keyboard of the virtues. There are approximately thirty of them, each one found between two vices, one by excess and the other by defect, often seeking to take on the appearance of virtue. In order to avoid every wrong note, we must have the inspiration of the song to be played. We must know the spirit of the melody. We must have a right and efficacious intention to practice these virtues right now in our activity. This brings us now to an important topic concerning a form of truth and certitude having a special character, namely, the truth and certitude of the prudential judgment.

* * *

---

18. See Cajetan, *In ST* I-II, q. 58, a. 5, n. 8.

THE PRACTICAL TRUTH AND CERTITUDE
OF EVERY PRUDENTIAL JUDGMENT

Is the prudential judgment always *true* and *certain*? St. Thomas responds,[19] following Aristotle, that it is always true, *if not speculatively*, then at least *practically*, for if it were practically false, this judgment would be imprudent and would spring from imprudence, not prudence. Furthermore, what holds regarding its truth must necessarily hold for its certitude, for in order to act prudently, we must have *practical certitude* that the act to be performed is morally good. Lacking such certitude, one would perform that act imprudently.

However, what is this truth and certitude found in the practical order? Likewise, how is it distinguished from speculative truth and certitude?

It can be espied easily enough by considering an example wherein the prudential judgment is itself at once speculatively false and, yet, practically true and certain, as happens when one suffers from invincible (i.e., non-culpable) speculative ignorance. For example, the person who invincibly does not know the extraordinary power of the wine offered to him judges, without prudential failure, that he can drink a glass of this wine, even though unexpected intoxication follows this drinking. This judgment is speculatively false in relation to the nature of this wine, but it is practically true with regard to the right intention of the person who judged thus without any fault on his part.

Likewise, as a result of an invincible (i.e., absolutely involuntary) error, one can believe that a host has been consecrated and thus adore it, while in reality, due to distraction on the part of the celebrant of Mass, it has not been consecrated. In this case, the prudential judgment, "I should adore this host," is practically true even though it is speculatively false.

How can this speculative falsity and this practical truth be reconciled in one and the same prudential judgment?

This reconciliation is possible because, just as Aristotle says, speculative truth is *the conformity of judgment with the reality judged* (*conformitas intellectus ad rem*), whereas prudential, practical truth is

---

19. See *ST* I-II, q. 57, a. 5, ad 3.

conformity of judgment with right appetite (conformitas intellectus ad appetitum rectum).

As we discussed in an earlier article,[20] this is a little-known point of doctrine that St. Thomas nonetheless places in high relief when he writes, in order to explain the fact that prudence is an intellectual virtue superior to opinion:

> The truth of the practical intellect (i.e., the practico-practical intellect, or prudence)[21] is taken in another different sense than is the truth of the speculative intellect, as is said in *Nicomachean Ethics*, bk. 6, ch. 2. This is so because *the truth of the speculative intellect* pertains to *conformity to the reality judged (per conformitatem ad rem).* Now, because the intellect cannot have infallible conformity in contingent matters (especially future things to be prudently foreseen) but only in necessary matters, therefore no speculative *habitus*[22] of contingent matters is an intellectual virtue. Only those virtues concerned with necessary matters are intellectual virtues (i.e., wisdom, the *habitus* of first principles, and the various sciences). *However, the truth of the practical intellect (i.e., practico-practical intellect, or prudence, distinct from that of moral science) pertains to conformity with right appetite.* This kind of conformity cannot be had in the order of necessary things, which do not depend upon our will, but does indeed hold for contingent things that are dependent upon us, as are human acts.[23]

---

20. Translator's Note: He is likely referring to Garrigou-Lagrange, "Du caractère métaphysique de la Théologie morale de saint Thomas, en particulier dans ses rapports avec la prudence et la conscience" ("Remarks Concerning the Metaphysical Character of St. Thomas's Moral Theology, in Particular as It Is Related to Prudence and Conscience").

21. Translator's Note: All parenthetical remarks are the added interpretations by Fr. Garrigou-Lagrange.

22. Translator's Note: With good reason, one should refrain from referring to the virtues as *habits*, which could lead the reader to think that they are mere subjective dispositions and not ones that give objective capacity with regard to choice. Accepting the conclusions of Yves Simon's life-long reflection, I am choosing to leave *habitus* untranslated. See Simon, *Definition of Moral Virtue*, pp. 47–68.

23. *ST* I-II q. 57, a. 5, ad 3.

Thus, one can have PRACTICAL CERTITUDE concerning the morality of the act one performs, even though it may coexist with an *invincible ignorance* or an involuntary speculative error. Such is the case when one of the faithful who, on account of an invincible error, believing there to be a consecrated host before him, judges, "I must adore this host." This judgment is true, practically speaking, through conformity to right intention, and false, speculatively speaking, for there is not conformity with the reality in question (the host is not really consecrated).

We need not worry about the danger of falling into subjectivism so long as we take care to restrict this kind of certitude *by conformity to right appetite* to the order of contingencies, recalling that *the right intention* of the moral ends of the different virtues itself has a rectitude founded immediately on the order of the *necessary* and the universal *by conformity to reality* [*rem*], for the truth of the first moral principles (*synderesis*) and of the moral science derived from them do indeed consist in conformity to the *object*.

However, this speculative rectitude of the first moral principles and of the necessary and universal conclusions of moral science cannot descend or radiate all the way to the *contingent singular* that is our human act and determine the golden mean that should measure it, except by the intermediary of *rectified appetite*, by the rectitude of will and of sensibility, a rectitude assured by the moral virtues.

Thus, we can understand why one can never legitimately act with a conscience that is *probable, practically speaking*, for that which is probable can be *false*, and if the judgment were false, practically speaking, the human act directed by it would not be prudent, but, instead, would be imprudent.

Consequently, we can also understand how each person, in the formation of his conscience, can pass from speculative probability to *practical certitude* concerning the fittingness of the act to be exercised, even if he does not know the reflex principles enumerated in the works of moral theology. The reflex principle, "the condition of the possessor is better," as well as how it is extended outside of matters of justice (an extension which, moreover, is questionable), is barely known by Christian men and women who nevertheless must form their consciences and do not always have the time, to this end, to take counsel.

Even without having recourse to this reflex principle, most Christians can, with the ordinary diligence that is possible for everyone, form their conscience and pass from probabilities for and against an action to the *practical certitude* of the prudential judgment *conformed to right intention.*

This conformity, as we have already noted elsewhere,[24] is not something artificial and mechanical, like certain comparisons of probabilities [undertaken by casuists]. It is something *vital* and *excellent*. Indeed, it is the *virtuous life* itself. It is the rectitude of the will and of sensibility, which makes the universal and necessary rectitude of synderesis and moral science descend all the way into the contingency and singularity of our human acts.

We can ask ourselves, given some man's knowledge [*science*], virtue, authority, and situation, whether one of his behaviors is conformed to humility and magnanimity or whether, perhaps, it may in fact contain some form of presumption or vainglory. It is often quite difficult to respond. To do so, *the tact of virtue itself* is required. Precisely because this man is truly humble and wishes in this moment to remain faithful to this virtue, asking for the grace for it, he will perceive that such an attitude to be taken is *conformed* or *not conformed* to the true humility that he carries in himself. The relation of *fittingness* (or, *suitability*) between the act to be performed and the virtue that he already possesses will (or will not) be established, and prudence will judge whether it exists or not. Therefore, only the virtuous man can render this judgment by inclination or by sympathy (*iudicium per modum inclinationis*), rendering a judgment in a domain into which the universal and necessary syllogism cannot descend, into the domain of ever-varied, individual contingencies. Now, it is precisely in this domain that one must act without confusing the false appearances of virtue with true virtue, the fake diamonds with true ones. This discernment is not accomplished without rectitude of will in him who judges. This is what Aristotle had noted in formulating the principle recalled so often by St. Thomas: "*Qualis unusquisque est (secundum appetitum), talis finis videtur ei.* [According

---

24. Garrigou-Lagrange, "Remarks Concerning the Metaphysical Character of St. Thomas's Moral Theology," pp. 257–58.

to the way that a man is well or poorly disposed (in his will and his sensibility), so does the end appear suitable or not suitable to him.]"[25] To the man who is truly humble, all that calls for humility appears good; to the man who is vainglorious, that which is inspired by the spirit of vainglory appears fitting or conformed to his interior dispositions.[26] What imprudences arise in teaching because one no longer retains sufficient love for truth because its worth is no longer recognized and because one maintains in oneself a supposedly charitable tendency not to contradict anyone and let everyone play with fire![27]

---

25. TRANSLATOR'S NOTE: I am expanding the form slightly based on Fr. Garrigou-Lagrange's way of explaining this in *Le réalisme du principe de finalité*.

26. See *ST* I-II, q. 58, a. 5, as well as Cajetan's commentary. Also, Aristotle, *Nicomachean Ethics*, bk. 3, ch. 5, and St. Thomas's commentary on this chapter, lect. 13.

27. For example, we can find the following sort of remarks regarding a choice to be made. "One must choose the *least evil* [act] in order to avoid the worst…" However, no distinction of any kind will then be made between the *least physical evil* (like the amputation of a member in order to avoid death) and the *least moral evil that is intrinsically evil* (like the lie in relation to homicide). Thus, it will be asked: Is it therefore permissible that one lie in order to prevent a murder? See *ST* II-II, q. 110, a. 3, ad 4. St. Thomas shows with evidence that it is illicit.

And is it permitted to vote for a candidate whose agenda is *instrinsically evil*, immoral, and irreligious, in order to avoid the election of an eviler candidate? Would it not at least be necessary that, in the agenda of the candidate for whom one votes there be enough good in order to permit one to *tolerate* the evil that is found beside it?

Acts are specified by their objects. If the object is intrinsically immoral, the act that approves it is intrinsically immoral and cannot be performed, even if one does so in order to avoid a greater evil. From concession to concession, one would eventually arrive at the denial of all principles.

Another obvious imprudence consists in expositing the question of divorce to young men and women in a catechism in the following manner: "Do spouses who are united by valid marriage have the right to *seek divorce* solely in order to obtain the cessation of civil effects, though without having an intention to remarry? Theologians are not in agreement on this point. Some respond 'no' by alleging that the law concerning divorce is intrinsically evil and contrary to divine and ecclesiastical law. Other theologians of great authority respond 'yes,' given that they hold that the law of divorce is not intrinsically evil, since it does not break the marriage bond itself. Indeed, *it is evident* that from the moment that the Church considers civil marriage as a pure formality there is no need to attach more importance to civil divorce than to civil marriage itself."

Will not this, "it is evident," and this manner of speaking of civil marriage as a "pure formality," produce the most untoward results? Most young men and women thus instructed retain only one fact: One can seek divorce if one does not have the intention to remarry. And they generalize that which cannot be tolerated except in rare circumstances. The broadest, quite contestable opinion is received as the truth itself, without any of the restrictions formulated by the theologians who sustain it.

Also, we have already shown elsewhere[28] how and why, according to these principles, the use of probability is legitimate in the formation of conscience when the measure of the act to be performed depends on our interior dispositions or, to speak in the language of St. Thomas, when there is a *medium rationis tantum* and not a *medium rei*. In this way, we can see prudence's place in the ensemble of moral virtues, which has often been compared to an edifice. The excavation that must be dug for its construction represents humility; the two columns that support the temple symbolize faith and hope; the dome and, above all, the keystone represents charity. The doorway with its two doors turns upon four hinges (*cardines*) that represent the four cardinal virtues: the two superior hinges represent prudence and justice and the two others fortitude and temperance. The brackets that lach onto onto these foundational parts symbolize the virtues annexed to the cardinal virtues.[29] And to each of these corresponds a gift of the Holy Spirit, represented by a precious stone embedded in the door, "*Portae nitent margaritis.* [Its portals shine with pearls.]" On the column of faith is fixed the lantern of the gift of understanding, and from the keystone of charity is suspended the burning lamp of the gift of wisdom, which illuminates the entire edifice.

In this way, we can see the use in treating moral theology not merely from the perspective of casuistry (a kind of contestable intermediary between moral science and prudence) but, rather, from a metaphysical perspective that enables one to determine the *nature* of each virtue according to its formal object and to deduce their properties as well as their relations with the other superior and inferior virtues. In this way, we come to see the place of each one in the spiritual edifice, and this is why St. Thomas divided the moral part of his *Summa* according to the division and hierarchy of the virtues and not according to the division of the precepts, for these latter are often negative, thus being

28. Garrigou-Lagrange, "Remarks Concerning the Metaphysical Character of St. Thomas's Moral Theology," pp. 258–60.

29. TRANSLATOR'S NOTE: Fr. Garrigou-Lagrange does not complicate the image by making a distinction between the acquired and the infused moral virtues. For an overview of his defense of this distinction, see Réginald Garrigou-Lagrange, *The Three Ages of the Interior Life: Prelude of Eternal Life*, vol. 1, trans. M. Timothea Doyle (St. Louis: Herder, 1947), pp. 57–66.

more directly concerned with vices to be combatted than with virtues to be practiced.

Coming to a close, we now see the profound contents of the Aristotelian definition of prudence as *recta ratio agibilium*, how this definition should be applied in the supernatural order to infused prudence, and why this latter, remaining discursive and at times hesitant, needs to be aided by the special inspirations of the gift of counsel, above all in difficult circumstances.[30]

While remaining quite inferior to faith and to the gifts of understanding and of wisdom, prudence so conceived does not cease to practically direct one toward the supernatural ultimate end. And, in the *purified soul*, it no longer teaches one only to disdain earthly things in order to prefer the contemplation of divine things but, moreover, is wholly turned toward the conquest of eternity and toward discerning what can dispose us for union with God here below.[31]

---

30. See *ST* II-II, q. 52, a. 2.
31. See *ST* I-II, q. 61, a. 5: "(Among the purifying virtues) prudence despises all worldly things for the sake of contemplation of divine things and directs all the soul's thoughts to God alone… (As a virtue of the purified soul) prudence sees nothing else but the things of God."

* * *

CHAPTER 2

The Instability of the Acquired Moral Virtues in the State of Mortal Sin

This rather delicate question has been treated a number times[1] in recent days in relation to Jacques Maritain's *Science and Wisdom*,[2] in which Maritain reproduces a theological argument which we ourselves briefly set forth in an article in *Vie spirituelle*.[3] This argument has been proposed many times by Thomists in the past, notably by Billuart, who summarizes many other members of the school in his own argument.[4] After having studied this topic many times while teaching this part of theology, we believe that it reconciles the various texts of St. Thomas related to these matters, as well as the interpretations offered by his best commentators. However, given that we set it forth in an abridged manner and thus did not undertake a comparative study of the relevant texts, some may have found our exposition to be too simple, indeed, perhaps negligent, regarding some of St. Thomas's precisions in these matters.[5]

For the sake of greater clarity, we would here like to recall various points related to this problem. It could easily become confused were we to forget certain elementary truths.

* * *

In order to rightly understand two capital articles of St. Thomas (i.e., *ST* I-II, q. 65, a. 1 and a. 2) concerning the state of the moral virtues in a subject who is in a state of mortal sin, and also in order to preserve the substance of the commentaries written by Cajetan, John of St. Thomas, and the Salamanca Carmelites on these matters, it is important that we distinguish the following from each other:

1. *False moral virtue* like the temperance of the miser;
2. The *natural disposition* to such a moral virtue;
3. The *acquired disposition* to such a moral virtue;

1. See Thomas Deman, "Questions disputées de science morale," *Revue des Sciences philosophiques et théologiques*, Vol. 26 (April 1937): p. 278. In this same article, the question of Christian philosophy in relation to moral science is taken up again. We will not return to this, for we have explained ourselves at sufficient length on this point at the last Thomist Congress held in Rome in November 1936. See Réginald Garrigou-Lagrange, "De Relationibus inter philosophiam et Religionem," *Acta secundi congressus Thomistici internationalis* (1936): pp. 379–405. [TRANSLATOR'S NOTE: This is included in this volume as the chapter "On the Relationship Between Philosophy and Religion."]
    Let us only note one thing that we would have thought would not need to be recalled: we have always admitted as an elementary doctrine of St. Thomas that *habitus* are specified by their *formal objects* and that, consequently, metaphysical wisdom, theological science, and the gift of wisdom are specifically distinct on account of their formal objects. What Thomist could doubt this? This is why we wrote elsewhere (Garrigou-Lagrange, "Le langage des spirituels comparé à celui des théologiens," *Vie spirituelle*, Vol. 49 (1936): pp. 257–76, esp. p. 274 and ibid., n. 1) that the language of the great spiritual authors, which is often the language of Scripture, is more elevated than the language of theologians, even though the former does not have the technical precision of the latter. Why? Because it expresses a higher form of knowledge. Despite its imprecision and obscurity, *infused contemplation is loftier than theological speculation on account of its formal object.* This is already true of *infused faith*, so for all the more reason is it true of savoring and penetrating faith [i.e., faith as animated by the gifts of the Holy Spirit]. How could this be doubted? By the formal object that specifies it, an essentially *infused habitus* is superior to an *acquired habitus*.

2. See Maritain, *Science and Wisdom*, pp. 137–241.

3. See Réginald Garrigou-Lagrange, "Les vertus morales dans la vie intérieure," *Vie spirituelle*, Vol. 41 (1934): pp. 225–28.
    TRANSLATOR'S NOTE: This selection is substantially what can be found in Garrigou-Lagrange, *Three Ages of the Interior Life*, vol. 1, pp. 58–59.]

4. See Billuart, *Summa sancti Thomae, De passionibus et virtutibus*, diss. 2, a. 4, §3: "Without charity, *true acquired moral virtues can exist*, just as there were such in many of the gentiles, though *they were imperfect* [acquired moral virtues]. I respond that virtue remains in the sinner as *a habitus* insofar as it is a virtue by way of *its intrinsic principles* on account which it seeks to be moved in difficult matters. However, *accidentally* and *on account of which the subject*, who is turned away from his ultimate end, it becomes *facile mobilis* and thereby has *the mode of disposition*. Whence, it remains essentially a virtue, though an imperfect one" (ibid., *in fine*).

5. See Deman, "Questions disputées de science morale," p. 291.

4. *True acquired moral virtue, in an imperfect and unstable state of disposition*, in particular when one begins to acquire it or when it increasingly declines in strength (here not concerning ourselves with the presence or absence of the state of grace);

5. *True moral virtue in the state of stable virtue* (*difficile mobilis*), *connected* in acquired prudence with the other acquired moral virtues and *united to charity* (therefore, in a subject who is in a state of grace);

6. *True acquired moral virtue* in a subject who is in a *state of mortal sin*.

However, let us note that the last case itself contains many nuances, depending on whether the subject never was in the state of grace or, on the other hand, he had acquired such virtues over the course of many years. Moreover, there is a notable difference if the latter only committed one mortal sin or if, on the contrary, he committed grave, repeated faults, in particular against that particular moral virtue. These various subtleties are often neglected in simplified expositions concerning this matter, but they obviously are worth taking time to reflect upon.

* * *

Taking each of the points of this enumeration in particular, we can quite easily show what St. Thomas said and, in accord with his principles and texts, render a judgment concerning the last case, which is of particular interest to us here in the matter at hand.

First, *false virtue*, like the *temperance of the miser*, is formally specified, not by the fitting [*honnête*] or reasonable good, but by the useful good pursued by the miser or by a delightful good that is sought, for example, by this or that dilettante. In *ST* II-II, q. 23, a. 7, St. Thomas speaks of this miser's "temperance" and his "prudence," which obviously are false virtues, having only appearances of true virtues. They are practiced for love of money, not so that this miser may live according to right reason. Thus, the miser pays his debts in order to avoid the expenses that would be incurred by a trial.

Second, *the natural disposition to a given moral virtue* is a praiseworthy inclination found in our individual nature, one that we do not need to acquire (for example, the natural disposition to meekness and not to courage or vice-versa). It disposes us not only to will the useful or delightful good but to will that which is a fitting or reasonable good, without, however, leading to it inasmuch as it is reasonable, formally speaking. This requires the very direction of right reason. It represents the difference between *facere bonum* and *agere bene* [to do something good and to act well] or between *bonum materialiter* and *bonum formaliter*. St. Thomas speaks of this inclination in *ST* I-II, q. 65, a. 1, where he says:

> An imperfect moral virtue (such as temperance or fortitude) is nothing other than a kind of *inclination* existing in us *directed to a given work concerning the genus of goods to be done*, whether such an inclination be in us by nature or by custom. And understood in this way, the moral virtues *are not connected*, for we may see that someone is prompt in performing a work of liberality on account of his natural constitution or on account of some custom, although this person is not prompt in performing the works of chastity.

Third, *the acquired disposition to a given virtue* is the result of the repetition of acts, as was said in the aforementioned text. For example, in the soldier who has often shown himself to be courageous, we find an acquired disposition to the virtue of fortitude, even though he often happens to yield to an inclination leading him to become drunk. The good disposition we are speaking of only differs from the preceding one because it is acquired and not innate. It leads one to perform a *good act*, though without yet disposing one to perform it *well*, precisely as the requirement of right reason, and it does not entail the connection of the virtues, since such a disposition often exists alongside notable vices.

Fourth, *next, we have true acquired moral virtue in the imperfect and unstable state of disposition*, in particular when one begins to acquire it or when it continually declines in strength. St. Thomas speaks of this in *ST* I-II, q. 49, a. 2, ad 3:

> A disposition, properly speaking, can be understood as being distinguished from a *habitus* in two ways. *In one way, they can be*

distinguished as the perfect is distinct from the imperfect within one and the same species, namely, as it is called *a disposition,* retaining the common name, when it is had imperfectly, such that it can be lost *easily.* However, it is called a *habitus* when it is had perfectly, such that it is not lost easily, *and in this way a disposition becomes a habitus,* as when a *boy becomes a man. In another way,* they can be distinguished as different species of one subaltern genus. Thus, we use the term "dispositions" for those qualities that *are easily lost on account of their very nature,* for they have changeable causes, for example, sickness and health. However, we use the term "*habitus*" for those qualities *that are such as not to be changed easily on account of their nature because they have unchanging [immobiles] causes* (e.g., *the sciences and the virtues*). And in this sense, a disposition does not become a *habitus.*

St. Thomas concludes some lines later saying that *a true acquired virtue* that merits this name *on account of its formal object* (the fitting good, formally willed) can exist *in an imperfect state (or an unstable state of disposition) on account of the subject in which it is found* (for example, because said subject is just beginning to acquire it or because it declines in him on account of actions opposed to this *habitus*). Indeed, in the same response, St. Thomas notes that, if *dispositions* that accidentally are *difficile mobiles* do exist, like, for example, deeply rooted low self-esteem, there are, by contrast, *habitus* that accidentally have little stability: "The opposite happens *with regard to qualities that by their very nature are difficile mobilis,* for if someone *imperfectly* has *science* in such a way that he can easily lose it, he is more properly said to be disposed to science than to have science." Such is the case when a young student has understood the first theorems of Euclid but thus knows only these rudiments of geometry. Likewise, we see this in the case of the person who *begins* to practice the acquired moral virtues in order to conduct himself well, out of love for the reasonable good as such. For now, we are not taking into consideration whether this subject is in the state of grace or not. Rather, we are only noting that he has a still-unstable beginning of true acquired virtue (for example, of temperance). And if he seeks to practice the other virtues (of courage, justice, and prudence), he must often combat lively inclinations that are contrary to them. In certain subjects who begin to develop true acquired virtues, there even are vices that must be uprooted. Consequently, these acquired virtues that are in a state of becoming [*in fieri*] are connected only *in fieri*. They are not yet *in statu virtutis* according to the expression frequently found in Cajetan,[6] and they certainly are not yet firmly connected in an established state of existence [*in facto esse*].

Fifth, *next, we have the case of true acquired moral virtue in the state of being a stable virtue (difficile mobilis) connected* in acquired prudence with the other acquired moral virtues and *united to charity*, therefore in a subject in a state of grace. These acquired virtues serve the infused virtues, most especially charity, a little like how the imagination and sense memory serve the intellect in the learned man and the agility of fingers serves [the *habitus* of] art and artistic inspiration in the artist. This is what normally takes place in the life of the righteous person who tends generously toward perfection.

Sixth, what are we to think about *true acquired moral virtue in a subject who is in a state of mortal sin*? St. Thomas tells us in *ST* I-II, q. 71, a. 4:

> Any mortal sin is contrary to charity, which is the root of all the infused virtues inasmuch as they are virtues, and therefore *through one act of mortal sin, charity thus being removed, consequently all the infused moral virtues are removed, inasmuch as they are virtues.* And I say this on account of faith and hope, whose *habitus* remain unformed after mortal sin and thus are not virtues... *So, therefore, mortal sin cannot exist together with the infused virtues; HOWEVER, IT CAN EXIST TOGETHER WITH THE ACQUIRED VIRTUES.*

A little earlier, the reason for this is given in these terms: "For just as a *habitus* is not generated through one act, so is it not corrupted through one act, as was said above (in *ST* I-II, q. 63, a. 2, ad 2)."

Therefore, true acquired moral virtue can remain in a subject in a state of mortal sin.

However, St. Thomas does not call it a perfect virtue without qualification [*simpliciter*]. He says, in *ST* I-II, q. 65, a. 2: "Only the infused

---

6.   See Cajetan, *In ST* I-II, q. 65, a. 1, nos. 1 and 11.

virtues are perfectly and without qualification [*simpliciter*] to be called virtues because they order man well to the ultimate end without qualification." Likewise, he says, in *ST* II-II, q. 23, a. 7: "If a particular good is a true good, for example, the preservation of the city or something of this sort, *it will indeed be a true but imperfect virtue,* unless it is referred to the final and perfect good. And in this way, *true virtue without qualification* [*simpliciter*] cannot exist without charity."[7]

He says again in *ST* II-II, q. 136, a. 3: "Patience cannot be had without the help of grace." He explains this in the response to the first objection to this article by saying:

> If human nature were in a state of integrity [i.e., unfallen], reason's inclination would prevail in human nature. However, what prevails in corrupt nature, instead, is the inclination of concupiscence, which is dominant in man. And therefore, man is more prone to suffer evils for the sake of the goods in which concupiscence delights presently than *to tolerate evils on account of a future good* that is desired in accord with reason. This latter is what pertains to true patience.

However, is the true acquired virtue in a subject in a state of mortal sin perfect in its order of acquired virtue? Does it remain stable, *difficile mobilis*? Is it *in statu virtutis* or only in a state of disposition, like geometry in the young student who knows only its first theorems?

Here, we must reflect on the fact that through mortal sin man is turned away not only from the supernatural final end but also from the *natural final end.* In other words, in such a state, *he cannot love God efficaciously as the Author of his nature* more than himself and above all else, as the natural law requires. St. Thomas shows well in *ST* I-II, q. 109, a. 3: "In the state of integral nature…man loves God more than himself and above all things. However, in the state of corrupt nature, man falls short of this on account of the appetite of the rational will, which on account of the corruption of nature *follows* [*its*] *private good, unless it is cured by God's grace.*" This is very important in the question

---

7. See also, ibid., ad 2.

that occupies us, as John of St. Thomas and the Salamanca Carmelites have justly noted.

One must not forget here that every mortal sin that turns us directly away from the supernatural final end likewise indirectly turns us away from the natural last end and is at least *indirectly* contrary *to the natural law*. Why? Because the natural law itself already obliges us to obey God in all that He commands (whether in the order of nature or in the order of grace).[8]

We must note well that in the present state of humanity, every man is either in the state of mortal sin or in the state of grace. Therefore, since the Fall, man cannot efficaciously love God, the Author of his nature, more than himself without the grace that heals, and this grace is not really distinct from sanctifying grace. So long as a man is in the state of mortal sin, his will is habitually turned away from God. Instead of loving Him above all else, the sinner loves himself more than God.

Can he who is in the state of mortal sin at least *efficaciously love* the fitting (or reasonable) good as such more than he loves himself? No, for this already would be to vaguely yet efficaciously love, more than oneself, God the Author of nature and the Sovereign Good. This is why fallen man cannot observe all the precepts of the natural law, for this requires *gratia sanans*.[9]

This means that every man in a state of mortal sin suffers from great weakness in his attempts to accomplish the moral good, even the moral good belonging to the natural order. And although he could have the true virtue of prudence, he cannot have it in the state of stable virtue, *difficile mobilis*. Indeed, acquired prudence requires the rectification of appetite (above all of the will).[10] Now, in the state of mortal sin, this rectification does not exist *even in relation to the natural last end*, and moreover, through this grave fault, the will is poorly disposed in relation to the *particular end* of the given virtue against which one has sinned. Hence, the rectitude of acquired prudence's judgment and

---

8. TRANSLATOR'S NOTE: On this, also see Garrigou-Lagrange, "Whether Aversion from the Supernatural End Cannot Exist Without Aversion from the Natural End," in *Grace*, pp. 504–506.

9. See *ST* I-II, q. 109, aa. 2–4.

10. See *ST* I-II, q. 58, a. 5, corp., and ad 3.

imperium[11] is compromised and, along with it, the stable inter-connection of the acquired moral virtues.[12]

Without a doubt, a single mortal sin does not suffice for *destroying* the acquired moral virtue of prudence and those that it directs. Nonetheless, upon the commission of such a sin, they begin to decline and stop existing *in the state of stable virtue*, and if such mortal sins come to be multiplied, the acquired virtue will come to disappear and be replaced by a vice.

Before this destruction, this virtue exists *in the state of being a decreasingly stable disposition*. If this were not admitted, one could never say when it begins to become unstable before being completely destroyed.

This is what Billuart said well and quite justly, here summarizing what many other commentators affirm:

I respond that virtue remains in the sinner as *a habitus* insofar as it is a virtue by way of *its intrinsic principles* on account of which it seeks to be moved in difficult matters. However, *accidentally* and *on account of the subject*, who is turned away from his ultimate end, it becomes *facile mobilis* and thereby has *the mode of a disposition*. Whence, it remains essentially a virtue, though an imperfect one.[13]

It would be easy to show that this conclusion is in conformity with what is said in St. Thomas's own texts, as well as in those of his best commentators.[14]

---

11. TRANSLATOR'S NOTE: On this point, see above, "Prudence's Place in the Organism of the Virtues." The theme comes up elsewhere in his corpus. See Réginald Garrigou-Lagrange, *God: His Existence and His Nature*, vol. 2, pp. 306–38 and 370–72. Also, a helpful summary of the same point can be found in the sixth chapter of the second part of *Bergsonian Philosophy and Thomism*, ed. McInerny. Also, see Jacques Maritain, *Scholasticism and Politics*, trans. Mortimer Adler (Indianapolis: Liberty Fund, 2011), pp. 118–43.

12. See *ST* I-II, q. 58, a. 5, ad 3: "Prudence not only is for *counseling* well but also for *judging* well and *commanding* well, which cannot exist unless the impediment of the passions corrupting the judgment and command of prudence be removed, and this is brought about through the moral virtues."

13. Billuart, *Summa sancti thomae, De passionibus et virtutibus*, diss. 2, a. 4, §3, *in fine*.

14. See Cajetan, *In ST* I-II, q. 65, no. 11: "In *virtue* as such, which is a species of *habitus*, there is found a quality that is essentially virtue *in a twofold manner*, namely, as *having the state of virtue* and as *not having the state of virtue*" (but having the mode of disposition, as was said earlier in no. 1). [CONT. NEXT PAGE]

The distinction that Billuart thus formulates, following many others, is elementary for every Thomist. St. Thomas (as we saw above in the fourth point, above) clearly enunciated it in *ST* I-II, q. 49, a. 2, ad 3, where he says: "The opposite happens *with regard to qualities that by their very nature are difficile mobilis*, for if someone *imperfectly* has *science* in such a way that he can easily lose it, he is more properly said

---

John of St. Thomas, *Cursus theologicus, De proprietatibus virtutum*, disp. 17, a. 2, no. 6: "Therefore, I say that from the absence of charity in a sinner, an acquired virtue directly loses the fact of being a virtue *simpliciter* [*sic*], meaning *in all ways*. However, it does not directly lose the fact it is a virtue *simpliciter* [*sic*], meaning *essentially* and absolutely… It clothes itself with the character [*rationem*] of a good disposition, which is an imperfect virtue." Ibid., n. 8: "*Because*, upon losing charity, *the sinner loses his conversion to the true ultimate supernatural and natural end*, virtue of any sort cannot make him who has it good, nor can it make him have a firm motive in the good that he does, given that the *motive* of doing the good *well and firmly* is taken from love of the end, by which one is strengthened in love and efficacity for the means. However, once the love of the end is lost, one will feebly carry on concerning the means, just as, once assent to the principles is lost, one cannot firmly assent to the conclusions." Cf. ibid., nos. 10, 11 (through a single act of mortal sin the connection of the virtues can be destroyed, as well as the firmness of one's motive) and no. 14 (virtue is not destroyed in an essential manner but, [instead] the state of virtue [is so destroyed]).

TRANSLATOR'S NOTE: This text is found in nos. 58, 60, 62, 63, and 66 in the Vivès edition. They are, however, the sixth, eighth, tenth, eleventh, and fourteenth numbers of the sub-section entitled, "The acquired virtues can essentially be virtues without charity, but not perfectively."

Salmanticenses, *Cursus Theologicus, De virtutibus*, disp. 4, dub. 1, no. 1; dub. 2, no. 26: "In the state of fallen nature, man cannot without grace and charity *acquire* a given virtue in perfect *esse* or, having acquired it in the aforementioned perfect state, *cannot preserve* [*it*]…because even perfect acquired prudence cannot exist alongside mortal sin." Again, see no. 27.

The Salmanticenses even say, ibid., dub. 1, no. 1: "Therefore, by the notion of an imperfect virtue in the present matter, we understand inclinations (namely, the natural disposition to virtue, an acquired disposition, and true virtue *in statu dispositionis*), *and in none of these acceptations do we contend that the virtues are interconnected*. Certain thinkers numbered among the adversaries believing that St. Thomas and the Thomists do not concede that true moral virtue (as regards their essence) can be found without the others are deceived in this matter, for the Thomists nowise deny this. Rather, they always speak *of perfect virtue*, which together with the essence [of virtue], has perfection and *the state of virtue*, which is excluded by the notion of imperfect virtue (just as a grown man [*vir*] along with his human essence also includes the perfection and state that are not included in the case of a boy who has not reached full maturity)."

The acquired moral virtues *of themselves and in the state of virtue* without a doubt must be interconnected, as Aristotle himself showed, but this latter is lacking *per accidens* if virtue (which *of itself is difficile mobilis*) is, *on account of the subject, in the state of disposition facile mobilis* because the subject is turned away from the last end, even the natural last end. The connection is at least compromised and the virtue declines as a virtue, no longer being as stable and firm as it should be.

to be disposed to science than to have science." Like virtue, science [i.e., a scientific *habitus*] which, of itself, is stable on account of its principles, can accidentally exist in an imperfect state as an unstable disposition, while low self-esteem can be strongly anchored up to the point of pertinacity.[15]

This elementary distinction, founded on the texts of Aristotle, is recalled by Cajetan in his commentary on *ST* I-II, q. 65, a. 1, no. 1, and is set forth by John of St. Thomas in his *Cursus philosophicus, Logica*, q. 18, a. 3: "Concerning quality and its species."[16]

It is even presented in the *Philosophia* of Goudin, *Logica Maior*, disp. 2, q. 5, a. 2 ("How many kinds of quality are there"), as being a common truth that every student ought to know.[17] For some time, we have thought that this distinction is a matter of great importance, and many of the critiques addressed to Jacques Maritain indeed seem to arise from the fact that these other thinkers have ignored it. On this point, he did not wish to say anything different [than what we have said].

Therefore, like Maritain, we think that there can be *true acquired moral virtues* in the state of mortal sin; however, they thus are accidentally *in the state of being wherein they are decreasingly stable dispositions* precisely because the subject in which they are found is turned away from the last end, even the natural last end. For this reason, such virtue only weakly attempts to accomplish the moral good, even in the natural order.

However, as we indicated at the beginning of this article, there are many nuances involved here, depending on whether the subject had

---

15. TRANSLATOR'S NOTE: The careful discussions of Yves Simon concerning objective and subjective potency can help one here as well. See Simon, *Definition of Moral Virtue*.

16. TRANSLATOR'S NOTE: See John of St. Thomas, *Material Logic*, pp. 376–87.

17. "It can happen that a *habitus*, which on the basis of its essential principles is *difficile mobilis*, accidentally is *facile mobilis* on account of the infirmity of the subject... Whence, the *habitus* sometimes clothes itself with the state of disposition... Science and virtue have principles that are unchanging of themselves, namely truth and moral fittingness, and nevertheless, in the beginner, each is unstable and *facile mobilis*."
TRANSLATOR'S NOTE: Fr. Garrigou-Lagrange does not cite the edition. The text slightly differs, only in minor ways, from Antoine Goudin, *Philosophia juxta inconcussa tutissimaque divi Thomae dogmata*, vol. 1: *Logica*, ed. Roux-Lavergne (Paris: Nouvelle bibliothèque, 1851), pp. 242–43.

never been in the state of grace or, on the contrary, had acquired the virtues in question over the course of a number of years. Moreover, if such a person has committed only one mortal sin, the acquired moral virtues only begin to decline in him. If grave faults are multiplied, their instability will increase until they finally come to completely disappear.

Therefore, this fragility of the acquired moral virtues in the sinner is completely different from the fragility of these same virtues and of the infused virtues in the righteous person. If it is true to say that the Christian in the state of grace has received a precious treasure in a fragile vessel, it is all the truer to speak of the instability of the virtue that still remains in the soul that has turned away from God. Such is, we think, not only St. Thomas's outlook concerning this matter, but also that of many other theologians.

* * *

CHAPTER 3

The Subordination of the State to the Perfection of the Human Person According to St. Thomas

The problem facing us is as follows. From the time of Kant and Hegel, controversies have scarcely ceased concerning the following question: is the State subordinated to the protection of the rights of individuals or, on the contrary, are individuals subordinated to the State?

According to Kant, who here self-admittedly follows Jean Jacques Rousseau, the individual, inasmuch as he is free, is *sui iuris*, the master of himself, and society was freely established by a "social contract" for the protection of the rights of individuals so that nobody may do harm to others. Thus, the police and tribunals were instituted to defend the rights of each individual.[1]

Herbert Spencer said something similar. According to him, society is ordered to the defense of the rights of each individual. In the past, this order was maintained in an authoritarian and military manner. Today, however, it is maintained in an industrial manner, which he claims is also more peaceful.

These individualist doctrines defend liberalism in opposition to Statist absolutism. They do not recognize well enough that society, far from resulting from a social contract, is posited by *the very nature of man*, who without the assistance of his fellow men could not exercise his own *specific activity* as a rational being. Indeed, without them his intellect would not come to know even the rudiments of grammar needed for speaking intelligibly, nor those of arithmetic in order to count, of geometry for surveying, of medicine for healing himself, etc.[2]

Kant obviously falls into an excessive individualism, even if the term "personalism" is used in defense of it.

Therefore, a reaction was inevitable, and it came from Hegel. In his idealistic pantheism, which held that *God comes into being in humanity*, social life is said to be, in the evolution of humanity, superior to the individual or patriarchal life of the first men, for the *common good* is superior to the individual good. According to Hegel, the common good is even something of the *divine in the process of its coming into being*. Consequently, this means that individuals are purely and simply subordinated to the State. Hegel himself said that *legality*, constituted by the State, *founds morality* because the *common legislation*, which is a form of objective spirit, becomes the norm of the subjective spirit of individuals. In this way, through the process of evolution, objective or social spirit (which, in this pantheistic evolutionism, is God in the process of His self-becoming) would gradually manifest itself. Thus, the State is set in the place of God, most especially the State that comes to successfully prevail over others, as was the case, once upon a time, for the Roman Empire. The rights of the State are the rights of God *in fieri* [in

---

1. See Kant, *Groundwork of the Metaphysics of Morals*, new trans. with introduction and notes by Victor Delbos (Paris, no date), p. 24 and above all 46: "The principle of the *autonomy of the will* expresses in the moral world the conception that Rousseau had held for the social order, holding that *man must prescribe for himself the law that he obeys*." Ibid., p. 64: "This restriction of religion to the requirements of rationally defined morality did not take place without disregarding essential, specific characteristics of it."
    TRANSLATOR'S NOTE: The comments appear to be those of Delbos.

2. TRANSLATOR'S NOTE: Note that there are also very positive reasons for this need for society. Throughout the various sub-species of justice, we see the profoundly interpersonal nature of human virtue, and how lofty indeed is friendship in all of its various forms! Human life bereft of society is quite impoverished in its potential, not merely because we have needs, but because society flows from us as a perfection. The deepest part of our being is oriented to the common good, above all God. (Indeed, all of this is enfleshed in us by our first bonds of society to the family and to the political community into which we are born. Our duties to parents and *patria* are something very noble indeed, and without social structures, we could not exercise this interpersonal life. We could even say that we have a natural right to the political life as a foundational human good. On this, see Lawrence Dewan, "St. Thomas, John Finnis, and the Political Good," *The Thomist*, Vol. 64 (2000): pp. 337–74.

the process of becoming]. This doctrine has inspired many Hegelian so-
ciologists, in particular Bluntschli and L. von Stein, as Leroy-Beaulieu
shows in his *L'État moderne*.[3] It is Statism, properly speaking.
Contemporary communists speak in a way akin to the Hegelian
Left, though from a materialist perspective. They set the State or political society in the place of God, and the rights of the State are said to be
the ultimate form of rights. Hence, individuals are totally subordinated
to it.

This is the principal reason, though not the only one, why communism has been condemned by the Church since the time of Pius IX,
as is clear in the *Syllabus errorum*. The first proposition condemned on
the Syllabus is: "God is identical with the nature of things and therefore subject to change; *God actually becomes himself in man and in the
world...*"[4] Henceforth, there is no longer any Immutable Truth since
God Himself, the First Truth, ever evolves, and He evolves so much
that, in reality, as Nietzsche said, *for this philosophy*, "*God is dead*," not
only in his human nature as on Good Friday, but in His Divine Nature.
Hegel expressed some regret over this state of affairs, but he said, we
must sacrifice the ancient form of Christianity so that the rational religion of the future might appear.[5]

God is replaced by society. But what then happens? Without God,
society is disaggregated; it is eaten away by atheism as by a cancer that
kills it, just as Donoso Cortès foresaw in 1852 in announcing what has
happened in the social domain for a century.[6]

---

3. Paul Leroy-Beaulieu, *L'État moderne et ses fonctions*, 3rd ed. (Paris: Gauillaumin et cie, 1900), pp. 14ff.
   TRANSLATOR'S NOTE: The full citation has been added. This pagination seems to match what he cites.

4. Pius IX, *Syllabus errorum*, no. 1 (Denzinger, no. 2901).

5. See G. W. F. Hegel, *Wissen und Glauben* (1802), in *Collected Works*, vol. 1, ed. [Hermann] Glockner, p. 433. Paulus Lenz-Medoc, "Déicide: La mort de Dieu," in *Satan: Ouvrage collectif des études carmélitaines* (Paris: Les Etudes Carmelitaines, 1948).

6. See Donoso Cortès, *Oeuvres de Donoso Cortès* [French trans.] (Paris: Librairie d'Auguste Vanton, 1862), pt. 2, pp. 271–82. "The generative principle of great errors of our days," a letter to Cardinal Fornari to be presented to Pius IX.
   TRANSLATOR'S NOTE: An English translation of this text is found in *Donoso Cortès: Readings in Political Theory*, ed. R. A. Herrera (Ave Maria, FL: Sapientia Press, 2007), pp. 141–57.

The other propositions on the *Syllabus errorum* all derive from this first one, in particular: "Right results from accomplished facts"[7] according to the laws of evolution, according to "the meaning of history," as many say today, without being overly preoccupied by the problem of avoiding relativism and without knowing what is prepared by Providence, which nonetheless continues to exist.

Pius IX also condemned two other consequences of these principles: First, "the rights of parents for the education of their children depend solely on the civil law," which evolves; second, likewise, "the right of individual property depends on the [state]," a right recognized as being necessary for a given moment of evolution so that the subsistence and the defense of the individual and the family may be assured.[8] According to the communists, individual property reminds one of the *armor* of the knights of the Middle Ages, an armor that should today be replaced by a modern garb made available to all by the state.

In order to philosophically and theologically explain the Church's condemnations in these matters, we must note that while individualism ever invokes *the dignity of individual freedom*, communism constantly

---

7.   Cf. Pius IX, *Syllabus errorum*, no. 39 (Denzinger, no. 2939).
       TRANSLATOR'S NOTE: Translated, the text reads: "'The state of the commonwealth, as the origin and source of all rights, exercises a right that is not circumscribed by any limits."
8.   See Denzinger, nos. 2892 (Pius IX, *Quanta cura*) and 3133 (Leo XIII, *Quod apostolici muneris*).
       TRANSLATOR'S NOTE: The full text reads as follows. No. 2892: "By impious opinions and machinations, these most deceitful men chiefly aim at this result, viz., that the salutary teaching and influence of the Catholic Church may be banished from the instruction and education of youth." No. 3133: "But Catholic wisdom, sustained by the precepts of natural and divine law, provides with special care for public and private tranquility in its doctrines and teachings regarding the duty of government and the distribution of the goods that are necessary for life and use. For, while the socialists would destroy the 'right' of property, alleging it to be a human invention altogether opposed to the inborn equality of man, and claiming a community of goods, argue that poverty should not be peaceably endured and that the property and privileges of the rich may be rightly invaded, the Church, with much greater wisdom and good sense, recognizes the equality among men, who are born with different powers of body and mind, inequality in actual possession, also, and holds that the right of property and ownership, which springs from nature itself, must not be touched and stands inviolate. For she knows that stealing and robbery were forbidden in so special a manner by God, the Author and Defender of right, that He would not allow men even to desire what belonged to another and that thieves and despoilers, no less than adulterers and idolaters, are shut out from the kingdom of heaven (cf. 1 Cor. 6:9ff)."

invokes the *dignity of the common good*, although it understands this good in terms of being a useful good rather than of a fitting [*honnête*] good, according to the principles of materialism and utilitarianism.

The denial of the immutability of truth opposed to error lies at the foundation of this absolute evolutionism, as well as the denial of the *real and immutable* value of the first principles of reason and of *the immutability of the true good* opposed to evil. This is what the first proposition of the *Syllabus errorum* said, and indeed, the condemned proposition ends thus: "All things are God and have the very substance of God; God is one and the same reality with the world, and so is spirit with matter, necessity with liberty, truth with falsehood, good with evil, and justice with injustice."[9] As evolution moves onward, the thesis is what is true today; tomorrow it will be the antithesis; the day after, the synthesis will be true, and so on. The result is complete relativism. There is only a *truth that is relative* to the current state of science. The relativists are caught in their own trap. Indeed, this is what happened for Hegel: evolution continued after him and worked against him, through the Hegelian Left. St. Paul said: "All these things are foolishness before God."

And therefore, to philosophically and theologically resolve this problem, we must grasp more deeply the nature of the individual human person's dignity *in itself* and always, as well as what the essential nature of the temporal common good is.

Now, let us note that *we Christians affirm the dignity of the temporal common good* much more than do the communists who constantly speak about it. This is so because we not only hold that it is a useful good but, above all, *a fitting [honnête] good: to live well in accord with legal justice and equity.* Otherwise this common good would not "specify" these two moral virtues of legal justice and equity, which far exceed utilitarianism and depend on the natural law impressed upon us by the Author of our nature.

However, on the other hand, *we Christians affirm much more and better than did Kant the dignity of the human person*, for we affirm that he is created in the image of God, called to adoptive Divine filiation,

---

9. Pius IX, *Syllabus errorum*, no. 1 (Denzinger, no. 2901).

that is, to eternal life, and that he always has the right to do its duty, *a duty* that is founded not upon the categorical imperative and the autonomy of the will but, rather, upon the rights of God, the Sovereign Good and Ultimate Legislator. The former would represent the pride of wishing to obey only oneself. The human will cannot impose moral obligation upon itself, for it is not superior to itself.

We can see all of this in St. Thomas's doctrine, which is opposed at once to individualism and communism, containing within itself a *superior and stable synthesis* above the fluctuations of these theories, just as the true virtue of prudence is superior to two defects, imprudence and craftiness, and as the virtue of fortitude is superior to cowardice and to temerarious audacity.

Only, in order to exposit objectively this doctrine of St. Thomas, one need not seek to reconcile it with the Hegelian dialectic, as one is sometimes tempted to do today. A good theologian said to me recently, "This would be to pour sulfuric acid into an excellent wine." Fr. Mattiuisi has written a book, *Il veleno Kantiano* [*The Kantian Poison*]. He could have spoken also "del veleno Hegeliano." Were he asked, "Is Hegel truly a great philosopher?" he likely would have responded, "He is a truly prestigious and grand sophist, who was himself taken by his own quibblings and by the ruses of the evil genius." Indeed, in Hegel, we do find a kind of genius, though it is a genius of denial and universal confusion. Between Hegel and us Christians, there is a *battle of spirit with spirit*, as St. John of the Cross said, a battle leading us to become increasingly aware of the value of the gift of God, indeed, a battle leading to the grave global conflicts faced by the world today.

By affirming that no truth is immutable, Hegel "perverted the eternal notion of truth," as Pius X said of the modernists.[10] From this new

---

10. See Denzinger, no. 2080 [old numbering].

 TRANSLATOR'S NOTE: This section is between ellipses in the new edition of Denzinger. It comes from *Pascendi*, no. 13. The official translation of the text reads: "Dogma is not only able, but ought to evolve and to be changed. This is strongly affirmed by the Modernists, and as clearly flows from their principles. For amongst the chief points of their teaching is this which they deduce from the principle of vital immanence; that religious formulas, to be really religious and not merely theological speculations, ought to be living and to live the life of the religious sentiment. This is not to be understood in the sense that these formulas, especially if merely imaginative, were to be made for the perspective, we are told that, in order to recognize what the new theory of evolution requires, the Church must *correct* the definitions of the Council of Trent concerning the first man and original sin. We would thus find ourselves in a state of utter intellectual shipwreck, saying with Günther[11] that dogmas need to be true only *provisionally* in relation to the current state of the science which exists at the time of their definition. This represents a form of complete relativism. Absolute truth would no longer exist.

For Hegel, even the truth of the principle of contradiction (or, identity) would disappear into universal becoming. Thus, we find ourselves returning to Hereclitus, who was refuted by Aristotle in the fourth book of the *Metaphysics*. And thus, the question is asked, "Can Hegel be Hegel and, at the same time, not be him?" If one denies the real value of the principle of contradiction, Hegel himself vanishes, and no affirmation is possible any longer, nor any probability. Indeed, universal becoming is only a realized abstraction; what exists is not universal becoming but, rather, this being that becomes, for example, this embryo that develops.

religious sentiment; it has no more to do with their origin than with number or quality; what is necessary is that the religious sentiment, with some modification when necessary, should vitally assimilate them. In other words, it is necessary that the primitive formula be accepted and sanctioned by the heart; and similarly the subsequent work from which spring the secondary formulas must proceed under the guidance of the heart. Hence it comes that these formulas, to be living, should be, and should remain, adapted to the faith and to him who believes. Wherefore if for any reason this adaptation should cease to exist, they lose their first meaning and accordingly must be changed. And since the character and lot of dogmatic formulas is so precarious, there is no room for surprise that Modernists regard them so lightly and in such open disrespect. And so they audaciously charge the Church both with taking the wrong road from inability to distinguish the religious and moral sense of formulas from their surface meaning, and with clinging tenaciously and vainly to meaningless formulas whilst religion is allowed to go to ruin. Blind that they are, and leaders of the blind, inflated with a boastful science, they have reached that pitch of folly where they pervert the eternal concept of truth and the true nature of the religious sentiment; with that new system of theirs they are seen to be under the sway of a blind and unchecked passion for novelty, thinking not at all of finding some solid foundation of truth, but despising the holy and apostolic traditions, they embrace other vain, futile, uncertain doctrines, condemned by the Church, on which, in the height of their vanity, they think they can rest and maintain truth itself. The Modernist as Believer: Individual Experience and Religious Certitude. Thus far, Venerable Brethren, of the Modernist considered as Philosopher."

11.   TRANSLATOR'S NOTE: He refers to Anton Günther (1783–1863), whose philosophical and theological conclusions were condemned by Pius IX.

In order to remain on the right path, we will begin by recalling the principal texts of St. Thomas that are opposed to individualism, then those that are opposed to communism, and we will see that, according to him, although man, inasmuch as he is *an individual* and *a part* of the State, is subordinated to it, the State itself is subordinated to the perfection of the *human person*. I do not say "subordinated to the human person," for he at times acts on his whims, but rather, "subordinated to the intellectual, moral, and religious perfection of the human person" according to the natural law.

By utilizing this distinction of the individual and the person, I am here reproducing and developing what was taught by my master, Marie-Benoît Schwalm, O.P., in his *Leçons de philosophie sociale*,[12] *Dictionnaire de Théologie Catholique* (the article, *Démocratie*, col. 283ff.), and in his article "Individualism and Solidarity."[13]

* * *

ACCORDING TO ST. THOMAS, MAN AS INDIVIDUAL AND PART OF THE STATE IS SUBORDINATED TO IT

Aristotle says in his *Politics*, bk. 1, ch. 1, "Every citizen belongs to the city as part to a whole, and, the part exists for the whole." However, for Aristotle, the citizen is not part of the city in the same way that the

---

12. M.-B. Schwalm, *Leçons de philosophie sociale*, vol. 2 (Paris: Bloud & Cie, 1911), pp. 417–40.

13. See M.-B. Schwalm, "Individualisme et solitarité," *Revue thomiste*, Vol. 6 (1898): pp. 66–99, esp. pp. 81ff.

I have already explained this distinction of the individual and the person in two places. See Garrigou-Lagrange, *Le sens commun*, 1st ed. (1908), and 4th ed. (Paris: Desclée de Brouwer, 1936), pp. 347–49. Also, in Garrigou-Lagrange, *The Trinity and God the Creator*, pp. 155–56. [TRANSLATOR's NOTE: See also Garrigou-Lagrange, *Christ: The Savior*, pp. 119ff, and *De beatitudine* (Turin: R. Berruti, 1951), pp. 85–87 and 372. The current English translation of *De beatitudine* by Patrick Cummins is not exact and should not be consulted as a final source regarding Fr. Garrigou-Lagrange's thought. (A translation of *Sens commun* is anticipated for publication by Emmaus Academic in the near future.)]

Jacques Maritain has also treated this issue in two articles where he responds to several recent objections. Jacques Maritain, "La personne et le bien commun," *Revue thomiste*, Vol. 46 (1946): pp. 237–78; "Personne et individu," in *Acta pontificiae academiae S. Thomae*, Vol. 12 (1946): pp. 3–33. [TRANSLATOR'S NOTE: See Jacques Maritain, *The Person and the Common Good*, trans. John J. Fitzgerald (Notre Dame, IN: University of Notre Dame Press, 1966).]

hand is the physical part of our body. The relationship is only analogically the same, according to an analogy of proportionality. Nonetheless, it is more than a metaphor, for the proper sense of the word "part" is maintained when one says, "The citizen is a part of the city."

St. Thomas himself says in *ST* II-II, q. 64, a. 2:

> Every individual person is compared to the whole community as a part to a whole. And therefore, if some man is dangerous to the city and corruptive of it on account of some sin, it is praiseworthy and advantageous that he be killed so that the common good may be preserved. As is said in 1 Cor. 5:6: "For a little leaven corrupts the whole lump of dough."

And immediately beforehand, St. Thomas says: "The part is ordered to the whole as the imperfect to the perfect; and therefore, every part naturally exists on account of the whole."

The Holy Doctor speaks in a similar manner in a number of other places in his treatise on justice in order to show that *suicide is contrary to the common good of the civil order [patrie]* and that *public authority can condemn criminals with the death penalty.*[14]

He also says, following Aristotle, in *ST* II-II, q. 58, a. 9, ad 3, while speaking of legal or social justice: "*The common good is the end of each person existing in the community, just as the good of the whole is the end of any given part.*" And it is clear that, for St. Thomas, *the common good* (which not merely a useful good but, rather, is a fitting one, the object of legal justice) *is not a mere juxtaposition of the private goods* of the citizens and their individual rights, just as the city is more than the juxtaposition of individuals. It has its own operations, above

---

14. See *ST* II-II, q. 58, concerning legal justice, aa. 5–9, a. 9, ad 3; a. 12; q. 64, a. 5, concerning suicide: "Any given part, as such, is [something belonging to] the whole; now, any given man is part of the community and thus, as such, is [something belonging to] the community; whence when he injures himself, he commits an injury against the community, as is obvious in the Philosopher [*Nicomachean Ethics*, bk. 5, ch. 11]." Again, *ST* II-II, q. 65, a. 1, concerning the punishing of wrongdoers: "*This same whole man is ordered as to an end to the complete community of which he is a part...* And therefore, just as through public power someone can lawfully be deprived of his life on account of certain major sins, so too he can be deprived of a member on account of certain minor ones." Cf. *ST* II-II, q. 66, a. 6, ad 2.

all the establishment of just laws according to the requirements of the common good and making them be observed. This doctrine is irreconcilable with Kantian individualism.

In *Politics*, bk. 1, ch. 1, Aristotle had said, "The common good of the city is better and more divine than the private good of one man alone." However, he does not thereby join Hegel's position that the common good is God *in fieri*. Moreover, the Stagirite never said anything like communists' claim that the temporal common good is the supreme good.

These texts from St. Thomas show that he is not an individualist. Likewise, with regard to the right to individual property, he does not join the individualists in saying, "It is lawful for everyone to use and to keep what is his own." Rather, he says: "With regard to the use of things (that he possesses), man ought to communicate them readily to others in their need."[15]

* * *

However, on the other hand, St. Thomas shows that the State is subordinated to the perfection of the human person, whose ultimate end is God Himself.

Thus, he is opposed to absolutism of the State or to the Statism of the Hegelians and communists.

In asking himself whether every human act, inasmuch as it is either good or bad, is meritorious or deserving of demerit before God, St. Thomas writes in *ST* I-II, q. 21, a. 4, ad 3:

> *Man is not ordered to the political community according to all that he is and has*; and, therefore, every act whatsoever of his need not be meritorious or deserving of demerit in relation to the political community.[16] However, all that man is, and what he has [and can do], must be ordered to God. And therefore, every good or bad human act has the character of merit or demerit before God, as regards the very character of the act.

---

15. See *ST* II-II, q. 66, a. 2.
16. This, however, is to what Marxist communism leads.

Moreover, St. Thomas shows that, in accord with distributive justice, the political society or the State should "order the common good to individual persons," for example through national roads, other means of communication, etc.[17] *Doubtlessly, this distributive justice is inferior to legal justice*, which is immediately ordered to the common good,[18] but nonetheless, *legal justice is inferior in turn to the natural law*, that is, to the natural right that comes from God, the Author of our nature. This is why *the State cannot make laws that deprive citizens of their natural right to what is necessary for their subsistence, their natural right to generation*[19] *and to the education of their children*,[20] as well as *their natural right to individual property*, "[a right] to the power of procuring and dispensing" concerning what is necessary to their life and that of their family.[21] This derives from human nature, which remains ever the same. It is not like an armor that is useful only in one given era of human history.

For the same reason, St. Thomas shows that the *citizen is not bound in conscience to obey unjust laws*, which are conformed neither to the natural law nor to the revealed divine law, sufficiently proposed.[22] And *indeed, man must not obey impious laws that would prevent the worship owed to God* but, instead, must suffer martyrdom rather than renounce the faith and obedience owed to God. As the Apostles and the first Christians said: "We must obey God rather than men" (Acts 5:29).[23]

It is also lawful for virgins to consecrate *their virginity* to God, for God, the Separated Ultimate Good, is infinitely superior to the

---

17. *ST* II-II, q. 61, a. 1, ad 2.
18. *ST* II-II, q. 58, aa. 5–8, a. 9, ad 3, a. 12.
19. See *ST* II-II, q. 61, a. 1, ad 2.
20. See *ST* II-II, q. 10, a. 12: "After leaving the womb but before having the use of free will, a child [*puer*] *is kept under the care of his parents*, as though he were being kept within in a kind of spiritual womb… Whence…before a child has the use of reason, the natural law holds that the child should remain under the care of the father. Whence, it would be contrary to natural justice if the child, before he has the use of reason, were to be taken from his parents' care or anything done concerning him against the parents' will."
    In this, St. Thomas corrects what Aristotle had said in granting the State too great a role in the education of children in *Politics*, bk. 8, ch. 1. Christian revelation provided St. Thomas with a loftier idea of the human person "created in the image of God and called to eternal life."
21. See *ST* II-II, q. 66, a. 2.
22. See *ST* I-II, q. 96, a. 4.
23. See *ST* II-II, q. 124, a. 1, ad 3.

temporal common good, and to the good of the preservation of the human species.[24]

Finally, *public authority must receive divine revelation sufficiently proposed and confirmed by manifest Divine signs.*[25] Moroever, this authority cannot legitimately establish laws contrary to Divine Revelation (for example, laws contrary to the indissolubility of marriage, to the Christian education of the youth, to the worship of God, and to the rights of the Church). *Even when it comes to the common good of the Church*, St. Thomas teaches that *schism*, which is contrary to the unity of the Church, *is less grave a mortal sin than infidelity*, which is contrary to the revealed Divine Truth. Why? Because, he says:

> Just as the good of the multitude is superior to the individual good of that which is a part of the multitude, so too *is the* [intrinsic] *common good of lower dignity than the extrinsic* (*or, separated*) *and supreme good*, to which the whole multitude is ordered [just as the good of the order of an army is less than the good of its leader precisely as its leader]. And similarly, the *good of ecclesiastical unity*, to which schism is opposed, *is less than the good of Divine Truth*, to which infidelity is opposed.[26]

In heaven, the separated common good, God seen face to face by all the blessed, will not be superior to the supreme good of each one; it will be *the same*. The Beatific Vision of one person will only be more penetrating than that of another according to the degrees of their merits.

This second series of texts from St. Thomas shows clearly that his doctrine is utterly opposed to State Absolutism (or, to Statism), whether of Hegelian idealism or of communistic materialism.

* * *

---

24. See *ST* II-II, q. 103, a. 4, ad 2.
25. See Aquinas, *De regimine principum*, bk. 1, ch. 15. Also, Leo XIII's encyclicals *Immortale Dei* and *Libertas*. [**TRANSLATOR'S NOTE:** This topic is also the final point of discussion in vol. 2 of *De revelatione*.]
26. *ST* II-II, q. 39, a. 2, ad 2.
     TRANSLATOR'S NOTE: This has been taken from the original Latin, although Fr. Garrigou-Lagrange translated it into French. The parenthesis represents something from his French text introduced into the translation; the text in the brackets is not found in his French.

However, how can these last texts of St. Thomas be reconciled with the preceding ones, which are manifestly opposed to individualism? Generally, people cite each set of texts separated from their context and then ask whether St. Thomas came to take a solid position in this problem. First of all, there clearly is no contradiction between these two series of texts if they are considered in context. Indeed, on the one hand, *in speaking of our obligations toward the civil order [patrie]*, St. Thomas says, "Man must not kill himself," but instead must preserve his life for the civil order because the *part is for the whole.*[27] He even adds, with regard to the criminal who should be punished with death, "This same, whole man is ordered, as to an end, to the complete community of which he is a part,"[28] and therefore, "if some man is dangerous to the city and corruptive of it on account of some sin, it is praiseworthy and advantageous that he be killed"[29] and not only maimed.

However, on the other hand, *in speaking of our obligations* not toward the civil order [patrie] but *toward God*, St. Thomas says in *ST* I-II, q. 21, a. 4, ad 3: "*Man is not ordered to the political community according to his whole self and according to all that he is...* Rather, the whole that is man, and all that he has and can do, is ordered to God."

Therefore, no contradiction exists between the two series of St. Thomas's texts. However, it is not enough merely to avoid contradiction. We must push further and reconcile these texts positively under the light of principles. How can we synthetically express this doctrine of St. Thomas so as to positively reconcile its various aspects, which are opposed both to individualism and to communism?

* * *

A SYNTHETIC ACCOUNT OF ST. THOMAS'S TEACHING
CONCERNING THE DIGNITY OF THE HUMAN PERSON
IN RELATION TO THE STATE

As we have said, this synthesis exceeds its contraries as the true virtue of prudence is elevated above imprudence and craftiness and as

---

27. *ST* II-II, q. 64, a. 5.
28. *ST* II-II, q. 65, a. 1.
29. *ST* II-II, q. 64, a. 2; q. 66, a. 6, ad 2; *ST* I-II, q. 105, a. 2, ad 10.

the virtue of fortitude is elevated above cowardice and temerarious audacity. We have formulated it as Fr. Marie-Benoît Schwalm indicated it: Although *man as an individual and as part of the state is subordinated to it*, nevertheless *the State itself is subordinated to the perfection of the human person*, created in the image of God, who has God as his ultimate end, something far superior to the end of the State, which is the temporal common good.

This problem belongs to the order of moral and social action. However, *operari sequitur esse*, action follows upon being, and the mode of action derives from the mode of being. Moreover, *actiones sunt suppositorum seu personarum* [actions are the actions of supposits (or, of persons)]. *My nature* is not what acts. *I* am what acts, through my nature, through my faculties, and through my will. Ontological personality is the foundation of psychological and moral personality.[30] Likewise, *these are human persons*—Peter, Paul, Madeline—*whom God loves*—and not merely their human nature. They are human persons whom He calls to the life of eternity. And thus, *the root of the solution to the present problem* should exist *in the order of being* so that we may find *an ontological foundation to the natural and immutable rights of the human person*. In this, we are concerned with a *certain truth* and not one that is merely provisional, concerning *the immutable truth* of these rights, meaning that one can then defend them energetically with certitude of defending the truth.

Moreover, these natural rights must be founded on man's very nature considered in his relation to God, the Author of our nature and ultimate end of our life, even already in the natural order. Therefore, we must thus consider the three causes: formal, final, and efficient.

Finally, the individual man cannot be, in one and the same respect, inferior and superior to the State. *Homo **non secundum idem** est infra Statum et supra eum.* This holds in virtue of the principle of contradiction. Therefore, we must find in each man a distinction in the order of being, prior to that of activity [*opération*]. *Operari sequitur esse.*

Now, man, like the beings that are inferior to him, like *this* molecule of water, like *this* plant, like *this* lion, is an *individual* "undivided

---

30. TRANSLATOR'S NOTE: The reader would benefit by consulting also Réginald Garrigou-Lagrange, *Christ the Savior*, pp. 108–199.

in himself and distinct from every other." However, man is superior to them inasmuch as he is a *person*, that is, inasmuch as he is an *intelligent, self-conscious and free subject, capable of knowing and loving God, his final end*, even already in the natural order. Therefore, why would it not be the case that the distinction we seek out in each man in the order of being is the distinction of *the individual* and *the person*?

Man, inasmuch as he is an individual (*indivisum in se et divisum a quolibet alio*) has *this body*, distinct from other bodies in space. St. Thomas often says, following Aristotle: "The individual has this flesh and these bones."[31]

Thus, inasmuch as he is an individual, man is born in a given place and at a given moment—*nascitur hic et nunc*—for example, in this city of this Italian, or French, or German state. Thus, he is a *pars Status*, a part of the State where he is born, a part first as a child, then as an adult and as a citizen. Now, the part is for the sake of the whole, as the imperfect is for the sake of the perfect, as St. Thomas says. Therefore, man is subordinated to the State as an individual, inasmuch as he is part of the State.

Beyond this, *if man were solely an individual* (and not a person), *he would be totally subordinated to the State*, just as many animals, which live in their forms of animal society, are *totally* subordinated to the latter—for example, bees and ants. These are animals that cannot exercise their *specific activity* (e.g., the building of a hive or the making of honey) without the concurrence of their fellow animals, and they live in peace in their animal society according to their natural instinct.[32]

---

31. Cf. *In VII Meta.*, c. 15, no. 2; *ST* I, q. 29, a. 2, ad 3, a. 4, corp.; q. 30, a. 4, corp.; q. 33, a. 2, corp.; q. 75, a. 4, corp.; q. 85, a. 1, ad 2. *De veritate*, q. 10, a. 5.

   This assertion is frequent in St. Thomas, as can be easily seen by reading entry no. 6 for the word *Homo* and entry no. 24 for the word *Individuum* in the general index of his works, the *Tabula Aurea*. It is also useful to compare what the index contains for the forty-three propositions that are found for the word *Individuum* and the forty-six that are found for the word *Persona*. Also, see the words *Princeps, Rex, Regnum, Bonum*, nos. 181 and 182, *Civitas, Servitus*, no. 7, *Matrimonium*, no. 113, etc., *Obedientia*, no. 42.

   St. Thomas says in *ST* II-II, q. 104, a. 5, corp., and ad 2; a. 6, ad 1; q. 122, a. 4, ad 3: "Man is the servant of another man *as regards the body but not as regards the soul or the mind*." Now, the citizen is less strictly subordinated to the state than the slave or serf was to his master.

32. Between an animal society and a human one, there is only *analogical* conceptual unity and not univocal unity. However, it is *more than a metaphor*, for the animals that live in this manner collaborate in the realization of their specific activity.

However, man is not only an individual, as are the beings that are inferior to him. He is also a *person* "created in the image of God" (Gen. 1:27; Wis. 2:23; Col. 3:10). That is, he is an intelligent, self-conscious, and free subject, capable of knowing and loving God, who is his ultimate end, even in the natural order. Now, God, the ultimate end of the human person, is infinitely superior to the temporal common good that is the end of the State.

More precisely: *If man were only what the materialists say he is,* without an immortal and spiritual soul, without an intellect *essentially distinct* from the internal senses, without freedom, properly speaking, *or if, as Hegel says, he were only a transitory phenomenon in the evolution of society—then, yes, truly he would be totally subordinated to his species and to society,* as bees and ants are subordinated to their species and their animal society. He would then be *an individual,* but not, properly speaking, *a person* in the true sense of the word: a subsistent being endowed with a spiritual and immortal soul.

However, this is not the case. Man is not only an individual. He is, properly speaking, a person, a subsistent being that has an intellect which is *essentially* distinct from imagination, freedom properly speaking, a spiritual and immortal soul capable of knowing God and loving Him. His final end is precisely to know God and to love Him. To arrive at this, he must live in peace with his fellow men in accord with virtue. To reach it, he lives in society in accord with just laws and equity. *Inasmuch as he is an individual, a part* of society, he is *subordinated* to it, but it itself is *subordinated* to the individual and moral perfection of the human person. Thus, we see what is required by the subordination of ends, in part from the very nature of these ends and in part from the superiority of spirit over matter.

Consequently, *individuated* human persons (living *here and now* in a given city of a given State) are part of society as individuated and must collaborate in social life. Nonetheless, it remains true to say with St. Thomas: "Man is not ordered to the political community according to his whole self and according to all that he is." On account of the fact that there is something superior in him, on account of the fact of his spiritual, intelligent, free and immortal soul, and *formally* inasmuch he is a person, he is *not subordinated* to political society. However, the latter is subordinated to the intellectual, moral, and religious perfection of the human person.[33] Also, one must not confuse the nation and the State.[34]

In the order of being (anterior to that of action), this represents *the ontological foundation of the natural rights of the human person*, a right to what is necessary for him and above all *a right to do his duty before God*, an imprescriptible right which cannot be denied without denying every moral obligation, properly speaking.

Moreover, this also means that *even the civic and political acts of the human person must be freely exercised*. The human person *cannot be obligated in conscience to obey an unjust law*, and *he even must not obey an impious law* contrary to the rights of God. Therefore, the State is subordinated to human perfection, a perfection to be obtained in the intellectual, moral, and spiritual order. St. Thomas said, "Man is not ordered to the political community *according to his whole self* and according to all that he is"—that is, not inasmuch as he is a person whose ultimate end is God.

One may perhaps object: *This distinction between the individual and the person is too speculative* for resolving practical problems in the social order.

We have already responded: "*Operari sequitur esse et modus operandi modum essendi*," act follows being, and the mode of action follows the mode of being. Hence, the intelligent and free being acts differently than individual beings inferior to him.

---

33. Society benefits from the worth and the intellectual and moral activity of persons. However, it is not the end of their moral life, just as the body benefits from the influence of the soul but is not the end of its activity. The soul is not subordinated to the body, but the body is useful to it. Cf. *ST* I, q. 76, a. 5. One must not confuse *ordination, subordination,* [and] *coordination*. The soul is ordered to the body but is not subordinated to it. Two equal soldiers are *coordinated* between themselves and *subordinated* to the leader whom they must obey in view of the end to be attained. Moreover, every coordination presupposes subordination in relation to the principle of order. See *ST* I-II, q. 100, a. 6.

    TRANSLATOR'S NOTE: Also, see Réginald Garrigou-Lagrange, *Le réalisme du principe de finalité*, pp. 130–33.

34. The State is the ensemble of countries submitted to the same government. The Polish nation has not always existed as a State; it has been split up.

    TRANSLATOR'S NOTE: Compare with Jacques Maritain, *Man and the State* (Washington, DC: Catholic University of America Press, 1998), pp. 1–27.

Others have objected: This distinction of the individual and the person remains *obscure* and *sic explicatur obscurum per obscurius* [*thus, the obscure is explained by the more obscure*].

We respond: This distinction between the individual and the person, such as we have proposed it, in the most straightforward of fashions, *is admitted by all, except by materialists*. Indeed, it is obvious that this tree and this lion are individuals and not persons, for they do not have intelligence or freedom; they cannot know God.

This distinction between the individual and the person is admitted, in particular, by St. Thomas. Indeed, for him, while the *dignity of the human person* comes from *spirit*, individuation comes *from matter* and from its relation to quantity, to extension. St. Thomas, following Aristotle, noted that two utterly similar twins are *two* only because the specific form of man is received in different parts of matter that do not occupy the same place. Likewise, two drops of water are *two* for the same reason. St. Thomas even teaches that the human soul is individuated by its relation[35] to *this* body—Peter's soul by its relation to *his* body, Paul's by its relation to *his* body; and according to Revelation, our bodies will be resurrected in order to reconstitute human persons in their integrity indeed forever, when political States will no longer exist.

Without a doubt, the human individual is not really distinct from the human person, but there is a real distinction between *spirit* (from which the dignity of the human person comes) and *matter* united to quantity (from which individuation comes).

Finally, this distinction between the individual and the person is *confirmed* for theologians by the revelation of the mystery of the Incarnation. Indeed, Christ, as a human individual, *hic homo*, was born in Bethlehem and was called a Nazarene, whereas on account of His personality he could say, "Before Abraham was, I am" (Jn. 8:58). According to Revelation, against the Nestorians, the person of Christ most certainly is not human, but instead, is divine. By this very fact, it is infinitely superior to the matter on which the individuation of the Savior's

---

35. TRANSLATOR'S NOTE: Its transcendental relation (*relatio secundum dici*), not as a true relation to a pure term (*relatio secundum esse*). On this topic, see above, Translator's Appendix to "*Cognoscens quodammodo fit vel est aliud a se* (On the Nature of Knowledge as Union with the Other as Other)," in Part II.

humanity depends. (In the treatise on the Incarnation, the distinction between the individual and the person becomes as bright as a flash of lightning, above all when it is a question of the infinite value of Christ's merits.) However, in this way, the distinction between the individual and the person is confirmed *ex alto* [from on high], and we see even better that *the human person*, however inferior he may be in comparison to the Divine (or, Uncreated) person of Christ, is superior to the individual, for—and we cannot insist too greatly upon this fact—his dignity is derived from *spirit*, whereas his individuation comes from matter.[36]

We need not here resort to St. Thomas's thesis concerning the individuation depending on matter. It suffices to note, here standing alongside natural reason and common sense, what St. Thomas says very simply in *ST* I, q. 29, a. 1: "The individual is found according to a special and more perfect mode in rational substances, which have dominion over their acts, and which, for this very reason, have received the special name of *persons*"[37] above that of inorganic beings, plants, and animals. He adds in ibid., a. 2: "'*Person' signifies that which is most perfect in nature, that is, a subsistent and rational being.*"[38]

Moreover, revelation speaks to us also about angelic persons, about St. Gabriel and St. Michael. It even tells us that there are three divine persons, not three divine individuals. Thus, we see that the notion of person (an intelligent and free subject) contains no imperfection in what it formally signifies.

All of this confirms *from on high* the doctrine that we have set forth. It is likewise confirmed by what St. Thomas tells us about *the secrets of the heart* that *God alone can know.*[39] The angels naturally know all the

---

36. The uncreated person of the Word can, without imperfection for it, play the role of created personality in Jesus (*gerere vices personalitatis humanae*), but it cannot play the role of matter without undergoing a manifest imperfection. Moreover, nobody speaks of Jesus's Divine Individuality. Rather, we speak of His Divine Personality. Similarly, moreover, in the treatise on the Trinity nobody speaks of the Three Divine Individuals. Rather, we speak of the Three Divine Persons. The Divine Nature is undivided and numerically the same in the three persons; it is not multiplied.

37. Translator's Note: The text slightly paraphrases the original Latin. I have taken this from Fr. Garrigou-Lagrange's French.

38. Translator's Note: Again, I am following Fr. Garrigou-Lagrange's French.

39. See *ST* I, q. 54, a. 4.

parts of the universe that are connected together, *concatenatae*, but *secrets of the heart* are not necessarily connected neither to our soul (since they are free) nor to anything exterior (since they are not manifest). Therefore, *they are not parts of the universe*, and God alone, *scrutator cordium* [He who searches hearts], can know them. This shows us the dignity of the human person, whose intimate depths are penetrated by God alone and who, when in the state of grace, takes part in the *kingdom of God* far above the temporal common good, which is the end of the State.

In the exposition of this doctrine, St. Thomas surpasses Aristotle greatly (in particular as regards the natural right of parents to rear their children).[40] St. Thomas received from Christian revelation a loftier idea of the person "created in the image of God" and called to eternal life.[41] Also, he distinguished much more explicitly than did Aristotle the individual and the person.

This doctrine, which at first can seem quite complex, can be expressed quite simply by the words of the Apostles and of the first Christians before their persecutors: "We must obey God rather than men" (Acts 5:29); "We cannot not speak about what we have seen and heard. *Non possumus*" (Acts 4:20).

We have a strict obligation to obey God, whose supreme rights found our first duties and every moral obligation properly speaking. *What we demand above all else* is not freedom for its own sake, as liberalism does but, rather, *the inalienable right to do our duty*—or, *the right of truth*, above all the ultimate truth to be known and loved. We can freely renounce some of our rights but not the right to do our duty. May it please God that [He lead] all peoples to recognize the truth of these

---

40. Aristotle, *Politics*, bk. 8, ch. 1, said that "the civil law ought to rule the education of children, which therefore must be public." Here, he does not sufficiently recognize the rights of parents. In contrast, St. Thomas said in *ST* II-II, q. 10, a. 12: "After leaving the womb but before having the use of free will, a child [*puer*] *is kept under the care of his parents*, as though he were being kept within in a kind of spiritual womb... Whence... before a child has the use of reason, the natural law holds that the child should remain under the care of the father. Whence, *it would be contrary to natural justice* if the child, before he has the use of reason, were to be taken from his parents' care or anything done concerning him against the parents' will."

41. Translator's Note: On this relation between revelation and philosophy, see the chapter below, entitled "On the Relationship Between Philosophy and Religion," pp. 361–97.

principles founded on the immutable natural law [*droit*], inscribed in our nature, and that they be united for the sake of respecting it.

In this form, at once very simple and very lofty, the doctrine that we have set forth is doubly certain: in the order of reason and in that of faith. It can be expressed in these words of the Savior: "Render to Caesar what is Caesar's and to God what is God's" (Mt. 22:21); "and do not fear those who kill the body but cannot kill the soul; rather fear him who can destroy both soul and body in hell" (Mt. 10:28, RSV).

No better affirmation can be spoken concerning the dignity of the human person whose superior duties are founded on God's imprescriptible rights, far above all the legitimate demands of the temporal common good that is the end of the State. In this way, the State is quite clearly subordinated to the intellectual, moral, and spiritual perfection of the human person, whose destiny immensely exceeds the end and temporal duration of political society. All the papal Encyclicals on this subject have strongly affirmed this fact.[42]

---

42. In particular, Pius XI said in the Encyclical *Divini redemptoris* against the communists: "Communism, moreover, strips man of his liberty, robs human personality of all its dignity, and removes all the moral restraints that check the eruptions of blind impulse. There is no recognition of any right of the individual in his relations to the collectivity; no natural right is accorded to *human personality*, which is a *mere cog-wheel in the Communist system*.... (And on the contrary) *He is a person, marvelously endowed by his Creator with gifts of body and mind.* He is a true 'microcosm,' as the ancients said, a world in miniature, with a value far surpassing that of the vast inanimate cosmos. *God alone is his last end, in this life and the next*... In the plan of the Creator, society is a natural means which man can and must use to reach his destined end. *Society is for man and not vice versa.*" Finally, Pius XI cites these words of St. Paul: "All things are yours, and you are Christ's, and Christ is God's" (1 Cor. 3:23).
     TRANSLATOR'S NOTE: I have followed the official ecclesiastical translation of the encyclical, although the Latin original was cited by Fr. Garrigou-Lagrange.

* * *

CHAPTER 4

The Divine Requirements of the Final End in Political Matters

In recent days, it is commonly asked what is the extent for the Church's power in the order of temporal questions and how her divine mission to lead souls to eternal life (in the light of dogma and of Christian morality) can permit her (or even make it obligatory for her) to intervene in political questions, which divide citizens and nations, while she herself leaves each person the full freedom in preferring this or that political regime.

We would merely like to recall that, according to the Church's own teaching, her intervention is measured by the divine requirements of the supernatural final end of our entire life: God loved above all. What is the radiation of this ultimate end? Must it be extended to all of our voluntary acts without exception, even those of the temporal order, and in what capacity is it extended even to them?

* * *

Let us first recall what is, according to Catholic doctrine, the foundation for the Church's powers in the spiritual order and in that of temporal affairs.

In the person of Peter, the other Apostles, and their successors, the Church has received directly from God, from our Lord Jesus Christ, the mission of leading souls, in light of revealed dogma and Christian morality, to eternal life. Her power corresponds to her divine mission; it extends to all men who have received the baptismal character, and to all that is necessary or useful for leading them to their final end. *In spiritual matters, this power is direct.* It is the order of faith and morals, that of salvation, where the Church exercises her *infallible magisterium* by teaching the supernatural and natural truths of the faith, the precepts and counsels contained in the deposit of divine revelation over which she has guardianship. It falls to her in this capacity to interpret what *revelation* says about the use of material things, about what one must render to Caesar and what is owed to God. Obviously, to this direct power also falls the administration of the sacraments, the sources of grace, *the religious government* not only of clerics but also of laymen considered as members of the faithful, the direction of theological studies, religious instruction in the schools, and everything that is of the sacred order or necessary for divine worship, such as the churches where the Holy Sacrifice is celebrated. Likewise, in this order of direct power, when it is not a question of the infallible magisterium but only of government or of discipline, the faithful are bound to submit themselves under pain, not of heresy, but of disobedience.

By way of consequence, the Church has an *indirect power* over *temporal affairs*, not taken in themselves, but taken, instead, *according to their relation to the salvation of souls*, depending on whether the use that the faithful make of them can impede or facilitate their salvation. And only the teaching Church is the qualified judge concerning the *relationship* of these temporal affairs with the supernatural last end to which they ought to lead us.

Under the influence of Protestantism, this point of doctrine, clearly affirmed by Pope Boniface VIII in the bull *Unam sanctam*,[1] was

---

1.   See Boniface VIII, *Unam sanctam* (Denzinger, nos. 873–74):
    "We are taught by the Gospel sayings that in his power there are two swords, that is, the spiritual and the temporal [reference is made to Lk. 22:38; Mt. 26:52].... [Both are therefore in the Church's power, that is, the spiritual sword and the material [sword]. But the latter is to be employed *for* the Church, the former *by* the Church;] the former [is by the hand] of the priest, the latter by the hand of kings and warriors, but at the priest's will and forbearance. Sword, however, should be subordinate to sword, and temporal power to spiritual... The spiritual should surpass any temporal power whatsoever in dignity and

misunderstood by the Gallicans, Jansenists, and liberals in their alleged defense of the rights either of the State or of the faithful.[2]

In his large treatise on the Church [i.e., his *Summa de ecclesia*], the Dominican Cardinal Juan de Torquemada, followed by Bellarmine and Suárez, determined in a very certain manner the nature of this indirect power in temporal affairs, doing so in accord with tradition and on the basis of the Church's own end. It is not a full and complete jurisdiction like that which the Church possesses in the order of spiritual affairs, but, as the great theologian says: "The sovereign Pontiff has, by his primacy, a kind of jurisdiction over the temporal order considered in its relation with the spiritual, to the degree required by the Church's needs

---

nobility, and we should confess this more clearly insofar as spiritual things surpass temporal things… [For truth bears witness that the spiritual power has to establish earthly power and judge it, if it has not been good…]

Therefore, if earthly power strays, it will be judged by the spiritual power; but if a lower spiritual deviates, [it will be judged] by its superior; but if the highest deviates, *it can be judged by God alone, not a man,* as the apostle testifies: 'The spiritual man judges all things, but he is judged by no one (1 Cor. 2:15)…

[This authority, however, although given to man and exercised through man, is not human but rather divine power, given to Peter by the divine mouth and confirmed for him and his successors in Christ himself, whom he, as the rock, confessed, as the Lord said to Peter himself: 'Whatever you bind,' and so on (Mt. 16:19).] Whosoever, therefore, resists this power ordained by God 'resists what God has ordained' (Rom. 13:2) [, unless, like a Manichean, he imagines that there are two first principles, which we judge false and heretical, because as Moses witnesses, not in the beginnings but 'in the beginning, God created heaven and earth' (Gn. 1:1).]

Furthermore, we declare, state, and define that it is absolutely necessary for the salvation of all human creatures that they submit to the Roman pontiff."

The [First] Vatican Council again affirmed the same doctrine. See *Pastor aeternus*, ch. 3 (Denzinger, no. 3064). Also, see Cajetan, *In ST* II-II, q. 60, a. 6, ad 3.

TRANSLATOR'S NOTE: The text in brackets was not included by Fr. Garrigou-Lagrange in the footnote, but is included here for clarity.

2.   See Alexander VIII, *Inter multiplices* (Denzinger, no. 2281), the condemnation of the first article of the Gallican Clergy, which they formulated in the following manner: "To blessed Peter and his successors, the vicars of Christ, and to the Church herself power over spiritual things and over those pertaining to eternal salvation has been given by God, but not power over civil and temporal affairs… *Therefore, by the command of God, kings and princes cannot be subject to ecclesiastical power in temporal affairs.*" Also, see Pius VI, *Auctorem fidei* (Denzinger, no. 2604). In the *Syllabus* [*errorum*], Pius IX also condemned this proposition (Denzinger, no. 2924): "The Church does not have the power of using force, nor does she have any temporal power, direct or indirect." See Reginald Schultes, *De ecclesia catholica* (Paris: Lethielleux, 1926), p. 349.

or by the duties of the Supreme Pastor charged with correcting abuses and preserving peace in the Christian people."[3]

It is not from the Pope, who does not have in this order of temporal things the full jurisdiction that he has in the spiritual order, that the Head of State draws his powers. Therefore, the pope cannot regularly intervene in a direct manner in the questions of propriety that must be ruled according to civil law, and in these matters, one cannot regularly appeal to him concerning the rulings proclaimed by secular judges.[4]

Therefore, this indirect power is solely concerned with temporal affairs, considered, not in themselves, but in their relation to the last end of all the baptized, of whom the Vicar of Jesus Christ is the Pastor. He is the one who is charged with leading them to eternal pastures, by the way traced out by our Lord Himself.

The Sovereign Pontiff can exercise this indirect power in two ways: either by way of counsel or by way of command. Of itself, a counsel is not obligatory, but it should be received with respect. A command, however, binds in conscience; to exempt oneself from it would not be heresy, so long as the infallible magisterium does not intervene, but rather, would represent an act of disobedience.

* * *

What follows in the order of political questions? How can the Church intervene in it and what freedom does each person have in this domain? Based on what we just said, the Church's intervention is measured by the divine requirements of our supernatural final end. Indeed, all our voluntary acts, whatever they may be, must be ordered to this end.

In order to avoid diminishing the magnitude of the question, let us first consider the case in which we enjoy the greatest freedom, namely, the case of acts that are said to be "indifferent" on account of their object. We will then see that we must think about acts whose object is no longer indifferent but, instead, are already morally evil (that is, in opposition with right reason, the divine law, and man's final end).

---

3.   Juan de Torquemada, *Summa de ecclesia*, bk. 2, ch. 113, concl. 2. Again, ch. 114.
4.   Ibid., ch. 113, props. 2, 4, and 6. See E. Dublanchy, "Turrecremata et le pouvoir du Pape dans les questions temporelles," *Revue thomiste*, Vol. 28 (New Series, 6) (1923): pp. 74–101.

It is certain that there are acts that are indifferent on account of their objects, that is, acts that, by their objects, are neither morally good nor morally bad. For example, it is morally indifferent to wish to teach mathematics or chemistry, to prefer the first of these sciences to the second; similarly, each person is free to prefer one or another legitimate form of government.

However, if one considers not only the immediate *object* of these voluntary acts but, moreover, *the end* to which they ought to be ordered, there cannot be, St. Thomas says, any indifferent deliberate act, taken individually in the concrete reality of life: "It is necessary that every human act proceeding from deliberative reason in the individual be considered as being either good or evil."[5]

The reason for this is that the rational being, as soon as he posits an act of will, must posit it for a fitting [*honnête*] end, for a morally good end. Otherwise, he prefers the useful or pleasing [good] to the fitting [good] and no longer acts reasonably.

Although it may be, for example, neither morally good nor morally evil to teach mathematics or chemistry, as soon as one *wills* to teach one of these sciences, this *willing* will be, on account of its end, not its object, either morally good (as in the case of the father of a family, who thus supports his family in an honest manner) or morally evil (as in the case of the anarchist who teaches how to make explosives in view of the worst of wrongdoings).

Similarly, in the political order, one is free to prefer monarchy to democracy and to work to show that a given country, such as France, will only find the tranquility of order by returning to the national traditions that established [its very character], to the regime that gave it greatness. One can even resort to all the legitimate means in view of this return. However, this work must be ordered to a morally good end, and in accord with the subordination of ends, to God Himself, more or less explicitly known and loved above all else. This is true already in the natural order, with regard to God, the Author of our nature, whom our intellect can know by its own powers alone. For all the more reason is it true after our elevation to the supernatural order: our supernatural last

---

5.   *ST* I-II, q. 18, a. 9.

end, God the Author of grace, indeed demands that all our voluntary acts be at least virtually ordered to Him. In other words, everything must contribute to our moral and spiritual progress, to our sanctification and our salvation. This is true not only of our specifically religious acts such as prayer, but also of all our free and voluntary acts, whatever they may be, even those that are indifferent on account of their objects. Each of them must have a good moral end, subordinated to the final end, namely, to love God above all else, more than ourselves, more than our family, and more than our country. "Whatever that you do," says St. Paul, "do all things for the glory of God" (1 Cor. 10:31). To the degree that all our acts are perfectly ordered to the Sovereign Good, the principle and end of all the others, to this same degree will peace (or, the tranquility of order) be established in our personal life, our family life, and our national life. Only in this way we will work to make known the rule of Christ over the nations. The subordination of ends requires it to be such.

However, as often happens, voluntary acts that are indifferent on account of their object, are altered as soon as this object is modified by being opposed to right reason and to the divine law. In this way, every legitimate form of government can be corrupted: democracy degenerates into demagoguery in the service of an omnipotent plutocracy, and monarchy degenerates into tyranny, into an oppressive militarism. Thus, in the object itself there is a truly condemnable disorder, for it becomes a serious obstacle for souls seeking out their final end.

Although Catholics have complete freedom to prefer this or that regime among the legitimate political regimes, still they must be certain, in following this preference, not to unconsciously subordinate religion to politics, nor to confuse these two orders. One would be inclined to this confusion if one said, "Modern peoples can live only in a democracy. Now, democracy is not durable without Christianity. Therefore, let us be Christians and democrats, or, better yet, let us be Christian democrats." Our motive for being Christians ought to be—it goes without saying—of an infinitely superior order. Obviously, neither can anyone claim that the formal motive for a Frenchman to be Christian and Catholic is because France can find the tranquility of order only by returning to the regime that gave her greatness, to a Christian and

Catholic monarchy. Such considerations could perhaps put one back upon the paths of faith, as has often enough happened, but it is important not to lose sight of the distance separating these two orders, as well as the subordination of one to the other.

Democracy, legitimate in itself, can degenerate into democratism, into a kind of religion that confuses the order of grace and the order of nature, or that tends to reduce the supernatural truth of the Gospel to a social conception of the human order, transforming divine charity into philanthropy, humanitarianism, and liberalism. The Church can, then, intervene, precisely in accordance with her magisterial authority. She cannot forget the principle: *corruptio optimi pessima*; the worst of corruptions is that which attacks that which is best in us, the loftiest of the supernatural virtues, which is the soul of all the others. If, here below, there is nothing better than true charity, which loves God above all else and one's neighbors for the love of God, there is nothing worse than false charity, which reverses the very order of love by making us forget the infinite goodness of God and His imprescriptible rights, so that we speak above all about the rights of man, equality, liberty, and fraternity. One thus confuses the formal object of an essentially supernatural virtue with that of a sentiment in which envy sometimes plays a large part. Is this not the essence of democracy understood as a kind of religion, something which completely distorts the notion of the virtue of charity and, at the same time, that of the connected virtue of justice? It would be illuminism to wish to find the spirit of the Gospel in it. To realize this fact, it suffices to apply here the principal rule of the discernment of spirits: "The tree is judged by its fruits." Those produced by the works of Rousseau are not those of the Gospel.

In order to react, as is fitting, against this democratism and against those who profit from it to the great detriment of their country, does it suffice to strike a vigorous blow [*un vigoreux coup de barre*] in the opposite direction in the human order? Does it suffice to recall the benefits of the natural hierarchy of values established in past days by the corporations in the work world, those of an aristocracy of intelligence, of a landed aristocracy, the advantages of monarchy, which brings unity, along with continuity in the internal and external politics of a large country, all in order to preserve it against enemies within and without?

If this reaction takes place only (or above all) in the human order, and not sufficiently in the supernatural order of faith and the love of God, it runs the risk of falling into the extreme opposed to that which it combats. Not only can it not efficaciously substitute, as it would like, the true idea of the virtues of charity and justice for the false notions of these virtues, but moreover, it can easily degenerate into an aristocratic naturalism that calls to mind Greek wisdom, with its intellectual pride which is opposed to the spirit of the Gospel. One would no longer understand the profound meaning of the Savior's teaching concerning humility and love for our neighbors: "I thank thee, Father, Lord of heaven and earth, that thou hast hidden these things from the wise and understanding and revealed them to babes" (Mt. 11:25, RSV). "This is my commandment, that you love one another as I have loved you" (Jn. 15:12, RSV).

In order to react against the naturalist notion of charity that is akin to the soul of democracy-religion, we must preserve ourselves against the other extreme, which would merely represent an opposed form of naturalism. We must elevate ourselves above these two extremes, turning toward the culminating point where the theological and moral virtues, lively faith, unshakeable hope, supernatural love of God and neighbor (and, indeed, of our enemies themselves), and divine charity, connected with true justice, all find themselves united together. In order to elevate ourselves toward this summit, Christian humility is required. A foundational virtue, it alone can repress the pride that tends to corrupt every political outlook and every form of government. Along with humility, docility of mind in relation to every kind of natural and supernatural truth is required. This is the only path that leads to the ultimate truth and to true wisdom.

The Church, who eminently possesses the grace that St. Paul called the discernment of spirits, intervenes in order to recall this fact to those who run the risk of going astray. She does not deny what is good in this reaction against the revolutionary dogmas. Indeed, she sees in this reaction excellent things that can be deformed. Thus, she speaks of the dangers that exist for Catholics in following this current of ideas, in letting oneself be absorbed by a natural activity that would be developed to the detriment of the life of grace. In speaking thus, the Church recalls once again the most important principles of Christian morality, which holds that our activity, in whatever order it is exercised, must be ordered to God, our final end, inspired from on high by divine faith, hope, and charity, without which the establishment of peace among the peoples is no more possible than it is in our individual lives.

If the Church is not content with merely recalling these principles admitted by all Catholics, if she intervenes practically by offering counsel or by issuing a command in the politics of a nation, she does so in virtue of her indirect power, on account of the relation of fittingness or opposition that temporal affairs have with the spiritual life of souls. When the Pope thus intervenes by issuing a command, this command obliges in conscience, and to exempt oneself from it would be a grave fault of disobedience. The Vicar of Jesus Christ is indeed the qualified judge (and here below the judge of last resort) concerning the extension of his indirect power *here and now* concerning a given temporal affair according to *the relation that it has with the life of souls and their supernatural last end.* We only see this relation according to our very limited understanding; he sees it under a superior light that he receives from God as the Supreme Pastor. In this capacity, it not only falls to him to teach *ex cathedra* by defining infallibly what is of faith for the universal Church; it also falls to him to govern. Indeed, just as his infallible magisterium demands faith, beneath such infallibility, his commands demand obedience. From the moment that he commands, one is bound to obey. As Boniface VIII said: "If earthly power strays, it will be judged by the spiritual power; but, if a lower spiritual power deviates, [it will be judged] by its superior; if the highest deviates, it can be judged by God alone, *not man.*"[6] The ultimate authority must be listened to when it commands, even where it is not infallible, and nobody here below can judge it.

Some may believe that they have incontrovertible reasons for *speculatively judging* that a condemned political movement whose overall institutional structure [*organe*], as directed and written out, is good in itself. However, they are not, for all that, dispensed from obedience. They must conform their practical judgment and their will to the

---

6. Boniface VIII, *Unam sanctam* (Denzinger, no. 873).

command issued, [precisely] as it is formulated. They are not forbidden to present to the competent authority facts and reasons that they estimate to have escaped his knowledge. However, they must do so with respect, by abstaining from every public protestation of such a nature as to lessen the prestige of that authority and to produce scandal. They must pray to God, accepting their suffering in a supernatural manner; this acceptance will purify what is good in their intention and their work, whereas their disobedience could compromise it forever.

If the ultimate authority does not believe that the facts and reasons which they invoke suffice for granting the desires of such objectors, then they must tell themselves that God watches over His Church and, consequently, that they must, in a spirit of faith, conform not only their practical judgment but also their speculative judgment to all that the Holy Spirit has in view in the pontifical order given. Let them think that twenty motives of general interest can escape their own sight, from the restricted perspective where they are habitually placed, and that a wisdom infinitely superior to their own directs, *fortiter et suaviter*, all events (whether happy or painful) by making them contribute to the Glory of God and that of His elect.

In this way, the act of obedience that they make will be all the more meritorious inasmuch as it is inspired by a greater faith and by a greater love of God. Do many things lead them to foresee that this obedience will have disastrous consequences for their country? Supernatural faith responds that God, who gives the grace for obeying in this way and who is the Master of all events, will not permit an act, so inspired by Him, to have disastrous consequences. In reality, He makes all things contribute, as St. Paul says, to the superior good of those who seek Him in sincerity of heart and who above all else wish to remain forever faithful to Him.

From this truly supernatural and peace-inducing [*pacifiant*] point of view, many wrongdoings committed by our fellow men are forgotten, one pardons one's adversaries with full sincerity, by upholding against them what truth requires without bitterness, one understands better one's own faults (negligence in the search for truth, and culpable indulgence for certain grave deviations), and finally, one sees all the better, in the end, how to save, with God's aid, everything that, in a national movement, is inspired by love for the common good, order, and the authority needed for the life of the country.

Thus, obedience makes one enter more profoundly into the Truth, into the thought of God concerning a Christian people, into the lofty idea of its destinies and of its relationship with the life of the Church, the mystical body of Christ. So too, one comes to understand more fully that, in the concrete reality of individual and social life, no single, deliberate act is morally indifferent, for each and every action must obviously be performed for a morally good end and, consequently, for God: "He who is not with me is against me."

Every deliberate act goes to the right or to the left, either to the side of the good and of God or to the side of evil, just as, at the watershed upon the summit of the mountains, every drop of water goes left or right toward opposite rivers and seas.

In the spiritual order, the watershed is above all known by those who have received the discernment of spirits, in particular by the Supreme Pastor, who has the mission of leading souls in the way of salvation. To him, more than to any other person, does it belong to discern the good grain from the tares, in order to save all that must be saved and thus bring all things into conformity with the supernatural good of those who in sincerity of heart seek God and truly wish to love Him above all else.

* * *

In a national movement that has captivated many intellects among the elite, there certainly is much that is good: that which it borrows from the great traditions of the French spirit, illuminated by Christian faith. Without delay, it is important to rectify these elements, which run the risk of deviation, and the first means for such rectification is to be obedient anew in order to benefit increasingly from the direction of the Church, who infallibly teaches us the word of God and places the accent where it is needed so that we may pass through the letter and thus penetrate all the way to the spirit of Christ's doctrine. Through obedience, God will save that which would be lost without Him.

In this superior light, we learn that, in order to be healthy and beneficial, nationalism must stand within the golden mean of the virtue of filial piety for one's mother country. As St. Thomas says in *ST* II-II, q. 101, a. 1: "*It pertains to piety to exhibit devotion for one's parents and fatherland.*" Thus, patriotism is a virtue that must accompany justice. We are debtors toward our country on account of its excellence as well as the sundry and manifold benefits that we have received from it. In the same text, St. Thomas says, "After God, it is to our parents and to our country that we owe the greatest debt."

From this superior perspective, we understand better that the principal treasure that our country has preserved and transmitted to us, under the direction of the Church, is the very doctrine of the Gospel, the Christian life, which has penetrated deeply into its institutions and which is the best aspect of family life and social life.

Then, we will love this country with something greater than a natural love. Our patriotism will not be only an already-noble acquired moral virtue, but under the light of supernatural faith and Christian prudence, it will be, as we see in figures like St. Louis and Joan of Arc, an infused virtue, perfectly subordinated to charity, vivified by the love of God, by the supernatural love of neighbor and of our very enemies.

So understood, patriotism—we must recall this fact when we forget the great duties that it implies—corresponds to the fourth commandment: "You will honor your mother and your father, so that you may live a long life." It ennobles, by elevating it, everything that is good in nationalism and prevents it from becoming a form of "us-ism" [*nosisme*], an egoism of the many, perpetually in conflict with neighboring egoisms.

Similarly, in the bright light of the Gospel, elites learn better and better *to serve* the common good of their countries, just as they learn to serve God, the supreme common good of all souls. True humility keeps them on the right path. In this way, they avoid an immense amount of wasted exertion, and charity renders their action more and more beneficial and fruitful.

Behold what the Holy Spirit obviously wills, the Holy Spirit who watches over His Church when He leads her to intervene in order to prevent this or that great national movement from deviating or from compromising forever what is best in it. He wishes to lead those who are passionate for the common good to know themselves better, to note their limitations, to see their defects in order to correct them, and to aspire higher and have recourse to loftier assistance in order to attain this loftier end. *The order of agents corresponds to the order of ends*, St. Thomas often says. God, the Supreme Agent, makes all things converge toward the final end. All events, whether happy and unhappy, contribute to it. His Church constantly calls to our awareness the great doctrine concerning the subordination of ends, above all of the moral ends which we *must* love and wish to attain. This is the very order of charity, that is, of love.

We must love—not only with a natural love but with a supernatural, theological love—God for Himself, our soul called to glorify Him eternally, our family, our nation, and the Church, who gathers together all nations in order to lead them to the Kingdom of God.

The warnings pronounced by the Supreme Pastor of souls have as their end the goal of preserving them from error, which is born from pride. A great deal of intellectual prowess, sometimes incredible in strength, as well as of voluntary energies, along with years of labor, are all lost by this aberration: "*Magni passus sed extra viam*. [Great strides are made, but not upon the path.]" The work of many generations comes to nothing if it does not follow the path of God. "Unless the LORD builds the house, those who build it labor in vain" (Ps. 126[7]:1, RSV). Let us build under the very direction of God; then, our work will be durable. That which is best in it, its spirit, will transcend time and bear fruits in eternity.

* * *

CHAPTER 5

Truth and Indifferentism

In one of his recent discourses, the Holy Father [Pope Pius XII] be-moaned a considerable lowering of moral conscience in the world. With the diffusion of materialism and atheism, the denial of moral and religious obligations has indeed taken on unbelievable proportions in many environments. Whence, [we have] the diffusion of bad faith and lying.

The denial of moral obligations is reflected in the most subversive slogans that stir up the young. In a society in which the psychoanalysis of Freud flourishes, continence is a word that elicits derision. The greatest freedom of morals becomes permitted and is even declared to be *normal*. Free love outside of marriage is displayed without any restraint, leading to frequent abortion [*avortement*] and a notably more elevated number of infanticides [*infanticides*] and suicides. These are the consequences of the *atheistic existentialism* that is freely allowed to be taught today and that becomes *a proof of God's existence by way of absurdity*, that is, through the despair and universal nausea to which it leads. It seems like the end of the world.

This denial of moral obligations is the consequence of the denial of religious obligations. Its ultimate outcome is limitless liberalism and indifferentism—as though religious truth no longer existed, nor truth of the supra-sensible order; as though one could just as well sustain the probability of atheism as that of the existence of God; Providence, and the future life, as though there were no certain sign of the divine origin of Christianity and the Church, and as though one could just as well deny as affirm the mysteries of the Redemptive Incarnation, the Eucharist, and eternal life.

Thus, one can see the incalculable evil caused by the reading of the works of Renan and, more recently, those of Gide and other similar books in various countries; they have led many souls to complete bewilderment.

Moreover, there is the increasingly widespread idea that, in the end, all religions are equal, that *dogmas have little importance*, that they divide more than they unite, and that *morality is the only thing that counts*. However, even such morality ultimately disappears, for it no longer has any immutable foundation.

This complete indifferentism represents the absolute denial of the true apostolate, which ought to bring men *the word of God* for which the martyrs shed their blood.

We would like to recall here the *rights of the truth*, without which, obviously, there would be neither *true freedom* nor a true human life worthy of this name, nor *true charity*.

To proceed in an orderly manner, we will first recall the principal forms of indifferentism and its consequences, such as we see them today.

I. INDIFFERENTISM, ITS DIFFERENT FORMS,
AND ITS CONSEQUENCES

Absolute indifferentism denies the necessity of every religion, even natural religion. It proceeds either from atheism, pantheism, or agnosticism. Indeed, if one can know nothing concerning God, there is no longer any talk about His rights, nor of our duties before Him. It becomes an indifferent or quite secondary affair to say, "God exists," or, "God does not exist," "God is the final end of man," or "He is not." *Religion becomes an indifferent, unnecessary, negligible affair*. At most one can say, with Hegel, that it proceeds, like art, more from the imagination than from reason. If it was necessary once upon a time, before the appearance of more or less generalized intellectual culture, *it is no longer necessary today. It is a luxury* like poetic art. Kant, who preserved a kind of moral faith in the existence of God and of the future life, *denied every specific duty before God*, as well as the necessity of every form of religious worship. He was content to say, "We must religiously fulfill our moral duties before ourselves and before other men." This absolute rationalism is obviously the foundation of utter laicism in laws and institutions; this laicism is the external form of absolute indifference, irreligion and impiety.

Mitigated indifferentism comes from the *Deists* who admitted the existence of God, but added that *God knows only the general laws of the universe* and not individual persons. Hence, they denied the usefulness and efficacy of prayer and of every external form of worship. This led them to say in these matters that, *among the various positive religions which exist, one can freely choose whichever one is more pleasing, just* as one can choose between the different forms of classical or romantic art. From this perspective, one is free to choose between Christianity, Islam, and Buddhism, as though Islam, which denies the mysteries of the Holy Trinity and the Redemptive Incarnation, were as true as Christianity, which affirms them—as though *yes and no* could be true at the same time.[1]

This indifferentism, which is found in Jean Jacques Rousseau's *Emile* ("The Profession of Faith of the Savoyard Vicaire") is formulated in propositions fifteen to eighteen of Pius IX's *Syllabus errorum*. These condemned propositions hold that *each person is free to choose the religion that pleases him* or which seems preferable to him according solely to the light of his individual reason.[2] Men can find the way of eternal

---

1. "Let what you say be simply 'Yes' or 'No'" (Mt. 5:37, RSV). As St. Paul said, "For the Son of God, Jesus Christ, whom we preached among you, Silvanus and Timothy and I, was not Yes and No; but in him it is always Yes" (2 Cor. 1:19, RSV). The Incarnation of the Word either *is* or *is not*; if it is, Christianity is the Truth, and Islam is an error. Two contradictory propositions cannot be true at the same time; one of the two is true and the other is false.

2. On the contrary, according to the Church, there is a true freedom of conscience, or the right to embrace and profess *the true* religion as soon as it is sufficiently proposed with certain signs of its divine origin. In this, there is a precept for us, *a duty* that we must *freely* fulfill like every precept. The moral obligation to believe in the mysteries revealed by God and evidently believable does not remove the psychological freedom of the act of faith; from the fact that the mysteries remain *obscure* and not demonstrated, we

salvation in each of these religions (indeed, finding it just as well in one as in the others).

Lammenais arrived at this mitigated indifferentism in the second volume of his *Essay on Indifference in Matters of Religion* and in *Words of a Believer.*

Modernism inclined one to think the same thing for religious faith, holding that it is only a *natural religious sentiment* that evolves and is found in all religions,[3] although in a superior manner in Christianity.

Many say: *It suffices that one embrace Christianity without professing Catholicism*; one can hope that, according to the spirit of the Gospel, this suffices for salvation. For these latter, Protestantism is a legitimate form of true Christian religion, a form in which one can please God just as well as one could in the Catholic Church. *It is as though one were to say,* again, contrary to right reason and to the Gospel, *that yes and no can be true at the same time* (e.g., the denial and affirmation of the value of the sacrifice of the Mass, sacramental absolution, and the necessity of good works for salvation). And nonetheless, *God cannot regard with equal benevolence two contradictory doctrines, the true and the false.*

This doctrine is utterly removed from all that which was thought by the Doctors of the Church and the Saints concerning the *free propagation of heresy.* Let us recall, for example, how St. Hermenegild and, later on, St. Casimir were opposed to the diffusion of the heresies of their times; how the Catholic cantons of Switzerland were ever opposed to the penetration of Protestantism and admirably guarded the integrity of the faith and the means of salvation, the sacraments and the sacrifice of the Mass; and how Canada and Ireland heroically knew how to defend their faith and continue to defend it very firmly. Nor should it be forgotten, either, that Protestantism, having become liberal Protestantism, hardly differs any longer from rationalism. Obviously, His Holiness Pius IX could only condemn mitigated indifferentism in the *Syllabus*[4] and, *a fortiori*, absolute indifferentism.

---

adhere to them freely by faith, by seeing that it is *a duty* for us to believe in them: "It is a freedom not from obligation but from necessity." Cf. *ST* II-II, q. 2, aa. 1, 9, and 10.

3.   See Pius X, *Pascendi dominici gregis*, no. 25 (Denzinger, no. 2093, old numbering). **TRANSLATOR'S NOTE:** This section is skipped in the most recent edition of Denzinger.

4.   See Pius IX, *Syllabus errorum*, nos. 15–18 (Denzinger nos. 2915–18).

Finally, *liberalism* held and still holds that *the civil freedom of different forms of worship* is, for modern society, *not a lesser evil to be tolerated* in order to avoid a greater one, but that it is *very useful* and *conformed to reason and the evangelical spirit* in developed peoples.

This comes down to saying that, even in a country with a Catholic majority, a country that owes, above all, its grandeur to true Christianity, not only is it tolerable, but *it is fitting*, according to right reason and the evangelical spirit, that Protestantism is *free* to publicly deny and combat all those the dogmas proposed by the Catholic Church which it rejects, as well to spread doubt concerning them.

Perhaps one will object that, contradictions can be found among the systems of Catholic theologians, as we find in matters concerning the efficacy of grace. However, it is easy to respond that, according to Catholic theologians, God does not regard these mutually opposed systems *with equal benevolence.* He knows infallibly which is true and which is false.

The principle upon which the liberalism of which we speak *rests is that it is only by persuasion* that true religion should be propagated and flourish and that, in these conditions, many will embrace it, indeed, with all the more freedom and confidence, given that one would not be obligated to embrace them, for *the truth ever prevails over error.*

From the times of His Holiness Pius IX, all the Popes without exception have responded: Certainly, *on the day of the last judgment, truth will prevail over error*, but in the present life in many men, dominated by their lusts and pride, *error ends up prevailing over the truth, if one accords, even in Catholic Countries, the same rights to false religions as to the true religion.* Many thus come to doubt the elementary truths of religion, which are the most profound and the most vital, like the *Our Father*. In the first generation, the number of unbelievers, atheists, and divorced is not very great. However, in the fifth and sixth generation, their number becomes considerable, and the consequences of mixed marriages are disastrous for faith. No one can deny this fact. An irenicism that refuses to recognize this itself leads to skepticism.

This is what led St. Augustine, cited by St. Gregory XVI,[5] to say that the freedom of teaching error as well as truth is a *freedom of*

---

5. Ep. 105 (166) c. 2, n. 9, M. L., 33, 399.

perdition, that is, the ruin of temporal society leading to the eternal loss of souls.[6] What, in fact, happened during the last century? What Pius IX foresaw. What Donoso Cortès[7] had announced a hundred years ago with astonishing precision. That is what has happened. *Liberalism*, he said, *not declaring itself to be either for or directly against Christian principles*, permits the endless prolongation of discussions in parliaments, but *it does not suffice for acting*; indeed, *for acting*, a determined direction must be taken, whether for or against the principles of the Gospel. Then, when it was necessary *to act* (for example, in order to establish a legislation concerning lay school or free school, concerning divorce, etc.) many of those who did not dare or did not wish to remain faithful to Christian principles descended from *liberalism* to *radicalism* in their denial, then to *socialism*, which replaces God and the Divine Law with society and universal suffrage. Finally, many descended to materialistic and atheistic *communism*, whose own denials we all know well, along with what then follows for each person's freedom, which disappears completely. Complete liberalism leads to its contrary, tyranny. The extremes touch each other, and the one leads to the other by the misunderstanding of the same superior truth.

And if, against communism, one would like today to defend freedom of teaching without going on further to speak about the rights of truth, *the defense of true liberty* (*as something distinct from license*) *will be deprived of its foundation*. Then, adversaries could ask for the freedom to teach materialistic atheistic communism, just as we ask for the freedom to teach the Gospel.

The disastrous consequences of such a liberalism are all too visible today. They recall to the words of of Cardinal Pie[8] to Napoleon III: "If the time has not come for Christ to reign, then, sire, the time has

6.   Gregory XVI, *Mirari vos* (Denzinger, no. 2731).

7.   Donoso Cortès, *Oeuvres de Donoso Cortès*. See vol. 2, pp. 212ff. "On the generative principle of gravest errors of our days," a thirty-page letter to Cardinal Fornari to be presented to Pius IX (1852) and the *Discourse on the General Situation of Europe* in 1850. TRANSLATOR'S NOTE: For these particular texts, the reader can consult *Donoso Cortès: Readings in Political Theory*, ed. R. A. Herrera.

8.   TRANSLATOR'S NOTE: Louis-Édouard-François-Desiré Pie (1815–1880).

not come for governments to last."[9] These words must have echoed in Napoleon's mind after the disaster of Sedan in 1870.

All of this has distanced many souls from the truths in which one must have faith, which is necessary for salvation.

Such a *religious syncretism* with an edifying appearance, presented to the faithful of all religions as a kind of a *super-religion* promising a renewed humanity, would be no less opposed to the salvation of souls. In this syncretism, which allegedly represents a lofty form of morality, a syncretism that is spreading, *Catholicism is not combatted.* On the contrary, it is *honored* with pomp, while, in the end, being annexed. Catholic dogma (which is held in infinite esteem, we are told) is gradually presented as being *obsolete.* It is not rejected; it is annexed. It is only an admirable part of an even more admirable whole. It comes to be integrated into a place of honor in the federalism of religions that must constitute the Universal Religion of the new era.

However, one no longer is concerned with Jesus's divinity, nor with the Blessed Virgin Mary, the Mother of God. One thus arrives at a kind of liberal Protestantism and does not progress beyond it. One falls into an irenicism that under the pretext of charity claims to reconcile contradictories: the yes and the no.[10]

Such are the different forms of indifferentism, which lead to the relativism spoken of in the Encyclical *Humani generis*: There is no longer absolute and immutable truth but only an ever-changing truth, relative to the mentality of our age and our momentary action. What is, by contrast, the Church's own teaching concerning the truth and its rights?

II. THE RIGHTS OF TRUTH

One of the documents that best shows the Church's teaching concerning truth is the Encyclical *Pascendi* of Blessed Pius X against the modernists.

---

9. Louis Baunard, *Histoire du Cardinal Pie, Evêque de Poitiers*, vol. 1 (Paris: H. Oudin, 1886), p. 636.

10. See *Humani generis.*

    TRANSLATOR'S NOTE: Fr. Garrigou-Lagrange does not cite a paragraph number. See nos. 11, 12, and 43.

The modernists denied the traditional definition of truth, as well as the ontological and transcendent value of the first notions and first principles of our intellect. According to them, the human intellect only reaches the phenomena and their experimental laws. The principle of causality would only have a value in the phenomenal order. Consequently, the modernists denied the demonstrative value of the traditional proofs of the existence of God, the Ultimate Cause, as well as the certitude of the fact of revelation and the miraculous signs that confirm it. Likewise, they denied the immutability of the first notions, which enable us to know analogically, but with certitude, the divine perfections and revealed mysteries: therefore, they rejected the immutability of dogma and said: "Truth is no more immutable than man himself, since it evolved with him, in him, and through him"[11]; truth would only be the conformity of our judgment with the requirements of human life, which ever evolves in its successive activities.

Pius X responded to the modernists in the Encyclical *Pascendi*: "They pervert the eternal concept of truth and the true nature of the religious sentiment."[12] He recalled the traditional definition of truth: *the conformity of judgment with being*, a truth that has a relation not only to the successive phenomena and their experimental laws, but to *intelligible being* and its necessary, immutable, and universal laws.

As St. Thomas shows,[13] whereas our sense knowledge attains only the phenomena, the sensible qualities, our intellect *intus legit*, attains intelligible being, the existing subject to which the sensible phenomena are attributed. Whereas the sense of sight attains *colored being* as *colored*, our intellect attains colored being as *intelligible being*, in opposition to non-being [*néant*].

Just as the colored is the proper object of sight, and the sonorous is the proper object of hearing, *the intelligible being of sensible things* is the proper object of our intellect.[14]

---

11.   Decree of the Holy Office, *Lamentabili*, no. 58 (Denzinger, no. 3458).

12.   **Translator's Note:** The text is taken from Pius X, *Pascendi*, no. 13. Fr. Garrigou-Lagrange cites the old Denzinger, no. 2080. This particular part of the text is ellipsed out in the 43rd edition of Denzinger.

13.   See *ST* II-II, q. 8, a. 1.

14.   See *ST* I, q. 5, a. 2; *De veritate*, q. 1, a. 1 and a. 9; *SCG* II, ch. 83, no. 32.

Therefore, truth, which is formally found in our act of judgment, is conformity with being. It consists in *affirming what is* and *denying what is not*—for example, affirming that Peter exists and that he is a man and not an animal, that he is *one* and the same under multiple and transitory phenomena.

Moreover, as St. Thomas notes, *it is in the intelligible being* of sensible things that *our intellect sees the truth of the first principles* as laws of the real, the principles of contradiction, of *raison d'être*,[15] of causality, and of finality, as was recalled recently in the Encyclical *Humani generis*.

To realize this fact, it suffices to formulate exactly these first principles in all their necessity and universality in function of being:

1. *No being can, at one and the same time, exist and not exist or, again, be what it is and not be it.* Hegel himself could not escape from this necessity; he could not at one and the same time exist and not exist, be Hegel and not be him.
2. *Every being has its raison d'être*, either in itself or in another.
3. *Every being that comes into existence needs a cause* and, ultimately, an *Uncaused Cause* that exists *of Itself.*
4. *Every acting being (or, every agent) acts for an end.* This is true not only of man, but of animal, plant, mineral, and all bodies, which are attracted to each other *for* the cohesion of the universe and its harmony, which is a good and an end.

These principles are *absolute, immutable truths* and not only truths that are relative to the mentality of a given age and our successive activities. These principles are the *primordial certitudes* of our natural intelligence, diamond-like certitudes that resist, like the first notions, all the sophisms of ancient skepticism or of modern relativism. They are *immutable certitudes* that *lead to God*, the First Cause and Final End of all things, so well that Holy Scripture declares "inexcusable" those who do not admit the existence of God (Wis. 13:1–9; Rom. 1:20).

---

15. TRANSLATOR'S NOTE: Concerning this expression, see the chapter above, entitled "On the Search for Definitions According to Aristotle and St. Thomas," pp. 24–25, note 6.

What greater absurdity is there than to say that the intelligence of the greatest geniuses and the goodness of the greatest saints arises from a material and blind fatality?

Against indifferentism, we must add: *Without the absolute truth of these first principles* as *laws of reality*, there is not a *true being* distinct from non-being [*néant*], nor a *true good* distinct from evil, nor a *moral life* distinct from perversity, nor a *true final end of man*, nor a *true God*, immutable in His nature and His attributes; all that remains will be an evolution in which *the more perfect constantly comes from the less perfect, and where all things are confused*, the true and the false, the just and the unjust. This is what was said in the first proposition of the *Syllabus errorum*.[16]

Finally, without the absolute truth of these principles, there is no longer *true freedom* distinct from false freedom (that is, from license), the source of all disorders against written or unwritten laws. Hence, one no longer can distinguish true freedom from *depraved freedom*, which leads to the incurable despair spoken of by atheistic existentialism today.

Thus one understands why not only Gregory XVI and Pius IX, but also Leo XIII, on the subject of indifferentism and liberalism, recalled these words of St. Augustine cited earlier: "The freedom of teaching error as well as truth is nothing other than a freedom of perdition."[17] Indifferentism, however mitigated one may suppose it to be, manifestly contains a fundamental error that is contrary to the final end of man and to the rights of God that we can easily know if the love of truth remains in us.

In 1888, Leo XIII said clearly in the encyclical *Libertas*[18]: "*Society as such must recognize that God is its author.* It must respect Divine

---

16. Pius IX, *Syllabus errorum*, no. 1 (Denzinger, no. 2901).

17. See Gregory XVI, *Mirari vos* (Denzinger, no. 2731), Alexander VIII, *Inter multiplices* (Denzinger, nos. 2281ff), and Leo XIII, *Immortale dei* (Denzinger, no. 3178). Also, see Pius IX, *Quanto conficiamur moerore* (Denzinger, no. 2865), Leo XIII *Immortale Dei* (Denzinger, nos. 3168–79); Leo XIII, *Libertas* (Denzinger, nos. 3252–55).

18. TRANSLATOR'S NOTE: I have chosen to translate Fr. Garrigou-Lagrange's French, which is cited from p. 231 of an unnamed text. It does differ from the current official French translation of the text. The official Vatican English translation of the section in question (taken from no. 21) is: "Wherefore, civil society must acknowledge God as its

authority. *Justice forbids, indeed reason forbids, that society be atheistic,* or, what comes to the same, *that society equally receive all religions and grant them all the same rights."*

Inasmuch as he is a rational being, man is ordered to knowledge of the truth and even knowledge of the ultimate truth inasmuch as it is accessible to him. Likewise, he is ordered toward love for the good, above all the Ultimate Good, the source of all the others.

Now, in order arrive at this knowledge and love, *man must do what is in his power for knowing God,* loving Him, and serving Him, recognizing in a practical manner that every good comes from Him, and he must ask Him to bestow upon him the aid needed for doing the good, which is sometimes difficult, and for persevering in it. This is a natural inclination for man, one that is no doubt weakened by sin, though, nonetheless, an inclination that remains and, indeed, is strengthened and elevated by grace.

These are our religious duties already in the natural order. This reminds us of our *final end,* and it is founded on *the rights of God,* the rights of the Supreme Truth to be known and to be recognized, and the rights of the Sovereign Good to be loved above all else, since it is infinitely better than us. Plato affirmed this clearly in his *Symposium.* This is even evident in the natural order, and in order to deny this evidence, one must do violence to right reason, as Scripture attests (Wis. 8:8).

Now, these are precisely the rights and duties that are denied by indifferentism. Moreover, *these duties toward God are the most fundamental of all duties.* Indeed, they are founded on the supreme right of God, the First Cause, the Author of every life, the Author of our intellects, of our wills, the Author of every good, the Author of society and of civil authority. These duties toward God *correspond to what is primordial in man, who first of all is God's creature,* and it is a question of our last end, namely, to love the Sovereign Good above all, more than ourselves, since that Good is infinitely better than every finite good. And, therefore, in the subordination of our duties, if one denies the supreme duty

---

Founder and Parent, and must obey and reverence His power and authority. Justice therefore forbids, and reason itself forbids, the State to be godless; or to adopt a line of action which would end in godlessness—namely, to treat the various religions (as they call them) alike, and to bestow upon them promiscuously equal rights and privileges."

founded on the rights of God, the First Truth and Sovereign Good, all our other duties are deprived of their deepest foundation. *The keystone has fallen*, and the edifice is crumbling and close to collapse. It is like a human body without a head to direct it or move it.

As Leo XIII said,[19] this means that *the true rights of man are born of his duties toward God*, for every duty is founded on a right, and every right on the supreme right of the very Author of our nature. *Man's very first right is that of doing his duty, above all his duty toward God*, the Supreme Truth and Sovereign Good. Man can *cede* many of his rights, but certainly not that of doing his duty. He cannot renounce it. Here is an inalienable and imprescriptible right, that of embracing and practicing, up to the point of death, the true religion; man *must* even undergo martyrdom rather than renounce God or cease loving and obeying Him. The rights of the Most High and the ultimate end of the soul's life are incomparably more precious than the life of the body, and if they cannot be defended except by war, one must not recoil from it, as the Holy Father recalled in one of his Christmas messages in 1948.

These superior truths can be obscured by the errors that are widespread among us, as the sun is sometimes hidden by dark clouds; however, despite all the sophisms, it nevertheless remains engraved upon the human soul, upon our natural understanding and our heart. These are the *unwritten laws*, νόμοι ἄγραφοι, spoken of by Socrates and recalled by Pius IX when he spoke against indifferentism.[20]

But man does not only have the duty to practice natural religion; he also has the duty to *receive Divine Revelation in a spirit of docility* when it is sufficiently proposed with certain signs of its Divine origin.[21] *Indeed, created reason must receive, in a spirit of docility, the light that is mercifully offered to it by the Uncreated Intellect and the Supreme Goodness.* Consequently, man has the duty to *pursue* the revealed truth as soon as he thinks there is a *serious probability* that it has been proposed to us for

---

19. Leo XIII, *Litteris encyclicis ad omnes antistites et catholicos Galliae* (February 16, 1892). Also, the Encyclical *Immortale Dei.*

20. See Pius IX, *Quanto conficiamur moerore* (Denzinger, no. 2865).

21. TRANSLATOR'S NOTE: To understand correctly Fr. Garrigou-Lagrange's position here, consult at length the two volumes of *De revelatione* (to be published in English translation in the near future by Emmaus Academic).

guiding us to eternal life. In this, we again are faced with the rights of the Divine Truth, rights that cannot be recognized by those who think that it is of little importance to know whether God has provided man with a revelation for guiding them to their destiny.

According to St. Thomas, *he who refuses to receive Divine Revelation which has been sufficiently proposed acts against the nature of our intellect, which is made for the truth.* As the Holy Doctor says in *ST* II-II, q. 10, a. 1, ad 1: "To have (supernatural, or, infused) faith is not in the power of human nature, but *human nature requires that man's mind not resist the interior inspiration* of grace and the external preaching of the truth."[22] This is what Leo XIII says in his Encyclical *Libertas*.[23] Certainly, the act of faith is *free*, but *it is also obligatory*; one must *freely fulfill this obligation*, like other obligations.

In the Encyclical *Immortale Dei* in 1885,[24] against the error of liberalism, Leo XIII also said in substance: *God is no less the Creator, Master, and Benefactor of civil society than He is of individual men*; He is the Author of our nature, which is made to live in society; *"every power comes from God,"* says St. Paul (Rom. 13:1), even that of the civil authority for promoting the temporal common good, to preserve it against all causes of division and of ruin, against the enterprises of wrongdoers [*malfaiteurs*]. *Therefore, if the civil authority rejects the authority of God by refusing to receive Divine Revelation sufficiently proposed, if it establishes civil laws contrary to Revelation* (e.g., concerning divorce), *it works to its own ruin and bestows death upon itself.* Such actions represent a veritable form of moral suicide, *as well as a grave fault entailing chastisements.* Society loses its equilibrium and no longer can find it; henceforth, it only lives by expedients and marches onward toward decadence. In acting thus, society acts against its own end, which is the temporal common good in accord with virtue, prudence, and social justice, a common good subordinated to the final end of man that Divine Revelation manifests with certitude.

---

22. TRANSLATOR'S NOTE: I have followed Fr. Garrigou-Lagrange's French rendering of the original Latin.
23. See Denzinger, nos. 3252–55.
24. See Denzinger, nos. 3168–79.

It is absurd to say that the human legislator can *propose laws contrary to those of the Supreme Legislator*. And if he does this, the human legislator will find that he thereby accrues a terrible debt to be repaid to God's justice.[25]

This would be to grant the same rights to error and to truth. Then what could we respond to the worst enemies of religion when they ask to have the freedom to teach such error? The defense of our rights would no longer have any superior norm. Society would thus end by sinking into immorality. As Hippolyte Taine said, when Christianity disappears from society, "it becomes an evil and cutthroat place," an anticipation of hell through despair and universal nausea.

Such are manifestly the requirements of the truth. How are they related to true liberty and charity?

III. TRUTH, FREEDOM, AND CHARITY

These requirements of truth are perfectly conformed (whatever some may say at times) *to true freedom*, which lies in *the power to choose* the means that lead us to our *true final end*, and not the power to choose what turns us away from it. Likewise, *reason is a faculty for reasoning correctly and not awry*; it is the faculty for knowing the truth, by avoiding error as much as possible. This point was explained by Gregory XVI in the Encyclical *Mirari vos* in 1832: "But what worse death of the soul is there than the freedom of error."[26]

Moreover, as Leo XIII remarked in his Encyclical *Libertas*,[27] *it is not true that all men*, nor even that the greater part of them, *seek truth and virtue*. And *if one grants the freedom of teaching the errors that flatter desire and pride, a great portion of mankind would no longer find the saving truth, except with great difficulty*. St. Thomas had said likewise: "The majority of men follow their senses rather than right reason."[28]

---

25. In moments of lucidity, even the enemies of the Church recognize this; here, one could cite in particular Proudhon and, later on, Clémenceau.

26. See Gregory XVI, *Mirari vos*, no. 14 (Denzinger, no. 2731).

27. See Leo XIII, *Libertas*, no. 23.

28. "In man alone is evil seen to exist as in the greater number… Most men follow their senses rather than reason." Cf. *ST* I, q. 49, a. 3, ad 5 and *Tabula aurea* for *malum*, no. 37.

Liberalism can *be defined*: The doctrine holding that *civil and social authority are not bound to receive Divine Revelation*, even if it is sufficiently proposed with certain signs of its Divine origin. This comes down to saying: *Civil society can prefer freedom to truth* and the freedom to act as one pleases to the Divine Truth which has been sufficiently made manifest. It means, for example, that the civil authority can refuse to practically recognize *the True God, refusing to invoke Him* for attaining light and wisdom *when it establishes its legislation*. From such a perspective, even if the true God forbade divorce, the civil authority could favor it by its purely secular laws. Even if revelation is sufficiently proposed, civil society could legislate without taking it into account. One understands why Pius IX in his Encyclical *Quanta cura* in 1864[29] and Leo XIII in the Encyclical *Libertas* in 1888 had said that this doctrine leads "to social atheism." These are fundamental truths, like all those that we recall here. One cannot deny them without bearing an utterly great responsibility for such a denial.

To prefer freedom to truth is obviously to favor license, the source of all disorders. Thenceforth, *true freedom disappears*, for true freedom only exists when it prefers, above itself, the truth that is its foundation, as the good is a *true good* only if it is *founded upon truth*, and the truth upon reality, that is, upon being and the nature of things. *Truth* consists in *affirming what is and denying what is not*. Truth is a property of being. Without it, there is neither a true good, nor a true freedom for choosing the true good in preference to evil, which is only an apparent good. "Nothing is willed unless it is first known." The freedom of choosing evil comes from the defectibility of the created will. God, who is sovereignly free, is incapable of sin by His very nature.

His Holiness Pius XII said (on November 11, 1948) to the delegates of the International Congress of the European Union of Federalists: "There was a time when Europe formed in its unity a compact whole... Now, the soul of this unity was Religion, which permeated into the very depths of the whole of Christian society. *From the time that the culture detached itself from religion, this unity disintegrated.* In the long run, pursuing its slow but continual progress like an oil stain, *irreligion has*

---

29.   See Denzinger, nos. 2890ff.

penetrated more and more into public life, and above all else, it is to this that the continent owes its tears, its malaise, and its anxiety. *Therefore, if Europe wishes to emerge from this situation, ought it not reestablish in itself the bond between religion and civilization?"*

Therefore, the principal freedom that we must defend is that of doing our duty, above all, our duty toward God, a duty that is founded on the rights of God, our principle and our end.

His Eminence Cardinal Gerlier, at the reopening of the Catholic Faculties of Lyon in November 1951, after having recalled a recent Declaration of the French Bishops and Archbishops, said, in defense of Christian schools, "Do not ask us—for we will never do it—to abandon the requests that simply intend to safeguard the *imprescriptible right of souls,"* above all *the right of doing their duty before God and of tending toward their final end.*

To bring our reflections here to a close, we must say something so as to avoid a misunderstanding in these matters. By losing sight of the rights of the Truth and of God, the Supreme Truth and the Sovereign Good, *some have often enough abused the distinction between thesis and hypothesis.* It has been said, *"The thesis* of the rights of God and of the obligations of society before Him is doubtlessly true in itself. Indeed, we must teach it in theology courses like a speculative truth. However, concretely, we must act according to *the hypothesis* of the freedom of all forms of worship, which is the only course of action practiced today, and we must draw every possible advantage from it."

From this perspective, *the thesis* of the rights of God, man's Last End, *becomes a purely speculative and practically negligible ideal.* This would lead to a very great error.

In reality, *the thesis* concerning the rights of God, the Supreme Truth and man's Final End, is not a purely speculative ideal. Rather, *it enunciates for us a primordial duty and the end that one must not cease to pursue,* namely, the true religion must be acknowledged by all, not only individually, but also socially, and this is sovereignly important for salvation and for not being turned away from it.

However, in order to arrive at this end, we must indeed consider the circumstances, and, consequently, *in the current circumstances,* which leave so much to be desired, prudence tells us that we should *tolerate one evil in order to avoid a greater one*, though all the while continuing to tend toward the end to be obtained, instead of being turned away from it. These are truths that are so elementary that one is not permitted to ignore them.

Otherwise, one ends by practically allowing the neutrality of the State, neutrality of schooling, and *a limitless freedom of conscience*. In following this route, *society as such would become radically irreligious and atheist*. To accord the same rights to the worst errors and to the highest truth is manifestly to deny the specific rights of the latter.

Also, on account of how the distinction between thesis and hypothesis has been abused, many theologians prefer to distinguish between the *end* that must always be pursued *and the means that are opportune here and now* for arriving at it in the current, infelicitous circumstances. It is only a question of prudence and not of doctrine, and the Church chose this course of action in her Concordats, without for all that admitting the liberal doctrine on this matter.

Thus, Leo XIII said in the Encyclical *Immortale Dei*:

> The Church, indeed, deems it unlawful to place the various forms of divine worship on *the same footing* as the true religion, but does not, on that account, condemn those rulers who, for the sake of securing some great good or of hindering some great evil, *allow* patiently custom or usage to be a kind of sanction for each kind of religion having its place in the State.[30]

Civil toleration is not the same thing as approval. An immeasurable distance separates the two. One can legitimately tolerate (but not will) an evil in order to avoid a greater one. Providence itself does this, but this Divine permission is never an approbation. An abyss separates the two, like that separating the most elevated good from the most perverse

---

30. Leo XIII, *Immortale Dei*, no. 36 (Denzinger, no. 3176).

TRANSLATOR'S NOTE: The text cited above is taken from the official Vatican translation, adding Fr. Garrigou-Lagrange's emphases in italics. His French reads: "If the Church judges that it is not permitted for one to grant the same *rights* to different cults and to the true religion, she does not, for that, condemn the heads of States that for some great good or to avoid an evil patiently *tolerate* the fact that room is made in the city for different religions."

evil. God, who has permitted or tolerated the sin of the demon, punishes the demon eternally.

One absolutely must maintain *the efficacious intention of the end to be attained*, an intention without which there can be neither rectitude, nor efficacy in one's choice of the means and in their execution. Only in this way are *the authority of God and the freedom of man* maintained in the harmony needed in order for the latter to differ from that *license* which leads to the ruin of temporal society and to the eternal death of souls. Here, a kind of poorly conceived "irenicism," thoughtlessly engaged in, could utterly distort one's judgment.

The Church has always proceeded in the way that we have come to call *fortiter et suaviter*, in accord with the subordination of ends. Thus, despite the greatest difficulties, the saints have proceeded in like manner in order to "restore all things in Christ" (Eph. 1:10) so that the "rule of God may come" not only into the hearts of the faithful, but into the human society whose Author is God, just as He is the Author of individual men. Thus, in particular, Blessed Pius X proceeded with a lofty wisdom, a great firmness, and in a perfectly disinterested manner.

Fr. Lacordaire understood well these rights of the truth when, after Lamennais' condemnation, he wrote in the conclusion of his *Considerations of the Philosophical System of M. de Lamennais*:

> I asked myself how a philosophy, whose vice I perceive so clearly today, had for so long held my reason in suspense. Upon reflection, I came to realize that fighting against an intellect superior to mine, and wishing *to fight alone* against it, it was impossible that I not be defeated. For the truth is not a self-sufficient auxiliary for reestablishing the equilibrium of forces. Otherwise, error would never triumph over the truth. *Therefore, the world needs a power that sustains weak intellects against strong ones, delivering them from the most terrible oppression: oppression of the mind [esprit]… I have learned from my own experience that the Church is the liberator of the human mind [esprit]… Neither peace nor freedom is possible outside the truth.*[31]

---

31. H.-D. Lacordaire, *Considérations sur le système philosophique de M. de Lammenais* (Paris: Derivaux, 1834), p. 201.

Léon Ollé Laprune said the same in *The Christian Vitality*:

If one practices the disastrous maxim of liberalism, "*Don't interfere with that action, let it pass*," on the pretext of intellectual largess, there comes to be *a growing misunderstanding of the value of the truth: in insecure minds a so-called charitable tendency not to contradict anyone and to leave everyone play with fire* and at last, in minds that are weak and soft, *a disposition to judge that everything can be held* and, moreover, that he who says, "I do not believe; I cannot believe," is more than half excused.[32]

Thus does one lose sight of the value of truth and that of true freedom.

A great woman who brought back to faith many unbelievers in a very cultivated milieu of Paris said, "I am struck by the fact that unbelievers experience more sympathy for persons having profound faith [*les êtres de foi profonde*] than for those whose convictions are flexible and utilitarian... However, the indomitable affirmation must be enveloped in the most intelligent sympathy, the most lively and delicate charity."[33]

To accord the same rights to error and truth is to deny the specific right of the latter, and one ultimately ends up foolishly according the worst errors the same rights as are accorded to the loftiest truths that are indispensable to society and to the salvation of souls. Therefore, we obviously must maintain the rights of the truth and reconcile it, as have the saints, with the requirements of charity.

In the saints, whoever they are, we find a *strong love of the truth and of justice* alongside *a great charity and mercy* for the lost and sinners. However, this all exists *without then falling into liberalism*, for the latter retains affinities with *indifferentism*, which is irreconcilable with supernatural love for God and souls. These saints are those who, in different eras, constitute *the vanguard of the Church* from the true supernatural perspective, which is that of living faith illuminated by the gifts of the Holy Spirit.

---

32. Léon Ollé Laprune, *La vitalité chrétienne* (Paris: Perrin, 1901), pp. 41ff.
33. Elisabeth Leseur, *Journal et pensées de chaque jour* (Paris: J. de Gigord, 1920), p. 162.

From this traditional perspective, we can avoid two deviations that are contrary to one another: sectarianism and indifferentism. In the middle and above these two contrary deviations, we find a summit where *absolute firmness of faith* is reconciled with *the radiation of charity*. These two theological virtues are like the two arcs of a gothic arch which mutually support each other. *They must be united very intimately* in us *so that the firmness of faith never degenerates into sectarian rigidity* and so that *charity* toward our neighbor *never degenerates into a form of culpable weakness and opportunism. This firmness of faith and this goodness of charity* are united *in the ardor of one and the same zeal,* namely, *zeal for the glory of God and the salvation of souls.* All the saints provide us with examples of it. This zeal is what attracts and converts those who seek the truth and who are delivered by it. The reign of error can be only transitory; the truth is what will ultimately triumph, indeed, God Himself, the First Truth. *One can do a true good to a sinner only by detesting the sin; one can only heal minds [esprits] from error through an utterly firm and strong love of the Divine Truth,* which alone can unite intellects and hearts.

* * *

CHAPTER 6

On Royal Government

In an era when politics is barely considered as being a virtue any longer, as being a form of prudence ordered to the promotion of the common good of the multitude, but is, instead, held to be the art of compromising for the sake of success, in order to safeguard the interests of a party, often by oppressing the elite among the citizens and by working to the ruin of a country, much benefit can be drawn from the publication of a translation of St. Thomas's *De regimine principum*, at least of the first book and of the first four chapters of the second book, which were certainly written by him.[1]

The "Common Doctor" of the Church ascends here to the first principles of social and political life. He first recalls the profound reason explaining why man is a *social being*. It is one of his properties, one that is deduced from his definition: *rational animal*. The least of intellects, man's intellect at first attains its object only in a very vague [*confuse*] and general manner, and ordinarily, without the help of a master, it would not reach the forms of knowledge [*aux connaissances*] needed for a somewhat-developed intellectual life, not even for the first theorems of geometry, which the surveyor uses in his activities. The young Pascal is cited as being a genius for having discovered them by his own effort without anyone's assistance.

"Man," says St. Thomas, "naturally knows what he needs for living, but only in general. Thus, he can, by his reason, by means of universal principles, arrive at a knowledge of the particular things necessary for his life. However, by his own reason, a solitary man could not attain all these kinds of things. Therefore, men must live in numbers in order to help each other, devoting themselves to various occupations, in relation to the diversity of their talents, for example, one to medicine, another to this, another to that" (ch. 1). This is not a [mere] "social contract" freely consented to. It represents a necessary consequence of our nature. Consequently, social authority, without which life in society would be impossible, comes from God, the Author of human nature, although it falls to men to designate the person or people who will hold power.

* * *

The purpose of [s]ociety thus constituted is the common good, which is superior to the proper good of each person (whatever individualism may say about it) but which nevertheless must not absorb it (as communism claims). "This common good of the multitude is greater and more divine than that of an individual" (ch. 9). It is peace, the tranquility of order in the city or the nation.

This common good is not only a *useful* good, like that pursued by the art of a cook, a tailor, a clockmaker, or a doctor. It is a *fitting good* [*bien honnête*], which has value by itself, by the moral order that it implies, independent even of the pleasure and the material usefulness [*utilités*] that result from it.

This fitting good is able to specify not only an *art*, but a *virtue* and even eminent virtues: the prudence of heads of state, the political prudence necessary for every citizen at least for voting well, legal or social justice, and equity. St. Thomas treated each of these virtues in his *Summa theologiae* in II-II, q. 50, a. 1 and a. 2; q. 58, a. 7; q. 120, aa. 1 and 2. And these articles show the full scope of the doctrine exposited in the *De regimine principum*.

This *fitting good*, the object of these superior virtues, is, like these virtues, subordinated to religion, to the worship owed to God, and to

---

1.   TRANSLATOR's NOTE: See Jean-Pierre Torrell, *Saint Thomas Aquinas*, vol. 1: *The Person and His Work*, trans. Robert Royal (Washington, DC: The Catholic University of America Press, 2005), pp. 169–71.

the theological (or, properly divine) virtues, which unite us to God and thus dispose us to the life of eternity.

Consequently, a government (*regimen*) is good to the degree that it succeeds at promoting the common good of the multitude, by maintaining unity and harmony in a society according to the natural subordination of ends. By contrast, it is wicked if it pursues a particular good opposed to the common good and thus begets discord.

Now, in order to tend toward a unique end, above all when it is superior and difficult to realize in the midst of many causes of division, there must be unity in direction and consistency. This unity multiplies powers tenfold by making them converge toward the same end. Thus, every government derives its strength from its unity, and the latter must be strengthened, as is well known, as soon as a people is menaced by its external or internal enemies. By contrast, when consistency is lacking, as much in internal politics as in external politics, when ministers begin [their rule] by undoing the work of their predecessors, a country will quickly move toward its ruin.

"Consequently," says St. Thomas (ch. 3), "monarchy is the best of governments," the most unified, the most durable, that which is the strongest for promoting the common good; "monarchy," he says in the same place, "is better than the aristocratic regime and the latter is better than a republican form of government." The same doctrine is maintained in the *Summa theologiae* where it is said, in *ST* I, q. 103, a. 3, in relation to the governing of the universe, "*Optima gubernatio est quae fit per unum.*" The best government is that of one alone. This is so because to govern is to direct a group of subjects towards an end (or, a good). Now, the good presupposes unity, as Boethius proves by showing that, just as all beings desire their own good, so too do all desire the unity without which they would not subsist. Indeed, we see that everything, to the degree that it is, is loath to allow itself to be divided, and its dissolution always comes from some defect or corruption. Also, that to which the intention of him who governs the multitude tends is unity or peace. Now, that which is one is what *of itself* causes unity. Indeed, the many cannot unite various elements and make them agree among themselves unless they themselves are united in some manner. Therefore, that which of itself is one can be a cause of unity better than the many that stand in need of being united. This is why the multitude is best governed by one alone than by many.[2]

Granted, as he says in the current work (ch. 3), in virtue of the principle *optimi corruptio pessima*, tyranny is worse than oligarchy, which represents the degeneration of aristocratic power, and oligarchy is worse than democracy, which represents, according to St. Thomas's terminology, the alteration or corruption of the republic.

The wrongdoings of tyranny are nonetheless carefully noted (ch. 3) in the spiritual order as well as in the temporal order:

> Those who aspire to command rather than contribute to the general interest instead paralyze any development in their subjects. Every superiority in the subjects gives the ruler the suspicion of some detriment being caused to their iniquitous domination. Tyrants suspect the good more than the wicked, and the virtue of another person always seems dreadful to them. Tyrants apply themselves to stifling in their subjects the awakening of this grandeur of soul, the fruit of virtue, which would prevent them from bearing the yoke of their unjust domination.

Nevertheless, St. Thomas adds (ch. 5) that if, in becoming tyrannical, the government of one alone nevertheless does not set itself disproportionately against the entire multitude, *it is still preferable to the others*. Collective government, as soon as discord is introduced into it, turns, perhaps more often, in fact, to oppression. Therefore, this means that it is more advantageous to live under a king. It is the best regime. We find the same conclusion in *Summa contra gentiles*, bk. 4, ch. 76, no. 4, with regard to the Church's government.

It is important only to deprive the monarchy of degenerating into a tyranny. To that end, St. Thomas says (ch. 6), the royal power should be tempered. This idea is developed in *ST* I-II, q. 105, a. 2, where it is shown that below the king there should be an aristocracy whose

---

2. TRANSLATOR'S NOTE: In the original, there is an end quote here. It appears that everything after the Latin quote is intended to be a translation of *ST* I, q. 103, a. 3. I have followed the French as it stands and have not marked off the text with quotes.

members are elected by the people and can be chosen from among the people themselves.

* * *

In *ST* I-II, q. 95, a. 4, St. Thomas, enumerates the different regimes and the way laws are instituted in each:

1. Monarchy and constitutions of princes;
2. Aristocracy and decisions of wise men, or decrees of the senate [*sénatus-consultes*];
3. Oligarchy and praetorian right;
4. Democracy and plebiscite;
5. Tyranny without justice and without true laws.

After this, he adds, "However, there is a certain regime made from these mixed together, which is best: and according to this we have the law 'sanctioned by the distinguished members of society [*maiores natu*] along with the people,' as Isidore says in *Etymologies*, bk. 5, ch. 10." In his commentary, Cajetan interprets this last phrase as meaning that, although monarchy is the best of regimes, the mixed regime, which, next to the king, makes room for aristocracy and for representatives of the people, is better not *according to the notion of a regime and without qualification*, but rather, for the good dispositions of the parts and in the order of purely human things.

Indeed, it is fitting that the government be officially informed of the variety of needs and interests of different branches of commerce, industry, agriculture, the arts, and even of the various sciences, including among them the moral and political sciences, without forgetting the eternal interests of religion. For, in the end, peace, which every government must wish to realize and maintain, is the result of the social life ruled in accord with all the points of interest that we just mentioned. The COMMON GOOD, which St. Thomas expresses often enough by the words BENE VIVERE, is not only the order of the economic life, but also the order of what he calls *vita secundum virtutem*, life according to virtue. This common good is the harmony of social life in all its amplitude and elevation; it is social life in accord with virtue, above all in accord with wisdom, prudence, and justice, subordinated to religion, which constantly reminds us that God is man's final end.

This is why under the *ancien régime* in France, the interests of different classes of society and of different regions were represented by the corporations and their delegates, by the Estates Provincial and the Estates General, the assembly of the clergy, the nobility, and the third estate.

Finally, in order that the monarchical regime not degenerate into a tyranny, the king must preserve a lofty idea of the power that comes to him from God. Also, St. Thomas strongly emphasizes the virtues which the king must have. They are, first of all, prudence (*prudentia regnativa*), justice, and equity, all ordered to the common good. But there is also grandeur of soul. The king must be a magnanimous man, who is elevated above desire, not only sensuous desire and the desire for riches, but above the desire for glory and honors. Besides, these honors would not suffice to repay him for the grave concerns of his office (ch. 7). The king, with a great spirit of faith, must await his recompense from God (ch. 8), and only the possession of God could render him truly and fully happy.

According to Scripture, prudent and just kings merit receiving an eminent recompense in the next life, for a greater virtue is required for governing a kingdom than for directing a family or directing oneself, and St. Thomas loves to cite the expression of Bias, "Power reveals the man" and shows what his virtue is worth. A Christian king who works to promote the temporal common good, subordinating it to the spiritual and supernatural good of souls, therefore merits a great recompense in eternity, and hence, here below, his subjects' profound affection, as well as their loyal and devoted attachment up to the point of sacrificing their lives if necessary. In this way, his power is strengthened, and peace, the tranquility of order, is maintained so that all may go about their work, accomplish their duties, and follow their destiny through the knowledge and love of God.

* * *

Such are the general lines of the part of this work that was written by St. Thomas's own hand. In order to understand this teaching aright, above all in relation to political prudence, one must bear in mind what is written in *ST* II-II, q. 47, on the subject of PRUDENCE in general, the RECTITUDE OF INTENTION that it requires, and its three acts: the COUNSEL that begins the deliberation, the PRACTICAL JUDGMENT that terminates it, and the COMMAND or *imperium* which presides over the execution of the thing decided.

COUNSEL considers the various means capable of conducting one to an end, and here it is important to envision means that are quite different from one another, so as then to knowingly judge what is truly the best. One must not forget that this best means is not always what first comes to one's mind; it often evades the common man's consideration. Consequently, even the most perspicacious and most informed head of state needs to have at his side a council composed of men who are superior and of greatly varied competence. They should propose to him opinions that are quite different from one another so as to see well the various sides of each problem to be resolved and to weigh the *pro* and *contra* as is fitting.

However, he must then rise from this multiplicity of opinions to the UNITY OF PRACTICAL JUDGMENT, which discerns, among the various means proposed as truly useful, that which is the best *hic et nunc*. Here, it is important not to jeopardize, through interminable discussions among parties, the unity and rectitude of one's PRACTICAL JUDGMENT. It is important to safeguard, as we said above, consistency in internal and external politics, and not only for a short period but throughout the entire history of a people, who must remain faithful to its past and proper genius so that it may preserve the treasure of its traditions and of its life.

To arrive at this unity in one's practical judgment, at consistency in the direction of internal and external affairs, and above all to maintain the efficacy of one's COMMAND, which is the third act of PRUDENCE, we must recall what St. Thomas says in the current work: The order of agents corresponds to the order of ends, and to attain this superior end, which is the common good of a people, to maintain its unity and harmony in the midst of so many causes of division, one must have recourse to a superior direction that is truly unified and persevering.

Moreover, let us note that the *imperium* or COMMAND, which directs the execution of the previously chosen means, proceeds in the opposite direction of DELIBERATION. Instead of descending from the consideration of the END to then consider the subordinate MEANS, all the way down to the least of the means involved, the command begins by applying these least means, then gradually elevating itself to superior means capable of realizing or obtaining the end pursued: *the end is first in intention and last in execution*. From this perspective, one understands that in the order of execution, not in that of intention, one can say, "politics first"[3]: in order for social life to be possible, the city or country must be inhabitable and disruptors must be expelled or made to submit by force.

Likewise, one must recall, as the Common Doctor teaches,[4] that PRUDENCE, in its three acts, requires rectitude of appetite or right intention; that is to say, it requires the MORAL VIRTUES, which rectify us vis-à-vis the principal subordinated moral ends: justice, fortitude, temperance, along with their various annexed virtues, including religion, humility, penitence, magnanimity, patience, and meekness. Nobody can be truly prudent without these virtues. Without them and without the tact that they give, one easily confuses humility and weakness, magnanimity and pride, meekness and softness, firmness and rigidity. Likewise, without a right and efficacious intention of moral ends, one cannot efficaciously choose and apply the means capable of making us attain them, nor can one arrive at the right and efficacious *imperium* which is the principal act of prudence.

Now, if such is the case for prudence in the conduct of private life, for all the more reason can the same be said when it is a question of what is more difficult, governing an entire people. Therefore, political prudence cannot exist without justice, equity, fortitude, and the other moral virtues which provide the equilibrium of the political life just as they do in the moral life. Now, these true virtues are rare, although many claim they have them, says St. Thomas (ch. 7) in recalling with Sallust that "ambition has compelled numerous mortals to falsity," to feigning, or to hypocrisy. Consequently, every regime that favors the

---

3. TRANSLATOR'S NOTE: The expression "*politique d'abord*" is that of Charles Maurras and *L'Action Française*. See the remarks above in "The Divine Requirements of the Final End in Political Matters," as well as in the Introduction to Part III.
4. See *ST* I-II, q. 57, a. 5, ad 3; q. 58, a. 4 and a. 5; II-II, q. 4, a. 1.

ambitions of demagogues who flatter the people in order to come to power, leads to political pharisaism and to ruin, for a durable union exists only in truth and justice.

This is why, if it is to last, the republican regime presupposes great virtue and great competence in the subjects who are called to participate, through elections, in the direction of the country. In the case of a canton whose interests are very simple, or a federation of cantons, as in Switzerland, such matters present no great difficulty. However, in the case of a populous nation, with very complex interests, having not only an economic life but also a superior artistic and intellectual life, which is a nation in the midst of multiple causes of division, must safeguard its unity and the continuity of its traditions—then, the difficulty increases terribly. How are we to find in its subjects, a good number of whom are peasants or workers, the competence and virtue necessary for choosing men capable of responding to the difficult questions that are posed, ones that often baffle jurists, financiers, or diplomats of the first order? The election will most often designate upstarts, ambitious, incapable men, who will become ministers when there is need for someone like Colbert, Vauban, or Louvois.

From this perspective, a disciple of St. Thomas chose to summarize his doctrine on the question of the regime by saying, "The perfect regime, according to the notion of a regime, namely, monarchy, is the regime of the imperfect; whereas, the imperfect regime, namely, democracy, is the regime of the perfect."

Democracy is an imperfect regime, as a regime (*in ratione regiminis* [according to the formal notion of what a regime is]), on account of the lack of unity and continuity in the direction of internal and external affairs. Hence, this regime is suitable only for perfect people already capable of directing themselves, virtuous and competent enough to express themselves as is fitting concerning the very complicated problems on which the life of a great people depends. But it is always true to say, as St. Thomas noted, that such virtues and competent authorities are extremely rare, and democracy, presupposing such perfection in its subjects, cannot give it to them. From this perspective, we here have in the political order something that is somewhat like what quietism is in spirituality: It presupposes that man has arrived at adult age or at the state of perfection, whereas he is perhaps still only a child, and treating him as though he were perfect, it does not give him what is necessary for him to truly become such.

Since true virtue, united to true competence, is a rare thing among men, and since most of them are incapable of governing and need to be led, the regime that is best suited to them is that which can supplement their imperfection. On account of the unity, continuity, and efficacy of its direction toward an end that is difficult to realize, monarchy is this *regimen perfectum in ratione regiminis*, above all a tempered monarchy, always attentive to different forms of national activity. Better than democracy or than the feudal regime, it assures the internal and external peace of a great nation, and enables it to endure a long time.

Such is St. Thomas's doctrine, as the present work shows quite clearly. The importance of these ideas is clear to all those who reckon that the internal and external peace of a people is one of the principal conditions needed for its moral and religious life. This is not an indifferent affair; truth exists in the political order, just as it does in the moral and metaphysical orders; and if one cannot always demonstrate it with evidence, it is important to draw as near as possible to it. Indeed, the durable union of intellects and of wills is realizable only in the truth, without which there can well be, according to majority rule [*la loi du nombre*], a collection of egoisms always ready to demand a liberty that degenerates into license; and without such truth, *justice and the common good*, which are the principle and end of the social order, cannot exist.

* * *

However, it will be said that all of this is doubtlessly true, but St. Thomas wrote at the time of St. Louis, when France received the benefits of a very Christian monarchy, tempered by a conservative, landed aristocracy and by the organization of the towns, which watched over the interests of the people in the different regions. Since then, the times have changed. Many peoples, like France, live in democracy. They consider universal suffrage as representing a kind of conquest, and, despite the disadvantages of such suffrage (disadvantages that are clear, indeed, only to the elite), they are not about to give it up. Consequently, the *de facto* question is much more complex than that of principles; there is room for flexibility on the margin when passing from theory to practice, from abstract considerations to directions that are opportune and efficacious *here and now.*

Quite certainly, this is all true, and indeed, this is what explains the great prudence and forbearance needed in these questions, as the concordats show; this is also why an attempt at a dictatorship in a country, even when many desire it, ought to be attempted only when one is sure [of its need and possibility of success], for otherwise, it could do more harm than good.

In any case, what is obviously important is that we return to an attentive consideration of the principles that St. Thomas enunciated in this treatise, for a good number of them apply to every legitimate regime. These principles, relative to the common good and to its subordination to man's final end, are those that are opposed to the pagan conception of the Modern State, descending from the Revolution, to this State that wishes to elevate itself above the most natural of institutions like the family, in order to enslave them, often claiming to impose a blind obedience to unjust and impious decrees that are laws in name only.

The Sovereign Pontiff [Pius XI], in his last Encyclical on the Kingship of Christ, said precisely against this anti-Christian and anti-natural conception of the State:

Men gathered together in society are not less under Christ's power than are individuals. The private good and the common good have the same source... Would that leaders of nations therefore not refuse to render their public homages of respect and obedience to Christ's power by themselves and by the people, if they wish, in safeguarding their authority, to promote and increase the prosperity of their countries!...

"With God and Jesus Christ having been excluded from legislation and public affairs, and authority no longer drawing its origin from God, but from men," we bemoaned at the beginning of Our Pontificate, "It happens that the very foundations of authority were overthrown as soon as the fundamental reason for the right of one group to command and of the duty of the others to obey were suppressed…" This is why, if men were to recognize Christ's royal power individually and in public, incredible benefits would result from such recognition, benefits that immediately permeate civil society, such as a just freedom, order and tranquility, concord and peace.[5]

These represent the very foundations of this doctrine, without which no form of government is durable, a doctrine that the *De regimine principum* sets forth excellently; and it is by returning to these principles that one will work efficaciously for the purification of intellects, without which any restoration of the social order is impossible.

---

5.   Pius XI, *Quas primas*, no. 18.

TRANSLATOR'S NOTE: The French text provided by Fr. Garrigou-Lagrange slightly differs from the current official French text of the encyclical. The equivalent text from the official English edition is as follows. (Note that I have included slightly more text so as to increase the readability of the selection.)

"Nor is there any difference in this matter between the individual and the family or the State; for all men, whether collectively or individually, are under the dominion of Christ. In him is the salvation of the individual, in him is the salvation of society… If, therefore, the rulers of nations wish to preserve their authority, to promote and increase the prosperity of their countries, they will not neglect the public duty of reverence and obedience to the rule of Christ.…

What We said at the beginning of Our Pontificate concerning the decline of public authority, and the lack of respect for the same, is equally true at the present day. 'With God and Jesus Christ,' we said, 'excluded from political life, with authority derived not from God but from man, the very basis of that authority has been taken away, because the chief reason of the distinction between ruler and subject has been eliminated. The result is that human society is tottering to its fall, because it has no longer a secure and solid foundation.' … When once men recognize, both in private and in public life, that Christ is King, society will at last receive the great blessings of real liberty, well-ordered discipline, peace and harmony."

* * *

PART IV

Garrigou pugnans:
Critical Philosophical Essays

* * *

INTRODUCTION TO PART IV

In this section, I have gathered a number of texts where Fr. Garrigou-Lagrange takes on the style of the "scholastic pugilist," fighting against a number of modern figures, as well as certain trends in early-twentieth-century thought that he held to be pernicious. A number of these essays date from late in Fr. Garrigou-Lagrange's career. Many of them are slightly simplified "echoes" of lengthier treatments of these topics in his earlier works, such as *God: His Existence and His Nature*, *Sens Commun*, *Le réalisme du principe de finalité*, *De revelatione*, and *Synthèse thomiste* (known to English readers in the slightly shorter form of *Reality: A Thomistic Synthesis*).

As in many other places throughout Fr. Garrigou-Lagrange's oeuvre, we here feel the attraction of theology speeding him along through philosophical questions. Again, I am offering this merely as an interpretive key, albeit one of my own making: Very often, "Garrigou the philosopher" is greatly comforted and strengthened by the intellectual light of faith and supernatural theology. He strides with confidence where a "methodologically pure" philosopher would undertake lengthy dialectical studies and textual criticism. Having spent many hours with his works, I can say with great certitude that he was aware of the difference between theological recapitulation of philosophical themes and the purely philosophical posture of mind. However, for his own part, he sometimes slips in and out of these *legitimate* genres, and one feels this quite strikingly in texts like those gathered here. Yet, who can blame him? Matters of great importance are at stake, as he notes in the final chapter of this section: "This does not represent a form of discovery. Rather, it is an aberration. Indeed, this is all the more clear when one considers its relationship with loftier problems such as the immutability of Christian dogma, the life of grace, and the life of eternity." Philosophical errors can indeed lead to foundational damage in the mind's (obedientially) receptive capacity for supernatural revelation.

The first chapter in this section, "The Thomist Critique of the Cartesian *Cogito*," provides a clear-headed analysis of how the Thomist should approach the great father of modern thought, René Descartes. Granted, today, we must be sure to contextualize Descartes's work both in terms of his own diachronic intellectual development[1] and within the context of his immediate intellectual milieu.[2] However, when it comes to basic ideas, Fr. Garrigou-Lagrange presents the primary "red flag" that the claims of the *Discourse on Method* and the *Meditations* should raise before a Thomist's eyes: *Neglect of the principle of non-contradiction undermines all the supposed certitude one would have in the insight loudly proclaimed by the mathematician who feared the evil genius: Cogito ergo sum. No matter all my doubts, I think and, therefore, exist.*

In this essay, Fr. Garrigou-Lagrange reflects at length on this central point, noting how significant figures in the history of the Thomist school (Antoin Goudin, Salvatore Maria Roselli, Tommaso Maria Zigliara, and Édouard Hugon) critiqued Descartes precisely by appealing to the true first principle: the principle of non-contradiction. Along the same lines as those taken by Fr. Garrigou-Lagrange, the response remains quite similar: without the principle of non-contradiction, the *cogito* may also be a *non-cogito*, and the self that is known through the

---

1.   For a recent study, see Peter K. Machamer and J. E. McGuire, *Descartes' Changing Mind* (Princeton: Princeton University Press, 2009).

2.   See Rogier Ariew, *Descartes and the Last Scholastics* (New York: Cornell University Press, 1999); *Descartes Among the Scholastics* (Leiden: Brill, 2011); *Descartes and the First Cartesians* (Oxford: Oxford University Press, 2015). For a brief treatment, with a slightly outdated but helpful bibliography, see Marjorie Grene, *Descartes Among the Scholastics* (Marquette, WI: Marquette University Press, 1991). Also, see the recent translation of Gilson's first study on the scholastic roots to Descartes thought, Étienne Gilson, *Theology and the Cartesian Doctrine of Freedom*, trans. James G. Colbert (South Bend, IN: St. Augustine's Press, 2018).

supposed direct insight of Cartesian thought will ultimately sink down into the endless stream of undifferentiated, ever-changing becoming. It may seem to be a minor point, but at the level of first principles, it is a response with significant and devastating consequences. A theme that we will see emerge throughout this section thus can be seen in our first essay in this section: One of the great intellectual "sins" of modernity is its lack of concern for the devastating consequences of underrating (or even, so to speak, contradicting) the principle of non-contradiction.

Thus, the brief second chapter, "The Empiricist Skepticism of David Hume: A *reductio ad absurdum* in Defense of Traditional Realism," presents a similar kind of rebuke to Hume's own empiricist skepticism. Fr. Garrigou-Lagrange does not here intend to present a detailed historical and textual study of Hume. Rather, he wishes to strike at the heart of the nominalism that is central to the latter's philosophy.[3] The phenomenalism and incipient positivism in an outlook such as Hume's undercuts the basic essential fixity of our knowledge (and, indeed, of reality), trading it for an *absolute* form of ever-evolving thought. None of the first principles can hold in such an outlook, and ultimately, one wonders how one can assert the positions of phenomenalism without falling into self-contradiction. Nothing remains fixed—not even non-fixity! (For non-fixity could at once be and not be non-fixity.) Nonetheless, we treat the world as though basic clusters of essential meaning are basic data in our knowledge and investigation. Without this, no valid form of positive science would be possible, for we would never have a stable *what* that we are seeking after. Granted, the philosophy of science requires a great deal more for a full defense of such claims. Fr. Garrigou-Lagrange's point, however, remains quite salient: The positions taken by pure phenomenalism or positivism ultimately represent a rejection of the first principles of reason and, thereby, surreptitiously (or, perhaps, openly) represent the denial of the very possibility of philosophy worthy of the name.

---

3.   Indeed, as a Dominican graduate-school classmate of mine quite amusingly once commented, the nominalism of Hume pales in comparison to the much more magnificent, if ultimately wrong-headed, edifice of great Medieval "nominalists" like Ockham and Buridan. The Scotsman's nominalist, my classmate said, is evidence to a great house falling into disrepair over the years, like a great old estate house, slowly falling into disrepair through the vagaries of history and politico-economic change.

The next chapter, "Hegelian Dialectic and Thomist Metaphysics," presents a response to the great post-Kantian whose influence remains ubiquitous throughout western culture, albeit as filtered through all of the various "Hegelianisms" that sprang up in reaction to Hegel's often-turgid prose. Fr. Garrigou-Lagrange's article presents a very brief summary of one possible reading of Hegel's account of history and the self-development of "Spirit" (or "Mind") throughout history. He reads Hegel primarily in a quasi-pantheistic, immanentistic sense, wherein God makes Himself in History—as if History were the continuous becoming of Spirit marching onward toward its full manifestation. Fr. Garrigou-Lagrange's own conflicts with certain vitalists such as Bergson and Le Roy[4] were doubtless of no small influence in this once-common reading of Hegel. However, he also reads (quite understandably and justifiably) Pope Pius IX's *Syllabus errorum* as opening with an anti-Hegelian salvo, a condemnation of great importance for subsequent ecclesiastical history, given the eventual relativizing claims raised during the modernist crisis. In contrast to this ever-changing outlook which merges being and non-being in the rolling tide of becoming and a ceaseless evolution without any fixity, Fr. Garrigou-Lagrange proposes and briefly defends the first principles of Thomist metaphysics as providing the only sure foundation for a sensible cosmology. As he reflected at greater length elsewhere, we here find ourselves faced with the great pair of choices that determine everything else: on the one hand, the path of the first principles leading to the True God and, on the other, radical absurdity.[5]

In the next chapter, "On Evolutionism and the Distinction between the Natural and Supernatural Orders" Fr. Garrigou-Lagrange returns to the tone of other essays in this text, for while this title likely leads one to think the great Dominican is going to reflect on the metaphysical questions involved in theories of evolution,[6] we actually

---

4. See Garrigou-Lagrange, *Le réalisme du principe de finalité*, pp. 61–94.
5. See Garrigou-Lagrange, *God: His Existence and His Nature*, vol. 2, pp. 436–45.
6. Fr. Garrigou-Lagrange did not devote lengthy reflection to the topic of the contemporary theory of evolution. His primary concern seems to be with evolution*ism* as a metaphysical doctrine which would have that which is *more* come forth from what is *less*, without some elevation by God. When he discusses the topic, he is quite brief, though he explicitly makes room for form of "moderate evolutionism."

find him primarily taking up concerns with the distinction between the natural and the supernatural orders. The theological perspective clearly guides the concerns in this essay. The primary context in the background here seems to be Henri de Lubac's *Surnaturel*,[7] although the more adventurous theories of Fr. Pierre Teilhard de Chardin, S.J., are certainly related to the topics considered herein. In any case, his primary concern herein is to defend the stability of human nature in distinction from the supernaturalized existence that we have through sanctifying grace and divinization. This entails a number of consequences, but the primary point is that if we do not affirm nature clearly enough, we shall never see the lofty character of the supernatural life of grace and of the theological virtues (as well as, he would add if treating the topic in full, the Spirit's gifts and the infused moral virtues). We risk "naturalizing" the supernatural order of mysteries (and, hence, ultimately, God) if we are not clear on this point: "If there is no nature, properly speaking, then neither is there any supernatural order, properly speaking."

As a point of contemporary reflection, I would add that this topic deserves great philosophical expansion, for we most certainly live in an era that gravely lacks a common vocabulary for articulating the shared

---

See Réginald Garrigou-Lagrange, "Verité et immutabilité du dogme," pp. 136–37:

"As regards the problem of evolution, it is important to clearly distinguish the domain of scientific hypotheses proposed for examination (i.e., that of sensible appearances) and the domain of being, which is that of metaphysics, where we must hold that God specially intervened in the production of vegetative life, sense life, and intellectual life and, *a fortiori* in a wholly special way in order to produce the life of grace in man.

"Finally, we absolutely cannot admit that the Incarnation of the Word and the Redemption would be moments in evolution. And if this evolution were explained along the lines of Hegelian metaphysics, which was condemned by the [First] Vatican Council, this would properly speaking be a heresy. Indeed, it would be even more than a heresy. It would be complete apostasy, for the absolute and pantheistic evolutionism of Hegel does not allow *any* Christian dogmas to survive. In denying the True God, who is really and essentially distinct from the world, he denies *all* the revealed mysteries and can only preserve their verbal forms."

Also, see Garrigou-Lagrange, *De Revelatione*, 5th ed., vol. 1, pp. 220–21.

7.   This topic has received masterful treatment in Lawrence Feingold, *The Natural Desire to See God According to St. Thomas and His Interpreters*, 2nd ed. (Naples, FL: Sapientia Press, 2010). Likewise, see *Surnatural: A Controversy at the Heart of Twentieth-Century Thomistic Thought*, ed. Serge-Thomas Bonino (Naples, FL: Sapientia Press, 2007).

and stable nature of the human person.[8] Without this fixity, given its proper ontological foundations, our theological reflection risks being an intermixed miasma of the natural and the supernatural. A clear articulation of the simultaneously fixed- and dynamic-creative character of human *nature* can help to clarify the necessary philosophical anthropology presupposed for a sane and traditional Christian theology. This is what Fr. Garrigou-Lagrange saw quite clearly in this essay, presented at the great University of Salamanca on the seven-hundredth anniversary of its official recognition as a University, even if his reflections ultimately remain pedagogical and somewhat surface-level.

The final chapter in this section, "The Encyclical '*Pascendi*' and Phenomenalism," represents an excellent and brief summary of so much of Fr. Garrigou-Lagrange's thought, which ever moved about within the context that was established by the modernist crisis in the early twentieth century. He was much more than an anti-modernist, but he was indeed that. This essay was written in 1958, on the fiftieth anniversary of Pope St. Pius X's famed anti-modernist encyclical, *Pascendi dominici gregis*.[9] Herein, many of the same principles articulated in this section (as well as in "The Threefold Foundation of Thomist Realism" in the second section above) are restated in light of the anti-modernist encyclical.

Let us draw some inspiration from the more pugilistic side of Fr. Garrigou-Lagrange. Let us also recall, however, that he takes up his pugilism with more charity than is often attributed to him in popular images as being "the sacred monster of Thomism." He is a pugilist precisely because he sees the damning effects of such errors in relation to the supernatural life so dear to any child of God, although uniquely important for a man called, as a son of St. Dominic, to preach the truth of this life. In contrast to what is usually said of him, his primary posture was rarely that of a pugilist fighting against the world and others. His

---

8.   The whole topic of evolution has elicited much discussion among Catholics in recent history. I personally hold that great Thomist strides can be made in the directions indicated in Maritain's late-in-life intuitions indicated in "Toward a Thomist Idea of Evolution," in Jacques Maritain, *Untrammeled Approaches*, trans. Bernard Doering (Notre Dame: University of Notre Dame Press, 1996), pp. 85–131.

9.   See Kerlin, "Réginald Garrigou-Lagrange: Defending the Faith from 'Pascendi dominici gregis' to 'Humani Generis,'" pp. 97–113.

concern was ever with knowledge of first principles, and his great synthetic works bear the mark of this fact. On occasion, however, he did indeed feel the need to directly address what he saw to be basic and fundamental errors being committed, often to the detriment of a sane epistemology and natural theology, thus having disastrous consequences for the life of faith. A devout Catholic philosopher or theologian should never fear the duty of charitably confronting error. Indeed, we should be constantly vigilant for errors to be corrected, for such things not only involve intellectual errors but also the salvation of souls. Granted, it is Christ, not philosophy, who saves, and Fr. Garrigou-Lagrange would quite readily admit that fact. Nonetheless, in a world awash with much philosophical foolishness, it is important to push back with the light of basic principles and primary truths. I hope that this section provides the reader with one particular model for this kind of task.

ORIGINAL TEXTS FOR THIS SECTION

"La critique thomiste du 'Cogito' cartésien." In *Cartesio: nel terzo centenario del Discorso del Metodo*, pp. 393–400. Milano: Vita e Pensiero, 1937.

"Sceptisme empirique de Hume, une preuve par l'absurde du réalisme traditionnel." *Doctor Communis*, Vol. 8 (1955): pp. 149–58.

"Dialectique hégéliene et métaphysique thomiste." *Communicationes IV. Congressus Thomistici Internationalis*, pp. 271–81. Romae: Offic. Libr. Catholici, 1955.

"De evolutionismo et de distinctione Inter ordinem naturalem et ordiinem supernaturalem." In *Actas del Congreso de Ciencias Eclesiasticas 1954, El Evolucionismo en filosofía y en teología*, pp. 227–36. Barcelona-Madrid: J. Flors, 1956.

"L'Encyclique 'Pascendi' et le phénoménisme.' *Divinitas*, Vol. 2 (1958): pp. 143–49.

CHAPTER I

The Thomist Critique of the Cartesian *Cogito*

In this article, we would like to recall the meaning of the *Cogito* according to Descartes's own thought, as well as the criticism which the Thomists have generally registered against it.

I. THE SENSE AND SCOPE OF THE "*COGITO*" ACCORDING TO DESCARTES

In his *Discourse on Method*, Descartes says:

> Having learned, even from the time of my college studies, that nothing can be imagined that would be so strange or so unbelievable that it would not, however, have been said by some philosopher, and then, while travelling, having recognized that all those who have sentiments than are quite contrary to our own are not, for all this, barbarians or savages but, rather, that many such people use reason as well as we do if not better.... I could not choose anyone from among these people whose opinions seemed should be preferred to the opinions held by others, and I found myself, as it were, constrained to strive to lead my own self-conduct by myself.[1]

Later on, he writes:

Thus, given that I desired to turn my attention only to the search for the truth, I thought that I needed to reject, as representing something absolutely false, everything which I thought contained the slightest doubt, so that I might see if, after this, there may not be left remaining in what I believe something which was utterly indubitable... However, I heeded the fact that, while I thus wished to think that everything was false, it was utterly necessary that I, who thought this fact, would be something. And noting that this truth—namely, *I think, therefore I am*—was so firm and so certain that all the most extravagant skeptical suppositions would not be able to shake it, I judged that I could accept it without scruple as being the first principle of philosophy which I was seeking.[2]

Now, is the "*Cogito ergo sum*" the result of discursive reasoning or, on the contrary, an immediate apperception, an intuition of the soul by itself? By looking at Descartes's *Responses to the Second Objections* and at the *Responses to the Objections Raised by Gassendi*, we can see that according to Descartes himself, the "*cogito ergo sum*" is an intuition. In response to Gassendi, he writes: "When you teach a child the elements of geometry, you will not make him understand in general... that *the whole is greater than its parts* if you do not show him particular examples."

As Étienne Gilson remarks on this:

Therefore, Descartes' intention cannot be doubted; it is not generally discussed. However, his critics or historians have often held that, whatever might have been Descartes' own intention, the *Cogito* was nonetheless the outcome of reasoning and could not fail to be such. Cf. Huet, *Censura philos. Cart.*, vol. 1, p. 11: "It is false to say that *I think therefore I am* is known by us through simple vision and not through discursive reasoning."[3]

---

1. Descartes, *Discourse de la méthode*, ed. Étienne Gilson (1930), pt. 2 (p. 16).
2. Ibid., pt. 4 (p. 32); Descartes, *Principes*, bk. 1, ch. 7.
3. Descartes, *Discourse de la méthode*, pt. 2 (p. 294).

Chronologically, in the order of discovery, it is possible that one could say, "I think; therefore, I am," after having said, "Everything that thinks exists." However, it is nonetheless true that, *de iure*, general truths found particular truths, and that the former is what is seen in a given particular example.[4]

* * *

This question becomes even more pressing if we consider the fact that, for Descartes (*Response to the fifth set of objections*), "God did not create only existences but even created essences." He freely created the eternal truths, logical, metaphysical, and geometric truths. "Without falling into blasphemy, one cannot say that the truth of something precedes the knowledge that God has of it, for in God, willing and knowing are one and the same thing, meaning that, *from the very fact that He wills something He therefore knows it, and therefore, only such a thing is true.*"

On April 15, 1630, we find Descartes saying to Mersenne that God would be subject to something, like Jupiter to the Styx, if outside and above Himself there were an order of truths that He would not have created.[5] Therefore, he did not hesitate to say: If the three angles of a triangle are equal to two right angles, and if mountains do not exist without valleys, this is because God has willed things to be such. Henceforth, what remains of the necessity of the principle of contradiction, founded on the opposition of being and non-being and, first of all, on the very nature of God, the First Being?

---

4. This point will be acknowledged if one admits, with St. Thomas (see *ST* I, q. 85, a. 3) that for the senses as for the intellect, more general [*commune*] knowledge precedes that which is less general: "Knowledge of particular things," he says there, "*quoad nos* is prior to knowledge of universals, just as sense knowledge is prior to intellective knowledge. However, both in the case of the senses and that of the intellect, more general [*communis*] knowledge is prior to less general knowledge."

5. "The mathematical truths which you call eternal were established by God and utterly depend on Him, just as much as do other creatures. Indeed, were we to say that these truths are independent from Him, we would thereby speak of God as though we were speaking of a god like Jupiter or Saturn, thus making Him subject to the Styx and to the fates. I pray you not to fear maintain and to proclaim everywhere that God is the one who established these laws in Nature, just as a King establishes laws in his Kingdom" (Letter to Mersenne, April 15, 1630).

Often, people have attempted to attenuate this Cartesian doctrine holding that God freely created eternal truths. However, as Gilson has shown, Descartes's texts on this point are formal in character.[6] Descartes held that the eternal truths were finite in character and, from this perspective something dependent upon the divine freedom. Thus, something that is contradictory for us, like a square circle or a mountain without a valley, is not, for all this, impossible or unrealizable for God. Descartes only makes an exception for the Divine Attributes (for example, God cannot lie) and for a purely formal contradiction, which does not involve the content of a definite essence (for example, "*ut quod factum est sit infactum*," that which has been made cannot have not existed, and creatures that were made by God cannot not depend on Him).[7] This Cartesian doctrine concerning the relationship of metaphysical truths to the divine freedom cannot be separated from the *Cogito*.

II. THE CRITIQUE REGISTERED BY THE THOMISTS

The first objection against the Cartesian *Cogito* which springs to the mind of a disciple of St. Thomas rests on the following words which were often formulated by the Holy Doctor and can be found in *De veritate*, q. 1, a. 1 (*What is truth?*):

I respond that we must say that, just as demonstrated things must ultimately be reduced to some principle that is *per se nota* for the intellect, this holds for the investigation of the nature (*quid est*) of any given thing, for otherwise there would be an infinite regress, leading to the destruction of all science and knowledge of things. *However, that which the intellect first conceives, as it were, as what is most evident* [*notissimum*], that notion *into which all of its conceptions are resolved, is being,* as Avicenna says at the beginning of his

6.   See Descartes, *Discourse de la méthod*, pt. 2 (pp. 335–72, 373). See the letters to Mersenne from May 6, 1630 and May 27, 1638; also, see the letter to Mesland on May 2, 1644; and the sixth response. Also, see Émile Boutroux, *De veritatibus aeternis apud Cartesium* (Paris: Germer Ballière, 1874).

7.   See [Letter to] A. Morus on February 5, 1649, cited by Gilson, in Descartes, *Discourse de la méthode*, pt. 2 (p. 335).

Metaphysics (bk. 1, ch. 9). Whence, all the other conceptions of the intellect are had as involving some kind of addition to being.

Thus, unity, truth, and goodness are indeed general modes of being, which belong to every being; and substance, quantity, quality, action, passion, relation, etc. are the categories of being. The same can be read in the *Summa theologiae*:

> *That which first falls into apprehension is being,* the understanding of which is included in all things that someone can grasp. Therefore, the first indemonstrable principle is that *we cannot affirm and deny* [one and the same thing at the same time from the same perspective] (or: being is not non-being), which is founded on the formal character [*rationem*] of being and non-being. And this principle is the foundation for all the other principles, as the Philosopher says in *Metaphysics*, bk. 4, ch. 3.[8]

Being, the most universal notion, is presupposed by all other notions, and the utterly first principle is that which enunciates what first of all belongs to being, namely, its identity with itself and its opposition to non-being: "Being is being; non-being is non-being. That which is, is; that which is not, is not; yes is yes and no is no. One and the same thing, from the same perspective and at the same time,[9] cannot both be and not be."

This fundamental assertion comes up consistently in Aristotle and also in St. Thomas. The latter says, in *ST* I, q. 5, a. 2: "*Being is the first thing that falls into the intellect's act of conceiving,* for any given thing is knowable on account of the fact that it is in act, as is said in *Metaphysics*, bk. 9, ch. 9. Whence, *being is the proper object of the intellect, and thus also is the first intelligible,* just as sound is the first thing heard." Also see *ST* I, q. 85, a. 5: "Both in the case of the senses and that of the intellect, more general [*communis*] knowledge is prior to less general knowledge."

---

8.   *ST* I-II, q. 94, a. 2.

9.   The word "simul" in the statement of the principle of non-contradiction is either temporal or supra-temporal; thus, making abstraction from time, one can say "Something cannot simultaneously and from one and the same perspective be finite and infinite."

* * *

Thus, following along these same lines, we can easily grasp the Thomist critique of the Cartesian *Cogito*, a critique found in the works of all Thomists writing about this matter from the seventeenth century onward. For example, we can read in Antoine Goudin's *Philosophia iuxta inconcussa tutissima Divi Thomae dogmata*, vol. 4, 11th ed. (Coloniae, 1724), p. 240:

The first complex principle[10] is, "One and the same thing cannot at once be and not be," as we can find in Aristotle, *Metaphysics*, bk. 4, ch. 4, and St. Thomas, *ST* I-II, q. 94, a. 2…

However, Descartes is not to be tolerated here when he commands that the mind, for the time being holding every other exposited principle in doubt, begin its knowledge of things with, "I think," from which it would immediately infer: "Therefore, I am." For, so without arguing about other points [*ut coetera non urgeam*], if the mind were to set aside even our own principle, along with all the others, as something that must remain doubtful, another doubt will remain: whether he who thinks exists or does not. For he could think and, nonetheless, not exist, if it were possible that *one and the same thing could be and not be*. And so, that very principle (or, rather, that very enthymeme) of Descartes rests upon our principle.

Likewise, Salvator M. Roselli, O.P., in his *Summa philosophica*, vol. 5 (Madrid, 1788), p. 9, asks himself whether there is an absolutely first principle which is needed for certain knowledge of reality. He first of all recalls the doctrine admitted by St. Thomas in *ST* I, q. 5, a. 2, concerning being, the intellect's first given, as well as the first principle which must enunciate what first of all belongs to being, namely, its self-identity and opposition to non-being. Then, he provides the following critique of the *Cogito*:

---

10.   Translator's Note: That is, the first principle formed by the second operation of the intellect by which complex enunciations and judgments are formed.

The very first principle of demonstration not only must be *maximally certain and evident* (for all universal, self-evident principles have this in common), nor must it only arise *naturally*, as St. Thomas says—that is, it does not need to be acquired through demonstration but, rather, through a simple perception of the terms, as has been said already—which is something also common to all self-evident principles. Beyond these characteristics, it *must also not presuppose any other truth*, for if it did suppose something else, it would not be the very first principle. Now, the Cartesian utterance, "I think; therefore I am," presupposes other principles, namely: *whatever thinks, is*; *whatever acts, exists*; *action follows on being*; *it is impossible that one and the same thing simultaneously be and not be.*

Indeed, unless these principles were true, I could not infer that I exist from the fact that I think. Hence, that utterance is a demonstration rather than a principle, for it includes the major premise, "Whatever thinks, is," which would not be true if the principles enumerated above were not true. Therefore, the conditions are lacking for the Cartesian utterance to have the character of being an entirely first principle of demonstration. Nor does it deserve to be called a self-evident principle, given that it comes to be known through demonstration and not merely through the perception of its terms.

Later Thomists would speak similarly. For example, among the most recent ones, we find Cardinal Tommaso Zigliara, O.P., saying in his *Summa philosophica*, vol. 1, 8th ed. (1891), 200:

By means of the hypothetical fiction of *an evil genius* which could possibly deceive him, Descartes placed the principle of contradiction in doubt, along with all other principles. Nay, once the principle of contradiction has been placed in doubt, even if only hypothetically, the *"cogito, ergo sum"* itself can be asserted as a certain principle only illogically for, by the very hypothesis in place, I must be in doubt whether I can *simultaneously think and not think, as well as simultaneously whether I exist and do not exist.* Therefore, wherever Descartes may turn himself, he will find himself in open self-contradiction.

Likewise, Édouard Hugon, O.P. wrote in his *Cursus philosophiae thomisticae*, pt. 1, *Logica* (1902), p. 336: "Obviously, the first fact, '*Cogito*,' from which is inferred, 'Therefore, I am,' holds only if it is contradictory to think and not think at the same time, which holds [*est*] from the principle of contradiction." Likewise, see Joseph Gredt, O.S.B., *Elementa philosophiae aristotelico-thomisticae*, vol. 2, 3rd ed. (1922), pp. 53–54. We also wrote, in 1908, in our work, *Le sens commun et la philosphie de l'être* (cf. p. 135 of the 4th edition):

> Descartes and the modern idealists do not wish to admit anything but a subjective form of evidence because, for them, the intellect knows itself before knowing being. It builds its foundation upon the *cogito*, but it could never conclude, "*ergo sum*," without surreptitiously presupposing the ancient axiom: "The object of the intellect is being." Kant and the phenomenalists saw this quite well. Therefore, one would need to be content with saying, "I think therefore I am thinking." And, in fact, this is not certain, for according to his own principles, the idealist does not know *the reality of his action*, but rather, only the representation that he fashions of it for himself, and he would know this reality through his consciousness, without being able to be absolutely certain whether it is indeed real, for if he doubts the objectivity of the principle of identity and of contradiction, as well as its value as a law of being, and if reality can, at bottom, be contradictory (like an utterly causeless becoming which would be its own self-sufficient reason), nothing can assure one that the action that he holds as being real truly is so. If being is not the first and formal object of the intellect, the intellect obviously will never attain it. Here, the phenomenalists are right a thousand times over. The case is closed. Finally, one will no longer even be able to say, "I think," for the "I" is, at bottom, inevitably ontological. One will need to be content with affirming with a German philosopher whose name I cannot recall, "*There is thought*," just as one says, "There is rain falling in my attic." And yet, even this is not certain,

for it could well be the case that such impersonal thought would in itself be identical with non-thought.

Even less will one be able to say, "Therefore, I am."

This represents the time-honored refutation of Cartesianism offered by the Thomists of the seventeenth century. The point of departure for knowledge is not the *cogito*. It is *being*, as well as the first principle which it implies: the principle of identity / non-contradiction [*sic*]. Every ancient philosophy proceeded from this primary certitude: *Obiectum intellectus est ens*; nothing is intelligible except in function of being; above all, the intellect is intelligible to itself only in function of being, which it knows as the first intelligible object before knowing itself through reflection. The first object known by our intellect is the intelligible being of sensible things and its primordial opposition to non-being. The first principles are *laws of thought* only because they are first *laws of being* and of reality. From the outset, it is utterly clear that reality cannot at once be reality and non-reality. The ontological formulation of the principle of identity / contradiction [*sic*] (being is being, non-being is non-being—being is not non-being) thus precedes its logical formulation (one cannot at one and the same time, from the same perspective, affirm and deny one and the same attribute of one and the same subject).

If the whole of ancient philosophy proceeded from this first certitude, "The object of the intellect is being," the whole of modern subjectivism is found in this other expression which does not, in fact, reach its conclusion: "*Cogito, ergo sum.*"[11]

Émile Boutroux said quite correctly in 1894:

> The central problem in Cartesian metaphysics is the passage from thought to existence. By itself, thought is inextricably innate within

---

11. We have developed these points in *Le réalisme du principe de finalité*, pp. 31 and 160–66. There, we showed that if the principle of identity (or, of non-contradiction) is the fundamental law of reality, there is more in *that which is* than in that which *becomes* and does not yet exist. *Therefore, becoming cannot be the first and fundamental reality*, for it is not related to being as A is related to A. If the principle of identity is the fundamental law of reality, then the first reality, the principle of all the others, must be *Being Itself*, "I am who am," in whom alone essence and existence are identical. See ibid., 14–35 on the primacy of being over becoming.

itself. How, therefore, by what rights and in what sense, can we affirm things that exist? … Existence, which for the ancients was a thing that is given and perceived, something merely there to be analyzed, here is a distant object that must be itself attained, so long as it can indeed be attained.[12]

Furthermore, let us note that, according to Aristotelian and Thomist realism, while the principle of contradiction (or, better, of non-contradiction) is indeed the fundamental law of reality, it is not, however, a judgment of existence. It precedes the first judgment of existence. With a primordial form of evidence, whose value then increasingly imposes itself through the intellect's reflection upon itself, it affirms *that it is not only* INCONCEIVABLE FOR US, *but is indeed* REALLY IMPOSSIBLE IN ITSELF *that any given reality would simultaneously exist and not exist.* Here, we have *a necessary law of reality in itself* and not a merely logical law of the mind (i.e., of reality inasmuch as it is conceived). This REAL IMPOSSIBILITY of absurdity is necessarily conceived as being distinct from SUBJECTIVE INCONCEIVABILITY, and by affirming it, the mind affirms, not yet the existence of an extra-mental being, but rather, the first law of extra-mental reality. It affirms it at least in this negative form: that which is manifestly absurd (like a square circle) is obviously UNREALIZEABLE outside of the mind, whatever God's power may be (if He exists) or even that of an evil genius. Behold the *objective* evidence which Descartes recklessly placed in doubt by saying that God can perhaps make a square circle or a mountain without a valley. Once this doubt has been admitted, the *cogito* could no longer reach the conclusion it proposes.

* * *

From this perspective, we can easily respond to a number of questions which arise today on [*se reposent à*] the occasion of the three-hundredth anniversary of the 1637 publication of Descartes's *Discourse on Method.*

12.   Émile Boutroux, "De l'opportunité d'une edition nouvelle des oeuvres de Descartes," *Revue de métaphysique et morale* (May 1894): pp. 248–49.

Is Descartes truly the father of modern philosophy? Yes, if the *Cogito* is proposed independently from the ontological value of the principle of contradiction.[13]

Does modern philosophy essentially differ from ancient philosophy? Yes, in the same sense as the first response, and this difference rests on idealism's opposition to the realism of the ancients.

Is the idealism coming from Descartes an aberration of thought? A form of progress? Or simply a new kind of thought? If it is conceived in the sense indicated in the first response, it is an aberration of thought, for if the ontological value of the principle of contradiction is set in doubt, *perhaps I simultaneously think and do not think, simultaneously am the self and am not the self, simultaneously exist and do not exist.*

Does the modern philosophy begotten by Descartes call for a rectification? If so, what kind? Yes, a rectification which reestablishes the value of the real scope of the principle of contradiction and of the notion of being presupposed by all other notions, as Aristotle shows in bk. 4 of his *Metaphysics*.

What is the most topically relevant subject still calling for further development[14] in Descartes's philosophy? At least one of the most topically relevant subjects would again be to show what Descartes held was the relationship of the *Cogito* with the real value of the first rational principles, as well as the nature of the relationship of this real value of the first principles with sense experience.

According to the Aristotelian and Thomist doctrine, the real value of the first principles *is founded* (or, *materially resolved*) in sense evidence which is presupposed for such knowledge and *is formally resolved* in the objective intellectual evidence of the real, necessary, and universal value of these principles, a necessity and universality which the senses could never perceive. This objective evidence is intelligible being in its evidential character, indeed, first of all: *the real extra-mental impossibility* of something which would exist and not exist at one and the same time from one and

---

13.   Clearly, we are not here attributing to Descartes the doctrine of Berkeley, nor that of Kant. However, whatever might have been his intentions to remain a realist, he introduced the principle of modern idealism by saying that the only object *directly and immediately* attained by the act of knowing is thought and not the intelligible being of things.

14.   TRANSLATOR'S NOTE: Reading "mettre encore au point" for "mettre encore ou point."

the same perspective. Thus, the real value of the *material resolution* of our intellectual evidence into sensible evidence is *formally judged* under the superior light of the intellectual evidence into which this same certitude *is resolved* (or, *formally founded*).[15] Here, we have the mutual relation between the senses and the intellect: The senses furnish *the matter* for intellectual knowledge, and the value of the senses is *formally judged* in the intellectual light of the first principles. A sensation without a real object sensed, without an efficient cause, and without an end, would violate the principles of contradiction, efficient causality, and finality. Doubtlessly, this doctrine claiming that our ideas come from the senses through abstraction is known only after we know the real value of the principles of contradiction and of causality. However, we do not come to know these principles without the senses furnishing us with the matter of knowledge.

Such is the perspective held by traditional philosophy, above all in the form that it takes in Thomism. The primordial certitude of this philosophy is that *the object of the intellect* is being and reality, indeed, a reality that obeys from the start the absolute necessity and value of the principle of contradiction as the law of non-contradiction. Thus obeying the principle of contradiction, being consequently cannot be a mere process of *becoming* which lacks an efficient cause superior to itself as well as an end, a becoming which would be self-explanatory, a *fieri* which would therefore be more perfect than *esse*. To hold that the first principle of the mind is the principle of identity (or, of non-contradiction) is to admit that *there is more in being than in becoming*, that *becoming cannot be self-explanatory*, and that it requires an efficient cause superior to itself, as well as a final cause. In the final analysis, these superior causes can only be found in *He who is*. All of this represents the affirmation of the primacy of being over becoming.

This traditional doctrine was profoundly underrated by Descartes because of the very way that he conceived of the importance of the *Cogito* by disregarding the absolute necessity and value of the principle of contradiction as the absolutely necessary and fundamental law of reality.

---

15. See *ST* I, q. 84, a. 6 and 5.
    Translator's Note: For a clear exposition of the point in the background concerning material and formal resolution, see Garrigou-Lagrange, *Sense of Mystery*, pp. 15–19.

* * *

CHAPTER 2

The Empiricist Skepticism of David Hume: A *reductio ad absurdum* in Defense of Traditional Realism

Every textbook on the history of philosophy dedicates a chapter to David Hume who, in eighteenth-century England, echoed the thought of Sextus Empiricus and, according to Kant's own words, woke the latter from his dogmatic slumber. We recently thought to read the principal texts of Hume in light of the intellectual notions—real notions, mind you, and not merely nominal ones—of *being, substantial being* (i.e., the notion of substance), *acting being* (i.e., the notion of efficient causality), and of *perfect being* which attracts and perfects (i.e., the notion of the end). In so doing, we found in the pages of Hume quite a striking *reductio ad absurdum* in defense of traditional realism. It so happens that his *radical nominalism*, which aroused Kant's *subjectivist conceptualism*, enables us to brightly highlight the truth of *traditional realism*. If this nominalism did not exist, we could just as well invent it so that we might see more clearly the true value of Aristotle and St. Thomas's realism.

Let us first consider what traditional realism teaches concerning our knowledge of the external world and concerning self-consciousness. Then, we will consider what Hume says about them, as well as how his subjectivist empiricism leads him to a phenomenalism that is a form of skepticism, one that represents an unacceptable and contradictory denial of the external world and of self-knowledge.

THE FOUNDATIONS OF TRADITIONAL REALISM

What does traditional realism teach concerning human knowledge of the external world?

We believe that Aristotle's principal text on this subject is found in *De Anima*, ch. 6 (lect. 13 of St. Thomas's Commentary, no. 396). There, he distinguishes the *sensible per se* from the *sensible per accidens*. The *sensible per se* is, *of itself, accessible to the senses*, whether as *a proper sensible* (e.g., the colored, which is the proper object of sight, or sound, which is the proper object of hearing, etc.) or as a *common sensible* which, of itself, is accessible to several senses (e.g., extension, which can be known by sight, hearing, and touch). The *sensible per accidens* is an *intelligible object immediately perceived by the intellect at the presentation of a sensible object.* St. Thomas writes, "Not everything that can be grasped by the intellect in the sensible thing can be called *sensible per accidens*. Rather, the only thing that can be so called is that which is *immediately* grasped by the intellect upon encountering the sensed thing, just as immediately upon seeing someone speaking or moving himself, *someone grasps (through the intellect and prior to every form of discourse) his life* and, hence, can say, 'I see that he lives.'" Indeed, *life, of itself,* is not *per se* accessible to the senses. It is not a proper sensible like the colored or the sounding, nor a common sensible like visible and tangible magnitude. *Life is not colored, sounding,* or *extended.* It represents *an intelligible perfection* in the plant, animal, and man, and we can analogically attribute it to God, the first living being, who is life *per essentiam.* Nonetheless, life is a sensible *per accidens* which my intellect grasps as soon as a living man speaks to me.

Now, in this capitally important text, Aristotle and St. Thomas are speaking about life, but the same observation applies to the *intelligible being* of sensible things, that is, of the *substantial being* of stones, plants, and of man. Already here, we vaguely know *substance.* They speak similarly of *the efficient causality* of the man who speaks to me or, again, of my right hand which *presses* against my left and is, itself, *pressed* by it. The *efficient cause* here is *substantial being acting*; action follows on being. Likewise, our intellect immediately grasps that *the eye is made to see* and the ear to hear; this is their finality. Through these examples, one sees that the *end* is something that is *sensible per accidens* and *intelligible per se*, something that the non-rational animal cannot know, just as it cannot know the intelligible being of sensible things, nor their substantial being (i.e., their substance), nor their acting (i.e., their action or efficient causality) upon us.

The Thomists say: when, through my power of sight, I grasp *a colored reality* precisely as *colored*, through my intellect, I attain this colored reality as such, that is, *the colored reality considered from the perspective of being*; similarly, when, through the power of hearing, I grasp a *sonorous being precisely as sonorous*, through my intellect I attain it *as a being*.

Thus, our intellect exercises an activity in our perception of the external world, and this human perception is not merely the simple sensation which exists in the animal that is inferior to us.

In his Commentary on *De anima* (lect. 13, no. 398), St. Thomas says: "The sheep knows *this lamb*, not inasmuch as *it is this lamb* (i.e., an individual of a given species in a given genus) but, rather, knows it inasmuch as it is *something from which it can draw milk*, and the sheep knows *this grass* inasmuch as it is its *food* (that is, inasmuch as it is the *terminus* or principle of a given *action to be performed here and now* or of a [similar sort of] passion)."

Without suspecting that Aristotle had said something similar, Jean Jacques Rousseau once said, "Man is distinct from animals because, through his intellect, he alone can give a meaning to this little word: *is*." Among all the animals, man alone can know *the verb to be*, its tenses, moods, and indeed, all verbs, which have the verb *to be* as an essential, radical element. As Aristotle said, "Socrates runs," means, "Socrates *is* running," and, "Socrates acts," means, "Socrates *is* acting."

What Aristotle and St. Thomas admit for our knowledge of *the intelligible being of sensible things* also holds true, according to them, for our knowledge of the thinking subject. When we are aware of our own individual act of knowledge and our own individual act of willing, we grasp the knowing and willing subject. As St. Thomas says in *ST* I, q. 76, a. 1: "*One and the same man is aware of the fact that he understands and that he senses.*" Here, we are not speaking of a kind of general knowledge but, rather, of *my act* of knowledge, *hic et nunc*, and of *my act* of willing. Psychological consciousness thus attains the knowing subject, the "*cogito*," as well as the willing subject. The knowing subject is grasped by our intellect in a given individual act of knowing, just as *a colored being* is grasped by the intellect *as a being* (i.e., as a subject of color), whereas sight grasps it as *colored*.

Let us now compare this traditional realism with Hume's empiricism, as well as with its consequences.

ABSOLUTE EMPIRICISM AND ITS CONSEQUENCES

My intention here is not to provide an exposition of Hume's skepticism but, rather, to show that this skepticism furnishes the Aristotelian with a *reductio ad absurdum* in proof of traditional realism or of the value of the intellect's natural power of understanding. These reflections, coming from an Aristotelian inspiration, are superior, in our opinion, to those of Thomas Reid, which themselves already represent a decent response provided by common sense. Obviously, however, Thomas Reid did not have the loftiness of Thomas Aquinas, and we must never confuse these two Thomases with each other.

Absolute empiricism holds that human knowledge can attain only that which is, of itself, accessible to the external or internal senses, the colored, the sonorous, the feelings of joy or of sorrow. However, it does not take into account what Aristotle called the sensible *per accidens*, which *of itself is intelligible*. Moreover, it denies the *essential* distinction between the senses and the imagination, seeing here only a distinction of degrees.

This absolute empiricism leads to complete phenomenalism. Since it neglects the *sensible per accidens*, which is something that is *per se* intelligible, in the end, we find that this perspective makes *the intelligible being of sensible things disappear*, along with *substantial being* (for the substance is nothing but a *collection* of phenomena [from this perspective]). Likewise, efficient causality becomes nothing more than a *succession* of two phenomena, as day follows upon night. (To this, Reid responded: Nonetheless, night is not the cause of day, and nobody says that it is.) Likewise, *the end*, which is the *raison d'être* for action, disappears as well. Finally, *the thinking subject*, my very substance, disappears. The only thing left standing are phenomena that are accessible either to the external senses or to the internal senses like the imagination and the sense memory which associates together its memories.

The intellectual idea is reduced to *an averaged-out or composite image accompanied by a common term, the intellect's judgment* to an *empirical association of two images,* and reasoning to *an empirical sequence of images,* which no longer manifests the *raisons d'être* of things and of their properties, nor the *raisons d'être* of our affirmations. The verb *to be,* the soul of our judgments, likewise disappears, since judgment is now nothing more than an empirical association without the verbs *to be, to act,* etc.

The intellect's own life and that of its three operations is suppressed by this absolute empiricism which becomes a radical form of phenomenalism[1] whether it is a question of the external world or of our own self.

This empiricism also leads to *radical nominalism: the universal* no longer is anything but a word, *a common term* which is attached, not to an idea, but to an averaged-out or composite image. For example, the idea that we form of the plant is only an averaged-out idea of a plant that is neither large nor small, connected with a common term: "plant." Likewise, the *intellectual notion of intelligible being* disappears, as well as those of unity, truth, goodness, efficient causality, and finality.

Substance is nothing more than a verbal entity, *a common term* which accompanies a *collection* of given phenomena. Likewise, the notion of causality and the principle of causality no longer have any ontological and transcendent value but, rather, have only a phenomenal value. Henceforth, this principle does not enable us to ascend from the effect to a supra-phenomenal cause. Instead, it is like a coat-hanger painted on the wall, on which nothing can be hung.

Likewise, given that the *universal,* properly so called, disappears, we would no longer even speak of there being a *succession* of phenomena but, rather, should speak of phenomena which follow upon one another, no longer speaking of *a collection* of phenomena but, rather, of phenomena gathered together without any uniting principle.

In short, after the disappearance of the intellectual notion of *the intelligible being* of sensible things, *the entire intelligible* (i.e., suprasensible) *order disappears for us.* The transcendental properties of being—unity,

---

1. TRANSLATOR'S NOTE: Reading "phénomène" as "phénoménalisme," given the antecedent structure.

truth, and goodness—all no longer have a meaning. Efficient causality and final causality vanish, like the verb *to be*, its tenses and moods, as well as all other verbs, above all: *to act, to produce, to realize, to actualize,* and *all active verbs*. They all should be stripped from our vocabulary. *Ontology disappears as well*, and all that remains is a phenomenology, indeed one that is completely empirical in nature and not a science, for the empiricists' induction cannot arrive at the universal. It says that up to now men have died, without being able to say whether this will be the case in the future. This would represent a kind of suppression of common sense (that is, of the intellect's natural power of understanding). The murderer could say to his judges, "I was not really *the cause* of this murder. It is a fact which *followed upon* my own actions, just as the day follows the night without being caused by it."

Thus, one arrives at a form of complete skepticism which falls into self-contradiction as soon as it wishes to say any little thing whatsoever concerning the external world or about ourselves.

This likewise holds true for Kant's subjectivist conceptualism which denies the ontological and transcendent value of the first notions and principles of reason. For him, speculative reason no longer can prove God's existence, nor that of my individual self.

Nonetheless, these nominalists and subjectivists *remain men*, and despite everything they hold, they *retain their natural understanding*, which prevents them from denying their own selves and from denying that they *really are the causes* of their own works. Kant cannot simultaneously be and not be Kant, nor can Hume simultaneously be and not be Hume. Despite everything, when they stop thinking in terms of their own philosophical system, these philosophers preserve their natural understanding, for otherwise they would fall into contradiction as soon as they would wish to say anything whatsoever about the external world or about their own selves. Aristotle, while speaking of Cratylus, said: "The role of the skeptic is to remain silent, like a plant, which cannot say anything."

We can ourselves quite clearly see that these represent the inadmissible and contradictory consequences of the empiricist and phenomenalist positions of Hume by reading section 12, pt. 1, of his work, *An Enquiry Concerning Human Understanding*, where he says:

These are the obvious dictates of reason; and no man, who reflects, ever doubted, that the existences, which we consider, when we say, this house and that tree, are nothing but (subjective) perceptions in the mind, and fleeting copies or representations of other existences, which remain uniform and independent...

> By what argument can it be proved, that the perceptions of the mind must be caused by external objects, entirely different from them, though resembling them—if that be possible—and could not arise either from the energy of the mind itself, or from the suggestion of some invisible and unknown spirit, or from some other cause still more unknown to us?[2]

Likewise, in pt. 2 of the same section: "There is no such thing as abstract or general ideas, properly speaking; but that all general ideas are, in reality, particular ones, attached to a general term, which recalls, upon occasion, other particular ones, that resemble, in certain circumstances, the idea, present to the mind."[3] The existence of external objects and that of our own permanent selves cannot be proven.

There are only more-or-less forceful states of consciousness, and the expectation of these states in certain circumstances.[4]

The consequence of this empiricism would be absolute phenomenalism. However, having pushed on to that point, in order to avoid coming to this conclusion, Hume presupposes a kind of pre-established harmony between the course of nature and the succession of our ideas (see *An Enquiry Concerning Human Understanding*, sect. 5). This represents a kind of recourse to God as to *an indispensable hypothesis*, after having said that His existence is indemonstrable. Does this not represent an act of self-contradiction?

In his *A Treatise on Human Nature*, bk. 1, pt. 2, sect. 6, Hume denies the existence of every substance, whether spiritual or material.

2.   David Hume, *Enquiries Concerning Human Understanding and Concerning the Principles of Morals*, 3rd ed., ed. P. H. Nidditch (Oxford: Clarendon Press, 1975), sect. 12, pt. 1 (pp. 152–53).

3.   Ibid., pt. 2 (p. 158, n. 1).

4.   TRANSLATOR'S NOTE: In the original, there is a closing quote here without a correlative opening quote.

He reduces not only the notion of matter but even that of spirit to a collection of sensations. In this text, he writes: "Let us fix our attention outside of ourselves as much as possible, to the utmost limits of the universe; *we never really advance a step beyond ourselves, nor beyond the universe of our imagination.*"[5]

Belief is distinct from fiction only by the sentiment that accompanies it, but this difference is purely subjective. (On this, see *An Enquiry Concerning Human Understanding*, section 5, pt. 2 and *A Treatise on Human Nature*, appendix B).

Note that Hume's empirical skepticism here, followed by John Stuart Mill and the positivists, had already been formulated by *Sextus Empiricus*.[6]

All of John Stuart Mill's objections against the Aristotelian syllogism can be found long before him in Sextus Empiricus. Aristotle would answer: These objections come from the confusion of the *universal* with the *particulars* which up to now have been the object of one's experience. We do not only say, "Up to now, all men have died, and it is probable that they will continue to die." Instead, we say, "*By his very nature*, man is mortal because he is composed of body and soul, and the organs of his body wear out and eventually come to die." Empiricism is unable to explain the value of the syllogism, just as it cannot provide a foundation for induction or the passage from the particular to a universal law. It denies the universal and suppresses every philosophy worthy of the name.

Hume's empiricism is even a kind of rejection of the intellect or of the *essential* distinction between the intellect and the senses, here seeing only a difference of degrees, not of nature. This is why it leads to phenomenism and to skepticism, which falls into self-contradiction as soon

---

5. TRANSLATOR'S NOTE: I have translated this from the French (though generally drawing on the English original), given its truncated form. For the full text, see David Hume, *A Treatise on Human Nature*, 2nd ed., ed. P. H. Nidditch (Oxford: Clarendon Press, 1980), bk. 1, pt. 2, sect. 6 (pp. 67–68): "Let us fix our attention out of ourselves as much as possible: Let us chase our imagination to the heavens, or to the utmost limits of the universe; we never really advance a step beyond ourselves, nor can conceive any kind of existence, but those perceptions, which have appeared in that narrow compass. This is the universe of the imagination, nor have we any idea but what is there produced."

6. See Sextus Empiricus, *Adversus mathematicos*, VII, 314–445 and *Hypotyposes pyrrhoniennes*, II, 18–84.

as it wishes to affirm anything whatsoever concerning the reality of the external world and concerning the reality of our own selves.

* * *

In sum, first, *the absolute empiricism of Hume leads to a phenomenalism which suppresses the notion of intelligible being,* the verb *to be,* the verb *to act,* and indeed, *all active verbs,* even though they are indispensable for thought and discourse. Does this not represent a form of self-contradiction?

Second, *from this perspective, one suppresses all personal pronouns, ego, tu, ille,* in order to no longer admit anything but phenomena which lack any real center of attribution. Only impersonal verbs would remain. Just as one says, "It is raining," one would say, not, "I am thinking," but, "There is thought in the appearance of my brain or of my mind." What, therefore, would remain of the human person…? In this way, one arrives at a form of complete nihilism.

Third, *every essence disappears,* along with all the properties that derive from it, like a circle deprived of the center which renders all of its properties intelligible. The idea of a circle would be replaced by an image of a circle having a kind of average size, along with the common term "circle." This represents the most absolute form of nominalism. One no longer has *the notion of an intelligible and universal idea* distinct from the sensible and singular image.

Fourth, *the first rational principles lose their necessity, universality, and real value,* but nonetheless, one continues to make use of them as if they retained this value, affirming with certitude that Hume was *really the author* of his own works and that the murderer is *really the cause* of a murder and deserves punishment.

Fifth, this is why, at the outset of this article, we said that *Hume's system provides a proof of traditional realism by way of a* reductio ad absurdum and that *even if it did not exist, one could invent it in order to demonstrate the true sense and scope of traditional realism.* In fact, Divine Providence only permits these errors in order to shed light on the truth, as it permits evil only for the sake of a greater good, which we will see uncovered in heaven, a good which sometimes shines forth on earth in order to aid all of those who sincerely seek after the truth and, at last, find it. God commands us to seek after it, and He never commands something impossible.

* * *

What we just said enables us to resolve the ever-contemporary question: In what way is *positive science* distinguished from *positivist science?* We can see quite clearly now that, like Hume, positivist science knows only phenomena and is phenomenalist, whereas positive, non-positivist science knows not only the phenomena, but also knows of *substances and causes*, at least vaguely, as does natural understanding. With true certainty, it attains *the nature* of things, which is the root of their properties, and can provide a foundation for a form of induction which arrives at the true universal (e.g., man by his nature is mortal). Positive, though non-positivist, science perfects our natural understanding and does not destroy it. In this way, zoology considers the animal not only as a collection of phenomena but also as *a living being* having certain properties: to nourish itself, to reproduce itself, and to sense. Likewise, he who possess this science sees or can see in the constitution of the animal and in its admirable instinct the effect of a First, Ordering Cause. So too, the astronomer who embraces his science in a single glance sees or can see in the harmony of the movement of the stars the effect of a Supreme Intelligence. Another example: Positive science does not only see a collection of phenomena in a chunk of bread but, rather, a substance, that of baked wheat flour. Positive science even sees or can easily see that *the substance of bread* is *wholly and entirely* in this chunk of bread and *wholly in each part of this bread, however small it may be.*[7] Positive science does not contain anything that is opposed to the dogma of Eucharistic transubstantiation.

We thus also see increasingly well *the subordination of the sciences* which is destroyed by Hume's phenomenalist empiricism because he did not see that *the first object known by our intellect* is not phenomena but, instead, *the intelligible being of sensible things.* If the first objection

---

7. TRANSLATOR'S NOTE: Given the complexities of "substance" involved in something like bread, however, see important qualifications provided from within the Thomistic outlook in Jean-Hervé Nicolas, *Synthèse dogmatique* (Fribourg: Éditions Universitaires, 1985), §889.

known by our intellect were phenomena, it could never escape the phe-nomenal order, as sight can see only the visible colored [thing] and as the sense of hearing can hear that which is sonorous. The principle of causality would not enable one to elevate oneself any higher. As we have seen, it would be like a coat-hanger painted on the wall, a mere appear-ance upon which nothing could be hung.

However, if, by contrast, the first object known by our intellect is indeed *the intelligible being of sensible things*, it can elevate itself, by means of the principle of causality (which has an ontological and tran-scendent value), to the First, Uncaused Cause, to the First Being which exists through Itself.[8] Thus, the positive scientist, through his science (into which his natural understanding is prolonged), can quite clearly understand what will be said by every man of good sense: what great-er absurdity can there be than to claim that the understanding of the greatest geniuses and the goodness of the greatest saints arises from a material and blind fatalism, from an unintelligent and lifeless matter! If the intellectual notions of *intelligible being* and of *cause* are retained, we must admit, in the final analysis, a Supreme, Uncaused Cause, which Aristotle called Pure Act, Thought of Thought, the Sovereign Good that draws all things to Itself. Divine Revelation calls this Cause, "He who is" (Ex. 3:14), He who alone can say, "I am the Truth and the Life" (Jn. 14:6).

---

8. That which exists, though not through itself, can exist only through another which exists through itself. Now, the composite and changing world does not exist through itself. Therefore, it can exist only through Him who is absolutely simple and immutable Existence itself, which is related to existence as A is related to A.

* * *

CHAPTER 3

Hegelian Dialectic and Thomist Metaphysics

There is no small use to be derived from comparing Thomist metaphysics to the Hegelian dialectic which has once again appeared in Marxism and in various contemporary philosophical works.

HEGELIAN DIALECTIC:
ITS PRINCIPLES AND ITS CONSEQUENCES

Hegel depended on his immediate predecessors just as much as he set himself in opposition to them. Kant had declared that speculative reason cannot demonstrate, with objectively sufficient certitude, the existence of God, the First and Transcendent Cause of the universe.

Now, Hegel thought that if this were indeed true, then speculative reason must explain the universe by a non-transcendent, immanent cause. To do so, he proposed the following explanation, thus establishing the outlines of his dialectic, one that is quite different from the dialectic spoken of by Plato.

He said that *only the rational*, that which has a *raison d'être, is real*. Reality is identical with the rational and metaphysics with logic. The rational is what constitutes reality. Destroy the rational element in any object and nothing remains.

Now, Hegel adds, in our own thought, *the rational* ever proceeds by way of a *thesis*, followed by an *antithesis*, before arriving at a superior *synthesis* which unites the thesis and the antithesis together. This is what is revealed to us by *becoming* (which is found in the order of bodies and in that of minds [*esprits*]): that which *becomes* in a sense *already is* while *not yet being* what it will be; the first opposition is that between *being in its initial state* [*l'être initial*] and *non-being*, which will then come to be united to each other in becoming itself.

Hegel calls the initial state of being or initial rational state of affairs [*le rationnel initial*] the Idea which is not yet self-conscious.

Before becoming externalized and self-alienated (through the opposition of non-being to being), *the Idea becomes Nature* and its universal becoming; then, returning back to itself and becoming self-aware, *it becomes Spirit*.

The Idea is the initial thesis. Nature is the antithesis. Spirit is the synthesis of the Idea and Nature.

Finally, Spirit itself in turn passes through three phases. It is sequentially *subjective, objective, and absolute*. Subjective spirit is the human mind [*esprit*] in individuals. Objective spirit is made up of [human] mores, laws, families, and civic orders [*cités*]. *Absolute spirit* is *art, religion*, and (above religion, which itself remains symbolic) *philosophy*. In philosophy itself, the idealistic evolutionism of Hegel represents the most complete expression of absolute spirit. Nothing higher exists. God does not exist in Himself as He who is really and essentially distinct from the human mind [*esprit*]. Rather, *God comes into being* in man's mind, and He above all becomes self-conscious in Hegelian philosophy itself.

Thus, we have a brief outline for the overall developmental trajectory of this philosophy, which at times does indeed contain quite excellent observations in its history of art and new insights, for example, in its history of philosophy.

* * *

What is the foundation of this dialectic, whose character is so different from the ascending and descending dialectic spoken of by Plato?

This forward march of spirit which is held to belong to the very nature of being, "Consists essentially in recognizing the *inseparability* (*Einheit*) of contradictories and in discovering the principle of this

union in a superior category." Moreover, Hegel uses the term, "A dialectic moment (*dialektisches Moment*)," for "contradiction itself and the
passage from one terminus of this contradiction to the other."[1]

Hence, we can see how it is that Hegel was able to say that *the
principle of contradiction* is only a linguistic law, of discourse and discursive reasoning [*raison raissonnante*], which speculates on abstract and
immutable ideas, while not, according to him, *being a law of superior
understanding*, which has *becoming* (wherein being and non-being are
identified) as the object of its intuitive knowledge.[2]

In our opinion, what above all implies a contradiction is the claim
that *becoming* would be self-explanatory (a *ratio sui*) and could exist,
contrary to what is asserted by the principle of causality, *without an
efficient cause that is superior to it* and, in the final analysis, *without a
First Uncaused Cause*. Because of the principle of causality, everything
which becomes or comes into existence needs an efficient cause, just as
the begotten being needs a begetter and, over and above its begetter, the
begotten being needs Him who is Being Itself and Life Itself, who alone
can give others being through participation.

The contradiction which sets being in opposition to non-being *most
certainly does not provide a sufficient replacement for the efficient cause of becoming*, nor for its final cause, nor for its subject, nor for what specifies it
or makes it be what it is (e.g., heating rather than physical displacement).
A contradiction which must be overcome furnishes an occasion for acting, just as difficulties in life are an *occasion for a struggle*, not the efficient
cause of the effort which struggles through such difficulties. The cause of
such effort is our will, as well as God who aids us by arousing our willing.

Theologians and the most traditional of philosophers are not the
only ones who have reproached Hegel for denying the real value of the
principle of contradiction. Nay, even minds that are quite independent
of every kind of tradition have registered such a reproach. Granted, others have indeed presented this denial as being something positive. Thus,
Alfred Weber, in his *Histoire de la Philosophie européenne*, remarks:

---

1. Cf. *Encylopédie*, no. 81. This is how the Hegelian dialectic is rightly characterized in A.
    Lalande's *Vocabulaire de la philosophie* (1926).
2. See *La Logique de Hégel*, 2nd ed., trans. A. Vera, vol. 1, no. 85 (pp. 393–412).

Becoming is at once being and still non-being (that which will be). The two contraries which beget being and non-being are found again in it, merged together and reconciled. A new contradiction will emerge from it, one that will be resolved in a new synthesis and so on until the arrival of the Absolute Idea. Therefore, *contradiction resolving itself into unity*, reappearing in a new form so as to disappear and reappear until the arrival of that which resolves itself into the definitive unity: *such is the driving [moteur] principle*[3] *and rhythm of Hegelian logic. Repudiating the principle of contradiction* held by Aristotle and Leibniz, in virtue of which a thing cannot simultaneously be and not be, it places itself, on this point, on the side of the sophists without, for that, concluding that skepticism must have the last word. According to Hegel, contradiction exists not only in thought but also in things themselves. *Being itself is contradictory...* From the moment that one looks upon nature and sees self-developing thought...the contradiction wherein the philosopher moves about ceases to be, in his opinion, an obstacle to understanding things and appears to him as being their very essence reflected in thought's own antinomies.[4]

WHAT ARE THE CONSEQUENCES
OF THE HEGELIAN DIALECTIC?

As we just saw, Hegel does not admit the ontological and transcendent value of the principle of contradiction, nor that of the principle of causality which is not formulated, "Every phenomenon requires a prior phenomenon," but rather, "Everything that comes into existence requires a cause and, in the final analysis, an Uncaused Cause which would be its own activity, Being Itself and Life Itself, who would be able to say: 'I am Him who is' (Ex. 3:14), and 'I am the truth and the life' (Jn. 14:6)." Therefore, according to traditional philosophy and the Christian faith, God, who is being itself, can exist without any creature and without the existence of any finite intellect. He is Intellection

---

3. In other words, in this system, *contradiction* replaces the first mover or the First Cause.
4. Alfred Weber, *Histoire de la Philosophie européenne*, 5th ed. (Paris: Fischbacher, 1892), p. 477.

(Thought) that is ever subsistent and Life through His very essence, without any admixed decay or death.

By contrast, things are quite different for Hegel, who held that *contradictories are inseparable, that being cannot exist without non-being*, which is identified with it in endless becoming. For him, *the one cannot exist without the many*, which is united to it in a superior harmony. Likewise, *the true cannot exist without the false*, which is a necessary moment of evolution. *Good cannot exist without evil*, which is another necessary moment of evolution. *The spirit of good cannot exist without the spirit of evil*, as was said by the Hegelian Benedetto Croce, who likewise said in a Hegelian fashion that *the future life cannot exist without death*, which forever accompanies it. Life could not be separated from death, nor good from evil.

Another consequence of this Hegelian dialectic is that, from this perspective, one can no longer admit *the existence of a God who is really and essentially distinct from the world and from human intellects.*

Likewise, one can no longer admit the existence of *Providence and the true finality of finite beings* known by Providence in an incomparably better way than by the Hegelian dialectic. Finally, one can no longer admit man's *free choice*, nor God's, for whatever appears to be free is in fact only a *necessary* moment of universal evolution. When applied to the State, this outlook leads to the suppression of individual freedoms, as can be seen in the history of the Hegelian left, which openly accepts the consequences of the system which fiercely rejected the personality of God and the individual immortality of the soul, while professing Marxist communism in its politics.

The recognition of these consequences is not limited to theologians but has also has been noted by historians of philosophy like J. Wilm.[5]

---

5. See J. Wilm, *Histoire de la philosophie allemande* (Paris: 1846), vol. 4. Also see the article "Hegel" in *Dictionnaire de Sciences philosophiques*, 2nd ed. (ed. Franck). On p. 686 of this article, Wilm says, concerning Hegelian philosophy: "In order for such a philosophy to be possible, it would need to equal the divine intellect... God alone possesses the supreme knowledge [*science*] of causes..."

In the aftermath of Hegel's death, the divisions which emerged between the Right Hegelians, the Left Hegelians, and the Hegelians of the center, gave the impression of being an utter state of confusion, like a tower of Babel, equaled only by the presumption with which the master had conceived of this supposed universal synthesis which hoped to unite all sciences and judge the Gospel's divine revelation from on high.

Hence, we should not be astonished to see the first of the eighty propositions condemned in the *Syllabus errorum* of Pius IX (December 8, 1864) being formulated like a summary of Hegelianism:

> There does not exist any supreme, all-wise, all-provident divine being distinct from this universe of things; God is identical with the nature of things and therefore subject to change; *God actually becomes himself in man and in the world*; all things are God and have the very substance of God; *God is one and the same reality with the world, and so is spirit with matter, necessity with liberty, truth with falsehood, good with evil, and justice with injustice.* This is a kind of summary of pantheism, naturalism, and absolute rationalism.[6]

The only truth that remains is one that is relative to a given moment of evolution. Today's truth will be an outdated thesis tomorrow. No longer is there any immutable truth, and all that remains are provisional truths.

The [First] Vatican Council condemned Hegelian pantheism in the following terms: "If anyone says that God is the universal or indefinite being which, by self-determination, constitutes the universality of beings, differentiated in genera, species, and individuals, let him be anathema."[7]

As Alfred Vacant observed: "This theory, which denies the principle of contradiction, utterly overthrows all the principles of reason..."[8] The same author adds: "The Rosminian propositions condemned in 1887[9] are in agreement with the systems of Hegel and Fichte in admitting that *undetermined being* is the common essence of God and the world."[10]

---

6. Pius IX, *Syllabus errorum*, no. 1 (Denzinger, no. 2901).
    TRANSLATOR'S NOTE: The final sentence is added in Latin by Fr. Garrigou-Lagrange.

7. [First] Vatican Council, *Dei filius*, can. 1, §4 (Denzinger, no. 3024).

8. Jean-Michel-Alfred Vacant, Études théologiques sur les constitutions du Concile du Vatican, vol. 1 (Paris: Delhomme et Briguet, 1895), p. 214.

9. See Decree of the Holy Office (under Leo XIII), *Post obitum*, no. 1 (Denzinger, no. 1891).
    TRANSLATOR'S NOTE: See my comments in the chapter above, entitled "*Cognoscens quodammodo fit vel est aliud a se* (On the Nature of Knowledge as Union with the Other as Other," pp. 75–76, note 22.

10. Vacant, *Etudes théologiques sur les constitutions du Concile du Vatican*, p. 214.

This is quite clear once you attentively read the first sixteen Rosminian propositions.[11]

THE FIRST PRINCIPLES OF THOMISTIC METAPHYSICS

Traditional metaphysics, which through a slow progress was prepared by Socrates and Plato, then systematized by Aristotle, developed by St. Augustine, then undergoing deeper and more precise developments by St. Thomas Aquinas, has ever defended the ontological and transcendent value of the principle of contradiction (or, of identity): "That which is, is; that which is not, is not." The Lord says in the Gospel: "But let your speech be yea, yea: no, no" (Mt. 5:37, DR).

One and the same reality cannot, at the same time and from the same perspective, both be and not be what it is; likewise, it cannot at one and the same time exist and not exist. St. Thomas dedicated fifty pages of his Commentary on Aristotle's *Metaphysics* to the defense of the real value of this principle, against Heraclitus and the Sophists. With Aristotle, he showed[12] that the denial of the *real value of the principle of contradiction* leads to the destruction of all language, the merging of all beings into one single being, the destruction of every kind of substance, and the admission of a becoming that takes place without anything that undergoes that becoming. Indeed, such a denial leads to the destruction of all truth, for truth follows upon being. Likewise, it leads to the suppression of all thought and of every opinion, which would thus come to deny itself at the very moment it affirmed itself. Every desire and action would likewise come to be destroyed, and movement or becoming would itself be eliminated, for there would no longer be a contradictory opposition between the point of departure and the point of arrival of movement. Thus, one would arrive before even setting forth! St. Paul said of Christ, "There was not yes and no; in him there was only Yes."[13]

Similarly, following Aristotle, St. Thomas defends the real value of the principle of causality in his commentary on the first book of Aristotle's *Physics*, there responding to Parmenides' objection to the

---

11.   See the article "Rosmini," in *Dictionnaire de théologie catholique*.

12.   See St. Thomas, *In IV Meta.*, ch. 4–8, lect. 6–17.

13.   2 Cor. 1:19 (RSV).

existence of movement. Parmenides said, "If something comes into being, this comes either from being or from non-being. Now, being cannot arise from being, for being already exists. *Ex ente non fit ens, quia iam est ens.* A statue of Zeus cannot come forth from a statue of Zeus, for it already exists. And nothing can arise from non-being. Therefore, becoming is impossible."

Aristotle responded that what becomes cannot come forth from *being that is determined* (*or, in act*), but it can come forth from a not-yet-determined *being in potency.* Thus, the plant comes forth from a plant seed, the animal from the *semen* of another animal of the same species, the statue from wood or marble which can be sculpted by the sculptor—*statua fit ex sculptibili.*

Moreover, St. Thomas adds: "*However, something cannot be reduced to act from potency except by some being that is in act* and, in the ultimate analysis, *through some Uncaused Cause,* which would be *its own action and its own existence.*"[14] The begotten being can be produced only by a begetting being, and in the final analysis, by Him who is Life itself, who is able to give life to others.

St. Thomas likewise defends the value of the principle of finality: "*Every agent acts on account of an end,* for otherwise one thing would not follow from a given agent's action than would some other thing, except by chance. (However, chance is a *per accidens* cause which presupposes a *per se* cause, ordered to its own proper effect.)"[15] If there were no finality, there would be no reason why the living eye could see, instead of hearing; it would no more be ordered to vision than to hearing.

Such are the first principles of Thomist metaphysics. They are the first principles of reason, explained by *the division of being into potency and act.* Act is either the determination of the agent, that which is received by the patient or subject of change, or the end of the generation or of some other operation.

This distinction between potency and act renders becoming intelligible in function of being, the first intelligible, and it is *necessary* for reconciling the principle of identity affirmed by Parmenides with the

---

14.   *ST* I, q. 2, a. 3 (First Way).
15.   *ST* I, q. 44, a. 4.

becoming affirmed by Heraclitus in accord with external and internal experience.

THE ASSIMILATIVE POWER OF THOMISM
MAKES IT INTO A SUPERIOR SYNTHESIS

This doctrine can assimilate what is true in different philosophical tendencies. Why? Because it is founded on necessary principles of great universality and elevation and because it has an extensive inductive basis which is ever renewable by a careful and attentive examination of the facts.[16]

As Leibniz noted with regard to the *philosophia perennis*, philosophical systems are generally true in what they affirm and false in what they deny, for reality is richer than they are.

Thus, materialism is true in its affirmation of the existence of matter and false in its denial of the existence of spirit, and vice-versa for idealistic or immaterialistic spiritualism. Truth is found at the elevated peak set in the middle of these two errors.

Likewise, it is elevated above the deterministic denial of freedom and the [libertinist] denial of the intellectual direction which freedom needs.

In this way, a thesis which is insufficiently comprehensive does indeed provoke an antithesis, as Hegel noted, before the mind arrives at a superior synthesis. St. Thomas himself also admitted this point, though he continued to give full respect to the real value of the principle of contradiction. In virtue of this principle, he firmly holds, like Aristotle, that *two contradictory propositions cannot be simultaneously true, nor simultaneously false*, for example: "Every man is just" and "A given person is not just." These two propositions are like yes and no. One is true and the other is false.

However, St. Thomas and Aristotle hold that *two propositions* which are *contrary* (and not contradictory) can be *simultaneously false in a contingent matter* and that between and above the two of them the truth is found like a summit, just as in morality the virtue of courage

---

16.   We have developed these insights in *La synthèse thomiste* (Paris: 1946/7), pp. 558–79.
    TRANSLATOR'S NOTE: See Garrigou-Lagrange, *Reality: A Synthesis of Thomistic Thought*, pp. 346–54.

294 REGINALD GARRIGOU-LAGRANGE, O.P.

is found between and above rashness and cowardice. Thus, these two *contrary* propositions are *simultaneously false*: Every man is just and no man is just. Indeed, there is a middle between two contrary propositions, namely, a particular proposition in which we can find the truth that is denied by two contrary universal propositions. By contrast, a middle does not exist between two contradictory propositions like, for example: "Every man is just" and "A given man is not just." A middle does exist between these two *contrary* errors: "Every man is just" and "No man is just." This middle is: "This man is just."

Thus, above and between mechanism and dynamism we find the Aristotelian doctrine *of matter* (the principle of spatial extension) *and substantial form* (the root principle of activity).

Likewise, above and between the psychological determinism which denies freedom and libertinism which asserts that the free act is not subject to intellectual direction, the Thomist conception of free choice soars on high.

Similarly again, above and between occasionalism which denies the activity of second causes and Molinism which, in order to defend freedom, denies the divine premotion, Thomism holds that, given that *the creature* is not its own existence, *it is likewise not its action* and can act only through the divine motion which makes it pass, without thereby doing violence to it, from potency in relation to the activity in question to act by actualizing our free choice, making it blossom and fructify, instead of destroying it.

We ever find ourselves faced here with *the same doctrinal leitmotiv concerning God, who is Pure Act*, elevated above all creatures composed of potency and act.

* * *

What absolutely cannot be admitted is that becoming would be a *ratio sui*, that it would exist *by itself* without an efficient cause superior to it, without a Supreme Uncaused Cause, and without a true ultimate end known by the Supreme Intelligence.

Aristotle would respond to Hegel as he did to Heraclitus: Becoming must obey the law of non-contradiction. It cannot at one and the same time both be and not be becoming. It is the passage from that which *can* be to that which *is*. Now, there is more in *that which is* than in that which *can* be and that which *is becoming*. There is more in a grown man than in the embryo. The more perfect cannot come from the less perfect; it requires a cause superior to becoming. There is no begotten without a begetter, and the statue can only be made by a sculptor. Becoming is not self-sufficient. It is not a *ratio sui*.

Hegel admits that "everything that is real has a *raison d'être*." We must add: "It has a *raison d'être* either in itself or in another and, in the last analysis, in Another which exists through itself." *Now, becoming*, the passage from potency to act, *does not exist through itself*, for potency is not act, and it cannot actualize itself. (Were it to do so, the more perfect would come forth from the less perfect without a fully sufficient cause.) In order for a potency to be actualized, a being already in act is needed and, in the last analysis, an Uncaused Efficient Cause who is Pure Act, acting in view of a supreme end.

Otherwise, one would place *absurdity at the root of all things and at each moment when ascending evolution would pass from the lesser to the greater, to a new perfection* (e.g., at the appearance of plant life, of sensation, of intelligence, and of morality).

Hegel wrote: "God is dead; universal evolution is self-sufficient without Him."

However, by a singular turn of events, *this denial of the true God only leads to a* reductio ad absurdum *demonstration* of *His existence* and of the mysterious harmony which exists in Him.

We must make a choice: *God* or *radical absurdity* placed at the principle of universal evolution and at each moment of its progress and ascent, with the more coming forth from what is less without a sufficient cause and without any form of finality deserving of that name.

One might as well say that the intelligence of the greatest geniuses and the goodness of the greatest saints arises from an unconscious and blind fatalism. What could be more absurd?

Thus, contradiction would be set in place of Him who is Being Itself, *Ego sum qui sum* (Ex. 3:14) and in place of *Him who is the Truth and the Life* (Jn. 14:6).

This proof of God's existence through absurdity is certainly not a negligible affair. Providence has permitted it for a superior good, namely, in order to make even clearer the Truth and Goodness of Him who is Being Itself, without any mixture with non-being or privation, the Truth and Goodness of Him who is Wisdom and Love, elevated above error and evil. Thus, the True God makes even radical error and evil serve the manifestation of His goodness. Such a fundamental error illuminates us by way of contrast and makes us once again find the path of truth.

Many excellent minds have thought that Hegelian philosophy was only a kind of "philosophical delusion," which consists in saying to oneself, "God has finally become self-aware in me. God? I am He!" It thus calls to mind the words of Leo XIII in his Encyclical *Aeterni Patris*, where he speaks of those who reject divine revelation: "[Such an idea is most false and deceptive, and] its sole tendency is to induce foolish and ungrateful men willfully to repudiate the most sublime truths."[17] Looking upon the animating inspiration of Hegelianism, many theologians have seen an echo of the sin of the angel, about which St. Thomas wrote,[18] "In this, he unduly desired to be like unto God because he desired as the ultimate end of beatitude that to which he could arrive at *by virtue of his own nature*, turning his appetite away from *the supernatural beatitude which is given through God's grace*." This is the sin of naturalism which denies the supernatural order, that is, the life of grace, so as to take his pleasure in nature, which he thereby completely disfigures.

The fragility of this Hegelian synthesis is equal to its seeming grandiosity, for it is constructed upon the denial of the real value of the first principles of reason. These principles, as well as the True God to whom they lead, do not cease to be true merely because Hegel denied them.

Hegel himself cannot exist without them. He cannot at one and the same time be Hegel and not be him, just as Aristotle himself said: "Protagoras cannot at one and the same time both be and not be Protagoras."

We do not completely deny the good that can result from Hegelianism, since, as we just said, the Hegelian dialectic represents an admirable *reductio ad absurdum* proof of God's existence, for it leads one to choose between the True God and radical absurdity.

---

17.   Leo XIII, *Aeterni patris*, no. 9.
18.   See *ST* I, q. 63, a. 3.

It remains the case that God alone is *He who is, Self-Subsistent Esse, Self-Subsistent Intellection, Goodness Itself,* the Truth and the Life, He alone in whom are essence and existence identical.

***

CHAPTER 4

On Evolutionism and the Distinction Between the Natural and Supernatural Orders

IF THERE IS NO NATURE, PROPERLY SPEAKING, THEN NEITHER IS THERE ANY SUPERNATURAL ORDER, PROPERLY SPEAKING
   On this seven-hundredth anniversary of this glorious University of Salamanca, the home of such teachers as Francisco de Vitoria, Domingo Bañez, Melchior Cano, and many other Spanish scholastics of the sixteenth and seventeenth century, it is a great honor for me to set forth the traditional doctrine concerning the distinction between the natural order and the supernatural order of grace in relation to certain recently-formulated objections which seem to have more or less revived Michael Baius's conception of the elevation of our nature to the life of grace, holding that this elevation is something *owed* to the former.

THE STATE OF THE QUESTION
   Many contemporary writers, working under the influence of *relativism* arising from evolutionism, positivism, or Kantianism, hold (like the nominalists of the fourteenth century) that *we cannot know the natures of things with certitude*, not even human nature and its immutability. Nay, according to them, human nature is not immutable but, rather, is a *complex of phenomena having only a relative stability*, like the transitory customs of various regions and eras. Thus, Marxists define human nature through variable historical facts, likewise speaking about the

natures of the family, property, society, and indeed even that of human authority in such a way that nothing which would be immutable could be found in these realities in the midst of such complete evolutionism. Many existentialists even wish to suppress the very notion *of nature* because, according to them, it would lead to determinism and the denial of freedom, the primacy of which they affirm without restriction.

These various positions all proceed from the relativism and evolutionism spoken of by Pius XII in his Encyclical *Humani generis.*

Now, all of these novelties are indeed rejected by believers. However, before the promulgation of the aforementioned Encyclical, some of them did not seem to sufficiently preserve the immutability of human nature, as well as the traditional distinction between the order of nature and that of grace.

According to these latter thinkers, human nature is indeed experientially apparent on the basis of man's end, inasmuch as this end manifestly surpasses the natural end of brute animals, for only man by his very nature tends toward truth and justice (and, consequently, to God), thus meaning that this nature is certainly something loftier than the variable complex of given, changing phenomena. However, these writers did not sufficiently distinguish man's natural end from his supernatural end, speaking of the distinction between the order of nature and the order of grace with much less clarity than did the [First] Vatican Council.

Their fundamental position can be reduced to this proposition: *human nature, conceived of in a Christian manner, depends on God's free choice and is ordered by Him to a supernatural final end, namely, to the Beatific Vision, meaning that it does not seem possible that human nature, conceived of in a Christian manner, could exist in a state of pure nature.* In other words, according to this theory, nature is no longer "*a center of determinate properties, a font of activity* that is strictly *limited in its own order.*" Instead, it must be thought of along different lines, namely, *as a nature in the midst of becoming, open to something superior*, thus desiring the immediate vision of the divine essence. In the end, this means that the state of pure nature (namely, without grace) would be impossible.

This theory, I believe, is not explicitly defended by anyone today, following upon the promulgation of the Encyclical *Humani generis.*

Those who defended it, with certain attenuations so as to avoid falling into Baianism, submitted themselves in a praiseworthy manner to the requirements laid out in the encyclical. However, it is useful to examine this theory in order to avoid a similar deviation ourselves. Indeed, already during the time of the modernist crisis, Fr. Laberthonnière had said this in almost a literal manner. This problem has been discussed quite excellently in recent history by those holding the opposite position.[1]

The whole difficulty that must be examined can be found in this expression: "*Nature conceived of in a Christian manner.*" Indeed, traditional theologians commonly hold that it is possible that there could have been a state of pure nature (namely, without the life of grace) for human nature, as it is conceived of in commonly received theology, and they believe that they are thereby conceiving of human nature "in a truly Christian manner."

Therefore, we must ask: *Does this new theory preserve the notion of nature, properly speaking, with a determinate proportionate (or, natural) end?* However, if this notion of nature, properly so-called, is not preserved in this new theory, how could the notion of the "supernatural," properly so-called, itself be preserved? This seems impossible, for in ordinary language [*communiter*] and even in the Councils,

---

1.   See Charles Boyer, "Nature pure et surnaturel dans le 'Surnaturel' du P. de Lubac," *Gregorianum*, Vol. 28 (1947): pp. 379–95. Also, see the articles by Fr. Rosaire Gagnebet, "L'amour naturel de Dieu chez St. Thomas," *Revue thomiste*, Vol. 48 (1948): pp. 394–446; Vol. 49 (1949): pp. 31–102. Likewise, see his more recent article, "L'enseignement du Magistère et le problème du surnaturel," *Revue thomiste*, Vol. 53 (1953): pp. 5–27.

Also, see what we wrote in *La synthèse thomiste* (Paris: Desclée de Brouwer, 1946/7 [1st ed.]; 1950 [2nd ed.]), pp. 699–725 (1st ed); pp. 701–804 (2nd ed.). Also, see Garrigou-Lagrange, *De beatitudine*, pp. 133–36 and 164–66.

TRANSLATOR'S NOTE: Fr. Garrigou-Lagrange merely cites Boyer's article as "in a given article from the periodical *Gregorianum* (1947), pp. 370ff and 390ff." The text from *La synthèse thomiste* is not reflected in the current English translation of this text. The text from *De beatitudine* can be partially found in Réginald Garrigou-Lagrange, *Beatitude: A Commentary on St. Thomas's Theological Summa, Ia-Iae, qq. 1–54*, trans. Patrick Cummins (St. Louis: Herder, 1956), pp. 104–107, 127–29. However, Cummins' translation is an unreliable (and often very brief) paraphrase of the original and should not be consulted as a definitive translation of Fr. Garrigou-Lagrange's own text.

"*the supernatural* is said to be *a perfection which surpasses the natural.*"[2]
Now, we do indeed concede the fact that in the writings of the Church
Fathers, the term "natural," is used as meaning "original" (that is, "that
which is connected with the origin"), and therefore, sometimes *in a
broad and improper sense* the term *natural* was used by them in order to
designate a truly *supernatural* gift of grace, namely, the original holiness
conferred upon Adam at his creation, as well as *the preternatural gift of
the integrity of nature,* namely, immunity from death, pain, concupiscence, and ignorance.

Whence, we must examine two things: (1) Whether human nature, properly so-called, as well as its immutability, can be known with
both philosophical and theological certitude; and (2) whether human
nature, properly so called, is ordered to the supernatural end in such
a way that the state of pure nature (namely, without grace) would be
impossible.

*   *   *

I. We say: *Human nature, properly so-called and immutable, can be
known with a certitude that is both philosophical and theological, and as a
nature, it does not depend upon God's free choice.* This is said in opposition
to the relativism born of empiricism, Kantianism, and evolutionism.

Indeed, quite correctly and with philosophical certitude, man is defined as a "rational animal," or something made up of rational soul and
body, or spirit and flesh, as the Church has declared on many occasions.[3]

In this oral exposition, I do not wish to develop at length the first
part of what I have here said. Were I to do so, I would present a defense
concerning the metaphysical certitude of the definition of man: "Man is
a rational animal." Here, I will present a brief summary of this defense.

First, this definition of man stands in harmony *with a philosophical induction* by which we compare man with beings that are inferior

---

2.   The [First] Vatican Council defined in *Dei filius,* can. 2, §3 (Denzinger, no. 3028): "*If
     anyone says that man cannot be called by God to a knowledge and perfection that surpasses
     the natural, but that he can and must by himself, through constant progress, finally
     arrive at the possession of all that is true and good, let him be anathema.*"
3.   See Lateran Synod of 649, can. 2 (Denzinger, no. 502); Eleventh Synod of Toledo
     (Denzinger, no. 536); Fifteenth Synod of Toledo (Denzinger, no. 567); [First] Vatican
     Council, *Dei filius,* ch. 1 (Denzinger, no. 3002).

to him, considering the similarities and differences that exist between them. In this way, we are able to methodically determine the proximate genus for our definition, as well as the specific difference, which is the root for the notes (or, properties) of man.

Second, this definition *is confirmed through a* per se *and adequate division of the genus of substance* into bodily substance and incorporeal substance, then into living and non-living bodily substance, then into sensate and non-sensate living bodily substance, and finally into rational and non-rational sensate living bodily substance. In this progressive dichotomous division of the various genera and sub-genera, brought about through members that are contradictorily opposed to each other, no middle exists between the divided members. Therefore, these divisions are necessary.

Thus, this definition of man, which is commonly admitted and known by all, is certain, notwithstanding the natural mystery involved in the union of the soul and the body (or, of matter and spirit) in one nature which is *per se* unified.

Third, moreover, this definition of man is, in turn, *confirmed through a deduction of man's properties*. We come to see that inasmuch as man is rational he *speaks* intelligently, *laughs* intelligently, *deliberates* about things to be done, and is *free* concerning whatever object is not good from every possible perspective, is *social in nature, religious, responsible*, and capable of both merit and demerit before God and other men. *Thus, we come to know the specific difference of man much better* that we know the difference of inferior beings (e.g., of lions, tigers, eagles, etc.), because the former (in contrast with the latter) *is not immersed in matter*,[4] and reason (or intelligence) is *intelligible* to itself inasmuch as it is essentially relative to *intelligible being* and not merely to sensible phenomena.

Fourth, *man's existence does indeed depend on God's free choice, but human nature does not*. It is necessary that human nature would be composed of soul and body, that his two superior faculties (i.e., the intellect

---

4. See *ST* I, q. 76, a. 1, ad 4: "On account of its perfection, human nature *is not a form immersed in bodily matter* or totally embraced thereby. Therefore, nothing prevents one of its powers from not being the act of a body, even though the soul, of its very nature, is the form of the body."

and the will) would flow from the rational soul, and that whatsoever [faculty] would be specified by its natural, proper object. The fact that the human intellect would be *the least of all intellects* does not depend on God's free choice, nor does the fact that its natural proper object would be *the lowest intelligible* of sensible things,[5] in which, as though in a kind of mirror, God's existence would be naturally known, as well as a number of His attributes.

Fifth, *were we to do away with human nature, properly so-called, nothing would remain of natural ethics* ordered to man's natural end; *similarly, nothing would remain of the natural law or of its immutability*, and we would find that we could not avoid falling into a legalistic positivism which wishes to legitimate grave injustices and the worst forms of violence through the omnipotence of the State against right reason.[6]

Sixth, *and finally, all of these truths concerning human nature are confirmed through revelation*, and thus the Church has declared, on many occasions, that man is made up of his spiritual, immortal soul and his body, nay, that the soul is not united to the body in a merely accidental manner but, rather, is the form of the body in a truly *per se* and essential way.[7] Thus, all the sciences that treat of man, from biology all the way to theology, confirm the aforementioned definition of man. *Whence, human nature*, properly so-called and immutable, *can be known with both philosophical and theological certitude, and it does not depend, as a nature, on God's free choice.*

* * *

---

5. See *ST* I, q. 76, a. 5: "As we already said above in *ST* I, q. 55, according to the order of nature, *the intellective soul stands at the lowest level among intellectual substances.*"

6. Hence, its proportionate object is *the least of intelligible things*, namely, the intelligible being of sensible things, knowable by the mediation of the senses.

    His Holiness Pius XII set this forth in a marvelous manner in his *Discourse to the Members of the Sixth International Congress Concerning Penal Law* (*L'Osservatore Romano*, October 4, 1953): "Ultimately, law is necessarily founded upon the ontological order, its stability, and its immutability. Wherever men and people are grouped together in juridical communities, are they not, quite precisely, *men with a substantially identical human nature? The requirements flowing from this nature are the ultimate norms of law... Their central nucleus*, because it reflects 'nature,' is ever the same. *It follows that an extreme legalistic positivism cannot justify itself before reason.*"

II. We say: *Man's nature, properly so-called, even when conceived of in a Christian manner, is not ordered, of itself and positively as a nature, to the supernatural end (or, to the immediate vision of the Divine Essence), though it can, in a free manner, be elevated to the life of grace; however, it could have not been elevated thereto.*

As is often said by theologians, to deny this would be to confuse man's natural end with his supernatural end, thus leading one to place in human nature not only a passive obediential (or, elevable) potency to the life of grace but, rather, a *positive inclination* (or, *innate appetite*) to grace as well as a kind of demand for it, prior to the infusion of faith and hope, nay, even before actual, natural cognition of God, the Highest Good.

However, as the Thomists say, this *innate natural appetite with a kind of demand* for the life of grace *would at once be essentially natural*, as a property of our nature, *and essentially supernatural*, as specified by a supernatural object, according to the principle: faculties, *habitus*, and acts are specified by their formal objects.[8]

This would be *to confuse* the two orders of nature and grace and, hence, *to destroy* them, just as if one were to confuse the intellect and the imagination, making up some kind of mixed faculty which would be neither the intellect, properly speaking, nor the true faculty of imagination subordinated to the intellect.[9]

However, were human nature, properly speaking, done away with, what would become of the properties of man, and, as we said, natural ethics, along with the natural law? And were grace, properly so-called, done away with, what would become of our free elevation to the truly and properly supernatural order?

---

7. See Lateran Synod of 649, can. 2 (Denzinger, no. 502); Eleventh Synod of Toledo (Denzinger, no. 536); Council of Vienne (Denzinger, no. 900); Leo X, Bull *Apostolici regiminis* (Denzinger, nos. 1440–41); Pius IX, Letter "Eximiam tuam" to the Archbishp of Cologne (Denzinger no. 2828); Decree of the Holy Office under Leo XIII, *Post obitum*, nos. 21ff (Denzinger, nos. 21ff).

8. See John of St. Thomas, *Cursus theologicus*, *In ST* I, q. 12, disp. 12, a. 3, no. 8. This is also held by Cajetan, Bañez, the Salmanticenses, Gonet, Billuart, et al. We have cited the texts of St. Thomas and his Commentators on this point in our work *De revelatione*, pp. 376–98 (1st ed., 1918); pp. 351–72 (5th ed., 1950).

    TRANSLATOR'S NOTE: Regarding this principle, see Garrigou-Lagrange, *Grace*, pp. 467–80.

9. See Pius X, *Pascendi*, no. 37 (On the method of immanence).

This can be understood quite easily. Especially after the condemnation of Baius, it is commonly taught[10] in the Church that: the grace of the first man was not something following upon creation [as such], nor something *owed* to nature itself; but God was able to create man, *without this supernatural grace,* even in the way that he is now born.[11]

Moreover, if the aforementioned new theory were admitted, what would become of the dogma *of the two natures in Christ?* There are two natures, properly so-called, in Christ. Likewise, how could[12] *the divine nature be known by way of analogy with our own nature,* if there were not a nature, properly so-called, in us? By saying that God could revoke the supreme precept, "Love your God with all your heart," Ockham implicitly denied that God, of His very nature, is the Highest Good. In this, we can clearly see the grave error of absolute nominalism.

Finally, what would become of the treatise on grace inasmuch as the latter is *a participation in the divine nature?* What would become of the *per se infused virtues,* which flow from grace, as the faculties flow from the *nature* of the soul?

When theology uses the term "nature," this term would never be taken in its *proper* sense. Thus, *a perpetual confusion of nature and grace* would ensue.

Whence, it must be said: *If nature, properly speaking, no longer exists, so too there will no longer be a supernatural order, properly speaking.* Nothing firm would remain in philosophy as regards any given nature. This deviation is much graver and more extensive than it appeared at first glance. As Blessed Pius X said: "Further, let professors remember that they cannot set St. Thomas aside, especially in metaphysical questions, without grave detriment. Just as is said in the words of St. Thomas himself: 'A small error in the beginning is great by the end'" (*Pascendi* and *Sacrorum Antistitum*).

---

10. TRANSLATOR'S NOTE: Reading "decetur" as "docetur."
11. See Pius V, *Ex omnibus afflictionibus,* nos. 8, 21, 23ff., 26, 55, 79 (Denzinger, nos. 1908, 1921, 1923ff., 1926, 1955, 1979), and Pius VI, Constitution *Auctorem fidei* (Denzinger, no. 2616).
     TRANSLATOR'S NOTE: The final Denzinger citation is listed as "15516." It almost certainly is 1516, which correlates to 2616 in the current edition of Denzinger.
12. TRANSLATOR'S NOTE: Reading "posset" for "possent."

* * *

III. *On the foundation of the distinction between these two orders, according to the [First] Vatican Council.* This Council spoke about this distinction much more clearly than does "the new theology." This Council said, in *Dei filius*, ch. 4[13]:

The perpetual common belief of the Catholic Church has held and holds also this: there is *a twofold order of knowledge*, distinct not only in its principle but also in its object; in its *principle*, because in the one we know by natural reason, in the other by divine faith; in its *object*, because apart from what natural reason can attain, there are proposed to our belief *mysteries that are hidden in God that can never be known unless they are revealed by God*...[14]

For divine *mysteries by their very nature so exceed the created intellect that, even when they have been communicated in revelation* and received by faith, they remain covered by the veil of faith itself and shrouded, as it were, in darkness as long as in the mortal life "we are away from the Lord; for we walk by faith, not by sight."[15]

Now, what is the foundation for this doctrine? It is the transcendence of the intimate life of God, that is, the transcendence of the divine essence *as such*.

St. Thomas says, "Sacred doctrine most properly pronounces determinations regarding God...as regards that which *He alone knows* about Himself and has communicated to others through revelation."[16] Likewise, "*A created intellect cannot see God through His essence except inasmuch as God joins Himself to the created intellect through His grace, as something made intelligible to it.*"[17] Otherwise, a created or creatable intellect, by its own powers, would attain the proper formal object of the uncreated intellect, namely, *the Deity, clearly seen.* This would represent a pantheistic

---

13. See [First] Vatican Council, *Dei filius*, ch. 4 (Denzinger, no. 3015–16).

14. See 1 Cor. 2:8–10.

15. 2 Cor. 5:6. Also see [First] Vatican Council, *Dei filius*, can. 2, §3 (Denzinger, no. 3028); ch. 2 (Denzinger, no. 3005).

16. *ST* I, q. 1, a. 6.

17. *ST* I, q. 12, a. 4.

confusion of created nature with the uncreated nature, for *"faculties and acts are specified by their formal objects,"* and a created faculty would thus be specified by an uncreated formal object not proportioned to it. In this way, we have a theological explanation for what was said in the selection from *Dei filius* cited above: "Divine mysteries *by their very nature* exceed the created (and creatable) intellect…"[18] They exceed the created intellect by their very nature, not merely on account of a free decree by God but, rather, on account of the transcendence of the divine nature over any given created and creatable nature, however perfect it may be. Whence, God was not able to will that the light of glory and the Beatific Vision might be *natural properties* of some utterly lofty angel or[19] that they would pertain to its natural beatitude.

In this, we can quite clearly see the distinction which exists between the order of nature and that of grace, not only in man but in the angels, even the loftiest among them. This distinction, not only in righteous men, but in the angels, was most excellently affirmed by St. Augustine: *"God created the angels, simultaneously establishing their nature and bestowing grace upon them."*[20] In many places, St. Thomas affirmed this even more explicitly, when he discussed the perfection of the angels in their existence of grace and glory.[21] Thus, we can understand why the Angelic Doctor said: *"The good of grace in one person is greater than the good of nature in the whole of the universe."*[22] Even the good of grace in one baptized infant is greater than all angelic natures taken together. Along the same lines, Pascal said: "The infinite distance separating bodies from spirits presents us with an image of the infinitely more infinite distance between spirits and charity, for the latter is *supernatural.* All bodies together do not have the value of the least of spirits…. And all (created) spirits together, as well as everything they may produce, do not have the value of the smallest of charity's movements. It is of another, infinitely more elevated, order."[23]

---

18.   See [First] Vatican Council, *De filius* ch. 4 (Denzinger, no. 3016).

19.   TRANSLATOR'S NOTE: Reading "aut" for "sut."

20.   Augustine, *De civitate dei*, bk. 12, ch. 9.

21.   See *ST* I, q. 62, aa. 1–4.

22.   *ST* I-II, q. 113, a. 9, ad 2.

23.   See Pascal, *Pensées*, art. 17.

Our natural knowledge of God, and even the natural knowledge of God that the loftiest angels can have, could forever grow without ever attaining, nor ever being able to demand, the least degree of the Beatific Vision. Nay, it could not even do so for the least degree of infused faith. Placed at these lofty heights, with tranquility and the greatest of certitude, traditional theology affirms, along with the [First] Vatican Council, the distinction of these two orders.

The aforementioned, recently proposed objections, were advanced, almost to the letter, by Fr. Laberthonnière at the time of the modernist crisis and were refuted in the Encyclical *Pascendi*.[24]

Thus, we can see with utter clarity that *neither the nature of our soul, nor an angelic nature, however lofty it may be, contains a seed of grace,* just as the animal's sense life cannot contain the seed of intellectual life. Sanctifying grace is indeed the seed of glory, but it is itself essentially supernatural and infused. Therefore, in angelic natures and in our own nature, we cannot find even the tiniest *seed of grace* but, instead, can only find *a passive obediential potency* (or, *a passive elevability*) to the order of grace. Such an elevation is indeed quite befitting, but it remains utterly *free*, like the divine adoption, because *the formal object of the divine intellect (namely, the Deity clearly seen) infinitely transcends the formal (or, proper) object of any given created or creatable intellect.*[25]

Whence, it remains the case that knowledge of God, the Author of grace and glory, utterly surpasses the natural powers and demands of any given created or creatable intellect.

---

24. See Pius X, *Pascendi*, no. 37 (On the method of immanence).

25. Obediential or elevable potency is "an aptitude for receiving whatever God may wish," so that it obeys God. (See St. Thomas, *De virtutibus in communi*, a. 10, ad 2 and ad 13, as well as in many other places indicated in the *Tabula aurea operum S. Thomae* at the word *Potentia*, no. 10). And *obediential potency* differs from the *befittingness* connected with it. For example, in all men's natures, there is an obediential potency to the Hypostatic Union, but not a befittingness to this. Likewise, in Christ's Soul, His *habitual grace* could ever grow from the perspective of God's absolute power (see *ST* III, q. 10, a. 4, ad 3), but this is not befitting.

TRANSLATOR'S NOTE: On the importance of the text from *De virtutibus in communi*, against those who hold that the notion of "obediential potency" is not St. Thomas's own notion, see Mark F. Johnson, "St. Thomas, Obediential Potency, and the Infused Virtues: *De virtutibus in communi*, a. 10, ad 13," *Thomistica*, ed. E. Manning (Leuven: Peeters, 1995), pp. 27-34.

Therefore, without grace, properly so-called, God's intimate life remains inaccessible. Indeed, we do have *a natural desire* to see God, the Author of nature, but this natural desire remains *conditional and inefficacious*, like the desire for rain in the midst of a drought, or like the desire for a doctorate experienced by a student who is insufficiently prepared for receiving such a degree.[26]

This *natural desire* to see God, the Author of nature, a desire which is conditional and inefficacious, is far less lofty a desire than is *the supernatural desire* of infused hope or infused charity.

This entire doctrine is confirmed by the fact that, according to revelation, man becomes *an adoptive son of God* through habitual grace. And let us recall that *adoption*, whether in the human order or the divine order, is *a gift that is free and not owed*, however befitting it may be.

Conclusion

The matters that we have spoken of pertain to human nature (or angelic natures) properly speaking, in relation to which grace is said to be, properly speaking, supernatural. *If there is no nature, properly speaking, then neither is there any supernatural order, properly speaking*, for the supernatural itself is defined (by the [First] Vatican Council) as "a perfection which surpasses nature."

And we must add: *Nature, considered in a Christian manner*, not only *can be elevated* to the life of grace, from which it is completely distinct, but moreover, following upon original sin, nature *was not destroyed*, even though our ability to freely choose what is good and to flee from what is evil is *diminished*, unless it comes to be healed through grace, which at once heals and elevates.[27]

All of this pertains to nature, properly speaking, conceived of in a Christian manner, but we cannot admit that human nature so conceived would depend on the free choice of God and would be *thus*

---

26. We have treated this at length in our work *De revelatione*, vol. 1, pp. 376–403 (1st ed. 1918); pp. 351–76 (5th ed. 1950): the existence of our nature's *obediential (or, elevable) capacity* for the supernatural order is suggested from a consideration *of the adequate object* of our intellect; the existence of this capacity is urged from a consideration *of our natural desire to see God through His essence* (resolution of objections).
    Also, see our *De beatitudine*, cited above (pp. 133–36).

27. See Second Synod of Orange, can. 8 and conclusion by Caesarius of Arles (Denzinger, nos. 378 and 396), Council of Trent, *Decree on Justification*, ch. 1 (Denzinger, no. 1521).

ordered by it to a supernatural final end, meaning that a state of pure nature would be impossible.

In this way, we come to avoid two mutually opposed errors. *On the one hand, we avoid naturalism,* which denies the supernatural order, as well as our elevation to the life of grace. *On the other hand, we also avoid the pseudo-supernaturalism* of Baius and certain others, who more or less confuse the order of nature and that of grace.

The Encyclical *Humani generis* (August 12, 1950) said: "Others destroy *the* [*true*] *gratuity* of the supernatural order, since God, they say, cannot create intellectual beings without ordering and calling them to the Beatific Vision."[28]

Whence, as happens in other matters as well [*ut alibi*], to change the order of nature by saying that *nature is not something immutable* but, rather, something ever in the midst of becoming, *would be to return to the nominalism of the fourteenth century.* Nature, properly speaking, would no longer exist, nor would a supernatural order, properly speaking.

What we have said makes the truth of this principle quite clear: *That which is supernatural* quoad essentiam *is supernatural* quoad cognitonem—for truth and being are convertible. Hence, the real possibility of the mysteries of the Trinity, the Incarnation, the life of grace, and the life of glory, all *cannot be apodictically demonstrated* solely by the natural powers of our intellect or those of an angelic intellect.

However, the possibility of these mysteries *is defended* against those who deny them and *persuasively argued for* by arguments of suitability having the greatest of profundity, indeed, even more so for the angels than for us. Nonetheless, these arguments from suitability offered for the Trinity, the Incarnation, and for the life of grace and glory will never be apodictic, no matter how profound they may be. Indeed, they do have a kind of tendential aim orienting them toward evidential knowledge, though not to the evidence of some demonstration but, rather, *to the evidential character of the Beatific Vision.* These arguments from suitability are like a polygon inscribed within the circumference of a circle. However small a polygon's side may be, it can be divided *ad infinitum*

---

28. Pius XII, *Humani generis,* no. 26.

without ever becoming as small as a mere point. Thus, no polygon will ever be the same as a circle's circumference. So too, arguments that of themselves are only probable will never be apodictic. This is so because of the transcendence of the supernatural order.

Therefore, the teaching of the [First] Vatican Council concerning the distinction of the two orders [of nature and grace] remains intact, for *quite obviously, the proper object of the uncreated intellect* (namely, the Deity, clearly seen) *infinitely surpasses the proper object of any given created or creatable intellect*. Whence, it is said: "What no eye has seen, nor ear heard, nor the heart of man conceived, what God has prepared for those who love Him."[29] And, the Only-Begotten Himself said: "I thank thee, Father, Lord of heaven and earth, that thou hast hidden these things from the wise and understanding and revealed them to babes."[30]

---

29. 1 Cor. 2:9 (RSV).
30. Mt. 11:25 (RSV).

CHAPTER 5

The Encyclical "*Pascendi*" and Phenomenalism

On the occasion of the fiftieth anniversary of the Encyclical *Pascendi*, we would like to recall how Saint Pius X in this document, promulgated on July 3, 1907, condemned phenomenalism, which denies (or places in doubt) the ontological value of the first notions and first principles of our natural power of understanding.[1]

I. THE NEGATIVE AND POSITIVE FOUNDATIONS OF THIS PHENOMENALISM

First of all, this Encyclical rejects the first, negative foundation of the apologetics of the modernists, one that resembled that of the liberal Protestants in significant ways. This negative foundation is what one calls agnosticism, the contemporary form of skepticism.

According to phenomenalist agnosticism, the principle of causality only has a phenomenal value. It holdes that its proper formulation is not, "Every being which comes into existence requires a cause and, in the last analysis, an Uncaused Cause," rather, holding that it is formulated, "Every phenomenon presupposes a prior phenomenon, and so forth, *ad infinitum* into the past." Thus, it follows that reason cannot prove the existence of God, the First Cause who exceeds the phenomenal order. Likewise, it follows that miracles are inconceivable, for a miracle would thus be a phenomenon without any phenomenal antecedent. One would need to be content with saying that the most extraordinary of phenomena arise *from unknown forces* which science will one day discover.

On the basis of this phenominalist agnosticism, modern thinkers derive what has been called "their scientific and historical atheism." As is said in no. 6 of this Encyclical (cf. Denzinger, no. 3475):

> We begin, then, with the philosopher. Modernists place the foundation of religious philosophy in that doctrine which is usually *called Agnosticism.* According to this teaching *human reason is confined entirely within the field of phenomena,* that is to say, to things that are perceptible to the senses, and in the manner in which they are perceptible; it has no right and no power to transgress these limits. Hence it is incapable of lifting itself up to God, and of recognising His existence, even by means of visible things. From this it is inferred that God can never be the direct object of science, and that, as regards history, He must not be considered as an historical subject. Given these premises, all will readily perceive what becomes *of Natural Theology, of the motives of credibility, of external revelation.* The Modernists simply make away with them altogether; they include them in *Intellectualism,* which they call a ridiculous and long ago defunct system. Nor does the fact that the Church has formally condemned these portentous errors exercise the slightest restraint upon them (especially in the [First] Vatican Council's Constitution, *Dei filius,* can. 2.1ff. [Denzinger, no. 3026ff] and 3.3 [Denzinger, no. 3033]).

* * *

Basing themselves on this phenomenalist agnosticism, the modernists then derive the positive foundation of their doctrine, namely,

---

1.   The citations from this document come from the official Vatican translation, along with the contemporary Denzinger numeration.

TRANSLATOR'S NOTE: The original footnote indicates that Fr. Garrigou-Lagrange is citing from Denzinger. In this English translation, only non-encyclical citations are taken from the current edition of Denzinger. Slight alteration was necessary on occasion because of the need to emphasize something missing from the English translation which is found in the Latin cited by Fr. Garrigou-Lagrange.

immanentism. If we cannot explain the origin of the Christian religion by appealing to a superior cause which surpasses phenomena, we must explain it through a cause which is immanent in us. As is said in no. 7 of the Encyclical (cf. Denzinger, no. 3477):

> The positive side of (the Modernist system) consists in what they call *vital immanence*… Religion, whether natural or supernatural, must, like every other fact, admit of some explanation. But when Natural theology has been destroyed, the road to revelation closed through the rejection of the arguments of credibility, and *all external revelation absolutely denied*, it is clear that this explanation will be sought in vain outside man himself. It must, therefore, be looked for in man; and since religion is a form of life, the explanation must certainly be found in the life of man. Hence *the principle of religious immanence* is formulated… (Hence) *faith*, which is the basis and the foundation of all religion, consists in a sentiment which originates from a need of the divine. This need of the divine…is at first latent within the consciousness, or, to borrow a term from modern philosophy, in the *subconsciousness*, where also its roots lies hidden and undetected.

Thus, divine (i.e., infused) faith comes to be identified with the *religious sentiment* belonging to the natural order, a sentiment which is found to various degrees in all religions. This identification represents a more or less explicit denial of the supernatural order, using the term "immanentism" or "evolutionism." From this perspective, Christianity would only be the most elevated form of natural religion, though an ever-perfectible form, one that could not be immutable in its dogmas, for the religious sentiment forever evolves, like human life and science which must forever progress in the phenomenal order.

The goal of the modernist apologist is not to show that the mysteries of the Christian faith have been revealed by God but, rather, that they are worthy of being *the object of religious experience*, which is ever-perfectible and not immutable.

History, we are told, shows that the diffusion of Christianity is not sufficiently explained by human means but, instead, contains *an unknown* which deserves to be experienced in its various manifestations. Moreover, according to the modernists, phenomenalism defines the truth through the conformity of our judgment with human life, which forever evolves, and not through the conformity of our judgment with extra-mental reality and its immutable laws. See *Lamentabili*, no. 58 (Denzinger, no. 3458): "*Truth is no more immutable than man himself, since it evolved with him, in him, and through him.*"

As regards the end that is proposed by the apologetics of the modernists, the Encyclical adds in no. 35 (cf. Denzinger, no. 3500): "The aim he sets before himself is to make the non-believer attain that *experience* of the Catholic religion which, according to the system, is *the sole basis of faith.*"

II. THE CONSEQUENCES OF THIS PHENOMENALISM

What consequences follow from this with regard to the ontological and transcendent value of dogmatic formulas, the immutability of dogmas, as well as the superiority of divine faith in relation to the human sciences?

The Encyclical responds in no. 13 (Denzinger, no. 3484):

> Hence, it is quite impossible to maintain that (*dogmatic formulas*, according to the modernists) *express absolute truth*: for, in so far as they are *symbols*, they are the images of truth, and so must be adapted to the religious sentiment in its relation to man... But the object of the *religious sentiment*, since it embraces that *absolute*, possesses an infinite variety of aspects of which now one, now another, may present itself. In like manner, he who believes may pass through different phases. Consequently, the formulae too, which we call *dogmas, must be subject to these vicissitudes, and are, therefore, liable to change.* Thus the way is open to *the intrinsic evolution of dogma.*

Likewise, see no. 26 (Denzinger, no. 3493): "First of all they lay down the general principle that in a living religion everything is subject to change, and must change."

For modernism, dogmatic formulas are not absolutely true, for the *notions that they imply do not have an ontological and transcendent value,* but rather, only have a phenomenal one. As we have seen, they hold that the principle of causality should not be formulated, "Every being which comes into existence requires a cause and, in the final analysis an *Uncaused Cause* who is *Being Itself, Ego sum qui sum.*" Rather, according to them, this principle should be formulated, "Every phenomenon presupposes a prior phenomenon, and so forth, *ad infinitum* into the past." If the notion of *being* does not have an ontological and transcendent value but, rather, only a phenomenal one, that of a verbal entity, as is said by nominalists, the same must be said of a host of other primary notions: *unity, truth, goodness, efficient causality, end, nature, substance, person,* etc. And what will thus become of dogmas which we cannot experience, such as the dogma of the Hypostatic Union and that of eternal life?

From this [modernist] perspective, the Nicaeano-Constantinoplitan definition of the *consubstantiality* of the Father and the Unique Son was true in relation to the state of sciences and philosophy in that era, a *truth that was relative* to the state of human knowledge at that moment of time. However, it was not an absolute and immutable truth.

As is said in no. 16 (cf. Denzinger, no. 3486) of the same Encyclical, it follows that *divine faith would ultimately be subordinated to human science* and that Jesus Christ could not have said, "Heaven and earth will pass away, but my words will not pass away" (Mt. 24:35, RSV) and "I am the way, and the truth, and the life" (Jn. 14:6, RSV).

The immutable word of the Savior surpasses the sciences which themselves evolve, and for this to be so, it is necessary that the first notions of reality, unity, truth, goodness, and so forth, all have a value that is not only phenomenal and transitory but, beyond this, one that is ontological, transcendent, and immutable.

It does not suffice that one say that dogmatic formulas have a *practical value* for the believer, *as a norm of action.*[2] Nor does it suffice that one behave in relation to Jesus Christ as though one were faced with a divine person. One must believe that *He is* truly God.

---

2. The modernists said: "The dogmas of the faith are to be held according to their practical sense; that is to say, as preceptive norms of conduct and not as norms of believing" (*Lamentabili,* no. 26; Denzinger, no. 3426).

As is clear, phenomenalism leads to disastrous consequences that ultimately lead one to lose one's divine faith. This fact is can be perceived well enough in the denials written by David Hume and by those of positivists whose thought lies in line with his own. This fact was seen above all during the period of the modernist crisis.

In recent years, have we not seen a kind of more or less explicit neo-modernism in a number of writings? The Encyclical *Humani generis*, which recalls the ontological and transcendent value of the first notions and first principles of natural understanding, responds to this question by showing the consequences of relativism in philosophy and theology.

* * *

Philosophically, this question comes down to the following, which has been subject to frequent examination by Thomists: *What is the first object known, not by our external and internal senses but, rather, by our intellect's natural understanding?*

St. Thomas responds that the first object known by sight is the *colored* being precisely as colored and not as a being. The first object known by the sense of hearing is *the sounding* [*thing*], and this sense can only hear that which is sounding, that which is audible. As for the first object known by our intellect's natural understanding, it is *the intelligible being* of sensible things, and we cannot know anything intellectually except under the notion of intelligible being…[3]

---

3. See *ST* I, q. 5, a. 2: "The first thing that the intellect conceives is being, for everything is knowable to the degree that it is in act. Whence, being is the proper object of the intellect, and thus is the first intelligible, just as sound is the first thing that is audible." See St. Thomas, *In II De Anima*, ch. 6, lect. 13 (*On the sensible per accidens*, which is intelligible per se, "*which is immediately grasped by the intellect upon the presence of the sensed thing.*") While the colored being is known by sight *as colored*, it is grasped by the intellect as *intelligible being*. Also see Cajetan, *De ente et essentia*, q. 1 (Whether being is the first thing known in the order and way of origin). [Cajetan, *Commentary on Being and Essence*, trans. Lottie H. Kendzierski and Francis C. Wade (Milwaukee: Marquette University Press, 1964), pp. 40–62.] Likewise, see John of St. Thomas, *Cursus Philosophicus*, vol. 2: *Naturalis philosophiae* (Turin: Marietti, 1933), pt. 1, q. 1, a. 3 (Whether being is the first thing known by our intellect).
    TRANSLATOR'S NOTE: The use of "proper object" by St. Thomas here does not directly correlate with the later use of the Thomist school in its careful (and important) distinction between the intellect's proper and adequate objects. our intellect's *proper object* (*the*

The efficient cause is *acting, efficient being*; substance is *being which exists in itself* and is one and the same under multiple and variable phenomena. Plants and animals are not only collections of phenomena, as Hume says, but, rather, are living beings. The animal is a living being endowed with sense knowledge. Man is a living being endowed with rational knowledge. The external and internal senses cannot attain the *intelligible being* of sensible things, nor know the meaning of the *verb to be*, nor grasp *the raisons d'être* of things and events.

Hume paid heed only to sensible phenomena and did not understand what is the object of the primary notions of substance and efficient causality. He was led to say that a substance is only a succession of phenomena, something limited to that order alone. However, in reality, an animal is not a mere collection of phenomena. It is *a living being* endowed with sense knowledge.

Hume did not grasp the importance of the verb *to be*, along with its tenses and its moods. He lost sight of the distance which separates the sensible from the intelligible. Whence, we have the ruinous consequences following upon his purely phenomenalist position, which certainly does not represent some sort of discovery, whatever some may say about it, but, rather, represents a profound ignorance of the value of the idea of being and of the verbs *to be, to have, to realize, to actualize, to attract*, and *to perfect*. Must we eliminate these primary notions and fundamental verbs from the dictionaries of all languages? This ontology stands at the foundation of "both ancient and Christian philosophy," as His Holiness Pope Pius XII said in one of his recent discourses.

We discussed these problems in the second edition (Paris: Desclée de Brouwer, 1950) of our *La synthèse thomiste* in the section entitled, "Étude sur l'immutabilité du dogme et le réalisme traditionnel."

---

quiddity or nature existing in corporeal matter; or, *the intelligible being of sensible things*) and its *common object*. The latter is divided into the *mediate object* (*that which is accessible through the intellect's proper object, being as being, analogically known*); or *extensive object* (*that toward which the human intellect is not opposed by its nature, that for which it has a negative obediential potency*). The *proper* and *mediate* objects are included in the *proportionate* object of the intellect. Its *adequate* object includes the *extensive* object as well. On this, see Austin Woodbury, *Natural Philosophy: Psychology* (St. Vincent College, Latrobe, PA: The John N. Deely and Anthony F. Russell Collection, Latimer Family Library), esp. nos. 902, 904, and 920; Garrigou-Lagrange, *Sense of Mystery*, pp. 146–47, n. 6.

According to this realism, the first object known by *the intellect's natural understanding* is not the sensible phenomenon (be it external or internal) but, instead, is *the intelligible being* of sensible things. If the first object of our intellect were the sensible phenomenon, the principle of causality would have only a phenomenal value and could not enable us to know a first, transcendent cause. As has been said [by others and also myself], it would be like a coat hanger painted upon a wall, upon which one could hang only an image of a cloak and not a real one.

Hume's supposed discovery, which gave birth to phenomenalism and lingered on in positivism and Kantianism, is not a philosophy but, rather, is the rejection of every philosophy worthy of the name, for it is the rejection of the proper object of the intellect. *It is the rejection of the intelligible*, which it reduces to the sensible, just as materialism always reduces the superior to the inferior. This does not represent a form of discovery. Rather, it is an aberration.

Indeed, this is all the clearer when one considers its relationship with loftier problems such as the immutability of Christian dogma, the life of grace, and the life of eternity.

By enumerating the consequences of phenomenalism, the Encyclical *Pascendi* shows that it represents the death of the intellect, which is here replaced with an artificial substitute from which every form of wisdom has disappeared. One thus arrives at the most radical form of empiricist nominalism, where the only thing that remains of *ideas* are words, *the common names* which express them.[4]

However, Providence permits all these errors only so that the light of truth may be made even more radiant. From this perspective, if the phenomenalism of Hume and of his successors did not exist, we would need to invent it so as to provide a proof through a *reductio ad absurdum*

---

4. It is true that these phenomenalists remain men and that their natural understanding continues to make use of the *idea of being* and of the verb *to be*, even though they disfigure it through their empirical nominalism, which no longer knows how to distinguish the *idea* from *an averaged-out* (or composite) *image*, accompanied by a common term. This is the source of perpetual equivocation in their writings and statements when they once again become trapped within their theories, instead of following the inclination of their intellect's natural understanding. In their own domain, they ultimately come to prefer artificial flowers to natural ones, and in the end, nothing remains of the intellect's natural understanding, which, by contrast, should be the foundation of every philosophy.

for traditional realism and for the value of the idea of *intelligible being*, which is elevated above the level of the sensible. It thus furnishes an indirect proof for the value of the verbs *to be*, *to realize*, and *to actualize*, which are the foundations for the classical proofs of the existence of God, the First Being and Supreme Cause.

By way of contrast, the inconsistency of Hume's empiricist skepticism shows the elevation and firmness of the genius of St. Augustine and St. Thomas.

According to them, one would mortally wound the intellect and, indeed, eliminate it (by eliminating its object) if one were to deny *intelligible being*, reducing it to sensible phenomena, and were to deny *being as acting*, which one would claim is merely an antecedent phenomenon. This denial of the intellect would lead to the denial of God, just as the affirmation of the intellect (and of the intelligible) leads to God, the Supreme Intelligible One and the First Being.

* * *

PART V

Philosophy, Faith, and Theology

* * *

INTRODUCTION TO PART V

This final section takes us to the borders between the natural and supernatural orders of knowledge. Although a number of the essays
found earlier in this volume were obviously written within the context
of supernatural revelation, this final section presents four essays that
are more thematically focused on the relationship between faith and
reason.

The first chapter in this section falls in the domain of "natural
theology," that portion of ostensive metaphysics[1] which is devoted to
what can be known about the First Cause of being precisely through
the principles of metaphysics (i.e., in terms of being). This essay presents a digest of what Fr. Garrigou-Lagrange discusses elsewhere at
much greater length in *God: His Existence and His Nature*.[2] In short,
its concern is with presenting an overview of the late Thomist school's
understanding of how various names—such as "Highest Good," "Self-
Subsistent Existence," "He who Eternally Knows," etc.—are attributed
to God without, on the one hand, reducing those notions to their mere
creature-derived content (God is forever more dissimilar from what we
can know on the basis of creatures than He is similar to them), while
also, on the other hand, avoiding any predication that would split up
the divinity (God pre-contains in His very eminence all that is said of
Him, though in a unified way). In other words, God "contains" all of
the divine attributes formally (i.e., indeed in a substantial and proper
sense), eminently (i.e., in a loftier *and unified* sense which somehow

outstrips all creaturely participations in His attributes), and analogically (i.e., in a way that is *simpliciter* different but *secundum quid* the same). There are great mysteries involved in this problem. On the one hand, we are faced with the problem of the particular kind of conceptual distinction found among the divine attributes: the minor-virtual distinction defended by the later Thomist school (though not without textual support from St. Thomas himself), as well as the extrinsic virtual distinction operative in case of certain attributes.[3] The various divine names are not *mere* names affixed indifferently to God. If that were the case, we would fall into nominalism, thus undercutting all language about God. Indeed, were they *mere* names, we could say rather meaningless things like, "God punishes through His Beauty," whereas the true thing to say would be, "God's Justice is beyond our justice, for in the eminence of the Deity it is merged with His Beauty, another pure perfection." The two expressions are not the same, and if we wish to have meaningful theological language, we must respect these points.[4]

---

1. On the distinction between the ostensive tasks of metaphysics and its defensive ones, the reader would benefit greatly from referring to the works of Fr. Garrigou-Lagrange's student, Fr. Austin Woodbury. The texts regrettably remain unpublished, but a copy of them can be found in the archives at St. Vincent College, Latrobe, PA, where the papers of John Deely and Anthony Russell are housed. This distinction seems also to have been that of Fr. Angelo Pirotta, O.P., and it generally follows the discipline structure that Fr. Garrigou-Lagrange himself held for metaphysics.

2. See Garrigou-Lagrange, *God: His Existence and His Nature*, vol. 2, pp. 1–267.

3. The topic only is explained with great brevity in most English texts in metaphysics wherein it is taken up, at least for beginners (as in Wallace's brief compendium, Owens's *Elementary Christian Metaphysics*, H.-D. Gardeil's metaphysics text, and the brief discussions in Fr. Garrigou-Lagrange in *The One God*, trans. Bede Rose [St. Louis: Herder, 1943], and *God: His Existence and His Nature*). Further consideration can be found in John of St. Thomas, *Material Logic*, q. 2, a. 3 ("On the Distinctions of Reasoned and Reasoning Reason, and on the Corresponding Unities"), pp. 76–88. The best English-language summary of this that I have been able to find is in Austin Woodbury, *Metaphysics* (St. Vincent College, Latrobe, PA: John N. Deely and Anthony F. Russell Collection, Latimer Family Library), nos. 882–88 and *Ostensive Metaphysics: Natural Theology*, nos. 1682–88. Likewise, see my detailed comments below, in the chapter entitled "On the Eminence of the Deity: In What Sense the Divine Perfections are 'Formally and Eminently' in God," p. 349, note 6.

4. No doubt, of course, the eminence of the Deity must lead us to remind ourselves always of the way that the divine attributes are interrelated. Otherwise, we would fall into a covert form of univocism that would break each divine name apart into a little separate domain hazily contained in the Deity. On this point, we can draw inspiration from the profound words expressed in Jacques Maritain, "Reflections on Theological

And yet, this distinction cannot posit anything *really distinct* in God Himself. God, He Who Is from Eternity, Ever-Actual and Unchanging, does not change and has no distinction within Himself, except where the Persons of the Trinity are distinguished from each other. As the famed adage runs in Trinitarian theology: "In God everything is one and the same where there is no opposition of relation." Therefore, the divine names are all somehow contained in the eminent and naturally unnamable reality that is the *Deity precisely as such*, that is, God precisely in His Godhead, God as He is known only to Himself. In God, being, oneness, goodness, truth, beauty, intellection, willing, love, mercy, justice, and so many other pure perfections are all united in the eminent reality that is God. This is a mystery of great light (in itself) and great shadow (for our weak minds), one that Fr. Garrigou-Lagrange has meditated upon at greater length elsewhere, drawing out its profound implications.[5] It is what gives the true meaning to the life of grace, for through grace, we are divinized and enabled to know and love with this same supernatural eminence, wherein all of the various divine names, whether they be known naturally or supernaturally, coalesce in God's utter loftiness.

Thus, the first essay provides a summary of these lofty matters which no doubt call for many subsequent technical reflections. Nonetheless, we all stand in need of first steps, and here the great Thomist pedagogue provides them for us. Moreover, because this chapter was given as a

---

Knowledge," in *Untrammeled Approaches*, pp. 243–71, especially pp. 249–50: "We know that the distinctions of reason that we use in this case are not only distinctions of reason founded *in re*, they are founded in a reality so much more real and rich with life than all created realities, that even *seeming* to treat them as if there were question of real distinctions is just a rather feeble way of paying homage to God's transcendence. Still, it is necessary that our thinking activity never let itself be caught in this trap of 'seeming.' And it should never be forgotten that the One about Whom the theologian speaks is not a mosaic of different perfections glued to the wall of aseity, but the living God in His sovereign and transcendent unity, the same Being, subsisting in itself, in which we are obliged by our human means to consider separately each of the perfections in question, each of which is in reality His very *esse* and His very life, and cannot be truly known by us except by our taking account of all His other perfections. This would require, it seems to me, that in the teaching of theology the study of each divine perfection be completed by the consideration of its relation to some other perfection, as by 'elevations' in which the mind would be made aware again and again of the infinite transcendence of the Uncreated."

5. See Garrigou-Lagrange, "The Eminence of the Deity, Its Attributes, and the Divine Persons," in *Sense of Mystery*, pp. 171–97.

paper at a conference, it also contains the questions that were asked of Fr. Garrigou-Lagrange, along with his responses. This provides a wonderful insight into how he responded to questions raised in these difficult matters of natural theology.

The next essay, "On the Relationship Between Philosophy and Religion," is situated within the context of the famed debates over "Christian philosophy" in 1930s France. It was delivered at the Second International Thomistic Congress. The overall francophone debate has been given admirable treatment and bibliographical work by Gregory Sadler, whose text *Reason Fulfilled by Revelation: The 1930s Christian Philosophy Debates in France* is an excellent source for the details of this history.[6] In this introduction, I will solely draw attention to several salient points, leaving the remainder to the attentive reader.

After opening with a brief exposition of "contemporary rationalism," taking Léon Brunschvicg's address "Religion et philosophie" as a point of departure, Fr. Garrigou-Lagrange moves on to "intramural grounds" within Catholic thought. As he does in many other works, he draws attention to his position by explaining the defects that "miss the mark," just as vices "miss the mark" of virtue. The general context for his expositions are the currents of European thought that ultimately led to the definitions enunciated by the First Vatican Council in *Dei filius*. In this case, his example by way of excess (vis-à-vis the claims concerning reason's powers) is the semi-rationalism of nineteenth-century figures such as Anton Günther, Jakob Froschhammer, and Georg Hermès. In this talk, Fr. Garrigou-Lagrange only briefly recounts their conflicts with the Magisterium, a topic that he takes up elsewhere in his oeuvre. [7] His primary concern here is their blurring of the natural and supernatural orders, especially regarding their claimed possibility of demonstrating essentially supernatural mysteries, at least non-contingent ones. He contrasts this excess to fideism as a defect (namely, a defect regarding the purported powers of reason). Here, he does not name proponents of this "fideism," although he

---

6.   Gregory B. Sadler, *Reason Fulfilled by Revelation: The 1930s Christian Philosophy Debates in France* (Washington, DC: The Catholic University of America Press, 2011).
7.   See Garrigou-Lagrange, *De revelatione*, 5th ed., pp. 111–14, 211, 316–18.

likely has in mind the account he gives of nominalistic and tradition-alistic fideism elsewhere.[8]

Having briefly remarked upon the opposed errors (rationalism and semi-rationalism by way of excess and fideism by way of defect), he then proceeds to set forth his personal position. Here too he sees two potential errors, again by excess and defect. On the one hand, there is a position that he likely means to be that of Blondel, namely, that the deficiency of our own natural, rational knowledge gives birth do a positive desire for the supernatural order. To Fr. Garrigou-Lagrange, this seems to be yet another kind of fideism, albeit in a mitigated form. In contrast, the other position is one that is at times found among Thomists, namely that philosophy is a discipline of the natural order to such an extent that it cannot be intrinsically altered in any way by a higher, supernatural wisdom.[9]

Fr. Garrigou-Lagrange attempts to articulate his position as being the golden mountain peak in the midst of these various other positions. Thus, he hews close to the account that was given by Étienne Gilson[10] and Jacques Maritain,[11] and indeed favorably cites most of Maritain's own accounts on this matter. According to Fr. Garrigou-Lagrange, Christian philosophy is positively and in itself Christian in character, not merely negatively "not anti-Christian" or "not contrary to revealed truth." Philosophy, even merely speculative philosophy, is positively

---

8.   See Garrigou-Lagrange, *De beatitudine*, pp. 21–23; *De revelatione*, vol. 1, pp. 377–96.

9.   See Sadler's account of Pierre Mandonnet, Fernand Van Steenberghen, and Léon Noël, as well as M. T.-L. Penido in *Reason Fulfilled by Revelation*, pp. 81–85. For a contempo-rary account somewhat along these lines, see the scholarly work of Van Steenberghen's student, Monsignor John Wippel, "Thomas Aquinas and the Problem of Christian Philosophy" in *Metaphysical Themes in Thomas Aquinas*, Studies in Philosophy and the History of Philosophy, No. 10 (Washington, DC: The Catholic University of America Press, 1984), pp. 1–33. Also, see John Wippel, *Medieval Reactions to the Encounter Between Faith and Reason* (Milwaukee, WI: Marquette University Press, 1995).

10.   For Gilson's position at the time of Fr. Garrigou-Lagrange's writing, see Étienne Gilson, *The Spirit of Medieval Philosophy*, trans. Alfred Howard Campbell Downes (New York: Scribner, 1936). A critique of certain conclusions flowing from Gilson's primary insights in these matters can be found in Thomas C. O'Brien, *Metaphysics and the Exis-tence of God*, ed. Cajetan Cuddy (Tacoma, WA: Cluny Media, 2017). For a summary of the controversy between O'Brien (along with those defending him) and several well-known students of Gilson, see Cuddy's Introduction to the volume, pp. i–xxxix.

11.   Maritain, *An Essay on Christian Philosophy*, and *Science and Wisdom*.

Christian in character, far more than anything extrinsically Christian such as, for example, "Christian geometry," which is Christian only from the perspective of the knower in whose soul the natural and supernatural orders come together.[12]

By saying this, Fr. Garrigou-Lagrange does not claim any change in the natural formal objects of philosophical disciplines. Instead, drawing on Maritain's *Essay on Christian Philosophy*, he comments that while the nature of philosophy is the same without the aid of the supernatural order, its *state* is quite different.[13] He explicitly draws a parallel to a topic discussed in the previous section of this volume, namely, the state of the natural, acquired moral virtues in the soul that is deprived of grace. When deprived of supernatural grace, one retains the same acquired virtue and, hence, the same formal object, but its state is no longer as vigorous as it once was. It no longer directs the moral life with the same vigor, for the agent is no longer oriented even to his or her natural human end.[14] Likewise, theological knowledge (as differentiated from faith) exists in an imperfect state in wayfarers, but in the blessed it exists in its perfect state wherein they will see with the clarity of vision the meaning and interrelations of the many revealed truths known imperfectly here below. Fr. Garrigou-Lagrange believes something analogous holds true with regard to the state of philosophy outside of the state of grace and revelation. Thus, among speculative topics, he believes that the Christian dispensation has brought to full light philosophical truths that were, at best, partially treated by other philosophers, including: free creation *ex nihilo*; God's universal providence; the spirituality and personal immortality of the soul; a full appreciation of free will; moral obligation in various personal, familial, and political matters (a point that he emphasized above in several of the essays in Part III of this volume); and even the full nature of the formal object of metaphysics and of the analogy of being.

---

12. One wonders how he would have responded to comments like those of Alvin Plantinga, who makes even stronger claims regarding Christianity as a structuring principle for human thought. See Alvin Plantinga, "Advice to Christian Philosophers," *Faith and Philosophy*, Vol. 1, No. 3 (1984): pp. 253–71.

13. Maritain notes that it is a question of *the order of specification* (nature) and the *order of exercise* (state). See Maritain, *An Essay on Christian Philosophy*, p. 11.

14. See Garrigou-Lagrange, "Whether Aversion from the Supernatural End Cannot Exist Without Aversion from the Natural End," in *Grace*, pp. 504–506.

Moreover, Fr. Garrigou-Lagrange supports Maritain in his controversial claims regarding "moral philosophy adequately considered," namely that there cannot be a moral philosophy that is at once truly scientific and practical without direct dependence upon revealed truths. Drawing on John of St. Thomas's account of the subalternation of sciences, Maritain holds that adequately considered moral philosophy is scientifically subalternated to theology by way of principles (though not as regards the subject of the science, which still remains human acts to be directed by practical reason).[15] At the end of Fr. Garrigou-Lagrange's talk, he clarifies that he prefers the term "subordination" to "subalternation." He does not explain, however, if this makes him differ from Maritain in any significant way. Elsewhere, in *The Sense of Mystery*,[16] Fr. Garrigou-Lagrange openly and fully ("*pleinement*") accepts all of Maritain's articulation as well, so it is possible that he merely wishes to retain the term "subalternation" for cases where the subject of the science is constituted by such subalternating.[17]

Following Maritain's terminology, he holds that there are two kinds of assistance offered to the Christian philosopher. First, there are the forms of "subjective" assistance that accrue to philosophical *habitus* because of the influence of theologically elaborated faith. Thus, while the infused, supernatural act of faith objectively presupposes the judgment of credibility ("it is naturally / rationally fitting to believe this revelation"), the light of faith then confirms these rationally credible signs and reasoning. When suitably elaborated, one is prevented from denying philosophical truths that would be at variance with what is revealed through faith. The philosopher who knows these things as revealed also will hold his demonstration in a more vigorous manner, even if it is only obscurely grasped. Here, each kind of knowledge remains in its order, formally speaking, but the

15. For a full exposition of Maritain's thought on this matter, see Ralph Carl Nelson, "Jacques Maritain's Conception of 'Moral Philosophy Adequately Considered'" (PhD diss., University of Notre Dame, 1961). Also, Matthew K. Minerd, "Revisiting Maritain's Moral Philosophy Adequately Considered," *Nova et Vetera*, Vol. 16, No. 2 (2018): pp. 489–510.

16. See Garrigou-Lagrange, *The Sense of Mystery*, p. 100, n. 44.

17. For an overview of the topic of subalternation, see John of St. Thomas, *Material Logic*, q. 26, a. 2 (pp. 510–18).

philosopher knows better his or her place in the order of wisdom. As
Maritain expresses the point:

> And in the light of theology, metaphysical truths take on a radiance
> so immediate and convincing that in consequence, the philosopher's
> labors are blest with a new facility and fruitfulness… In one sense,
> the advent of Christianity did dethrone philosophical wisdom and
> raise theological wisdom and the wisdom of the Holy Spirit above it.
> Once philosophy acknowledges this new arrangement, its condition
> in the human mind is thoroughly changed. I think that every great
> philosophy harbors a mystical yearning, which in fact is quite capa-
> ble of throwing it out of joint. In a Christian regime, philosophy
> understands that even if it can and ought to sharpen this desire, it is
> not up to philosophy itself to consummate it.[18]

---

18.   Maritain, *An Essay on Christian Philosophy*, pp. 26–27. On p. 28, he also notes the way
      that healing *gratia sanans* helps to heal the natural powers of man as well. Maritain's
      late life comments on "Christian" philosophy help to show that it is not so much
      "Christian" as "fully philosophical." Thus, nature is brought to perfection *in its own line*
      by healing grace. See Jacques Maritain, "Along Unbeaten Pathways" in *Untrammeled
      Approaches*, p. 421: "'The same problem [of terminology] arises with the expression
      'Christian philosophy' which I have often used as well, and is just about as worthless;
      What I propose in its place is 'philosophy considered fully as such' or 'philosophy forg-
      ing ahead' as distinguished from 'philosophy considered simply as such' or 'stumbling
      philosophy.'" He clarifies this comment in "Reflections on Theological Knowledge," in
      ibid., p. 266: "Such an expression [i.e., "Christian philosophy"] runs the risk of being
      completely misunderstood, as if the philosophy in question were more or less reined
      in by confessional proprieties. The reality is quite different. Given the naturally high
      estate proper to philosophical problems and at the same time the limitations of human
      intelligence, as well as the wounds of nature which affect the human mind itself, we
      should not be surprised that even among the greatest minds philosophy *considered
      simply as such* might well become a stumbling block. All the same we feel sorry for those
      who have felt the flame burn brighter in them on reading Plato or Plotinus… Whether
      there is question of a philosopher or of any man of faith, that faith impregnates the
      Christian intelligence completely. It deputizes philosophical reason to the single search
      for Truth, delivering it from its subjection to the world and from any form of servil-
      ity to the fashions of the times. This is why what we call 'Christian philosophy' is a
      philosophy set free, and ought to be called philosophy *understood fully* as such. This is
      no guarantee of course against any possibility of error, but it does permit this philos-
      ophy to move forward indefinitely and to maintain the integrity of the philosophical
      undertaking as it advances from century to century, even if, as in present times, it is
      encumbered with the frivolous and vainglorious declarations (but there is always some
      truth in them) of philosophical superstars to the enthusiastic delight of journalists."

This brings us to the other kind of "assistance" or strengthening, whereby the threshold is crossed: namely, when natural wisdom receives revealed data on its own, philosophical plane. This happens not only with regard to the natural "reverberations" of theologically explicated revealed data (e.g., the nature of relation as applied to the Trinity) but also as regards merely natural data revealed (e.g., all the topics listed above including free creation *ex nihilo* and universal providence).[19] On this topic, the reader should pay heed to where Fr. Garrigou-Lagrange responds to the comments of Fr. Jacques de Blic, S.J., and, especially, to Fr. Anicetus Fernandez-Alonso, O.P. There he explains that revelation proposes both a truth and the general manner by which one is to proceed in proving that truth. However, this process does not provide the full objectively illative reasoning that would lead one discursively to the revealed conclusion: "Even though it provides neither the major premise nor the minor premise of the demonstrative syllogism, it positively reveals the terminus at which it must arrive." To appreciate this, one must remember that the way that we know a conclusion is precisely colored by the fact that it is known mediately, in a syllogistic fashion.[20] He proposes an analogy with the way that angels illuminate each other by materially proposing an object to be believed. This topic deserves fuller philosophical treatment in light of the tradition of which Fr. Garrigou-Lagrange was a member. Such a treatment would likely help in shedding light on a position that he and Maritain both supported with such conviction and depth.

The third chapter brings our reflections to a domain that, at first glance, appears to be "between" philosophy and theology. In "Apologetics Directed by Faith," Fr. Garrigou-Lagrange defends the view of apologetics that he set forth at length in the massive two tomes of his *De revelatione*. To call this latter work a "manual" risks conjuring up images unworthy of the profound reflections that he undertakes therein concerning the nature of an all-important property of revelation: rational credibility. A clear understanding of this property is of

---

19. On this difficult topic, one should consult Maritain, *Science and Wisdom*, pp. 174–98.
20. See Ioannis a Sancto Thoma, *Cursus philosophicus*, vol. 3 (p. 4), q. 11, a. 3, 372a7–373b17 (especially 373b28–373b17).

great importance for understanding the boundaries between faith and reason. Hence, this third chapter has been included in this section to help "round out" the discussion of the distinction between philosophy and theology.

The "rational defense" of the faith may at first appear to be purely a work of human reason. Apologetics seeks to study and to make evident the *rational credibility* (or "rationally believable character") of supernatural revelation.[21] This is not to say that it takes as its task rationally proving the supernatural truth of faith. Instead, according to Fr. Garrigou-Lagrange and the tradition he represents, the apologete[22] merely defends the reasonable nature of divine revelation. The matter is well expressed in a remark made by Charles René Billuart that Fr. Garrigou-Lagrange cites elsewhere:

> Nor also can the *possibility* of this mystery (of the Trinity) be proven by means of natural reason alone. I deny that it can be proven that this mystery does not involve a contradiction *positively* and *evidently*; however, I concede that it can be proven that this mystery does not involve a contradiction *negatively* and *by ways of probable arguments*. Indeed, this suffices so that this mystery not be judged to be impossible, not however that it be known to be *evidently possible*.[23]

Apologetics is thus located on the intriguing border between the natural and the supernatural. Is it the philosophical science of Christian

---

21. For a general history of apologetics, see Avery Cardinal Dulles, *A History of Apologetics* (San Francisco, CA: Ignatius Press, 2005). On p. 284, he praises Fr. Garrigou-Lagrange warmly, although his comments are not utterly lacking in scorn: "In establishing apologetics on a firm theological basis, Garrigou-Lagrange made a clear step forward, but unfortunately his apologetical method remained imprisoned in the narrow rationalistic framework of the Roman textbook tradition."

22. Concerning Fr. Garrigou-Lagrange's distinction between an apologist and an apologete, see Réginald Garrigou-Lagrange, *De revelatione*, 5th ed. pp. 38–39, esp. p. 39, n. 2: "Similarly, he who writes an apology is 'an apologist,' and he who teaches apologetics is called 'an apologète.'" Although he uses the term "apologète" instead of "apologiste," it is not clear whether or not he means to strictly deploy this distinction here. However, since he does use the latter term in a citation near the end of the essay, I have maintained the terminological distinction.

23. Billuart, *Summa sanctae Thomae, De Trinitate*, diss. proem., a. 4.

good sense? Or is not apologetics rather a task of theology, defending
its principles against objections raised from the perspective of reason
alone? The matter is not in doubt for Fr. Garrigou-Lagrange. According
to him, it is a theological task, for theology is not only a science that deduces conclusions in light of virtual revelation from what is known on
faith; it also is a form of wisdom that finds itself tasked with the defense
of its own principles.[24] In the natural order, this sort of self-defense falls
to metaphysics.[25] In the order of reasoning which is objectively illuminated by faith (i.e., in the domain of acquired supernatural theology),
this defense falls to theology. Apologetics *is* this rational defense, made
under the direction of revealed truth.

Thus, apologetics *is not* a kind of philosophy of religion in defense
of Christianity. Instead, it is a theological task that has a theological
goal and receives from on high the very means by which it is to undertake its demonstrations. These methods differ from the "Christian philosophy" that Fr. Garrigou-Lagrange defends in the first chapter of this
section. Even when such a philosophy receives objective aids, it only receives a conclusion to be reached without the explicit manifestation of
the middle term (or, means) by which it will be demonstrated. Therein
lies all the work of manifesting a philosophical truth in a philosophical
manner. In apologetics, the means are also revealed, thus implying that
the apologete (or apologist) must have faith, even though his hearers do
not need to have this supernatural light.

This third chapter is offered as a summary of the central matter
treated in the lengthy two tomes of *De revelatione*, which I am at present translating for Emmaus Academic. This lengthier text will provide
many resources for Thomists concerning these topics with its important insights into the developed Thomistic position on these matters.
Among all of Fr. Garrigou-Lagrange's many works, it is a unique text
which was the fruit of years of teaching, providing a profound exposition of an important domain within traditional Thomistic theology,
one that is often underrated nowadays.

---

24. And as noted in "Theology and the Life of Faith," theology (and the theologian as such)
also meditates upon the principles revealed by faith and gives them precision.

25. For example, Fr. Garrigou-Lagrange believes that this is the case in the fourth book of
Aristotle's *Metaphysics*.

The final chapter is a brief but no less edifying text on the nature of theology, "Theology and the Life of Faith."[26] Although our concerns have been primarily philosophical throughout this volume, it also has been quite clear that Fr. Garrigou-Lagrange's own philosophical thought is "magnetized" by his primary vocation as a theologian. A man with a powerful philosophical intellect, he nonetheless remains a theologian.[27] By allowing ourselves to reflect on the nature of theological wisdom with Fr. Garrigou-Lagrange, we will simultaneously be illuminated regarding his positions concerning philosophical wisdom in comparison to theological wisdom. In this essay, he is more concerned with showing the relationship between acquired theological knowledge and the formal assent of faith than with the relationship between such theological knowledge and philosophical wisdom. By paying heed to his reflections, however, one will also sense the importance played by philosophical wisdom in the life of the believer.

At first, Fr. Garrigou-Lagrange stresses the ways that the theologian uses philosophical truths to defend the faith, giving special consideration to the notion of truth and the importance of the Thomistic school's conclusions on this matter.[28] As the essay develops, he begins to discuss some of theology's proper tasks.[29] As a form of wisdom, theology must defend its principles and make them more intelligible. Before even coming to theological *conclusions*, he notes that much must be done by the theologian in order to elaborate *revealed truths in a*

---

26. An altered and shortened version of content from this essay was included in Fr. Garrigou-Lagrange's *De deo uno*. There is significantly more content on more technical matters in the essay that we present from the *Revue thomiste*, thus justifying its inclusion here. See Garrigou-Lagrange, *The One God*, pp. 31–37.

27. No doubt, this is the source for some of his brevity when reflecting on philosophical themes. There are many topics that require further sounding out than what Fr. Garrigou-Lagrange can often provide for them. He did not, however, seem to be unaware of this fact. The theologian can often provide very profound philosophical insights, but his or her concerns lie elsewhere. No matter how much theology articulates its philosophical tools, there are forever tasks to be accomplished by philosophy in its own right.

28. Without drawing attention to their properly philosophical character, he provides a list of philosophical topics that are given great depth by being reflected upon in the light of theology, including the analogical notions of the divine names, the notions of nature and person, the distinction between substance and accident (which is given profound treatment in the discussion of quantity in relation to transubstantiation), and freedom.

29. See also, Garrigou-Lagrange, *De revelatione*, 5th ed., pp. 7–37.

more distinct manner. Here, he interprets the reality of dogmatic development by using a tool that was discussed in the first section of the present volume: the process of arriving at a fully formed definition on the basis of an initial, vague one. Beyond this kind of work, theology must indeed draw many properly scientific conclusions from revealed data, thereby passing beyond the domain of what could potentially be defined as holding *de fide*, even though such conclusions are far more than mere opinions.[30]

Unlike philosophy, theology plunges its roots down into faith, but it has its own *obiectum formale quo* (i.e., its objective light, virtual revelation). It is acquired by human study as reason is illuminated by faith to judge of things concerning the inner mystery of God and all things related thereto.[31] As Fr. Garrigou-Lagrange says elsewhere, without faith, theology is like a corpse.[32] Theology must ever draw on the life of

---

30. I say *properly* scientific because scientific knowledge *as such* is objectively illative knowledge of conclusions drawn syllogistically in the light of principles and through scientifically defined middle terms. On this topic, the reader would benefit greatly from the studies presented in Kieran Conley, *A Theology of Wisdom: A Study of St. Thomas* (Dubuque, IA: The Priory Press, 1963); Francisco P. Muñiz, *The Work of Theology,* trans. John P. Reid (Washington, DC: The Thomist Press, 1958); and Mark F. Johnson, "God's Knowledge in Our Frail Mind: The Thomistic Model of Theology," *Angelicum,* Vol. 76, No. 1 (1999): pp. 25–45. As will be clear in the article itself, Fr. Garrigou-Lagrange thereby opposes himself to his fellow Dominican, Fr. Francisco Marín-Sola, on the topic of the dogmatic definability of theological *conclusions,* strictly speaking.

31. On this topic, see my comments in Garrigou-Lagrange, "Remarks Concerning the Metaphysical Character of St. Thomas's Moral Theology, in Particular as it is Related to Prudence and Conscience," pp. 261–66 ("Translator's Appendix 1: Concerning the Formal Object of Acquired Theology").

32. See Garrigou-Lagrange, *De revelatione,* 5th ed., p. 17: "Indeed, formal heretics do not deduce conclusions from principles believed by divine faith, for when they pertinaciously reject the authority of God and of the Church concerning one article, they do not preserve divine faith concerning other articles but, instead, retain only a human faith or opinion founded on their own judgment and their own will (*ST* I-II, q. 5, a. 3). Hence, when faith perishes, Sacred Theology necessarily is destroyed as a habitus. Certainly, the heretical theologian retains a kind of material coordination of theological concepts; however, this coordination lacks the light of faith which provides for their formal connection. It is akin to how once the soul leaves the body the parts of the human body remain materially ordered in the corpse for a time, even though it is nothing more than a human corpse, lacking its substantial form. Therefore, in the formal heretic, there cannot be anything but the corpse of Sacred Theology, or better, a sophistical dialectic concerning divine things jumbled up among themselves, for having rejected the external authority of God and the Church and having lost the internal light of faith, heretics lack the cognitive rule and principle for rightly

grace, the theological virtues, and the gifts of the Holy Spirit. In its own way, the mature, theological explication of these mysteries strengthens and illuminates the intellect of the believer, leading the mind to assent evermore strongly to the formally revealed principles utilized in theological reasoning.[33]

In concluding this volume, these four chapters present explicit reflections by Fr. Garrigou-Lagrange on the inter-relations among the various kinds of wisdom: philosophy, theology, and the gifts of the Holy Spirit.[34] Fr. Garrigou-Lagrange philosophized in faith. Stated another way, he was a philosophical theologian—more theologian than philosopher in the final analysis, but a philosopher nevertheless. It is fitting, therefore, to end on the level of wisdom wherein he primarily situated himself during his many years of laboring on behalf of the Church.

ORIGINAL TEXTS FOR THIS SECTION

"De Eminentia Deitatis: In Quo Sensu Perfectiones Divinae Sunt in Deo 'Formaliter Eminenter.'" *Acta Pontificiae Academiae Romanae S. Thomae Aquinatis et Religionis Catholicae*, Vol. 2 (1935): pp. 162–75.

---

judging concerning things of faith. Therefore, they often confuse supernatural things with natural ones, frequently falling into error. So then, it is not surprising that they say theology is not a science but, rather, a collection of opinions, for their theology in fact is nothing other than that."

And he remarks in a footnote to the penultimate sentence: "Even if the formal heretic sometimes can arrive at true theological conclusions and write about them without error, nonetheless, he knows these conclusions only in a material manner and not in the same way that they are known by the Catholic theologian. For in theological conclusions, the formal connection between the subject and the predicate depends on the light of revelation proposed by the Church and upon the internal light of faith. However, the formal heretic has lost the light of faith and believes only the dogmas that are pleasing to him by means of his own judgment and will."

33.   An interesting parallel text on the relationship between revelation, dogma, and theology can be found in Ambroise Gardeil, "Épilogue: Valeur du dogme et de la théologie pour la vie surnaturelle," in *Le donné révélé et la théologie*, 2nd ed. (Paris: Cerf, 1932), pp. 319–58.

34.   For reflections on the various kinds of wisdom, see Garrigou-Lagrange, *Sense of Mystery*, pp. 3–39.

"De Relationibus inter philosophiam et Religionem." *Acta secundi congressus Thomistici internationalis* (1936): pp. 379–405.

"L'apologétique dirigée par la foi." *Revue thomiste*, Vol. 24 (New Series, 2) (1919): pp. 193–213.

"La théologie et la vie de foi." *Revue thomiste*, Vol. 40 (New Series, 18 (1935): pp. 492–514.

CHAPTER I

On the Eminence of the Deity:
In What Sense the Divine Perfections
Are "Formally and Eminently" in God

Today, our discussion turns to the meaning of the commonly received expression, considering it in accordance with St. Thomas's
doctrine: simply simple [*simpliciter simplex*] perfections are found in
God "formally-eminently."

Now, in the excellent paper he presented this conference, the Most
Rev. Pietro Parente showed us how we must indeed preserve this doctrine in order to avoid the nominalism of contemporary agnostics who,
in a way, resurrect the opinion of Maimonides (Rabbi Moses) holding
that the divine attributes are found in God *virtually*-eminently, as is the
case for mixed perfections, rather than being *formally-eminently* there.

However, this last expression is not understood by all thinkers in
the same way, so we must look into its exact meaning. Therefore, let
us first begin our investigation by recalling what is generally admitted
about this matter, following the order of the articles in *ST* I, q. 13.

I. WHAT DOES THE ADVERB "FORMALLY"
MEAN IN THIS EXPRESSION?

First, these simply simple perfections are said to be *formally* in
God inasmuch as they are *substantially and properly* found in Him
(aa. 1, 2, 3). That is, they are found in Him substantially and not in
a solely causal manner, as if, following Maimonides, we were to say

that the assertion, "God is Good," means only, "God is the cause of goodness in things" (cf. a. 2). This is also said of Him *properly* and not in a merely metaphorical manner. Thus, God is called just in the proper meaning of this word, whereas He is only metaphorically said to be angry (a. 3).

Now, the reason for this twofold assertion is the fact that simply simple perfections such as goodness, wisdom, and love *involve no imperfection in their formal meanings* inasmuch as this formal meaning is distinguished from the finite manner in which these perfections are found in creatures. It is quite clear that the First Cause eminently should have all the perfections that creatures have, so long as those perfections do not intrinsically involve any imperfection.

This is the most certain point in this matter.

Second, contrary to what the nominalists hold, the names by means of which the aforementioned perfections are expressed are not synonyms. According to them, the distinction among the divine attributes is only a verbal distinction of discursive reasoning [*rationis ratiocinantis*], like the distinction between Tullius and Cicero. If this were the case, just as we can write "Cicero" anywhere we could write "Tullius," so too could we indifferently write, "the divine justice" where we write, "the divine mercy," thus being able to say, "God punishes through His mercy and shows His pardon through justice" (a. 4). This second assertion is equally most certain and is commonly received by Thomists, Scotists, and Suárezians.

Third, the aforementioned perfections are said of God *analogically*, not univocally, nor equivocally. Whence, the sense of the words "formally-eminently" means *formally-analogically*, not *univocally*. Indeed, St. Thomas says in a. 5:

> Every effect which does not equal the power of its efficient cause receives a likeness of that agent *in a lower manner than how it is found in that agent* and *not according to the same formal character as it has there* (i.e., as is obvious from the context, *not univocally*). This means that what is found in a divided and manifold manner in effects is found in the cause simply and in the same manner... All the perfections of things exist in created things in a divided and

multiplied manner, whereas they pre-exist in God in a united and simple manner.

This is a text of great importance, giving rise to the definition of analogy which separates Suárez from St. Thomas.[1] For some thinkers, in accord with Suárez's principles, analogous terms [*analoga*] are those that use the same term but signify through that term a formal notion [*ratio*] which is *simpliciter the same* and *secundum quid diverse*. However, the Thomists hold that for St. Thomas analogous terms are those that have the same term while signifying through that term a formal notion that is *indeed simpliciter diverse* and *secundum quid the same*. In other words, they are alike according to a kind of proportion (i.e., are *proportionally the same*).[2]

This formulation expressed by the Thomists perfectly coincides with the aforementioned text from St. Thomas (a. 5), where he expressly speaks about this matter and says: "Every effect which does not equal the power of its efficient cause receives a likeness of that agent *in a lower manner than how it is found in that agent* and *not according to the same formal character as it has there* (i.e., as is obvious from the context, *not univocally*)." And a little bit further along in the same article, He says, "The term 'wisdom' is *not* said of God and man *according to the same formal notion.*" In truth, it is said according to a formal notion that is proportionally the same, inasmuch as wisdom in general is knowledge

---

1. In treating the unity of the concept of being, seeming to draw closer to Scotus than to St. Thomas, Suárez says in *Disputationes metaphysicae*, disp. 2, sect. 2, no. 34: "Now, I only assert that everything that we have said *about the unity of the concept of being* seems much clearer and more certain than the idea that *being is analogous*. Therefore, it is not right to deny the *unity* of one's [analogous] concept in order to defend *analogy*. But if one of the two must denied, it should be *analogy*, which is uncertain, rather than the *unity* of the concept, which seems to be demonstrated by *right reasonings*." Likewise, see *Disputationes metaphysicae*, disp. 28, sect. 3, nos. 9 and 11; disp. 32, sect. 2. Also, see Delmas, *Metaphysica*, p. 61; Frick, *Ontologia*, no. 23. In the opposite sense, see A. Martin, "Suárez: métaphysicien et théologien," *Science catholique* (July–September 1898). Norbert del Prado, *De veritate fundamentali* (1911), pp. 196ff: "Suárez, drawing back from St. Thomas, walked down the Scotist path…"

2. Thus Cajetan, *De analogia nominum*, ch. 6 and *In ST* I, q. 13, a. 5, no. 15. John of St. Thomas, *Cursus philosophicus, Logica*, q. 13. Goudin, *Philosophia, Logica major*, pt. 1, diss., 2, q. 1, a. 2. J.-M. Ramirez, "De analogia secundum doctrinam aristotelico-thomisticam," *La ciencia tomista* (July 1921, extracted in 1922): p. 16.

through the highest causes, although God's wisdom is the cause of things, whereas created wisdom is caused (or, measured) by things.

St. Thomas's manner of speaking here is completely in conformity with what is taught in logic, where analogous terms are distinguished from univocal ones. Thus, it is said that the generic and univocal term *animality* expresses *a formal notion that is simpliciter the same*, namely "a body living a sensate life," in both a superior and inferior animal, both in the lion and in the worm.[3] However, the analogous term "knowledge" expresses a formal notion that is *simpliciter* diverse and only *proportionally the same* in sensation and intellection inasmuch as sensation is related to the sensible just as intellection is related to the intelligible. Likewise, "love" expresses a formal notion that is only proportionally the same in sensate love and in spiritual love. Hence, whereas a univocal perfection can be *perfectly abstracted* from the inferior cases to which it is applied (e.g., as the formal notion of animal makes abstraction from what is specific to the lion and the worm, not considering the extrinsic differences of the genus), an analogous perfection *cannot be perfectly abstracted* from its analogates,[4] because a likeness of proportions cannot be conceived without the members of the proportionality being conceived vaguely [*in confuse*] (or, *actu implicite*). Hence, great difficulty is involved in attempting to define knowledge in its general sense, in such a way that it can be verified in its proper sense in the cases of sensation, in created intellection, and in the divine intellection. Likewise, it is difficult to define the analogous notion of being so that it can be verified of God, created substances, and accidents.

However, precisely because the analogical *ratio* is only *proportionally the same*, it follows, as St. Thomas notes (cf. *De veritate*, q. 2, a. 11),

---

3. Thus, in the genus of animality, we already find ourselves faced with that which Suárez says is the definition of analogy: a formal notion signified by a term is *simpliciter the same* (a body living a sensate life) and *secundum quid diverse*, inasmuch as a superior form of animality brings with itself all the internal and external senses, in contrast to inferior forms of animality.

4. See Cajetan, *De analogia nominum*, ch. 5.

    Translator's Note: Likewise see John of St. Thomas, *Material Logic*, q. 13, a. 5 ("Whether an analogous concept enjoys unity by way of abstraction from its inferiors"), pp. 167–83; Simon, "On Order in Analogical Sets," in *Philosopher at Work*, pp. 135–71; M. T.-L. Penido, *Le rôle de l'analogie en théologie dogmatique* (Paris: Vrin, 1931), pp. 53–61.

that *an infinite distance can separate two analogates.* Indeed, the distance separating sense knowledge and intellective knowledge is immense, but nonetheless, both of them are called forms of knowledge *analogically and properly* and not in a merely metaphorical sense.

Moreover, St. Thomas's terminology, holding that the formal notion of an analogical perfection is not *simpliciter* the same but, instead, only *proportionally the same* in God and in creatures, is completely in conformity with the words of Lateran VI: "Between Creator and creature no similitude can be expressed without implying a greater dissimilitude" (Denzinger, no. 806). Therefore, when we say the perfections that involve no imperfection are *formally* found in God, we must understand that we mean that they are there *formally-analogically,* not univocally, while nonetheless being there properly and not only metaphorically, as already in the created order, sensation and intellection are analogically but properly called forms of knowledge.

In this way, we have our explanation regarding the meaning of the adverb "formally." Now, let us turn to our explanation of the adverb "eminently."

* * *

II. WHAT IS THE MEANING OF THE ADVERB "EMINENTLY" IN THE AFOREMENTIONED EXPRESSION?

First, from what we have said, it follows that *the utterly eminent manner* in which the divine attributes are found in God *remains hidden from us* and can only be expressed *negatively and relatively* (e.g., as when we say [negatively], "non-finite wisdom," [and relatively] "the supreme and loftiest of wisdom").

Whence, St. Thomas says in a. 5:

When the term "wise" is used to describe a man, it in some manner describes and fully embraces the thing that is signified (distinct from man's essence, from his very existence, from his power, etc.). However, this is not the case when the term is said of God. In that case, it leaves behind the thing that is signified as something *not fully embraced* and *exceeding the term's signification.*

This already provides an explanation for the adverb "eminently" in the expression "formally-eminently." However, this matter still calls for further explanation.

Second, from what we have said thus far, it similarly follows, against Scotus, that *there is not a formal-actual distinction on the side of the reality in question* [*ex natura rei*] among the aforementioned divine perfections. Indeed, according to Scotus, this distinction is more than a virtual distinction inasmuch as he holds that it precedes the consideration that our mind undertakes concerning the matter. However, the distinction which precedes our mind's consideration is already one that is *real*, however minor it might be. Now, a real distinction between the divine attributes is incompatible with God's utter simplicity, on account of which the Council of Florence stated: "In God everything is one and the same where there is no opposition of relation."

Therefore, the most we can admit is that there is a *virtual distinction* between the divine attributes, and indeed, it can only be a *minor virtual distinction*, according to the mode of that which is implicit and explicit, inasmuch one attribute contains the others *actu implicite*.

Nonetheless, against the nominalists, we must hold that the divine names are not synonyms. (That is, we must hold that justice and mercy are not only verbally distinct, like "Tullius" and "Cicero.")

Third, next, we find ourselves faced with the difficult question concerning *the identification of the divine perfections in God*, so that *they are not destroyed* through such identification but, rather, remain in God *formally* (i.e., substantially and properly) without being synonyms. Here, we find ourselves faced with the great difficulty involved in joining together the two adverbs *formally* and *eminently*. At first glance, it seems that the meaning of the second would destroy that of the first. Indeed, we can understand quite easily that the seven colors of the rainbow are *eminently* contained in white light while being found there only *virtually* and not formally. Formally, white light is neither blue nor red, whereas the Deity is formally true, good, intelligent, merciful, etc.

Scotus gave particularly strong pushback in this matter, defending his assertion that there is a *formal-actual* distinction among the divine attributes on the very side of the divine reality [*ex natura rei*] because he thought that their formal identification was impossible. To his eyes, if the divine attributes are *formally* found in God, they must be *formally distinct* in more than a virtual manner.

However, is not this kind of identity impossible?

To this Cajetan responds in no. 7 of his commentary on *ST* I, q. 13, a. 5:

> (This can be understood in two ways.) First, we could think that the proper formal character *of wisdom* and the proper formal character of *justice* were one formal notion so that *that one formal notion would not be a third formal notion* but only that which is the proper formal notion of wisdom and justice. And *this mode of identity is indeed utterly impossible*, implying two contradictories...
>
> Second, this can indeed be imagined if we were to think that the formal notion of *wisdom* and that of *justice* are enclosed in an eminent manner IN ONE FORMAL NOTION OF A SUPERIOR ORDER and *formally identified*. And this identity is not only possible but in fact is the case for all the perfections that are found in God. Indeed, we must not think that the *proper* formal notion of wisdom is found in God but, as is said in the words of the article in question, the formal notion of wisdom in God is not there according to what is proper to wisdom but as something proper to a superior notion, namely, *the Deity*, indeed being common there, in a formal and eminent manner, to justice, wisdom, goodness, power, etc. For just as the *reality* [*res*] that is wisdom and the *reality* [*res*] that is justice in creatures is elevated *into one reality* [*rem*] of a superior order (namely, the Deity) and thus are one reality [*res*] in God, so too *the formal notion* of wisdom and *the formal notion* of justice are elevated *into one formal notion of a superior order*, namely, the proper notion of the Deity and are a singularly unified formal notion, *eminently containing both of them, not in a merely virtual manner* as the formal notion of light contains that of heat but, instead, *formally*, as the formal notion of light contains that of the heating power.[5] Whence, the divine genius of St. Thomas most

---

5. Today, we would say: Just as white light does not formally contain the seven colors but does indeed formally contain the power for producing these colors.

subtly infers from this...: Therefore there are two different formal notions of wisdom in God and in creatures."

That is, as Cajetan says later on in no. 15: "It is not one formal notion *simpliciter*" but, instead, is *proportionally one*, as he had said in ch. 6 of his treatise *On the Analogy of Names*.

This is the Thomistic sense of the expression, "Formally-eminently." "Formally" at once means *substantially* (not causally) and *properly* (not metaphorically), although *properly* in an *analogical* sense. To say that they are there "eminently" excludes the formal-actual distinction of God's attributes and expresses their identification—or, rather, their identity in the utterly eminent formal notion of the Deity, whose proper character can only be known negatively and relatively here below *in via* while remaining hidden regarding what it is in itself.

This point is expressed in an equivalent manner by St. Thomas when he writes in *ST* I, q. 13, a. 4: "Indeed, these perfections pre-exist in God in a *united* and simple manner, whereas they are received in a *divided* and multi-form manner in creatures... Thus, to the various and multiple concepts of our intellect there corresponds *something entirely simple* and *unified* [in God], understood imperfectly by means of conceptions of this kind." Likewise, in ad 2: "The many notions corresponding to these terms are not empty and vain because to all of them there corresponds *one simple thing* imperfectly and multiply represented through all of them." And this is how he likewise speaks in the body of a. 5. Whence, the divine attributes are thus *identified* in the utterly eminent formal notion of the Deity and hence *are not destroyed*. They remain *formally* in the Deity *without, however, being* formally distinct.

Fourth, nay, rather, the divine perfections are thus identified in the eminence of the Deity without being destroyed in such a manner that it is only in the Deity that they exist *in their utterly pure state*, unmixed with any imperfection. Thus, God alone is Existence Itself in its pure state [*per essentiam*], Goodness in its pure state [*per essentiam*], etc.

Fifth, this identification is more easily explained as regards the perfections that belong *to the same line* and are not virtually distinct except in an extrinsic manner.[6] Thus, intelligence, intellection, and the divine truth always [and eternally] understood are quite clearly identified inasmuch as God is Self-Subsistent Intellection, the same as the Highest Truth of itself and eternally understood in act.

6. TRANSLATOR'S NOTE: As regards the even-non-virtual distinction of intellect and intellection in God, see the remarks made by Fr. Garrigou-Lagrange in *De revelatione*, 5th ed., p. 297, n. 1: "The reason for this is because if existence and essence (or even essence [*sic*], intellect, and intellection) were virtually distinguished in God, then *something in God would be conceived of as being potential with a foundation in reality*. Now, since God is the height of actuality, we cannot conceive of Him as having some distinction with a [virtual] foundation in reality in potency to existence, operation, or to something else. Nonetheless, we can admit that there is an *extrinsic virtual distinction* between these divine perfections, namely one that has a foundation in creatures, not in God, inasmuch as pure act has in itself that which in creatures pertains to potency and to act."

Moreover, he cites: "John of St. Thomas, *Cursus theologicus, In ST* I, q. 14, disp. 16, a. 2, solv. arg., nos. 19, 20, 28, and 33. Billuart, *Summa sancti thomae, In ST* I, diss. 2, a. 1; diss., 5, a. 1, dico secundum. Cf. *ST* I, q. 25, a. 1, ad 3."

Also see Garrigou-Lagrange, *God: His Existence and His Nature*, vol. 2, pp. 225–46 (esp. pp. 229–36). In p. 231, n. 29, he cites Billuart, *Summa sancti thomae, In ST* I (*De deo*), diss., a. 1, sect. 4, obj. 3; Contenson, *De Deo*, bk. 1, diss. 2, ch. 2, spec. 2 (although the latter holds that there must be a virtual distinction between the divine intellect and its primary object); also, *ST* I, q. 14, a. 2. Also, see Garrigou-Lagrange, *God: His Existence and His Nature*, vol. 2, pp. 63–64, n. 5. There, he also cites: Gonet, *Clypeus thomisticus*, disp. 2, a. 3, sec. 1; Salmanticenses, *De Deo uno*, tr. 4, disp. 2, dub. 2, nos. 21 and 34.

In *God: His Existence and His Nature*, vol. 2, p. 229, n. 28, he states: "In this case, however, we can concede an *extrinsic virtual distinction*, inasmuch as the pure actuality of God is equivalent eminently to potentiality and act, which are distinct in the created order. But then, we see that the foundation for this distinction is *entirely extrinsic* to God; it has not its *raison d'être* in the formal notions of the perfections so distinguished, but in their created mode which could not be found as such in God." He cites *ST* I, q. 25, a. 1, ad 3, as well as pp. 196ff of Gredt, *Metaphysica*. The latter seems to be found in no. 801 (p. 244ff) of Joseph Gredt, *Elementa philosophiae Aristotelico-Thomisticae*, 13th ed., vol. 2, ed. Eucharius Zenzen (Friburg: Herder, 1961).

In sum, Fr. Garrigou-Lagrange, following these highly technical (but important) discussions within the Thomist school, distinguishes between: (*a*) perfections that are not even virtually distinct from each other (e.g., *essence and existence, intelligence and intellection*); (*b*) those which are virtually distinct solely because of the diverse relations of creatures to God, whether actual or possible (e.g., *knowledge of simple intelligence, knowledge of vision, providence, justice, mercy*, etc.); and (*c*) perfections that are virtually distinct, independent of any relation creatures have to God (i.e., *intellection* and *volition*).

As encouragement for research by able Thomists looking to recover knowledge that has been basically lost in recent history, this point (concerning a virtual distinction which involves an intrinsic conceptual distinction as opposed to an extrinsic nominal distinction) is summarized in the diagram on the following page, drawn from Austin Woodbury, *Ostensive Metaphysics* (St. Vincent College, Latrobe, PA: John N. Deely and Anthony F. Russell Collection, Latimer Family Library), no. 886.

DISTINCTION, i.e., lack of identity, is . . .

Either MENTAL, i.e., distinction not existing on the part of the thing, which is . . .

Either NOMINAL, i.e. distinction of name without intrinsic diversity of objective concept, which is . . . .

Either merely CONVENTIONAL, i.e., a distinction according to name only, without any diversity according to priority of signification or according to connotation of extrinsic equivalence

Or SYNONYMOUS, i.e., distinction according to name only, but according to priority of signification or according to equivalence to diverse perfections in something else, which is . . .

Either MINOR, i.e., distinction according to name only, but according as the names have diverse priorities of signification.

Or MAJOR (or, EQUIVALENTIAL), i.e., distinction according to name only, but according to equivalence to diverse perfections in something else.

or CONCEPTUAL, i.e., distinction between intrinsically diverse objective concepts of the same thing, which is . . . .

Either MINOR, i.e., distinction between objective concepts of the same thing, which are intrinsically diverse, though only as implicit and explicit.

Either MAJOR, i.e., distinction between objective concepts of the same thing, which are diverse according to actual and potential.

or REAL, i.e., distinction existing on the part of the thing, so that the members distinguished are diverse realities, which is . . . .

Either REAL-MODAL, i.e., distinction between diverse realities whereof one is nothing else than a mode whereby the other is mannerized.

Either REAL-REAL, i.e., distinction between two realities whereof neither is a mere mode whereby the other is mannerized.

However, we understandably find it more difficult to explain how perfections belonging to different lines are identified (e.g., intellection and love or justice and mercy). Nonetheless, from what we have said, it is clear that they are identified in the eminence of the Deity, which at once is formally-eminently intellection and love, as well as mercy and justice.

Sixth, in the same way, we have an explanation for the fact that there is only a virtual distinction, not a formal-actual one, between the divine nature and the subsistent relations constituting the Divine Persons (e.g., between the divine nature which is communicable *ad intra* and the incommunicable Paternity).

Whence, Cajetan says in no. 7 of his comments on *ST* I, q. 39, a. 1: "*Of itself*, and not merely from our perspective, there is *one formal notion* in God, one that is neither purely absolute nor purely relational [*respectiva*], not purely communicable nor purely incommunicable, but rather, *most eminently and formally* containing both whatever belongs to the perfection of being absolute and whatever is required by the relational character of the Trinity [*Trinitas respectiva*]... This is so because *the divine reality* is prior to being and to all of its differences, for it is *above being, above one*, etc." Therefore, the Divine Reality is likewise above the absolute and the relational, which are formally-eminently found in it.

* * *

This doctrine concerning the eminence of the Deity is particularly illuminating for three questions of great importance in dogmatic theology.

First, it makes clear that reason by itself can demonstrate the existence *of a supernatural order of truth and life* in God inasmuch as *the Deity* (or, the intimate life of God) exceeds the proper object and powers of any created or createable intellect. See *ST* I, q. 13, a. 4 and *SCG* I, ch. 3 where St. Thomas writes, "It is most evidently clear that there are certain truths about God which utterly surpass the powers of human reason."

Second, likewise, this also makes it clear that we must say that *sanctifying grace* is a participation in the divine nature inasmuch as it is a physical, formal, and analogical *participation in the Deity as it is in itself.* Thus, it places in our depths an ordination to the vision of God as He is in Himself. Thus, it seems rather insignificant to ask, "Is grace a participation in the divine infinity?" Certainly, the divine infinity is not subjectively participated in by us, for in that case it would be limited. However, grace orders us to the vision of the Deity, and such vision is a true participation in it.

Already, stones are like unto God according to *existence*, plants according to *life*, and human and angelic intellects according to *intellection*. Grace alone renders us like unto Him according to the *Deity*.

Third, and finally, this doctrine concerning the eminence of the Deity enables us to explain from on high why we cannot here below *in via* know *how God's universal salvific will is intimately reconciled with the mystery of predestination.* This would be to know how God's infinite mercy, infinite justice, and sovereign freedom are reconciled in the eminence of the Deity, knowing why this person was mercifully chosen rather than that other person.

Provided it be united to a growing love of God in charity, this theological contemplation of the eminence of the Deity normally disposes one for infused contemplation proceeding from living faith under a special inspiration from the Holy Spirit, through an illumination by the gifts of understanding and wisdom, each of which attaining in a loftier manner the Deity, who is, "The inaccessible light, whom," as St. Paul says, "no man has seen or can see" (1 Tim. 6:16) until we reach the glory of the hereafter.

QUESTIONS AND RESPONSES

Bartolomé M. Xiberta, O. Carm.

1. In the Reverend Father's excellent talk, mention was made of the analogy of proportionality. I wonder whether this type of analogy should be the only one mentioned? I ask this because in recent authors I everyday see a growing tendency to extol this analogy and at the same time to disparage the analogy of attribution. However, I feel that I must rise up forcefully against this tendency, for it would threaten to diminish the value of scholastic doctrine[s in these matters]. To my eyes, both types of analogy seem to be of equal importance in predicating names

of God and creatures. Indeed, the analogy of attribution has its place whenever many things are analogized according to efficient and final causality, whereas the analogy of proportion [*sic*] holds sway whenever they are analogized on account of a relation in the genera of formal and exemplar causality. But, now, the relation of God and creatures is found in all the genera of causes in an equally principal manner. In truth, one cannot deny that St. Thomas's examples are generally taken from the analogy of attribution.

Moreover, I was surprised that Fr. Garrigou-Lagrange did not speak about that aspect of analogy which St. Thomas sets before others in this matter, namely, the analogy of one to another and of two to a third, that is, the analogy between a principle analogate and secondary analogates, as well as the analogy of secondary analogates among themselves. From this particular doctrinal perspective, we must insist that God is the first analogate in complete and simple perfection, indeed to such a degree that (*a*) nothing is superior to God (not even logically); (*b*) in no common formal notion (not even analogically) does God come together with creatures so that He would in some way fall into the same rank as them; (*c*) that the relations between God and creatures are above all ruled by the metaphysical principle, "that which is first in any given genus is the cause of all those things in that genus,"[7] so much so that whatsoever simple perfections creatures have are from God (indeed in the genera of efficient and final causality as well as that of formal and exemplar causality). Whence, it follows that whenever a simple perfection is detected in creatures, some knowledge is obtained concerning the divine perfection formally, although in a diminished manner. However, if this aspect of doctrine is overlooked, I fear that the aforementioned truths will not be able to remain standing and that what will thus remain concerning the doctrine of analogy would not be of service in trying to avoid agnosticism [given our seeming inability to connect the

---

7. TRANSLATOR'S NOTE: On this famed maxim, the reader may consider the work of Vincent de Couesnongle, "La causalité du maximum: l'utilization par saint Thomas d'un passage d'Aristote," *Revue des Sciences Philosophiques et Théologiques*, Vol. 38 (1954): pp. 433–44; "La causalité du maximum: pourquoi saint Thomas a-t-il mal cité Aristote?" *Revue des Sciences Philosophiques et Théologiques*, Vol. 38 (1954): pp. 658–80; "Mesure et causalité dans la 'quarta via,'" *Revue thomiste*, Vol. 58 (1958): pp. 55–75 and 244–84.

analogates together in such a case]. Indeed, we are able to ascend from knowledge of a given secondary analogate to knowledge of the primary analogate, and this is so because of the aforementioned metaphysical principle. However, we cannot pass from knowledge of one secondary analogate to another because the aforementioned principle cannot be applied in such cases. Certainly, when the blind man knows the *bright* sound of the trumpet, he does not know anything about a *bright* color red, notwithstanding the analogy of proportion [*sic*].

2. I do not completely understand the notion of the Deity which the Reverend Father extols in comparison to whatsoever perfections that can be known from creatures. In the end, the term "deity" is only an abstract expression derived from the concrete expression "God." Given that the term is a proper name (whatever its etymological origin may be), it adds nothing beyond the bare designation of the subject except what may be known about the same subject *from another source*. Thus, under the formal notion of the Deity each person knows that very thing which is implied by the other notions which he himself draws from creatures. However, the advantages that the Reverend Father designates as pertaining to the notion of the Deity seem to me to be found in the formal notion of Self-Subsistent Existence, by which God is conceived of as the primary analogate in the order of existence, which certainly includes all the others in a most united way and in the purest state, without destroying their distinct formal notions because, on the contrary, it confers upon each one of them everything that it has.

Fr. Garrigou-Lagrange's Response

I will begin by responding to the second question. Here, I am making use of the classic terminology utilized by Thomists when they say that the *subject of Sacred Theology* (inasmuch as it is distinct from metaphysics, which contains natural theology) is *God considered from the perspective of the Deity*, that is, not God considered from the common formal perspective of being, but instead *from the most proper formal notion* of the Deity (i.e., God inasmuch as He is God). This is said in order to briefly express what St. Thomas says in *ST* I, q. 1, a. 6: "Sacred doctrine *most properly* determines matters concerning God, inasmuch as He is the highest cause, doing so not only in relation to what is knowable through creatures...*but also in relation to that which He Himself knows about Himself and has communicated to others through revelation.*" As regards the explanation of this classical expression, "God from the formal perspective of the Deity," see the commentators on *ST* I, q. 1, a. 6 and 7, especially Cajetan, John of St. Thomas, Gonet, Gotti, and Billuart, who all make use of these terms which I have explained at length in my books *De revelatione* and *God: His Existence and His Nature*. (Consult the term *Deity* in the alphabetical indices of these works.)

As I show there, in the question concerning the divine attributes in general, the Thomists commonly hold that the term "Deity" is to be understood as referring to the very essence of God inasmuch as it contains the divine attributes *actu explicite* (and not only *actu implicite*). By contrast, God considered from the formal perspective *of Self-Subsistent Existence* contains the attributes deduced from Him only *actu implicite*, for a deduction is required in order for them to be explicitly known.

Thus, the Thomists generally distinguish natural theology which is concerned with God from the formal perspective of being (i.e., as the First Being), thus forming a part of metaphysics, from supernatural knowledge about God, which attains God from the formal perspective of the Deity, that is, as is often said, according to His *intimate life*.

However, the Deity is known in multiple ways: (1) *Negatively*, as the eminence in which the simply simple perfections are formally-eminently found (or, identified, though without being destroyed). This is the way that philosophical knowledge attains the Deity. (2) *Positively*, the Deity is known in multiple ways, either (*a*) *clearly and immediately* through the Beatific Vision, which alone attains *God as He is*; or (*b*) *obscurely*, and here too one can know it in two ways, either through infused faith under [the light of] formal revelation or through sacred theology under [the light of] virtual revelation. On this matter, see the works of all Thomists, especially those who were cited above.

* * *

Allow me to briefly respond to the other question, which does not, however, directly pertain to the current discussion. I indeed admit that a twofold analogy exists between God and creatures, namely an analogy of proper proportionality and one of attribution. I gave special attention to the analogy of proper proportionality because it is verified in all the simply simple perfections which were being spoken about in the earlier discussion.

However, regarding the analogy of attribution between God and creatures, I have set forth in another work the common opinion of the Thomists which seems to me to be rather different from what is now being indicated in the question being posed [by Fr. Xiberta] and would stand in need of specific treatment in order to avoid every possible form of confusion concerning this matter.

For our purposes here, let me merely summarize the lengthier exposition that I present in *De revelatione* (vol. 1, p. 304). The analogy of attribution is taken according to a proportion of one or many [analogates] to another principal [analogate]. Of itself, *it conveys only an extrinsic denomination* in the analogates that are distinct from the principal one, as air and food are said to be healthy in relation to the healing of an animal. Nonetheless, the analogy of attribution *does not exclude an intrinsic denomination* in the inferior analogates.[8] However, if we wish to determine the character of such an intrinsic denomination for them and how it is similar to the perfection existing in the supreme analogate, we then must have recourse to the analogy of proper proportionality, which thus simultaneously exists along with the analogy of attribution. However, in the current discussion, our primary concern was with this second kind of analogy; hence, joining Cajetan and other Thomists, we spoke of the analogy of proper proportionality.

---

8.   TRANSLATOR'S NOTE: This important point is at play in the insightful work of Steven Long, *Analogia entis: On the Analogy of Being, Metaphysics, and the Act of Faith* (Notre Dame, IN: University of Notre Dame Press, 2011).
   Yves Simon (citing q. 13, a. 4, p. 165, of John of St. Thomas's *Material Logic*, as well as the appendix on analogy in Maritain's *Degrees of Knowledge*) explains this very important point well in "On Order in Analogical Sets," 147: "...it follows that the analogy of attribution, whenever it combines with proportionality, is reduced to a state of virtuality. It cannot retain its form when the denomination is intrinsic, for its form implies extrinsicality in all cases but one. We still may speak of mixed analogy, but, of the two types combined, only one, viz., the analogy of proportionality, exists in its own form; the other, viz., the analogy of attribution, has lost its own form, and the effect of attribution—the connection of meaning by causal relations—takes place within a system ruled by the form of proportionality."

Gabriel of S. M. M. O. Carm. Disc.

The divine "eminence," as it is set forth by the speaker, most clearly is something of such lofty beauty as to excite true admiration in the mind, as well as a sense of satisfaction. Therefore, it is not surprising if mystical theologians had that as the particular object of contemplation, even of that contemplation which is had as the fruit of our activity under the aid of divine grace.

Fr. Garrigou-Lagrange's Response
Indeed, and when a special inspiration of the Holy Spirit comes according to the gifts of understanding and wisdom, then this infused contemplation already exists in various degrees.

Fr. Pietro Parente
In *ST* I, q. 13, St. Thomas proves that many names are said of God in a substantial and proper manner, not accidentally and metaphorically (and, hence, are not synonyms).

However, in a. 5, the primary concern is with the predication of certain perfections of God and Creatures. There, he excludes univocity and equivocity. However, he admits analogy and indicates this by saying that an analogical perfection exists "*excellently*" in God but does not exist in Him "according to the same formal character [*rationem*]" as in creatures.

Thereafter, the Reverend Father states that those perfections do not exist in God *according to the same form* [*eamdem formam*] as in creatures, on equal footing with formal character of the form [*rationem formae*]. Afterwards, he concludes that the adverb "eminently" affects the adverb "formally," so that the very form of the divine perfection, on account of its eminence, is *simpliciter* different from the creature's form.

However, for my own part and in contrast to Fr. Garrigou-Lagrange, I believe that St. Thomas does not here hold to the equation *ratio = forma* in the current question. Nay, based on *ST* I, q. 4, a. 3, the contrary seems to be the case: "In a third way, certain things are said to be similar when they communicate *in the same form* but not *in the same formal character* [*rationem*], as is clear in *non-univocal* agents." Likewise, in q. 13, a. 3, St. Thomas very carefully distinguishes the thing signified from the *mode* of signification. He places that properly and formally in

God, though he constantly says that the mode by which God has it is *more eminent* and *more excellent*.

However, remembering the distinction of simple perfections from mixed ones, I say that according to St. Thomas, simple perfections are *formally* found in God (i.e., according to their proper form just as they are in creatures), though in a more eminent manner (i.e., according to the notion of Pure Act). Non-simple perfections in God are diverse (eminently) both as regards their form and their mode.

It must be noted that his term "mode" is taken intrinsically and substantially (not accidentally) so as to express a degree of being. If analogy implies diversity both regarding the form and mode, it seems difficult to avoid equivocity. However, formal likeness does not beget univocity on account of a diversity of mode or degree, which provides a foundation for an analogy of proportionality.

Fr. Garrigou-Lagrange's Response

The same perfection or form (e.g., wisdom) does indeed exist in God and in the creature, though not according to a formal character [*rationem*] which would be *simpliciter* the same but, instead, according to one that is proportionally the same (so that that the proper meaning of wisdom is preserved rather than a metaphorical meaning). Thus, *this perfection*, wisdom, is *proportionally the same* in us and in God, not *simplicter* the same. This is the general explanation of the commentators on St. Thomas when they explain these words from *ST* I, q. 13, a. 5: "The term 'wisdom' is *not* said of God and man *according to the same formal notion*." Indeed, this perfection, wisdom, is only proportionally the same in them, for God knows all things in Himself, such that His wisdom is the cause of things, whereas the created intellect knows many things through the highest cause in the mirror of created things, so that its wisdom or [*seu*] science is caused (or, measured) by things. A proportionality (or, likeness of proportions) is thus established: Just as *homo sapiens* is related to all things known through the highest cause, so too in some way is God related to all things known through the highest cause, noting well this great difference, namely, that God's wisdom is the cause of things and is not caused by things. We could speak similarly about being, one, true, etc.

Moreover, as St. Thomas says in the same text:

> When we apply the term *wisdom* to God, we do not intend to signify *something distinct* from His essence or power or His very existence. And thus, when the term *wisdom* is said of man, in a certain way, it describes and embraces the thing signified. However, this is not the case when it is said of God. Instead, when it is said of Him, it leaves behind the thing signified as unembraced and exceeding the term's signification. Whence, it is clear that the term "wisdom" is *not* said of God and man *according to the same formal notion*.

The analogical common *ratio* of wisdom (or of being, one, true, etc.) *cannot be perfectly abstracted from its analogates* but, instead, is only *imperfectly* abstracted from them, because it expresses something that is the same *secundum quid*, not *simpliciter*, and this proportionality cannot be known unless its members are known in a vague manner.

Hence, when it is said that "wisdom formally-eminently is in God," this eminence affects the very perfection of wisdom and not only the mode in which it is found in God. By contrast, if habitual grace is said to eminently exist in the Blessed Virgin Mary, such eminence affects only the *mode* (and indeed intrinsically) according to which grace is found in her in a lofty degree. Thus, the *same formal character* of habitual grace is found in the Blessed Virgin Mary and in any given righteous person, namely, *a participation in the divine nature*.

However, if one is speaking *of the* very *divine nature* in God (that is, the Deity), then the formal character is not simpliciter the same in God, where it exists in a substantial manner, whereas it is found in the Blessed Virgin Mary as an accidental participation in the divine nature.

In *ST* I, q. 4, a. 3, St. Thomas indeed says: "In a third way, *certain things are said to be similar* when they communicate in the same form but not in the same formal character [*rationem*], as is clear in non-univocal agents." This terminology agrees with the preceding terminology, for the form (or, perfection) of wisdom remains *in some way the same* in God and in creatures. However, it is not *simpliciter* the same but, rather, is proportionally the same. Otherwise, it would not exist according to diverse formal characters. Hence, St. Thomas says later on in the same text: "Therefore, if some agent is not contained in a genus, its effect will have *an even more distant likeness to the form of the agent*, not however, such that *it would participate in a likeness of the agent's form* according to the same formal character of the species or genus but, rather, only *according to some kind of analogy*, just as existence itself is common to all."

Thus, *being* signifies that which is or can be, and regarding the former, it signifies that which exists from itself, from another, in itself, or in another. And among the members of a proportionality, likeness does exist, though according to a *formal notion that is proportionally the same.*

This would be univocity if the formal character signified through the common term were *simpliciter the same* (like a specific formal notion or a generic formal character). It would be equivocity if the formal notion signified through the common term were *totally diverse*, as when "dog" is said of the earth-bound animal and of the constellation "the dog star." In analogy, there is a *formal character that is proportionally the same*, either *properly* (as when God is said to be just) or *metaphorically* (as when God is said to be angry).

Thus, it remains the case that, according to St. Thomas, simply simple perfections exist in God and in creatures according to a formal character that is proportionally the same, not one that is *simpliciter* the same. Thus, they are *formally-eminently* found in God, whereas mixed perfections do not formally exist in God but, rather, are there only *virtually-eminently* inasmuch as God can produce them. Whence, in the expression "*formally-eminently*," the word *eminently* affects not only the *mode* of this simply simple perfection in God but also *the very formal character* according to which it is found in God, so that it may not be distinguished from the other divine perfections. Rather, they are all identified in the eminence of the Deity without, for all that, being destroyed.

* * *

CHAPTER 2

On the Relationship
Between Philosophy and Religion

A s is well known, the problem concerning the relationship between
philosophy and religion has been expressed in various ways by rationalists and by Christian philosophers. Therefore, it is fitting to begin
by considering how it is expressed and resolved by contemporary rationalists and then to examine how it is resolved by Catholic philosophers
in our times, according to their various tendencies, above all when they
treat of the very spirit of Christian philosophy.

I. HOW IS THIS PROBLEM EXPRESSED AND SOLVED
BY CONTEMPORARY RATIONALISM?

In order to understand the outlook of contemporary rationalists concerning these matters, we can listen in particular to M. Léon Brunschvicg,
professor of philosophy at the Sorbonne, who, in 1934, at the last international congress of philosophy in Prague, read a special communication
concerning this matter under the title, "Religion et philosophie."[1]

This communication, whose principal assertions we will cite immediately below, represents a kind of compendium of many works by the
same author[2] and it lucidly manifests the mentality of many contemporary rationalists.

In this exposition, two parts can be distinguished with ease: namely, the negative part, which reveals the foundation of rationalism and

of all its denials; then, the positive part, which intends to restore the concept of religion in a rationalistic manner.

In the negative part, the foundation of this rationalism is that the *notion of truth is one and indivisible*. While [Thomist] theologians say, "The notion of truth is analogous, or said proportionally of divinely revealed truth and of human truth, which itself is also manifold, namely, metaphysical, mathematical, physical, and even morally certain," this rationalism asserts:

> What constitutes the philosopher, inasmuch as he is a philosopher, is the fact that, to his eyes, *the idea of truth remains one and indivisible*. He can only allow, by changing his terrain, by uniting an attribute to a substantive, that the mind releases [*relâche*] whatever there may be of a *rigorous method of verification* that remains its inflexible requirement. *Religious truth must be truth without qualification. Therefore, there is no need to search for another foundation for religion or for another content.* And this itself is a solution that the true religion will be defined by the identity of its foundation and content. [*Et cela même est une solution que la religion véritable se définira par l'identité du fondement et du contenu.*][3]

From the aforementioned foundation based on the unity and indivisibility of the truth, the conclusion is drawn that no assertion can be admitted unless it is recognized in a rigorously scientific manner as being true, according to the requirements of reason and the rational interpretation of experience. Hence, the truths of divine revelation or supernatural mysteries (e.g., the Trinity, the Incarnation, and eternal life) cannot be admitted, for these mysteries can never be rigorously proven, nor can the

---

1.   This communication has been committed to type in Léon Brunschvicg, "Religion et philosophie," *Revue de métaphysique et de morale*, Vol. 42 (1935): pp. 1–13.

2.   See Léon Brunschvicg, *Spinoza et ses contemorains*, 3rd ed. (Paris: Alcan, 1923). *Introduction à la vie de l'esprit*, 5th ed. (Paris: Alcan, 1932). *Les âges de l'intelligence* (Paris: Alcan, 1934). "De la vrai et de la fausse conversion," *Revue de métaphysique et de morale*, Vol. 37 (1930): pp. 279–97; Vol. 38 (1931): pp. 29–60, 187–235.
     Translator's Note: The series was brought to a completion in *Revue de métaphysique et de morale*, Vol. 39 (1932): pp. 153–98.

3.   Brunschvicg, "Religion et philosophie," p. 6.

signs of revelation be historically and philosophically certain; there will ever be doubts concerning their existence and value.

Nay, according to the aforementioned foundation, the very notion of divine revelation cannot be the object of rational discussion. In other words, no religion, indeed most certainly not the Christian religion, can arise from divine revelation which is confirmed by certain signs.[4]

Nor is it remarkable that, according to this outlook, the intervention of a supernatural God in the world could not be known with certainty because, as they say, following the critique established by Kant, it is quite clear that the traditional proofs for God's existence contain a *petitio principii*, on account of an illegitimate use of the principle of causality whose ontological and transcendent value is not at all apparent outside the order of phenomena.[5]

This absolute rationalism openly confesses that it acknowledges the position of the nominalists[6] and that it retains nothing from classical ontology.[7]

* * *

After this negative part (by which it rejects every divine revelation and natural certitude of the existence of God, who is really and essentially distinct from the world), in the positive part, the notion of religion is restored in a rationalistic manner, one that retains certain Christian terminology.

According to the aforementioned principles, *religion* can only be conceived, as Kant said, *within the limits of pure reason.*[8]

---

4.   See ibid., p. 5.

5.   See ibid., p. 3: "Since Kant, if not since Socrates and since Descartes, we know that this function (reason) consists in grasping a natural phenomenon, or a voluntary act, so as to put it into connection with other phenomena or with other acts in a manner to form the unity of scientific experience or of moral conduct."

6.   See ibid.: "The victory of nominalism over the systems of conceptual dialectic that have succeeded one another from Aristotle to Hegel is the victory of good sense."

7.   See ibid., p. 4.

8.   See ibid., p. 12: "The only path that humanity has not yet attempted is to give credit to reason for which, according to Kant's expression, despite the diversity of beliefs, there is only one religion. Now, religion, in order to be wholly united must be wholly and entirely a spirituality." Again, p. 11: "Its essence is to make an effort in breaking away from the letter and from the symbol in order to satisfy more nearly the requirements of the interior ideal."

However, what is in this religious notion *par excellence*? M. L.
Brunschvicg responds:

> From this entirely speculative and rationalist perspective, we do not say
> that the religious notion *par excellence* still needs to be discovered: it is
> the *Word*, which Greece received from Egypt and which was to become
> the center of Judeo-Christian theology; it is the interior light, illumi-
> nating every man coming into this world, and to the degree that he
> understands and coordinates his thoughts, he will experience its boun-
> tiful universality and unlimited fecundity. Behold what is affirmed by
> the religion where the Word is God: the intimate, irrecusable certitude
> that there is in each of us a presence thanks to which our intellect is
> something other than a passive accumulation of images and our love
> something other than the egoistic thrust of instinct, of such a kind that
> it does not need to separate us from our own selves in order to unite us
> at the depths of our interior being to the community of minds [*esprits*].[9]

In this religion, according to requirements of reason so constituted,
the Word of God is not, as in the Prologue to the Gospel of John, "The
Son of God who for us men and for our salvation descended from
the heavens." Instead, here for rationalism, it is nothing other than the
word of the human mind or our reason, which perpetually evolves and
progresses amid innumerable contradictions.

Hence, in this religion, which calls itself "ascetic rationalism," *the
cult of human reason* comes to replace the worship [*cultus*] of God who
is really and essentially distinct from humanity:

> *God is not an object of truth*, which could be detached for itself in one
> knows not what region of reality, *nor even an object of love*, which
> one would make to enter into competition with other objects. *He is
> that by which we are capable of understanding and of loving*, without
> ever drying up the source of our understanding, without ever limit-
> ing our affection or returning it to our personal interest.[10]

---

9.   Ibid., p. 6.
10.   Ibid., p. 10.

The Word of God so understood, according to the doctrine of immanence, as being the word of the human mind (for, in this doctrine
human reason is utterly independent), is truly the Absolute Itself.[11]

In other words, the only religion that can regenerate humanity is
the cult of human reason. In this rationalist "religious" worship [*cul-
tu*] pure love is required, without self-interest, along with a eulogy on
pure love cited from the doctrine of François Fénelon.[12] That is, the
greatest of sacrifices are demanded for obtaining the progress of humanity, a progress whose existence however, not only fails to be recognized by all [*non solum non rigorose recognoscitur*] but indeed often
seems stand in stark contrast to the most certain facts of our past and
current experience.

Nevertheless, thus is the principle of rationalism preserved: Human
reason is the supreme arbiter and judge of the truth and falsity, not
only of scientific truth, but of religious truth, just as said in Spinozism,
Kantianism, and Hegelianism. Hence, religion, as conceived of by the
Catholic Church, represents only an inferior form of human knowledge, an inferior form of evolution, which prepares the way for the
superior, "According to the progress that is accomplished with a kind
of spontaneity, from an *elementary* religion to a more elevated type—let
us say, so as to give precision to what we mean, from the religion of
sublimated nature to the religion of nature which has been *overcome*."[13]
Thus religion is subordinated to philosophy, which judges all things and
is judged by no one.

* * *

It is not very difficult to critique this rationalistic conception of
things, one which would lead to a species of nihilism.

In the first place, the fundamental assertion of this rationalism is
gratuitous, namely, that the notion of truth is one and indivisible such

---

11. See ibid., pp. 6–7: "There can be for philosophy no other God than the *Word*, under-
    stood in the immanence that assures its perfect spirituality without any relation, conse-
    quently, to the exterior forms that would render it, even were it only in appearance,
    dependent upon the conditions of space and of time."
12. Ibid., p. 9.
13. Ibid., p. 7.

that no proclamation could be admitted unless it were recognized as true in a rigorously scientific manner.

Even if the discussion were only concerned with truth as it is known by man himself, outside of experimental truth rigorously proven through scientific experience, why could there not be, outside the limits of experience and above mathematical truths, metaphysical truths, at least the first principles, for example, the principle of causality whose most universal formula is not, "Every phenomenon presupposes an antecedent phenomenon," but, "Every contingent being requires a cause and, in the final analysis, an uncaused cause, which is Self-Subsistent Being, Truth Itself, Goodness Itself, and Life Itself"? Moreover, why could there not be revealed truths? It is irrational to affirm *a priori* that the notion of divine revelation cannot be an object of rational discussion.

Nay, just as this absolute rationalism holds its position concerning truth's supposedly indivisible character, it must, without any evidence, reduce all things—extra-mental being, the will, and every religious idea— to subjective human reason given that our reason is the Absolute Itself. In this way, it unjustly reduces to subjective experience *extra-mental being* and its laws, which would be nothing other than subjective laws of our mind. Nevertheless, in reality, the principle of contradiction (which, for example, makes a square circle self-contradictory) excludes with evident certitude not only what is *subjectively unthinkable* but, indeed, what is *really impossible* outside the mind. This [self-]evident principle is not a mere subjective law of reason but, rather, is an objective law of being, whether possible or actual. Moreover, outside of our reason, other things most certainly exist: other men and sensible beings such as the stars, which certainly are not effects of our reason.

Likewise, absolute rationalism cannot maintain its assertions unless it reduces to human reason the will itself, which would be identified with the activity of the intellect, according to these words of Brunschvicg: "To summarize everything in a word: it is one and the same thing to learn to think and to learn to love."[14]

However, the will is, in fact, something distinct from the intellect, according to the commonly admitted adage: "I see what is better and

---

14. Ibid., p. 13.

approve it, but follow what is worse" (Ovid, *Metamorphoses*, VII, 20–21). A man of great intellectual culture can be profoundly perverse, for beyond the rectitude of the intellect, rectitude of will is needed. Only the man of good will is, without qualification, good, that is, rectified concerning the good, not only the good of the intellect but, indeed, that of the whole human person.

In addition, absolute rationalism unjustly reduces all religious faith and worship of God to reason and the cult of reason. This represents a gratuitous identification of human reason with the Divine Intelligence. However, this identification is contrary to the notion of religion and the notion of the true God. In this conception of things, humanity is said to be *God in fieri* [in the midst of becoming], but this rationalist God is one who is feeble, ignorant, senseless, able to sin, a sinner, wretched, and afflicted. Equally, the aforementioned rationalistic conception opposes contradictorily the history of Christianity and the true sense of its dogmas. The Word of God that is discussed in the prologue of St. John's Gospel differs infinitely from the word of the human mind, however much its evolution may become to its perfection.

Finally, the progress of humanity is not so clearly established an affair as such rationalists affirmed. Nay, often with material progress great backsliding takes place in things intellectual and moral, as we now see in Russia and many other regions. Hence, it is not surprising that this rationalistic doctrine, whatever it may say about the purest love of humanity and of its hoped-for regeneration, may ultimately lead many of its authors to pessimism.

Brunschvicg indeed does admit that this rationalistic conception of merely philosophical religion will appear deficient and incomplete to many.[15] For this reason, he says another religious conception seeks its foundation in religious traditions and gladly accepts the disciplinary rules and authority of a given hierarchy.[16]

Finally, he concludes, "Both conceptions will mutually accuse each other of being utopian; but what would be the worst utopia, in any case, the *sin against the spirit*, would be to leave the two schemes

---

15. See ibid., p. 7.
16. See ibid., p. 11.

[*plans*] to be blurred together at risk of inevitably missing both ends at once."

In reality, however, these two tendencies, namely the philosophical tendency and the traditional Christian faith, can be very agreeably reconciled, provided that it be freed from every kind of deviation, to the degree that rational philosophy not be rationalistic, and traditional faith not decline into fideism and false traditionalism. Thus, both are reconciled in the Church's own doctrine, which we must now discuss.

II. HOW IS THE AFOREMENTIONED PROBLEM EXPRESSED AMONG CATHOLICS TODAY?

This problem concerning the relationship between philosophy and religion often came into discussion among Catholic philosophers in the nineteenth century during the pontificate of Pius IX, when two mutually opposed errors, namely, fideism and semi-rationalism, arose. Today, however, we can see this problem once again in more recent discussions concerning the nature and spirit of Christian philosophy.

The importance of these recent discussions can be more clearly understood if we briefly recall the opposition between semi-rationalism and fideism.

Semi-rationalism, as it was proposed by [Anton] Günther and [Jakob] Frohschammer, in line with a rather Hegelian tendency, and by Georg Hermès according to a Kantian spirit, does indeed differ from rationalism in that such semi-rationalism does not deny the divine origin of Christianity. However, semi-rationalism wished to demonstrate the revealed mysteries (that is [*seu*], to reduce them to philosophical truths) and if in addition to those revealed mysteries, there remain certain, so to speak, contingent mysteries which cannot be demonstrated, this is not because they are *essentially supernatural* but, rather, is only impossible because they are *contingent*, like the day when the world will end, as well as future contingent events of the natural order.

Thus, semi-rationalism preserved Christian dogmas in a kind of material way, but did so ultimately according to the spirit of rationalism. This doctrine blurred together the essentially supernatural order of God's intimate life with the natural order, and the ultimate source of this confusion was the exaggeration of the powers (or, at least, the judgment) of human reason, which proclaims its absolute autonomy.

On the other hand, *fideism* wished to reduce to religious and Christian faith all philosophical truths that exceed experience, namely, certitude concerning the existence of God the Author of Nature, certitude concerning His transcendence (that is, His real and essential distinction from the world and from the human mind), and certitude concerning the spirituality and personal immortality of our soul. Thus, under the pretext of affirming the value of the Christian spirit, the value of rational philosophy is denied and, by that, the value of the rational defense of the preambles of faith and the divine origin of Christianity. Thus, we here once again find ourselves faced with the confusion of the two orders of nature and grace. However, in this case, this is not due to an exaggeration of the powers and judgment of reason but, rather, is due to a serious diminution of reason, which such fideists hold cannot, without religious faith, have certitude concerning those things that exceed experience.

Thus, in the nineteenth century the question concerning the relations between philosophy and religion emerged from the opposition between rationalism or semi-rationalism and fideism.

* * *

Now, however, among Catholic philosophers, there are two particular tendencies giving rise to the new state of the question.

Some people so strongly defend the *Christian spirit of Christian philosophy* that they do not seem to acknowledge the essential distinction between human nature and grace clearly enough, more so on account of reason's supposed indigence than on account of an exaggeration of its powers and its judgment. These Christian philosophers often insist on the *deficiency of our rational knowledge* gradually leading to the emergence of a desire in us for a superior form of knowledge, one which is nothing other than the immediate vision of God, promised to those who believe. Therefore, although they reject the doctrine *of immanence* as a doctrine, they make use of the method of immanence for apologetics, so that they seem to acknowledge in human nature not only a capacity and fittingness for the supernatural order but, even more than this, a kind of demand for it. Thus, whenever they speak, grace seems in some manner to be something justly owed to the indigence of our nature. In this claim, we seem to be faced with a kind of vestige of fideism, endangering the rational demonstration of the preambles of faith.

On the other hand, other Catholic philosophers and theologians rightly wish to preserve *the rational value of philosophy* and the essential distinction between the orders of nature and grace. However, many seem not to preserve the spirit of Christian philosophy well enough, for they sometimes say: as a discipline of the natural order, *philosophy* can be called *Christian* only in a *negative* sense, namely, inasmuch as it must never contradict Christian revelation, and only *by reason of the subject* in whom such philosophy exists, but it cannot be called Christian *in itself.* If Christian philosophy had this character, it could no more be called Christian than could geometry existing in a Christian mathematician without contradicting revelation in any way. However, nobody speaks of a Christian geometry, while all use this expression "Christian philosophy" in order to signify a wisdom that is distinct from theology, though philosophically elaborated under the influence of Christian revelation.

From these various, mutually opposed opinions, the state of the question to be resolved is now clearer, and now it seems that the true solution must exist above and between these mutually opposed extremes, at once as a golden mean and a peak [of excellence].

For us Catholics, the true solution is certainly to be found between and above the opposed excesses of rationalism or semi-rationalism on one side and fideism on the other. Nay, it seems that it is even between and above the two current tendencies related above, one of which thus affirms the *Christian spirit* of Christian philosophy in such a way that it seems to disparage its rational value, and the other which so strongly affirms its *rational value* that it seems not to acknowledge its Christian spirit well enough. The true solution must be found in the reconciliation of these two conceptual notes of Christian philosophy, namely, its rational value and its Christian spirit.

Our concern is not only with the letter of Christian philosophy but with its spirit. It must not be considered only in a quasi-external manner from the perspective of a kind of logical formalism, nor on the contrary, according to its material documentation, but rather, must be considered according to its intimate nature, as it existed in the great teachers such as in St. Augustine, Boethius, and in St. Thomas. Having thus posed the question, let us see the principles of its resolution.

* * *

III. CHRISTIAN PHILOSOPHY IS NOT ONLY CHRISTIAN NEGATIVELY AND BY REASON OF THE KNOWING SUBJECT, BUT RATHER, IS CHRISTIAN POSITIVELY AND IN ITSELF

This was already hinted at above, according to the Church's mind, in relation to the condemnation of the three propositions of the semi-rationalists that must be called to mind.

The first of them is this: "As there is a distinction between the *philosopher* and his *philosophy*, he has the right and the duty to submit himself to the authority he acknowledges as legitimate; but *philosophy neither can nor must submit to any authority*," that is not even to the authority of God who reveals.[17] Before this, Pius IX[18] had explained that even though philosophy has a right to make use of its own principles, its own method, and its own conclusions, nevertheless, it cannot say something contrary to divine revelation, nor call revealed truths into question, nor not support the judgment that the authority of the Church has established regarding a given philosophical conclusion. Likewise, the [First] Vatican Council says in *Dei filius*, ch. 3: "*Created reason* is absolutely subject to uncreated truth,"[19] which holds not only for the philosopher but also for philosophy itself, given that it is an expression of human reason.

The second proposition of the semi-rationalists to be noted is a corollary to the preceding, namely: "The *Church* must not only abstain from any interference with philosophy; *she must also tolerate the errors of philosophy and leave it to philosophy to correct itself*."[20]

---

17. Pius IX, *Syllabus errorum*, no. 10 (Denzinger, no. 2910).
18. See Pius IX, *Gravissimas inter* (Denzinger, no. 2858).
19. [First] Vatican Council, *Dei filius*, ch. 3 (Denzinger, no. 3008).
20. Pius IX, *Syllabus errorum*, no. 11 (Denzinger, no. 2911); Letter "Gravissimas inter" to the Archbishop of Munich-Freising (Denzinger, no. 2860ff).

The third proposition follows from the two others, namely: "Philosophy is to be treated without any regard to supernatural revelation."[21] Often, in contrast, the teaching of the Church concerning this matter is briefly enunciated thus: "Revelation is the negative norm of philosophy." This brief or succinct expression "negative norm" especially intends to say that philosophy must not found its demonstrations on principles revealed and accepted by faith, as theology does, but must proceed in accord with its own naturally known principles and its own method, as Pius IX declared.[22] However, this brief expression, "negative norm," does not deny what has been affirmed elsewhere by the Church, namely: *revelation frees reason from errors, positively illuminates and confirms it,*[23] *fosters the certitude and purity of natural knowledge,*[24] *and is the infallible rule of philosophy.*[25] Thus, we here have an affirmation of philosophy's positive subordination to divine revelation.

* * *

This positive subordination comes to light more clearly in several Encyclicals by Leo XIII concerning the philosophy of St. Thomas. Fr. Norbert del Prado, O.P., explains this well in his book *De veritate fundamentali philosophiae christianae.*[26] He says: "The philosophy of St. Thomas by right merits to be called Christian… (Nay, rather, in it) the true and perfect characteristics or notes of Christian philosophy shine forth (not only positively but) in a marvelous manner." To explain this assertion, Fr. del Prado reminds the reader of these words of Leo XIII

---

21. Pius IX, *Syllabus errorum*, no. 14 (Denzinger, no. 2914).

22. See Pius IX, Letter "Gravissimas inter" to the Archbishop of Munich-Freising (Denzinger, no. 2858).

23. See Pius IX, *Qui pluribus* (Denzinger, no. 2775ff); Allocution *Singulari quadam* (Denzinger, no. 1642ff [former numbering]); [First] Vatican Council, *Dei filius*, ch. 2 (Denzinger, no. 3005), ch. 4 (Denzinger, no. 3019), Leo XIII *Immortale dei*, no. 35 (Denzinger, no. 3172).

24. See [First] Vatican Council, *Dei filius*, ch. 2 (Denzinger, no. 3005).

25. See Pius IX, Brief "Eximiam tuam" to the Archbishop of Cologne (Denzinger, no. 2829); Letter "Tuas libenter" to the the Archbishop of Munich-Freising (Denzinger, no. 2877).

26. Norbert del Prado, *De veritate fundamentali philosophiae christianae* (Fribourg: 1911), pp. xvi and following.

from the Encyclical *Aeterni patris* and from other apostolic letters: "We exhort you, venerable brethren, in all earnestness to restore the golden wisdom of St. Thomas, and to spread it far and wide for the defense and beauty of the Catholic faith, for the good of society, and for the advantage of all the sciences."[27] Leo XII also wrote:

> In the end, the philosophy of St. Thomas is nothing other than Aristotelian philosophy. The Angelic Doctor has truly interpreted this in the most scientific manner of all thinkers, and he made *this philosophy Christian, having freed it from the errors* that easily were beyond the powers of the heathen writer. This philosophy is itself of use in the vindication and exposition of Catholic truth.[28]

Finally, everyone knows these other words of Leo XIII, which in a large measure apply to St. Thomas's philosophy and not only to his theology:

> Again, clearly *distinguishing*, as is fitting, *reason from faith*, while happily associating the one with the other, *he both preserved the rights and had regard for the dignity of each*; so much so, indeed, that reason, borne on the wings of Thomas to its human height, can scarcely rise higher, while faith could scarcely expect more or stronger aids from reason than those which she has already obtained through Thomas.[29]

The expression "Christian philosophy" used in these Encyclicals by Leo XIII shows that Christian philosophy is so called not only negatively and on account of the knowing subject, but *positively* and *in itself*. Nay, it is so called in accord with its positive and marvelous conformity with Christian revelation. Through this subordination to divine revelation, not only is the *philosopher* positively perfected, but *philosophy itself* is so perfected.

---

27. Leo XIII, *Aeterni patris*, no. 31.

28. "*Litterae apostolicae*, quibus Constitutiones Societatis Iesu de doctrina S. Thomae Aquinatis profitenda confirmatur" (December 30, 1892).

TRANSLATOR'S NOTE: This letter may also be found under the title *Gravissime nos*.

29. Leo XIII, *Aeterni patris*, no. 18. This is also taken up below in my final response.

However, a problem remains regarding how we can say that a science (or, rather, *a wisdom of the natural order*), one specified by a naturally knowable formal object, is *positively* and *in itself Christian*, all the while preserving it its nature. For the resolution of the problem thus posited, great aid is derived from the very useful distinction between the *nature of a philosophical science* and *its more or less perfect state*. This distinction was rightly proposed by Jacques Maritain.[30]

IV. THE NATURE AND STATE OF PHILOSOPHY: ITS TWO FORMS OF ASSISTANCE

Any given science, while preserving its nature, can exist in two states, in an imperfect state, e.g., in the learner, and in a perfect state, as in a great teacher. Again, the acquired moral virtues can exist either in an imperfect state, namely, without charity,[31] or in a perfect state when, with the advent of charity, man no longer is in a state of mortal sin. Again, theology, while preserving its nature, exists in an imperfect state in the wayfaring theologian who believes the principles of theology, and it exists in a perfect state in the beatified theologian who sees the principles of this theology.

Similarly, philosophy, while preserving its proper nature as the wisdom of the natural order, can be either in an imperfect state, when it exists without subordination to divine revelation, as in Aristotle, or *in a more perfect state*, with the aforementioned subordination, as it existed in St. Thomas.

Now, this *more perfect state* is correctly explained by Jacques Maritain by means of a twofold assistance, namely, an objective and subjective assistance, which philosophy accepts from revelation or from theologically explicated faith.[32]

---

30.   See Jacques Maritain, *De la philosophie chrétienne* (Paris: Desclée de Brouwer, 1933), pp. 27, 37, 48. Jacques Maritain, *Science et sagesse, suivi d'éclaircissements sur la philosophie morale* (Paris: Labergerie, 1935), pp. 123, 228, etc.

31.   TRANSLATOR'S NOTE: See the chapter above, entitled "The Instability of the Acquired Moral Virtues in the State of Mortal Sin," pp. 171–82.

32.   TRANSLATOR'S NOTE: This phrase "theologically explicated faith" is important, for it seems to be referring to the kind of reflection that theology performs when it *directly* considers its *De fide* principles (though reflectively and no longer under the light of formal revelation but, rather, under the light of theological speculation), not limiting itself to merely theological conclusions. On this, see the chapter below, entitled "Theology and the Life of Faith," pp. 421ff. Traditionally this light was called

* * *

An objective form of assistance arises especially from the supernatural revelation of the natural truths of religion, which reason could indeed know by itself alone, but which in its actual state, after original sin, cannot easily attain with certitude and without error. This is clearly affirmed by St. Thomas in the first article in the *Summa theologiae*, and is declared by Vatican I, sess. 3, ch. 2, in a text known by all: "It is to be ascribed to this divine revelation that such truths among things divine that of themselves are not beyond human reason can, even in the present condition of mankind, be known by everyone with facility, with firm certitude, and with no admixture of error."[33]

However, among the natural truths of religion the following ones must be cited in particular:

1. *Utterly free creation ex nihilo*, namely, from no presupposed subject, *for the manifestation of the divine goodness*. Neither Plato, nor Aristotle, nor the other Greek philosophers reached this threefold truth, which is proposed to us in the form of one truth; and the majority of modern philosophers, Christians excepted, have deviated from it.

2. *Universal providence*, which even in the natural order extends to the smallest of details. Nor did the Greek philosophers arrive at this truth without admixed error, and how many modern philosophers withdraw from it! In addition, together with this truth of the natural order, revelation hands on the notion of the divine conservation of created

---

"virtual revelation." For an explanation of this term, see Garrigou-Lagrange, "Remarks Concerning the Metaphysical Character of St. Thomas's Moral Theology, in Particular as it is Related to Prudence and Conscience," pp. 261–66 ("Translator's Appendix 1: Concerning the Formal Object of Acquired Theology). Because theology has these other tasks, precisely as a form of wisdom, Fr. Francisco P. Muñiz proposed that the *lumen sub quo* of theology should be described in broader terms than virtual revelation. His essay on this matter is a text of great penetration, and while I believe further terminological meditation is necessary on this particular point, his overall views concerning the nature of theology are among the best articulations that are to be found among Thomists writing on this particular topic. On the whole, his insights can be harmonized with Fr. Garrigou-Lagrange. See Muñiz, *Work of Theology*.

33. [First] Vatican Council, *Dei filius*, ch. 2 (Denzinger, no. 3005).

things and of the divine motion by which God acts in every agent without, however, falling into the excesses of occasionalism or determinism.

3. *The spirituality and personal immortality of the human soul.* Indeed, this truth was affirmed by Plato, though not without admixed error, and in addition, great doubts remain for philosophers, whether ancient or modern, concerning the way the separated soul knows, and for many, these doubts diminish the probative force of the very demonstration of personal immortality. By contrast, the Christian faith holds with firm certitude not only the existence of a future life, but of eternal life, which is a formal participation in the intimate life of God.

To this truth is connected another, namely, that *concerning free will*, which is required for there to be merit, or concerning freedom not only from constraint but from necessity. In all these things, as is obvious, Christian philosophy is objectively assisted by revelation.

4. It is also assisted objectively through revelation *of the obligations of the natural law even in its secondary [precepts]*, concerning which human reason is darkened after original sin on account of the wounds of ignorance and of concupiscence. This is especially true concerning the unity and indissolubility of matrimony as well as concerning various other truths pertaining to the individual, familial, and social moral life. Above all, on the basis of revelation alone, we know that mankind has been ordered to the supernatural final end, and that, hence, one cannot tend solely toward the natural final end as though one had been constituted in a merely natural state.[34]

---

34. In this respect, *moral philosophy*, as Jacques Maritain has noted well, in the texts cited above, is especially subordinated to divine revelation. For it does not consider only the natures of things in an abstract manner, but moreover the *ultimate end* to which man in a concrete manner, in his actual state, must tend, amidst many difficulties and problems that are quite complex, which require not only the theologian's examination but also that of the Christian philosopher.

In all these truths and other similar ones, Christian philosophy *positively* accepts objective assistance from theologically explicated faith, as revelation accepted by faith is truly, as Pius IX said, *a guiding star* from on high showing the end to be sought, although philosophy must arrive at this end of philosophical knowledge by its own naturally known principles and according to its own method.

* * *

Subjective assistance is also caused by the infused virtue of faith and by the very act of faith, for although, as St. Thomas shows,[35] one and the same thing cannot simultaneously be *seen* (or, *known*) and *believed* (that is, simultaneously be *evident* and *obscure*), nevertheless, the act of faith, e.g., in the existence of God the Author of grace and of reward, subjectively confirms from on high our philosophical certitude concerning the existence of God the Author of nature, a certitude which is had through demonstration from effects. Likewise, the certitude of supernatural faith concerning eternal life subjectively confirms from on high philosophical certitude concerning the spirituality and personal immortality of the human soul.

Indeed, in one and the same faculty (e.g., in the intellect of a Christian philosopher) there cannot be *two subordinated habitus* without the superior exercising a vital influence on the inferior. This subordination is dynamic, not merely static. Again, the very *act* of a superior

---

This special subordination is similar to that which is preserved by the lawgiver [*iurisperito*] when he must elaborate just laws in the civil order, e.g., concerning matrimony, not abstracting from the revealed truth concerning the indissolubility of matrimony.

Likely, in the practico-practical order, *acquired prudence*, most excellently defined by Aristotle as "right reason in things to be done", must, in our actual state, be subordinated in the just man *to infused prudence*, which under the light of divine faith directs our life in particular matters.

Something similar holds true in the case of moral philosophy, adequately considered. The Christian philosopher, in the moral order, is analogically akin to the the doctor who must care for a person consecrated to God; here, the doctor must consider the state of this person and in his medical prescriptions require nothing against the sanctity of this person's state. However, he remains a doctor, and his medical prescriptions in no manner are the counsels of spiritual direction. Equally, the Christian philosopher, even in the moral order, thus remains a philosopher, and does not become a theologian, even though he knows the positive subordination of philosophy to theologically explicated divine revelation.

35. See *ST* II-II, q. 1, aa. 4 and 5.

habitus (in the case of the act of faith, especially the act of faith illuminated by the gifts of wisdom and understanding) assists from on high
the natural certitudes required as prerequisites concerning the existence
of God and concerning many similar truths.

This is affirmed clearly enough by St. Thomas when he treats of the
subjective assistance of the rational certitude of the judgment of credibility regarding the signs of divine revelation through the infused light of
faith. The act of infused faith indeed presupposes the judgment of credibility but afterwards confirms it. St. Thomas says in *ST* II-II, q. 1, a. 5, ad
1: "Concerning the things that are of faith…the faithful have knowledge,
not in a quasi-demonstrative manner, but inasmuch as *through the light
of faith, they see that they ought to be believed.*" Likewise, see ibid., a. 4, ad
2: "For the (believer) would not believe unless he saw that they should
be believed, whether on account of the evidence of signs, or on account
of something else of this sort"; and ad 3: "The light of faith makes them
see the things that are believed ([or] to be believed). For just as through
the other *habitus* of the virtues man sees what is befitting for him in accord with that *habitus*, so too through the *habitus* of faith is man's mind
inclined to assent to those things that are befitting to right faith and not
[to assent] to others," e.g., to assent to the preambles of faith.

Hence, many Thomists rightly note:

> In the case of believers, nothing prevents the *habitus* of faith that
> they have from concurring in knowledge of credibility, for although
> the *habitus* of faith primarily and principally is ordered to an obscure
> assent [to revealed truths], this does not, however, mean that it
> cannot *concur with certain previous operations* which of their very
> nature tend toward its own principal end and effect. The judgment
> concerning the credibility of the things of faith is something of this
> sort [i.e., tending to the principal end and effect of faith], for by the
> mediation of it [i.e., the judgment of credibility] is the intellect led
> to assent to the truth which it does not see.[36]

---

36. Thus, Billuart, *De fide*, diss. 1, a. 6, and Wiggers cited in the same place.
       TRANSLATOR'S NOTE: He likely is referring to Johannes Wiggers (1571–1639), a
       Thomist at Louvain.

* * *

As we intimated above, this is confirmed in two ways. What is here being affirmed in the intellectual order is commonly admitted in the moral order for *the acquired moral virtues*, which without charity exist only *in imperfecto statu dispositionis facile mobilis*, at least from the perspective of the [acting] subject, although they still indeed have a due, fitting object; however, with the advent of charity, they come to be *in statu virtutis difficile mobilis*. Nay, rather, then their acts, under the influence of charity, become meritorious of eternal life.[37] Nevertheless, these acquired moral virtues are intrinsically of the natural order on account of their specifying object. Therefore, upon the advent of infused charity, the acquired moral virtues preserve their nature in the just man; however, they now exist in a more perfect state than they existed in before.

Similarly, the Thomists generally hold that *theological science* can exist in two states while preserving its proper nature in both of them. On the one hand, it exists *in an imperfect state* in the wayfaring theologian, who [precisely because of this state as a *viator*] does not have evidence of the principles of theology but, instead, holds them through infused faith. On the other, theological science exists *in its perfect state* in the beatified theologian, who under the light of glory has evidence of the principles of theology. There, with much greater ease than was possible when he was a wayfarer, he can deduce many conclusions from them beyond his immediate knowledge of the Word.[38]

In the same way, while preserving its nature as a science belonging to the natural order, philosophy can exist either *in an imperfect state* in a pagan philosopher (e.g., in Aristotle) or *in a more perfect state* in a Christian philosopher (e.g., in St. Thomas), for then, he is perfected by a twofold assistance (namely, objective and subjective as was said

---

37. Thus are many texts of St. Thomas on this matter explained by Cajetan and many other Thomists. See *ST* I-II, q. 65, aa. 1 and 2; II-II, q. 23, a. 7, and Cajetan, *In ST* I-II, q. 65, a. 1, nos. 1–3. TRANSLATOR'S NOTE: Again, see the chapter above, entitled "The Instability of the Acquired Moral Virtues in the State of Mortal Sin," pp. 171–82.

38. See John of St. Thomas, *Cursus Theol.*, q. 1: *De Sacra Doctrina*, a. 3 (Whether theology is, properly speaking, a science).

above). Christian revelation is indeed *the extrinsic norm* of philosophy, but under its direction, philosophy becomes *intrinsically Christian* on account of the aforementioned twofold assistance.

* * *

V. CONCERNING THE SPIRIT OF CHRISTIAN PHILOSOPHY: ITS OPPOSITION TO BOTH RATIONALISM AND FIDEISM

Quite clearly, from the aforementioned twofold assistance through theologically explicated faith, philosophy receives a superior spirit.

Now, the spirit of Christian philosophy can be defined in opposition to the spirit of rationalism and that of fideism even though, of themselves, these two contrary deviations must be conceived in light of how they are opposed to the truth which is conceived first (for they recede from this truth and therefore must be defined in relation to it).

Against fideism, Christian philosophy must firmly defend three fundamental subordinate truths: first, the ontological value of the first principles of reason (namely, the principles of contradiction, of causality, and of finality); second, the ontological value of the *"cogito"* itself (that is, of the existence of the knowing subject); third, the real value of experience inasmuch as one cannot have and experience, properly speaking, (whether internal or external) without the existence of a thing that immediately falls under that experience. Without these fundamental truths, Christian philosophy cannot avoid fideism and cannot defend the preambles of faith as it must. Thus, *the value of rational philosophy*, especially ontological philosophy, finds a firm defense against fideism.

However, against rationalism (and, also, against semi-rationalism), we also must affirm *the spirit of Christian philosophy*, which is in particular born of its twofold assistance (i.e., objective and subjective) through theologically explicated Christian revelation. Thus, Christian philosophy indeed remains *per se* a discipline of the natural order which must prove its conclusions through naturally known principles and through experience, thus being specifically distinct from theology, which proves its conclusions through revealed principles, known by faith.

Still, the twofold objective and subjective assistance which Christian philosophy receives from revelation directs its investigations from on high in the direction of the revealed truth concerning all the questions of greater importance: for example, concerning the demonstrability of God's existence, His transcendence or His distinction from the world, likewise concerning Providence, human nature, the limits of our natural knowledge, human personality, the subordination of our intellect to the Divine intellect, and perfect beatitude.

As is quite clear from what we have said, this is indeed how Christian philosophy is conceived of in the Encyclical *Aeterni patris* itself, wherein the discussion is concerned with St. Thomas's philosophy, which is distinguished from theology with sufficient clarity in his works.

This position represents the golden mean and peak [of excellence] between and above rationalism and semi-rationalism on the one hand and fideism on the other. Again, this conception overcomes the two tendencies exposited above, one of which affirms the spirit of Christian philosophy while, however, seeming to diminish its rational value, whereas the other affirms this value but does not acknowledge its Christian spirit well enough.

The truly Catholic conception of philosophy must acknowledge all its intelligible notes and qualities without any diminution. In this way, we find that these notes can be reconciled in accord with philosophy's due subordination to divine revelation.

COMMENTS AND RESPONSES

Remarks by Fr. [Jacques] de Blic S.J., Professor in Collegio Max. Valseni

My precise concern is not to contradict Fr. Garrigou-Lagrange, whose principal thesis I substantially agree with, as regards the reality of the claims he has made. However, I would like to present him with certain observations concerning the philosophy he speaks of as being affected in itself through an objective assistance. Clearly, when the illustrious speaker declares that one must speak of philosophy not only as being negatively Christian but also as being positively Christian, this does not cause any difficulty for me; however, when he wishes that philosophy be Christian not only on account of the knowing subject but also in itself through an objective assistance, such remarks seem less felicitous to me.

First of all, the concept of a philosophy that is Christian in itself is not, in reality, indicated in the texts of Leo XIII that the Reverend Father has presented.

Second, it is difficult to conceive how, through God's revelation, philosophy could be objectively assisted so that it would be Christian in itself. If the Reverend Father were to have said that revelation aids the philosopher because it adds to his individual understanding a kind of social assistance through the diffusion of the true faith in the whole of society, that is, through the creation of a kind of atmosphere that is favorable to inquiry into philosophical truth, I would understand and acknowledge this to be the same thing that is taught by the [First] Vatican Council, as alleged above. However, what would be the meaning of an objective assistance that would make philosophy intrinsically Christian? I confess that I do not see what is meant by this claim.

Moreover—and this will be my third observation—the alleged texts from the [First] Vatican Council do not explicitly make mention of such a positive diminution in the powers of reason after original sin, which the Reverend Father believes cause our philosophical reasoning to stand in need of some form of objective assistance. This theological idea, one which was a principal source of traditionalism (as I could historically prove), is neither easily understandable [*bene intelligibilis*], nor dogmatically obligatory, nor—although it is Augustinian—proven without qualification by St. Thomas. Therefore, it cannot provide a foundation for a theory of Christian philosophy that is Catholic in a strict sense.

Fourth, nor does what the Reverend Father says in note 34 above (thereby adopting the opinion of the illustrious Monsieur Maritain) concerning the necessary subalternation of moral philosophy to divine revelation seem to be a theological position having significant probability in its favor [*neque magis probabile videtur*]—even speaking Thomistically. This would seem to mean that a purely rational ethics would be impossible, as though Christianity would essentially alter the rational moral order. And I do not see how such assertions may be reconciled with St.

Thomas, first, inasmuch as he holds (as Fr. Leonard Lehu has most excellently shown)[39] that reason is, without qualification, the adequate moral norm, and likewise, he holds Aristotle as the Philosopher κατ᾽ ἐξοχήν [*par excellence*] in ethics no less than in metaphysics.

On account of the importance of this question, permit me to cite the great Thomist Francisco de Vitoria in his *Commentario ad Secundam-Secundae* (ed. rec. III, 37). He says, "We determined in the *Prima se-cundae*, along with St. Thomas, that all the precepts of the evangelical law are matters of natural right, as well as all the counsels, except the precepts concerning faith and the sacraments. And so, the evangelical law contains no other precept outside the natural precepts, with the exception of the precepts concerning faith and the sacraments."

Fifth, and finally, I have the greatest desire for further clarification, because whereas the Reverend Father fully speaks of the laudable assistance which Christian philosophy enjoys, he says nothing concerning the danger that is proper to it, namely, the danger that, under the pretext of making a philosophy Christian (that is, ruled by faith), we may, in fact, rule our philosophy by mere theological opinions—which would truly be deplorable. For if the received adage is that "philosophy is the handmaiden of theology," considering the matter thoroughly, it seems certain that philosophy ought to be the handmaiden of faith rather than of theology and theologians.

Finally, allow me to say that all these critical observations by no means prevent me from approving in substance the remarks of Fr. Garrigou-Lagrange—and, indeed, not only "on account of the subject" (whose genius I admire), but also "in themselves."

Remarks by R. D. Franc. Kuraitis, Dean of the Faculty of Theology and Philosophy at the University of Kaunas in Lithuania

When a philosophy is handed on by Catholic philosophers, it is neither necessary, nor fitting that it be called intrinsically Christian.

---

39. TRANSLATOR'S NOTE: In particular, see See Leonard Lehu, *La Raison: règle de la moralité d'après Saint Thomas* (Paris: LeCoffre, 1930). Also, Leonard Lehu, *Philosophia moralis et socialis* (Paris: LeCoffre, 1914), pp. 72–166.

1. Philosophy is a discipline of the natural order and it uses natural sources, depending upon natural principles, performing all of its tasks by way of a natural method. What is established and concluded in philosophy ought to be placed under the verification of natural reason (either directly, indirectly, or through a *reductio ad absurdum*). Hence, nothing that can only be known by revelation can properly pertain to philosophy.

Certainly, the Catholic person [*homo catholicus*] who is conscious of his Catholic character should shun those things that are contrary to Revelation and the Church's doctrine. In fact, the sincerely Catholic person knows that God is the Author both of the natural and supernatural orders and that He cannot contradict Himself. Hence, such a person knows that disagreement cannot exist between those things that, on the one hand, revelation teaches and the Church proposes and, on the other, those things that natural reason reveals as being true and certain. The Catholic philosopher also has great aid from faith and from the Church's doctrine in those truths of religion which he himself must discover philosophically. Such truths are given in revelation by God so that man may know them more easily, without the mixture of error, and with certainty. But the Catholic philosopher must propose in a philosophical manner (namely, on the basis of natural sources, depending upon natural principles, according to a natural, critical method, and not on the basis of the authority of revelation and the Church) even all those things that under the influence of faith and the Church's teaching he denies or affirms in philosophy.

Hence also, the philosophy of a Catholic philosopher cannot contain anything *per se* that would not be philosophical, that is, that cannot be shown from natural sources, not depending on natural principles, and in which he would not proceed according to a critical, natural method. But if such things were contained in a philosophy true to its name held by a Catholic philosopher, then we would find nothing in those things that would provide a reason that such a philosophy be called Christian in itself.

2. Our opinion in this matter (one that we in no way have invented) has nothing in common with the three propositions of the

semirationalists condemned by the Church,[40] for we fully acknowledge that the Catholic philosopher, as a man who is aware of the doctrine of the faith, must respect every law of the Church. Nor is our opinion contrary to the doctrine of Leo XIII who calls philosophy Christian when one is concerned with applying St. Thomas's philosophy in the exposition and vindication of Catholic truth. For philosophy is apt for vindicating Catholic truth and for defending it [precisely] when its strength and certainty does not depend on theology and on the doctrine of faith.

3. Thus, philosophy, even that which is held by a Catholic person, is indeed a discipline of the natural order and must prove its conclusions through naturally known principles and experience. In this way, it specifically differs from theology, which proves its conclusions through revealed principles known by faith. Hence, in order for the rational value of philosophy (and by that fact, the value of the rational defense of the preambles of faith and of the divine origin of Christianity) not to be overshadowed, philosophy should not call itself Christian in itself.

Remarks by Fr. Anicetus Fernandez-Alonso, O.P.

According to the express declaration of the most eminent President of this Congress, not only are objections permitted but also observations that can serve in clarifying the thesis being discussed. To this end, allow me to insist on the doctrine concerning the specification of *habitus* through their order to their formal objects, which, as Fr. Rector [Michael] Browne said most excellently on the occasion of Fr. De Blic's paper, must be held before one's eyes prior to everything pertaining to this question. In fact, the question concerning Christian philosophy is a question concerning the relationship between philosophy and revelation or between the natural *habitus* [pl.] of philosophy and the supernatural *habitus* [pl.] of faith, of the gifts, and also of theology itself, which also is supernatural in its origin. Therefore, if *habitus* are specified and distinguished through their ordering to their formal objects,

---

40. See Pius IX, Letter "Gravissimas inter" to the Archbishop of Munich-Freising (Denzinger, no. 2858 and 2860); Pius IX, *Syllabus errorum*, no. 10 and 11 (Denzinger, no. 2910 and 1911).

it follows that in order for those relations to be understood aright, one must pay special attention to their formal objects, and everything must be assessed and discussed in light of these objects.

Now, on the basis of this doctrine concerning the specification of *habitus*, to my eyes, it seems quite clear that the positive, objective subordination of philosophy to revelation (or that the positive, objective direction and assistance of philosophy by faith) is something altogether impossible and self-contradictory. For what would this positive, objective direction, assistance, or subordination mean? Indeed, if these words mean anything distinct from what is expressed by the negative assistance and subordination which others concede and defend, it seems that we must say that the philosophical and natural assent to a given natural truth is positively and objectively assisted or becomes stronger and clearer through the influence of faith, the gifts, or theology because we are held to assent certainly to the same truth (or another truth connected to it) through these supernatural *habitus*. For from the object of faith there is derived a light by which certain truths appear more clearly even to the natural light of reason, and in this way philosophy is positively and objectively illuminated and assisted through faith and the other supernatural *habitus*. The idea that revelation would provide philosophy with such true assistance or influence implies a contradiction, both from the perspective of revelation and from that of philosophy, for no *habitus* can depart from its formal object (unless one were to allow oneself to fall into contradiction). In fact, either, on the one hand, such an objective and positive assistance is produced because faith positively and formally (not only occasionally and negatively, or indirectly) makes it clearer, so that through the natural light or *habitus* [sg.] of philosophy some natural truth would thereby be seen; or on the other hand, lest the greater clarity would appear in the natural order, the Christian philosopher, on account of the fact that he holds certain a given natural truth through faith or theology, likewise assents to the same truth more strongly through philosophy as well, in comparison with how he would assent if he did not know it in any way through revelation. However, in the first case, faith passes out from its formal object by naturally illuminating, and in the second, philosophy passes out from its formal object by assenting on account of a supernatural light or motive. Now, this is impossible lest faith be converted into a natural *habitus* or philosophy into a supernatural *habitus*. In other words, what is at stake is the distinction between supernatural and natural *habitus*. And so, its seems that we must completely reject expressions like "positive, objective direction, assistance, or subordination," as describing any way that philosophy might be considered (whether in its perfect state or in its imperfect state, as much in the process of coming into being [*in fieri*] as in full existence [*in facto esse*], in the state of integral nature, that of original justice, or that of fallen nature). However, this does not mean that philosophy is, objectively speaking, entirely independent from revelation. Outside that positive subordination or assistance (or, direction), there is a kind of negative subordination, direction, and assistance by means of which the Christian philosopher or philosophy is prevented from making every denial or affirmation that directly or indirectly would be contrary to a given truth of revelation. And in this way, philosophy (especially in the state of fallen nature) is often freed from many errors and often is placed upon and directed along the way of truth—negatively but in a real manner. In fact, in my opinion, this doctrine can be enunciated briefly and exactly as follows: Revelation is the negative norm of philosophy.

However, in order for this doctrine to appear with greater clarity, it helps to note that human reason is one thing and philosophy another, as are the supernatural *habitus* [pl.] of faith, the gifts, and theology. Human reason positively and objectively is illuminated and confirmed in our knowledge of many natural truths through revelation, and through faith, the gifts, and theology, is thoroughly made subject to the First Truth supernaturally revealing Himself. However, in our knowledge of natural truths, philosophy cannot be illuminated and confirmed in such a manner through revelation nor thus be made subject to the First Supernatural Truth, lest it ceases to be philosophy and is converted into faith or theology. Nevertheless, it is still, in some way, illuminated and confirmed by revelation and in the Christian philosopher and also is subjected to the First Truth who is already supernaturally known, namely, since the philosopher must teach nothing contrary to revelation. Therefore, every form of progress made by reason even in knowledge of natural truths though under the direct and positive-objective influence of revelation is theology or faith, not philosophy.

Explained in this way, this distinction between reason and philosophy, or better yet, between theological reason and philosophy is not condemned by these propositions cited by Fr. Garrigou-Lagrange, namely: "As there is a distinction between the philosopher and his philosophy, he has the right and the duty to submit himself to the authority he acknowledges as legitimate; but philosophy neither can nor must submit to any authority"; "created reason is absolutely subject to uncreated truth." In fact, these propositions and others similar to it condemn the idea that philosophy would be absolutely independent of revelation, which they do indeed wish to deduce from their distinction. But we cannot infer from these that philosophy is positively and objectively illuminated by revelation in its knowledge of natural truth and positively subjected to the Uncreated Truth supernaturally revealing Himself, as are faith and theology. I believe I can make this teaching plain by means of a single example. It can happen that someone does not perceive the distinction between substance and quantity solely by the light of natural reason or that he only perceives it as being probable. However, because such a distinction is more greatly conformed to the things that revelation teaches concerning the Sacrament of the Eucharist, he holds it as being certain. Then, that greater certitude caused by revelation is not philosophical but, instead, divine or theological.

Moreover, it must be noted that said negative direction and subjection is always necessary in Christian philosophy, however one happens to consider philosophy. And neither the texts of the Church nor the words of St. Thomas require anything more. Also, in order for a given philosophy to truly and properly be called Christian, inasmuch as there is such a philosophy, it suffices that one say that it would not exist in such a state of perfection without the negative direction of revelation, especially in the actual condition of human nature. Such a philosophy requires faith in the philosopher. However, the mere possession of faith does not suffice so that it may be called Christian. In addition to this, such faith must truly be the negative practical norm in the inquiry into the truth. Hence, not any philosophy whatsoever expressed by any Christian philosopher whatsoever is to be called Christian, but rather, only that which is truly constructed under the negative direction of revelation. The more that a given philosophy fulfills this condition, the more truly and more exactly is it called Christian. This is especially the case for the philosophy of St. Thomas.

And only in this sense can philosophy be called objectively Christian unless we wish to confuse it with faith or theology. And I think that Fr. Garrigou-Lagrange in reality does not defend a complete [*majorem*] influence of revelation in philosophy, nor that the philosophy of St. Thomas is called Christian in any other manner, although his words sometimes seem to imply something else.

And pay heed, lest, on account of our contrary manners of speaking, one might think that I suppose Fr. Garrigou-Lagrange, whose great merit in this question I gladly acknowledge, defends the doctrine here combatted by me, a doctrine which often is so obviously erroneous that it could be neither defended nor disregarded by anyone. As I said at the start of my remarks, my intention was neither to exposit nor to judge Fr. Garrigou-Lagrange's opinion, but rather, to insist upon the doctrine of the specification of *habitus*, which seems to me to be of great importance in this question, and to show how, according to this doctrine and according to my own opinion, philosophy could be assisted by revelation and be called Christian.

Other things ought to be said concerning the subjective assistance of philosophy through revelation and about other indirect aids of revelation, as well as concerning the interpretation of certain texts promulgated by the Church and ones found in St. Thomas. However, the space granted to us here does not permit fuller explication.

Responses by Fr. Garrigou-Lagrange

To Fr. de Blic: "Christian philosophy is Christian in itself on account of objective assistance." Allow me to make a distinction: It is not such on account of its formal and specifying object, for its object remains ever the same whether philosophy is Christian or not, just as any given science in whatever state always preserves its same formal object. However, the very *habitus* of philosophy or of science can be considered in various states, preserving the same formal object, for a *habitus* may be had either in an imperfect state or in a perfect state. Now, this is admitted by the majority of theologians and is a commonly accepted truth. However, philosophy is perfected from the perspective of its object through easier knowledge of this or that material object, which is proposed to it from on high by divine revelation, an object which, then, is more easily demonstrated philosophically. For example, Christian philosophy not only knows in a vague manner [*in confuso*] that the world was produced efficiently by God, but that it was produced through a most free creation from nothing for the manifestation of God's goodness.

It seems that the [First] Vatican Council in its definition does not abstract from original sin.[41] Nevertheless, I do not insist upon this, and the fact suffices, as is obvious from history and experience.

With regard to moral philosophy, I use the word "subordination" rather than "subalternation." And I affirm specifically this subordination for moral philosophy, for it does not consider only man in the abstract but, instead, man in the concrete along with the direction of life which is *de facto* ordered to the supernatural end. However, this does not mean that philosophy is essentially changed. Rather, the same specifying object remains, and moral philosophy judges according to a resolution to naturally known principles.

Nor does there seem to be a danger that philosophy would be regulated by theological opinion. For this subordination is not to theology but, instead, to revelation theologically explicated. That is, one can explain something in such a way that a theologically certain truth can be connected to revelation, and if the opinion of a given great theologian is cited, it is only cited according to his degree of authority.

There was an allusion to the philosophy that would be only Christian collectively as, for example, there is a philosophy that is called Greek because it was developed by Plato, Aristotle, the Stoics, and the Epicureans. However, then it would be a merely historical and superficial denomination. For were we to use the term "Christian philosophy"

---

41. See Jean-Michel-Alfred Vacant, *Études théologiques sur les constitutions du Concile du Vatican d'après les actes du concile*, vol. 1, pp. 648 and 662. Nay, rather, as is said in the latter place, in the preparation of this chapter of the Council it was said, "When we say concerning the present state of man, we certainly also understand man as fallen through sin."

in this way, we would need to say that such philosophy includes the doctrines of Ockham, Descartes, Leibnitz, and others. However, we are not speaking about this philosophy, but rather, understand it as it was understood by Leo XIII in his Encyclicals and especially in the Encyclical *Aeterni patris* in which he speaks of the perennial philosophy, especially as it appears in St. Thomas.

Also, true objectivity certainly must not be confused with material consideration.[42]

To PROFESSOR KURAITIS: I completely admit and, indeed, said in my talk that philosophy must not found its demonstrations on principles revealed and received by faith as theology does; but, rather, it must proceed under its own naturally known proper principles and according to its own method. This is presupposed as something admitted by all; nay, it was declared many times by Pius IX.

However, now, it is asked how the philosophy that is called "Christian" would deserve thus to be named, even though it has a naturally knowable formal object and must demonstrate its conclusions on the basis of naturally known principles.

To explain this, we recall the same testimony holding that, even with regard to truths of the philosophical order, revelation frees reason from errors, positively illuminates, confirms and fosters the certitude and purity of natural cognition, and is the infallible guide of philosophy.

To FR. FERNANDEZ: Many times, over the course of many years, I have defended the value and utmost importance of this principle: faculties, *habitus*, and acts are specified by their formal objects,[43] and hence in the aforementioned discussion above, I said: "How can we say that a science (or, rather, a wisdom of the natural order), one specified by a naturally knowable formal object, is positively and in itself Christian, all the while preserving its nature?"

---

42. TRANSLATOR's NOTE: That is, the character of the formal object, precisely as an object, must not be confused with the material object that is attained by means of that formal object.

43. TRANSLATOR's NOTE: On this topic, see the remarks in the Translator's Introduction to this volume.

Indeed, it is often said, "Revelation is the negative norm of philosophy." However, as I noted in my talk, "This brief or succinct expression 'negative norm' especially intends to indicate that philosophy must not found its demonstrations on principles revealed and accepted by faith, as theology does, but instead, must proceed under its own naturally known principles and its own method. But this brief expression 'negative norm' does not deny what has been affirmed elsewhere by the Church, namely that 'Revelation illuminates reason (even in the order of natural truths), confirms it, and fosters the certitude and purity of natural cognition and is the infallible rule of Philosophy.'"[44]

Leo XIII explains this well when he says in the Encyclical *Aeterni patris*: "Those, therefore, who to the study of philosophy unite obedience to the Christian faith, are philosophizing in the best possible way; for the splendor of the divine truths, received into the mind, helps the understanding, and not only detracts in nowise from its dignity, but adds greatly to its nobility, keenness, and stability."[45]

This aid does not imply a contradiction. Even less does it presuppose a confusion of formal objects. No *habitus* passes out of its formal object. However, the authority of God who reveals from on high proposes not only supernatural mysteries but also truths of the natural order which thereafter become much more easily knowable for philosophy. The demonstrative middle term is indeed not revealed to us; however, its end or terminus is so revealed, and sometimes it is formulated vividly and perfectly. In this divine revelation of the natural truths of religion, we have something more than a mere occasion for philosophical inquiry; indeed, errors to be refuted already are occasions for this labor, as well as, in another manner, the revelation of supernatural truth. However, the revelation of natural truths determines the end of the inquiry and the direction to be taken for laboring philosophically—just as a great philosopher profoundly illuminates the mind of a given disciple when he excellently and vividly formulates for him a conclusion to be proven, leaving his disciple then to undertake the labor of efficaciously proving it.

---

44.   TRANSLATOR'S NOTE: The self-citation is slightly different from what is presented in the body of the talk, although the sense remains the same.

This is how an objective assistance is given to philosophy, in the sense that revelation objectively proposes many naturally knowable truths concerning God, His providence, the soul, human act, man's beatitude, and even concerning the physical world. Nay, it already reveals in some manner the subordination of these truths and provides a general indication of the way the human mind may be naturally guided to them, although it does not metaphysically demonstrate them.

In particular, revelation shows the importance of these words of God, "I am He who is," in which is expressed what Fr. Del Prado called the fundamental truth of Christian philosophy, namely, that God alone is self-subsistent existence, in God alone are essence and existence the same, and whatever is other than God has existence only through participation.

This is, as it were, the golden key of metaphysics. In this, Divine Revelation is related not only to human reason, but properly speaking, to philosophy itself, as a guiding star for travelers. It reveals from on high where this golden key must be placed and what it is, but it does not determine how it must be metaphysically established according to the ascending *via inventionis*, nor later what must be deduced from it according to the descending *via iudicii*.[46] For this, the great labor of the metaphysician is required; however, under the light of this guiding star, this labor is made much easier. In this sense, Leo XIII says, "St. Thomas makes Aristotelian philosophy Christian."[47]

This objective assistance so considered is what is commonly admitted, at least vaguely [*in confuso*] by Catholics; it positively reveals to the philosopher the direction to be taken. Even though it provides neither the major premise nor the minor premise of the demonstrative syllogism, it positively reveals the terminus at which it must arrive.

Here, then, we can see how this direction notably differs from the way Revelation directs the theologian, who explains revealed truths and deduces theological conclusions, not from naturally known principles, but from principles that are formally revealed as such.

---

45. Leo XIII, *Aeterni patris*, no. 9.

    TRANSLATOR'S NOTE: The citation is taken from the official translation of this passage.

46. TRANSLATOR'S NOTE: See the chapter above, entitled "On the Twofold *Via inventionis* and the Twofold *Via iudicii* According to St. Thomas," pp. 11–20.

47. See text associated with note 28, on p. 373, above.

Thus, we have the subordination of philosophy to Divine Revelation, without any confusion of the formal object of philosophy and the formal object (*quod* and *quo*[48]) of infused faith.

Faith does not depart from its formal object, nor does philosophy. Rather, they are subordinated, just as their formal objects are.

For faith believes all revealed things on account of the authority of God who reveals. Among these revealed things there are many truths of the natural order whose manifestation from on high gives aid to the labors of the philosopher, who proceeds under the inferior light of natural reason.

For example, as Aristotle shows in the first book of the *Metaphysics*, first philosophy is the science of all things, or, of being inasmuch as it is being, through its highest cause, under the light of natural reason.

Indeed, this remains the case in Christian philosophy, but it is greatly perfected. Aristotle only vaguely determined how the world causally depends upon God. He speaks most especially about Pure Act inasmuch as it is the final cause of the world; however, he is unable to determine how God is its efficient cause. For Aristotle, the world exists *ab aeterno* according to a hidden dependence upon God, and the Stagirite certainly does not allude to the freedom by which God thus produced the world, just as He could have not made it.

However, under the light of Divine Revelation, it is proposed from on high that the Highest Cause of all things most freely created all things *ex nihilo* for the manifestation of His goodness. In this way, a truth of greatest importance in the philosophical order is proposed to us, although the demonstrative middle term [*medium*] for this truth to be metaphysically proven is not explicitly manifested.

However, the direction to be taken in our metaphysical inquiry is indicated, as well as the terminus at which we must arrive. Nay, then, it is easy to see that, if every being other than God exists through participation, God created the world *ex nihilo* (that is, that He produced

---

48. TRANSLATOR'S NOTE: That is, the formal object understood from the perspective of the thing known, namely the Deity (formal object *quod*) and the formal object understood precisely as it is an object, that is conformed to a particular "objective light," (formal object *quo*) here, formal revelation (as distinct, from, e.g., virtual revelation by which theological knowledge is attained).

matter out of no presupposed subject), as well as the spiritual soul, which is not educed from matter.

Consequently, we likewise come to see all the more easily and profoundly that the *obiectum formale quod* of metaphysics, namely, *being insofar as it is being*, is analogically said of the Creator and of created being. Aristotle did not arrive at this in his speculations concerning the analogy of being.

Finally, we also come to see more clearly that the *obiectum formale quo* of metaphysics (namely, the natural light of reason) comes forth from the same supreme font as extra-mental being. Thus, the value of the light under which metaphysics proceeds is confirmed, and a positive determination is offered for the direction according to which its investigations ought to take place in this matter, even though metaphysics does not argue from the very principles of faith, thus specifically differing from sacred theology.

Hence, when the Christian philosopher, as a philosopher, adheres to a given metaphysically demonstrated conclusion, this adherence proceeds from evident principles under the natural light of reason. However, before the Christian philosopher thus arrives at this demonstration, he often receives from on high the best direction for passing from the vague concept to the distinct one[49] (e.g., from the vague notion of the production of all things by God, to the explicit notion of an utterly free production *ex nihilo*). Neither Plato nor Aristotle arrived at this explicit notion, but Christian philosophers arrive there rather easily, and indeed in a properly philosophical manner, under the direction of Revelation.

Nay, when it is said that Revelation is the negative norm of philosophy it must be noted that revelation prevents an error (e.g., the error of pantheistic emanation proposed by Neoplatonists) only because it first positively gives a good direction for finding the truth (e.g., by announcing the way all things were divinely produced through an utterly free creation *ex nihilo*).

Whence, the objective assistance which I discussed comes about, as is obvious, through the proposition of a new object, not indeed one

---

49. TRANSLATOR'S NOTE: See the chapter above, entitled "On the Search for Definitions According to Aristotle and St. Thomas," pp. 21–34.

that is formal and specifying, but rather, of a material object to be con-sidered philosophically. So too, under the guiding light of revelation, we come to investigate more profoundly, in a metaphysical manner, into the nature of metaphysics' *obiectum formale quod* (i.e., being, an-alogically said of the Creator and of the creature) and likewise come to understand more fully the value of the very light of natural reason coming forth from the Creator.

However, the subjective assistance which I discussed in the body of my talk, is explained in that place. But the texts of St. Thomas cited above ought to be read with an understanding of their context, and often they are explicated by his great commentators as I have exposited at greater length elsewhere.[50]

When St. Thomas says in *ST* II-II, q. 1, a. 5, ad 1, "Of the things that are of faith...the faithful have knowledge, not in a quasi-demon-strative manner, but inasmuch as through the light of faith, they see that they ought to be believed," he understands this, as I said, in light of what he explains in the preceding article, ad 3: "The light of faith makes them see the things that are believed ([or] to be believed). For just as through the other *habitus* of virtues (e.g., chastity) man sees what is fitting for him in accord with that *habitus*,[51] so too through the *habitus* of faith is man's mind inclined to assent to those things that are fitting to right faith and not [to assent] to others." For example, one is thus in-clined to assent to the preambles of faith, and to the miracles by which revelation is confirmed, even though he does not yet have scientific knowledge of them, as I explained in the same text. Having understood these points, we see why the Christian philosopher can arrive much more easily at the philosophical contemplation spoken of by Aristotle.

* * *

For a fuller understanding of the objective assistance about which we have spoken, we must cite those things that St. Thomas says in *ST* I q. 106, a. 1, ad 2, concerning the illumination of the angels: "One

---

50. See Réginald Garrigou-Lagrange, *De revelatione*, vol. 1, p. 533–36.

51. It is a judgment in the manner of inclination, e.g., concerning those things that are fitting with regard to chastity, even if one does not know moral theology concerning this matter. See *ST* II-II, q. 45, a. 2.

angel does not illuminate another by giving it the light of nature, of grace, or of glory, but rather, by assisting the light of its nature and by manifesting to it truth concerning those things that pertain to the state of nature, of grace, and of glory." Again, and at greater length, see also *De veritate*, q. 9, a. 1, ad 2.[52]

As a number of commentators explain, the illumination of the angels does not occur through the infusion of a new light or a new *species* but, rather, only through the proposition of an at-first-unknown object displayed and artfully arranged in line with the capacity of the inferior angel. Thus, by proposing the object in this way, the superior angel illuminates the inferior one, and its superior light radiates in the very object proposed in this way. Thus, it assists the power of the inferior angel, just as the teacher, by his method in explaining principles, assists the intellect of the student.

---

52. TRANSLATOR'S NOTE: On this, also see Maritain, *Science and Wisdom*, p. 88, n. 1, pp. 189–90.

* * *

CHAPTER 3

Apologetics Directed by Faith

Quite recently, Albert Michel, professor at the Faculty of Theology of Lille, published an article composed before the [First World] War in which he defended the *radical distinction* of apologetics and theology by reproducing the proofs presented by several authors, such as the late Fr. de Poulpiquet.[1] In substance, he said that these are two sciences that are very clearly and specifically distinct by their formal object and by their method. *Theology* has for its formal object *theological conclusions*, which can be deduced from principles of faith, and it proceeds principally according to the *method of authority* since it invokes above all else the authority of God who reveals and gives us assurance concerning the principles of faith, from which theological conclusions are deduced. *Apologetics*, by contrast, has for its formal object *the evident credibility* of the mysteries of faith and proceeds according to an *essentially rational method* so as to establish such credibility. Thus, it would be "a science of the rational order, given that it is related by its formal object and its method to *the human sciences, of which philosophy remains the ever-authorized guardian and director.*"[2]

From this perspective, apologetics would not *make use* of philosophy but, rather, would exist *under the direction of philosophy*, and not under the positive direction of faith and of theology. Apologetics would be subordinated to philosophy, which would be superior to it.

Its nature is understood along these lines by all those who conceive of it as being a philosophy of religion and not at all as a part of fundamental theology.

The alleged motivation for this position is that the apologete[3] does not make use of the method of authority, or call upon the authority of God the Revealer, in order to prove to non-believers the value and the existence of the signs of revelation. This would be to fall into a manifest *vicious circle.*

This elementary consideration of the vicious circle to be avoided, which has been insisted upon in recent years, certainly has the great advantage of requiring one to distinguish more clearly than had been the case heretofore in many works of apologetics or of fundamental theology those arguments which have a rational value accessible to the non-believer and those from authority which have a value only for a believer. However, it would be wrong to claim that this wholly elementary distinction was misunderstood by the authors who are critiqued. If this

---

1.   At the beginning of this article, A. Michel was astonished to have found in my work (*De revelatione per Ecclesiam catholicam proposita* [Paris: Gabalda, 1918], vol. 1, p. 52, a. 1) a reference that seems to class him among the proponents of the contrary opinion. I confess that there was an oversight on my part in this reference. In reading Michel's article, "Fondamentale (théologie)" in the *Dictionnaire de théologie catholique*, I had been quite satisfied with many of the explanations given concerning the nature of fundamental theology, properly speaking, or, apologetic theology (col. 518–20), of which I took note. Only slightly struck by the restrictions indicated in the course of the same article, I forgot them and later transcribed the reference to *Dictionnaire*, col. 519, the content of which coincides on the whole with the doctrine of Fr. Gardeil, who is cited therein, which is the doctrine I myself follow as being the just interpretation of the true thought of St. Thomas.

   If we mistakenly attributed to Michel an opinion that is not his, it is because we have been habituated for some time to seeing in him a faithful disciple of St. Thomas and because it appeared to us wholly natural that he would teach concerning this matter what is certainly, according to us, the doctrine of the holy Doctor.

2.   A. Michel, "L'apologétique et la théologie fondamentale," *Revue du clergé français* (June 1919), p. 322.

3.   **Translator's Note:** On Fr. Garrigou-Lagrange's distinction between an apologist and an apologete, see Garrigou-Lagrange, *De revelatione*, 5th ed., pp. 38–39, esp. p. 39, n. 2: "Similarly, he who writes an apology is 'an apologist,' and he who teaches apologetics is called 'an apologete.'" Although he uses the term "apologète" instead of "apologiste," it is not clear whether or not he means to strictly deploy this distinction here. However, since he does use the latter term in a citation near the end of the essay, I have maintained the terminological distinction.

were so, all their work would rest upon a *petitio principii* that jumps to one's eyes at first sight like a kind of enormous and ridiculous blunder.[4]

Therefore, the most basic point consists in distinguishing clearly an apologetic proof of such a nature as to convince a non-believer from a properly theological proof, founded on the authority of revelation, already accepted by faith.

Does it follow that apologetics would be a science that is *radically distinct* from theology, even from fundamental theology? Does it follow that it would *be no more directed by the light of revelation and of faith* than is, for example, metaphysics, physics, or mathematics? Moreover, would it follow that it would be *directed by philosophy* and subordinated to this science instead of *making use* of it according to the profound sense of the word *uti* [*to use*] in St. Thomas's language?[5] Must it be connected to the purely human sciences "of which philosophy remains the ever-authorized guardian and director"?

Must *the directive light* of apologetics be exclusively rational? And would the apologetic demonstration [of the rational credibility of the mysteries] lose its probative force for the non-believer if, while wholly avoiding *relying* upon faith, it was normally and positively *directed* by this superior light, if it was a rational demonstration performed under the light of faith: *demonstratio ex ratione quidem, sed sub directione fidei* [a demonstration that indeed is from reason, though under the direction of faith]? Must this direction, precisely because it would presuppose the apologete's faith, through a *petitio principii*, presuppose such faith in its still non-believing hearer?

This question is not without importance. To realize this fact, it can be posed in other terms as follows.

---

4. The fideists themselves did not fall into the quite obvious absurdity that would consist in saying, "Only the *Catholic faith* can lead one to admit the value of the signs that guarantee its divine origin." They only said: "Common sense (which for them was the *common faith of humanity*, founded upon primitive revelation, transmitted by the traditions of various peoples) must supply for the impotence of individual reason so that we may have certitude concerning the value of the signs of the divine origin of Christianity."

5. See *ST* I, q. 1, a. 5, ad 2: "This (sacred) science does not take things from other sciences as from superiors, but instead, *makes use* of them as inferiors and handmaidens, just as architecture makes use of those crafts that minister to it."

Must the apologete, who wishes to manifest to a non-believer the evident credibility of the mysteries of the faith, *as a rule*[6] proceed as though he himself did not have faith, as though he were a *seeker* in search for religious truth? Must he come to consider Christianity and the Church from the outside like Buddhism and Islam? Must he, by his powers alone, *without any positive superior direction*, elevate himself laboriously from the domain of philosophy (or philosophical discussions) and of history up to the summit of apologetics, a preamble of faith? Must he, without any other directive light than natural reason alone and philosophy, fight all the objections of philosophical and biblical rationalism, as well as all those of semi-rationalism in its most varied forms, so that he may scientifically reach a conclusion regarding the evident credibility of the revealed mysteries, in the exact sense in which these words (credibility, revealed mysteries) are understood, not only by philosophers worthy of this name but by the Catholic Church herself?

Or, on the contrary, ought not the apologete *normally* say to those who seek religious truth: "*Credidi propter quod locutus sum* [I believed, for which cause I have spoken]" (2 Cor. 4:13, DR)? I belong to the Catholic Church, who herself has taught me how it is *reasonable* to believe and unreasonable not to believe. I find the proofs that she herself proposes to me convincing, and I wish to make you come to know them. You must judge concerning their value for your own part. If you have objections, we will examine them sincerely, but I warn you beforehand that, even after the rational resolution of your difficulties, you cannot believe without grace, for faith is not the conclusion of a syllogism, but a gift coming from God, and one must ask for this gift with humility, confidence, and perseverance. Before proving anything, I will explain to you the *exact meaning of the terms* of the problem, according to the Church herself, who considers herself to be illuminated by God. I will tell you exactly what she understands by these words, the meaning of which rationalism and semi-rationalism have often altered: supernatural, mystery, revelation, divine faith, credibility, miracle, etc. I will also indicate to you *the signs* that, according to the Church, are valuable

---

6.   It is not here a question of what he can do *per accidens* in a given circumstance because of the distrust expressed by a given listener.

in the eyes of God Himself (that is, those which are conformed to the requirements of your reason and to those of faith). Next, I will philosophically prove *the value of these signs* and, historically, *their existence.* The apologetics that I will set forth for you is not a science invented or constructed by Christian philosophers. According to the testimony of the Catholic Church, it is the apologetics transmitted by Christ to His Apostles and preserved in Scripture and tradition. It is an essentially traditional apologetics, one that the Church has never ceased to teach, for she has always presented a *twofold teaching*: that which prepares for faith, by showing the rational path, and that which proposes the mysteries to be believed and the duties to be practiced.

Such is the question facing us: Ordinarily, must apologetics set forth *from below*, elevating itself slowly toward heaven like a tower that would recall to certain critical minds the Tower of Babel? Or, on the contrary, does it come *from on high*, similar to the ladder that Jacob saw, a ladder that descended from heaven and rested upon the earth: on it the angels (or envoys) of God rose and descended, with Yahweh standing at the top (Gen. 32:12)?

To put it another way: Must we confuse apologetic teaching with the rational research into the religious truth, the apologete with the seeker? If he must *normally* act as though he had no more faith than does his non-believing hearer, why does his name mean, "Defender of the faith?" Can one defend what one does not yet have? Or, on the contrary, ought not the apologete normally set forth and defend the truth that he possesses, by tracing, *under the direction of revelation*, faith, and the magisterium of the Church, the luminous way that *will rationally lead* souls of good will to believe in the Truth that sets us free?

And if these souls sincerely seek the truth, by which of these two apologetes will such souls prefer to be approached in order to be illuminated?[7]

---

7. A luminous intelligence that has done much practical apologetics in recent times wrote: "I am struck by the fact that non-believers experience more sympathy for people [*les êtres*] of profound faith than for those whose convictions are pliable and utilitarian. They go more, these dear non-believers, to the 'intransigents' of faith than to those who by the force of compromise and of subtleties, seek to make one 'accept' the faith. Nevertheless, it is necessary that the indomitable affirmation be enveloped in the most intelligent sympathy, the most lively and delicate charity." Élisabeth Leseur, *Journal et pensées de chaque jour.* TRANSLATOR'S NOTE: This has been most recently republished by Éditions du Cerf in 2005.

Is apologetics a purely human doctrine, *subordinated to philosophy and directed by it*, constructed by Christian philosophers, in which we would above all need to take as our guides Plato, Aristotle, and their scholastic successors? Or, has it been ordinarily taught (*per se loquendo et non solum per accidens*) by *God Himself*, by *Christ* and *His Church*, and should it be *directed by them*?

To respond to the question thus posed, we must consider the following points:

1. Whether revelation necessarily contains an apologetic teaching.
2. Whether theology, the science of revelation, can and must, inasmuch as it is the supreme science, defend its own, proper principles, or instead, must abandon this defense to an inferior science.
3. Whether apologetics normally must proceed by depriving itself of the positive direction that comes to it from revelation and from faith.
4. How, following after Our Lord and the Apostles, have the greatest traditional apologetes (someone like St. Augustine, St. Thomas, or Bossuet) proceeded?

In all of this, it is important not to confuse the normal with the accidental, what is *per se* with what is *per accidens*.

* * *

I. DOES REVELATION CONTAIN AN APOLOGETIC TEACHING, AND MUST IT CONTAIN IT?

There can be no doubt concerning this point. The prophets learned from God Himself (and, indeed, had to learn from God) how they should act to prove their supernatural mission. God promised them that He would work signs through them. They announced and performed them.

Likewise, Jesus Christ and the Apostles, illuminated by the divine light, predicted and performed the divine works by which their preaching was confirmed in an irrefutable manner.[8]

---

8.   On this point, see *De revelatione*, vol. 1, pp. 85–94.

And it was not in a *per accidens* manner that God revealed to the prophet how a given miracle to be performed was connected with the revelation to be confirmed. The prophet needed to have such knowledge concerning the divine origin of such a miracle precisely so that he could announce the sign and declare with certitude that it was done in confirmation of God's word.

Thus, the Church received from God Himself the signs of her divine origin and the *absolute certitude* of their probative force: a supernatural certitude that greatly surpasses that of philosophy and of history. Also, she has solemnly defined the probative force of miracles,[9] not as a philosophical conclusion that would result from the rational examination of the miracles performed, but as a truth revealed by God Himself and by His Christ: "But the testimony which I have is greater than that of John; for the works which the Father has granted me to accomplish, these very works which I am doing, bear me witness that the Father has sent me" (Jn. 5:36, RSV).

Positive theology has gathered all the apologetic teaching contained in Scripture, the Fathers, and the Church's definitions, as one can see in works of biblical theology, the *Enchiridion Patristicum* of Fr. Rouët de Journel, and the *Enchiridion symbolorum et definitionum* of Heinrich Denzinger.

Should speculative theology neglect these matters or limit itself to deducing theological conclusions from what is revealed on this point, thus leaving the rational defense of revelation to an inferior and radically distinct science which would have the name "rational apologetics"?

* * *

II. CAN THEOLOGY, AS THE SUPREME SCIENCE, RATIONALLY DEFEND ITS PROPER PRINCIPLES, OR MUST IT ABANDON THIS DEFENSE TO ANOTHER SCIENCE?

Today, one hardly considers speculative theology as anything but *a science that deduces* from the principles of faith the theological conclusions that are virtually contained within them. And Michel concedes that fundamental theology must do this work for what pertains to revelation, the credibility of the mysteries, miracles, and so forth, just as will be done in the special treatises on the Trinity and the Incarnation.

Thus, he adds, the theologian will develop these theses according to the method of authority, for "the theologian's direct end is not to convince a non-believer—*for then he would fall into a vicious circle*—but rather, is concerned with *deducing* from these principles all the virtualities that they contain, doing so through a reflexive study of the supernatural principles to which he adheres by faith."[10]

However, it is important to not forget what St. Thomas, with all of the tradition, teaches concerning the subject of theology inasmuch as it is not only a science but, rather, is *a supreme science*, or *wisdom*. From this perspective, it has a special property, a function that is *not deductive*, but *defensive*, analogous to what Aristotle attributes to the supreme science of the natural order (i.e., to metaphysics). The teaching of St. Thomas concerning this point is very clear in *ST* I, q. 1, a. 8:

> Like the other sciences, theology does not argue in proof of its principles (which are the articles of faith), but instead, *deduces* the conclusions that they contain. However, we must note that among the philosophical sciences, certain subordinate ones neither prove their principles nor defend them against those who deny them; they abandon this defense to a superior science. The supreme science among them (i.e., metaphysics) *argues* against him who denies its principles, if he concedes something; and if he concedes nothing, it cannot argue with him, but it can nonetheless *resolve his objections*. Thus, since no other science exists above sacred science, *it argues with him who denies its principles* (the articles of faith). It undertakes such argumentation against heretics by arguing in reference to some reveal truth if the adversary concedes it. However, if the adversary does not believe any revealed truth, theology can only resolve the objections that he proposes.[11]

In this last case, theology does not use its principal method, which is the method of authority, but instead makes use of reason "*utitur ratione*

---

9.   See [First] Vatican Council, *Dei filius*, ch. 3, can. 4 (Denzinger, no. 3034).

10.   Michel, "L'apologétique et la théologie fondamentale," 328. Likewise, his article "Fondamentale (théologie)" in the *Dictionnaire de théologie catholique*, col. 518–19.

11.   TRANSLATOR'S NOTE: I have taken this directly from his French instead of from the Latin. The parentheses are his additions to the text.

humana" as it is said in *ST* I, q. 1, a. 8, ad 2. And inasmuch as it is a supreme science or wisdom, it judges from on high the value of the principles of the inferior sciences of which it makes use: "It does not fall to it to prove the principles of other sciences but only *to judge concerning them.*"[12]

Just as metaphysics, the supreme science of being inasmuch as it is being has a special function, which is called critical metaphysics or the defense of the ontological value of its first principles (*the criticism*[13] set forth by Aristotle in the fourth book of his *Metaphysics*), so too does theology, the supreme science in a superior order, have a special function, for it *defends* the articles of faith against those who deny them prior to *deducing* theological conclusions.

This is a prerogative of *wisdom*, which as Aristotle and St. Thomas show, is a perfection or *habitus* of the mind, *essentially superior* to *mere science*. "As wisdom is knowledge through the most elevated causes, it *judges* and *orders* or *directs all things*... It resembles the other sciences inasmuch as it *deduces* conclusions; however, it has a special and eminent property inasmuch as it judges of all things, not only conclusions, but principles."[14]

Will it be said that this role played by theology is understood only with regard to the resolution of objections against the possibility of different mysteries (as is done in the treatises on the Trinity and on the Incarnation) but that it is not understood with regard to the defense of the divine origin of the Christian and Catholic religion?

---

12. *ST* I, q. 1, a. 6, ad 2.

13. *This critical metaphysics* avoids falling into a *vicious circle*, for it does not claim to give a *direct demonstration* of the ontological value of reason and of its first principles; rather, it furnishes an *indirect proof* for them (or, a proof by *reductio ad absurdum*). That is, *it makes use* of logic so as to reduce the skeptic or the agnostic to illogicality and so as to obligate him to at least remain silent. Thus, theology, in its critical or defensive part, *makes use* of philosophy so as to reduce rationalism to absurdity, and to show it that it cannot deny the fact of revelation without rejecting the foundations of speculative rational certitude or those of historical certitude.

     TRANSLATOR'S NOTE: Thus, for example, one would have a text such F.-X. Maquart, *Elementa philosophiae*, vol. 3: *Metaphysica defensiva seu critica* (Paris: Andreas Blot, 1938). Also, see the lengthy text for the "Defensive Metaphysics" course taught by Fr. Garrigou-Lagrange's faithful student, Austin Woodbury. See Austin Woodbury, *Defensive Metaphysics*.

14. *ST* I-II, q. 57, a. 2. TRANSLATOR'S NOTE: I have here taken, again, from his French translation.

However, a concession is indeed made to us, acknowledging that fundamental theology must treat of everything that is reveled and defined concerning *revelation itself, credibility, miracle*, etc. Therefore, in these matters, it should not be limited to deducing theological conclusions but, instead, just as much and even more than in the treatises on the Trinity and on the Incarnation, it must *rationally* defend the faith against the objections of rationalists by avoiding the use of the argument from authority in such cases. Natural reason and history are also theological *loci*, as Melchior Cano showed at length after St. Thomas.[15]

Rational credibility is a *property of the object of faith*; theology, which is the science of faith, must therefore treat of this property.

Such is manifestly the opinion of St. Augustine and of St. Thomas. St. Augustine defined theology: "To this knowledge [*scientiae*] is attributed only those things by which that most wholesome faith is *begotten*, nourished, defended, and strengthened."[16] Theology is the science that begets saving faith, nourishes it, defends it, confirms it. St. Thomas refers to this text,[17] and explains it by saying: "Faith cannot be begotten and nourished by a science except by way of external persuasion,"[18] for faith is a gift coming from God. And, as John of St. Thomas remarks,[19] theology clearly does not thus beget faith in the theologian himself but, rather, in the unbelievers whom the theologian succeeds at illuminating. Thus, he adds, inasmuch as it is supreme science, theology can, in a way that is analogous to what happens in metaphysics, prove the evident credibility of the miracles by *making use* of philosophy and of history *without thereby falling into a vicious circle*.[20]

"Sacred science," says St. Thomas himself, "*makes use* of philosophy in three manners: to prove the preambles of faith...to give some

---

15.   In many other places, St. Thomas shows that theology need not only deduce theological conclusions but also defends the principles of faith against heretics and against non-believers by refuting by reason the objections posed by these latter. See *SCG* I, ch. 2, 8, and 9; *Quodlibet* IV, q. 9, a. 3.

16.   Augustine, *De trinitate*, bk. 14, ch. 1.

17.   See *ST* I, q. 1, a. 3.

18.   *ST* II-II, q. 6, a. 1, ad 1. TRANSLATOR'S NOTE: I have here taken, again, from his French translation.

19.   See John of St. Thomas, *Cursus theologicus*, q. 1, disp. 2, a. 12, no. 4.

20.   Ibid.

understanding of the mysteries by analogy with natural things…and to respond to objections against the faith."[21] In the Prologue of his *Commentary on the Sentences*, q. 1, a. 5, in treating of theology's proper manner of proceeding, St. Thomas expresses himself as follows:

> The principles of this science are received from revelation… Now, the preaching of revealed truth was confirmed by miracles. Therefore, this science must report on the signs that confirm the faith.[22] Next, it must refute errors through proofs from authority or based on reasoning. Moreover, through analogies, it must set forth the precepts, and lead us, ultimately, to contemplation of the divine truth.[23]

St. Thomas applies this method not only in the *Summa contra gentiles*, but also in the *Summa theologiae* where we can easily find the materials from which to compose a complete treatise on *Revelation*, considered in its possibility, its suitability, its necessity, and its credibility, a treatise on [the nature of] miracles and on the miracles of Jesus Christ—all proven not only through arguments from authority but also defended rationally against non-believers and established in a manner to convince those who seek to know whether Catholicism is indeed divine in its origin.[24]

An objection may be raised against this claim. St. Thomas, it will be said, incorporated natural theology into his *Summa*. Now according to his own words,[25] such natural theology is distinct from sacred theology. Therefore, must we not also say that apologetics is incorporated into theology in like manner, even though it nonetheless remains radically distinct from theology?

21. Aquinas, *In Boetium de trinitate*, q. 2, a. 3. TRANSLATOR'S NOTE: I have here taken from his French translation.

22. "Oportet etiam quod modus istius scientiae sit narrativus signorum, quae ad confirmationem fidei faciunt."

23. TRANSLATOR'S NOTE: I have here taken, again, from his French translation. The selection is a paraphrase. The Latin footnote is inserted by him, likely both for emphasis and because he slightly simplifies the sentence.

24. See *ST* I, q. 105, aa. 6–8; II-II, qq. 171–75; III, qq. 43, 44, 53–55.

25. See *ST* I, q. 1, a. 1, ad 2.

It is easy to respond to this. No parity exists here between natural theology and apologetics. The first, conceived of by Plato and Aristotle, and given precision by scholastic philosophers, considered only naturally knowable divine truths and did not treat of the fact of revelation. By contrast, apologetics has as its precise end the tasks of proving the fact of revelation and of defending the faith. Therefore, it is connected to theology because the latter, precisely because it is the supreme science, cannot abandon the defense of its principles to another science.

Yet, it will be insisted: However, even if theology has this rational and defensive office, why not admit that apologetics can be constituted as a purely rational science, independent of all positive direction that would come from revelation? This is the question that we must now consider.

* * *

III. MUST APOLOGETICS NORMALLY PROCEED BY BEING DEPRIVED OF POSITIVE DIRECTION COMING TO IT FROM REVELATION?

1. *This is not necessary.* This would only be necessary so as to avoid a vicious circle. Now, such circular reasoning is perfectly avoided if the apologete expresses himself thus: "I am going to set forth for you the motives of credibility, which are taught to me by the Church herself, who declares herself to be illuminated by God. I will then show you philosophically and historically their probative force and will respond to your objections."

Moreover, it is important here to consider what apologetics *must normally* do (*per se loquendo*) on account of its object and of its end and what the apologete *can* do *accidentally* (*per accidens*), in this or that circumstance, on account of a given disposition in a listener whose sensitivities he must respect and whose prejudices he must not offend in too vigorous a manner. This second consideration is wholly material and secondary since it is not taken from the object, nor from the end, but instead, from a defect in the subject that must be acted upon. To put this concern in the foreground would lead to a *materialization of apologetics*, just as one can fall into a kind of materialization in Exegesis and in Church History. It would be profitable to undertake a study on this point.[26] [*Il y aurait un étude à faire sur ce point.*]

2. *Ordinarily* [normalement], *apologetics must proceed under the positive direction of faith*. Without a doubt, in order to avoid a vicious circle, its argumentation must *rest on* rational principles and not on the principles of faith. However, it is *directed* by faith. What is meant, in fact, by *directing*? It means to show the end to be attained and to indicate the means for arriving at it. Now, the faith of the apologete shows the *end* to be attained: to manifest the evident credibility of the revealed mysteries. And as, in all things, we must first consider the end (*finis est prior in intentione*), the apologetic demonstration presupposes that the apologete has exact *notions* of the divine faith that he defends, the evident credibility that he manifests, as well as of supernatural revelation, the supernatural order, miracles, and prophecy. Exact notions of all these matters do not come from philosophy but, instead, from revelation, being set forth in Scripture and explained by the Church's Magisterium, whereas they are distorted [*altérées*] by rationalism and semi-rationalism.

For example, before starting to prove the *evident credibility* of the mysteries, we must say what the Church understands by these words, for semi-rationalism understands them in a wholly different manner than she does.[27] And this exact notion of credibility must be determined not only in accord with reason's requirements but also *in accord with*

---

26. One *materializes* exegesis and the history of the Church by reducing them to their inferior function: that function which, making abstraction totally from the light of faith, considers scripture only as a human book and stops at the material details of the external facts of the life of the Church. Does not the historian who thus claims to abstract totally from the light of faith, so as to furnish the bases for an apologetics that is more convincing for non-believers, expose himself often to *explaining*, like materialists, *the superior by the inferior*, the supernatural by the natural, the Church and the progress of religious life by human institutions and their development? When one proceeds in this manner, does he not forget to kindle the light of his lantern? How is one thus to write, without being deceived, the history of dogmas, that of heresies, that of the various religious orders, that of the saints? Between this history and the truth, there is the same difference as that found between stained glass viewed from the outside and the same stained glass viewed from the inside. In order to know the intimate life of a family, it does not suffice to see the façade of the house in which that family lives and to survey those who pass in and out of it.

27. See Garrigou-Lagrange, *De revelatione*, vol. 1, pp. 137, 169, 191, 430; vol. 2, pp. 35, 107.

the requirements of divine faith, which beyond being merely prudent must be *irrevocable*, consequently requiring a truly certain judgment of credibility. The same remark holds for the notions of supernaturality, mysteries, revelation, divine faith, miracles, and prophecy.[28] The modification of the first of these notions leads all the others to be modified. In setting forth the exact *meaning* of these words, the apologete clearly must be directed by the teaching of revelation, explained by the Church and in a more detailed way by theology.

Moreover, revelation *indicates* to the apologete not only the goal to be attained and the meaning of the terms of the problem, but also the *means that are efficacious* for convincing the non-believer's reason and for leading him to recognize the divine origin of the Christian and Catholic religion. God has not, in fact, left us with the task of discovering these means. Given that this is concerned with a matter of sovereign importance, and likewise, given that every superior agent itself prepares the superior effect that it wishes to produce, God Himself gave the prophets, Christ, the Apostles, and His Church sensible testimonies such as miracles and has revealed that *this* miracle to be performed in confirmation of *this* revelation has an irrefutable value, one perfectly "appropriated or accessible to the natural intelligence of all men."[29]

Indeed, human reason by itself is not what formulated this principle: In order for a positive religion to be believable, it must be confirmed by miracles. God is the one who has judged that miracles are the

---

28. See Ibid., vol. 1, pp. 515–20.

29. See [First] Vatican Council, *Dei Filius*, ch. 3 (Denzinger, no. 3009). Our Lord said, declaring from on high the probative power of the miracle: "The works that I do in the name of my Father, these give testimony about me… If you do not wish to believe in me, believe in the works so that you may know and believe that the Father is in me and I in the Father" (Jn. 10: 25–38). "If I had not done among them works that nobody else did, they would not have sin; however, they have seen and hated both me and my Father" (Jn. 15:24). "For there is nobody who does a miracle [*virtutem*] in my name who can before long speak evil of me" (Mk. 9:38).

And *the Church, speaking in the name of God*, and not only of natural reason or sound philosophy, declares infallibly: "If anyone says that no miracles are possible…or that miracles can never be recognized with certainty and that the *divine origin of the Christian religion* cannot be legitimately proven by them, let him be anathema" ([First] Vatican Council, *Dei filius*, ch. 4, can. 3, Denzinger, no. 3034).

most suitable means of confirming it.[30] This certainly does not prevent those who listen to apologetic preaching from recognizing, solely by their reason, the probative force of the miracle thus proposed.

Normally, therefore, apologetics exists under the *positive* direction of faith since the latter shows it the end to be attained, the exact meaning of the terms of the problem, and the means to be employed. Apologetics *proposes all of this* under the direction of faith, and then *it rationally proves* the value and existence of the signs proposed. "Apologetics *proponit* sub directione fidei, et *probat* ex ratione."

Thus, it differs from the argumentation both of theology, properly so-called, which rests upon the principles of faith and sound philosophy, which proves by means of reason without contradicting faith. Philosophy is directed by faith only in a *negative* fashion, for it finds by it only the end to be attained, [not][31] the terms of the problem and the means of the proof.[32]

The apologete so directed proceeds onward with surety and is preserved from the error, which involves diminishing the value of miracles and augmenting unduly the value of internal motives. Moreover, he can thus, as he should, declare to his listeners that the act of faith will not be the conclusion of the apologetic demonstration but, instead, the fruit of a grace that he must petition from God with humility, confidence, and perseverance.

---

30. TRANSLATOR'S NOTE: Among which miracles is included the miracle of the Church herself. In *De revelatione*, Fr. Garrigou-Lagrange discusses at length the various kinds of intrinsic and extrinsic motives of credibility with great subtlety. In English, the interested reader would benefit much from the pedagogical text by Fr. Garrigou-Lagrange's student, the great sacramental theologian Emmanuel Doronzo, *Revelation* (Middleburg, VA: Notre Dame Institute Press, 1974). The corresponding section of his *Theologia dogmatica* can be profitably consulted as well.

31. TRANSLATOR'S NOTE: It seems that this negation is necessary to make sense of this sentence by Fr. Garrigou-Lagrange. See the comment in the next note regarding his use of this explanation elsewhere.

32. One thus has the following formulas:

Sacra theologia argumentatur ex fide. [Sacred theology makes its arguments from faith.]

Apologetica argumentatur ex ratione, sub directione positiva fidei. [Apologetics makes its arguments from reason, under the positive direction of faith.]

Philosophia argumentatur ex ratione, non contradicendo fidei. [Philosophy makes its arguments from reason, in such a manner as not to contradict faith.]

TRANSLATOR'S NOTE: However, to understand his exact position on this, see the extended discussions above, in "On the Relationship Between Philosophy and Religion," pp.

3. Per accidens, *the apologete can choose to avoid speaking of the superior direction that he follows; nonetheless, he could not completely deprive himself of it.* Per accidens, that is, on account of particular circumstances (e.g., the defiance of philosophers imbued with the principle of the absolute autonomy of reason), the apologete can choose to avoid speaking of the superior direction that he follows. In this way, a believer or a theologian, seeking to convince one of these philosophers in a more thorough manner, will be able to say, "I come to you to demonstrate the rational credibility of the mysteries of faith by making abstraction from every directive light superior to pure reason." However, in reality, even in this case, this apologete will only avoid *speaking* of this superior direction. He will in no way, in fact, abstract from it, for faith will always propose for him what he must defend, as well as the end to be attained, likewise indicating for him even the means he should use. Thus, it will direct the demonstration in a positive manner without taking away its rational force.

Moreover, absolutely speaking, nothing prevents it from being the case that a non-believer, instructed in the doctrine of the faith, would demonstrate its credibility for a completely human motive (e.g., to show that he is well-versed in these questions like a historian of ideas, or for a given literary goal, such as Voltaire writing *Zaïre*).

But even then, the knowledge of the things of faith that this unbeliever has will direct the apologetic demonstration thus made.

However, it will be objected: "Nonetheless, a non-believer can, in good faith, seek out on his own behalf religious truth and find it in the Gospel and in the Church. His apologetics will take place without any superior direction. Therefore, it is the case that apologetics ordinarily (i.e., *per se loquendo*) does not need to be undertaken under the direction of faith."

It is easy to respond that this non-believer is a seeker and not an apologete (i.e., not a defender of the faith). Moreover, in studying the Gospel, St. Paul, or the Church's doctrine, we find a twofold kind of teaching: apologetic and dogmatic. He has not constructed an apologetic. He has

---

361–97. There, he maintains this same model concerning the way that faith interacts with philosophy, although he attenuates the "negative" aspect, allowing it to have a more direct and objective influence upon philosophy.

allowed himself to be convinced by what has been thus proposed to him, the value of which he has verified from a solely rational point of view.

However, one may well register the counter-example: Nonetheless, God, the prophets, Christ, and His Church could have not given any apologetic teaching and have left the concern for constituting it in the hands of philosophers.

Let us say in response, however, that if such were the case, God, in revealing, would not have Himself indicated and given the signs of revelation, and the ministers that He chose for transmitting it would not have given proofs of their divine mission—something which is inconceivable.

Finally, let us note that the apologete who wishes to truly make the most possible abstraction from every form of superior direction will need to take care to avoid the point of departure taken by Georg Hermès who, in order to proceed along lines that were more rationally delimited, declared that at the beginning of an apologetic demonstration one must place faith in doubt inasmuch as one has not arrived at proving its legitimacy scientifically.[33]

Although some apologetes have not fallen into this Hermesian error, one can write of them without injustice:

[They] are receptive and feverish persons—receptive because they too easily take on the state of mind of their contemporaries; feverish, because from a fear of wounding these various states of mind, they are troubled by a continual apologetic restlessness. They themselves seem to suffer from the doubts which they are combatting. They lack sufficient confidence in the Truth. They are too eager to justify, to demonstrate, to adapt, or even to excuse. This nervousness and fever are not a sufficiently pure homage to the Truth, and they indicate too imperfect commerce with it. They diminish faith in the mission received and weaken its grace.[34]

---

33. Concerning this error, condemned by the [First] Vatican Council, see Vacant, *Études théologiques sur les constitutions du Concile du Vatican d'après les actes du concile*, vol. 2, p. 167.

34. Humbert Clérissac, *The Mystery of the Church* (Tacoma, WA: Cluny Media, 2016), pp. 68–69.
    TRANSLATOR'S NOTE: This translation is taken from the Cluny edition.

By contrast, at the beginning of an apologetics course, one will need to exposit *the doctrine of the Church concerning the true method to be employ*ed in defending the faith rationally. One cannot postpone to a later time the examination of what is taught on this point by the [First] Vatican Council, as well as in the declarations of the Magisterium against modernism. Otherwise, one would exposit I know not what personal apologetic, the fruit of one's individual thought, but not that same apologetic that the Church has ever proposed in its general lines, an apologetic whose merits we must rationally set forth.

IV. HOW HAVE THE GREAT, CLASSICAL APOLOGETES PROCEEDED FROM THE TIME OF THE CHURCH'S VERY BEGINNINGS?

It is clear that the Apostles proposed the motives of credibility for Christianity by doing so under the positive direction of faith. The same holds for someone like St. Justin, Tertullian, St. Augustine in *The City of God*, St. Thomas in the *Summa contra gentiles*, Bossuet in the *Discours sur l'histoire universelle*, Pascal in the *Pensées*, and more recently Lacordaire in his *Conférences*.[35]

Such is indeed the *classical* form of apologetics, a claim that could be easily demonstrated. "This notion of apologetics," says Fr. Ambroise Gardeil, "is, without a doubt, the most adequate notion on which one could settle. Credibility is formally a property of a supernatural object. Therefore, we will deal with this property of faith in the same order as the science that is occupied with faith's own object... Moreover, this way of understanding apologetics is that of the ancients who connected apologetics to the theology of the object of faith. Ultimately, this is the

---

35.   On this subject, read the fourteenth Conference at Notre-Dame: "The chief design of a doctrine…is to conquer minds… The aim of doctrine, then, is to govern minds: it does not hide this; and I, living doctrine, to whom it has been said in the persons of my ancestors, 'Go and teach all nations,' I…why should you wish me to hide my ambition from you? … And if you have a doctrine, this ambition is also yours. Let us not dissemble…. *This certitude* so difficult for all…this certitude, which has only enemies, *we possess it.*"

TRANSLATOR'S NOTE: I have taken much of the translation from the excellent translation by Langdon, making only minor changes. See Jean-Baptiste Henri Lacordaire, *Conferences Delivered in the Cathedral of Notre Dame in Paris*, trans. Henry Langdon (London: Thomas Richardson, 1853), pp. 190–94.

perspective taken up in the *Summa contra gentiles*."[36] This terrain is truly ours.

And after more or less happy experiments, the general tendency today is to return to the traditional conception of apologetics.

In recent years, Léon Ollé-Laprune wrote in *Le prix de la vie*: "Intellectual honesty requires us to declare all that is of Christian origin in our preoccupations, in our very questions, in our investigations... A solution like the one that we have proposed comes from positive religion; in a sense, this solution is quite philosophical since it was accepted by reason and proven through reasonings."[37] Likewise, in the historical order, Fr. Antoine Lemonnyer, discussing after Fr. William Schmidt, the problem of *Primitive Revelation and the Current Data of Science*, writes: "This little book is an apologetic work, and it is openly so, which is the frankest and the best way for it to present itself. It is also, so it is believed, a work of solid and honest science."[38] More explicitly, we likewise read in *Christus*: "In order to be efficacious, apologetics must blossom, as by a kind of overflow, from an assured religious philosophy, from a theology renewed at the sources of faith, and from a knowledge of history acquired through a lengthy and methodical effort. But yet (at the beginning of the nineteenth century), this dangerous genre was cultivated for its own sake."[39]

The recent works of Frs. Rousselot and Huby lie in the same lines, though with some exaggeration, which we have noted elsewhere.[40]

---

36. Ambroise Gardeil, *La crédibilité et l'apologetique*, 2nd ed. (Paris: Gabalda, 1912), p. 251 and p. xi of the preface.

37. Ollé-Laprune, *Le prix de la vie*, pp. 345–47.

    TRANSLATOR'S NOTE: It is not clear what edition Fr. Garrigou-Lagrange is citing.

38. See the preface to G. Schmidt and A. Lemonnyer, *La révélation primitive et les données actuelles de la science* (Paris: Lecoffre-Gabalda, 1914).

39. Joseph Huby et al., *Christus: Manuel d'histoire des religions* (Paris: Beauchesne, 1913), p. 966.

    TRANSLATOR'S NOTE: The author goes on to discuss how at this time many apologists / apologetes were laymen or priests who were not trained well enough in theology, much to the detriment of apologetic science, whatever may be said for the power of their personalities and brilliance.

40. See Réginald Garrigou-Lagrange, "La grâce de la foi et le miracle," *Revue thomiste*, Vol. 23 (New Series, 1) (1918): pp. 289–320

    TRANSLATOR'S NOTE: One should also consult Garrigou-Lagrange, *Sense of Mystery*, pp. 199–216; likewise, in the forthcoming translation of *Le réalisme du principe de finalité*, see pt. 2, ch. 5.

In Études, Fr. d'Alès, writing a review of our work *De revelatione*, noted with us: "The perspective of a seeker advancing toward the truth is one thing, while that of the apologist, who is aware that he possesses it and undertakes tracing the avenues of light for the benefit of another person is another."[41]

A little later, his eminence, the Cardinal Secretary of State deigned to write us concerning the subject of the same work: "Eager to set forth the apologetic questions of fundamental theology against the various forms of contemporary naturalism, you have taken care to consider them and develop them in the light of supernatural faith itself and under its direction. In this, you make use of the singularly fecund method that makes resplendent, before souls that are eager for the light, the radiant splendor of the Divine Truth, in order to draw them toward the tranquil and serene possession of this liberating truth."

* * *

However, the objection from the beginning of this article may perhaps still be on the reader's mind: Does not apologetics have a formal object and a method distinct from the object and method of theology?

Quite easily, we can respond to this concern by saying that even if apologetics is a rational office of theology (as criticism is an office of metaphysics), it can very well have its own proper object (which comes under the extensive object of theology) and a rational method that is different from the method of authority that theology principally, though not exclusively, uses.[42] St. Thomas admits that a potential part (or even an integral part) of a virtue like prudence is concerned with a special matter. The same can be said as regards a particular office of a science, a branch whose special matter is given increasing precision.[43]

If we needed to admit the possibility of two radically distinct sciences, one purely rational and the other theological, one would still have the burden of explaining why neither St. Thomas, nor any great

---

41. D'Alès, Études (October 20, 1918): p. 498.
42. See the development of these ideas in *De revelatione*, vol. 1, pp. 62–65.
43. See *ST* II-II, q. 48, a. 1.

theologian up to the end of the nineteenth century spoke of this radical distinction and why they even spoke in a manner opposed to it.

Moreover, between these two sciences, not only would one have an overwhelming variety of choices and tedium arising from repetition, but moreover, both of them would be incomplete. Hence, we have endeavored to define less what one *can* do from various perspectives than what one *must* do in order to be complete, in order to present apologetics in all its radiance. And is this not a suitable aim, above all in a course that has forming apologetes as its immediate goal, rather than converting non-believers?

Recently, a Thomist metaphysician wished to write on the subject of the work whose method we have defended here:

> The clarity and order of this apologetic work manifestly comes from the *theological direction* which has subordinated its parts to the whole and to the goal to be attained. Theological wisdom has weighed the arguments to see whether they are truly efficacious and correspond not only to the requirements of reason but also to those of faith, *sapientis est ordinare*. If one wishes to understand the necessity and the manner of this superior direction, one must recall *that it falls to theology, the supreme science, to defend its principles*. To this end, it *makes use* of inferior sciences such as philosophy and history. However, *the inferior can attain that which belongs to the superior only under the direction of the latter*. Moreover, theology, as the supreme science or wisdom, *judges* in a superior manner the philosophical principles to be *utilized*[44] in apologetic demonstration. It alone can judge them in this manner because it alone knows the nature of the divine faith to be rationally defended.[45]

Doubtlessly, in a *per accidens* manner, one could choose to avoid speaking about this superior direction. However, this silence,

---

44. See *ST* I, q. 1, a. 6, ad 2.
45. Rohner, *Analecta ordinis praedicatorum* (July 1919).
    TRANSLATOR'S NOTE: Fr. Garrigou-Lagrange openly notes that this is his French summary of the original Latin review.

recommended by this or that circumstance (e.g., the mentality of the listener to be convinced) is only an accidental affair and, therefore, is not what determines the very *nature* of apologetics. Now, apologetics must have a determinate essence. It does not suffice to say, "One *can* place oneself within this perspective just as well as within this other one." Rather, one must determine what one *must* do. *Classical* apologetics clearly and frankly says what it is. It does not forget the principle of finality: *Omne agens agit propter finem* [every agent acts on account of an end], on which rests this other principle, namely, *ordo agentium correspondet ordini finium*, the order of directing agents corresponds to the order of ends. Theology, the science of faith, ought therefore to direct the rational defense of faith.

From this way of seeing things, explained as we have, Michel seems to draw much nearer to our position by what he has recently written concerning the same work in *L'Univers*.[46]

After having recalled the task that is imposed upon the apologete from the philosophical and historical perspective, he adds: "Apologetics presupposes all this, but it *requires* more still. All this work, however complex it may be, *requires* that it be *ordered* not only according to the requirements of reason, but, even more, that it be *conformed to the teaching of the ecclesiastical magisterium*, which, in the course of recent controversies, has made pronouncements on more than one point concerning the Catholic demonstration." And we are particularly grateful to Michel for what he means to say about the text he is reviewing: "On account of their magnitude and their very richness, these two volumes (each approximately five-hundred pages in length) sometimes seem to test the patience of the overly hurried reader; however, their scientific value will be quite obvious to the eyes of all and, through the abundance of the documentation and references that they contain, they are presented, in all truth, like a *summa* of fundamental theology that is quite complete and methodically ordered."

If some divergence remains between us, it must be quite minimal, and I hope that it will disappear through meditation upon the principles of the master whom we both endeavor to follow most faithfully.

---

46.   See *Univers* (June 15, 1919): p. 377.

* * *

CHAPTER 4

Theology and the Life of Faith

B y "the life of faith," we here mean the vitality of Christian faith, whether in the Church in different ages or in each believer from the perspective of his or her intimate relations with God.

It could seem unnecessary to treat of the importance of theology for the life of faith understood in this way, for in principle, it is quite clear that—above all for a priest—the positive and speculative study of Christian dogmas is sovereignly useful to the interior life and to the apostolate. Christian faith is indispensable for salvation, and theology (or, the science of faith) is of great use in becoming well aware of the relations of the various truths of faith in the *doctrinal body* that is *Christian doctrine*, or the teaching of the Savior and of the Apostles.[1] It is so obvious that it is almost tautologous to state the fact.

THE PROBLEM, SUCH AS IT IS POSED TODAY
However, it in fact does happen that one loses sight of this truth and, consequently, of the difficulties that are encountered in the study of theology. Sometimes, these difficulties render this work quite arduous and can fatigue certain minds who are content with a more superficial knowledge of things. From the perspective of positive studies, theology is the patient study of Scriptural texts, the documents of tradition, of various interpretations that have been proposed concerning

them, and of errors old and new. From the speculative perspective, it is the thorough study of the notions without which one cannot know revealed truths: analogical notions of the various divine perfections (Wisdom, Goodness, Mercy, Justice, Providence, Predestination, etc.); the notions of *nature* and of *person* in the treatises on the Trinity and the Incarnation; the notions of *substance* and *accident* in that of the Eucharist; the notions of *freedom, merit, grace, sin, eternal punishment, beatitude,* etc. Some might think that the abstract considerations needed for thoroughly studying these notions are quite distant from our habitual preoccupations. The interior life, we are told, is simpler, above all in what is superior in it, and it does not seem necessary that it should get tangled up with the metaphysical study of all these problems. Great saints, like the sublime beggar Benedict-Joseph Labre, lived profoundly upon the Eucharist without ever having read a treatise on the sacraments.

It suffices, some say, to adhere to the fixity of faith and, for action, to the directions of ecclesiastical authority. As regards *theological opinions—the ensemble of which,* they think, *constitutes theology!*—they are merely disputed questions to which are dedicated the teams of laborers belonging to various religious orders. These groups and their doctrines all hold an equally probable certitude, allowing the mind complete freedom of choice among them and even the possibility of choosing none of them. The vital questions would lie elsewhere.

Some believe that nothing of great importance is involved for the Catholic when it comes to the question of choosing between the *definition of truth* to which St. Thomas always returns (conformity of the intellect with reality) and the definition of truth proposed some years ago by Maurice Blondel when he wrote, "For the abstract and chimerical *adaequatio rei et intellectus* [the adequation of the thing and the

---

1.   In its decree *Lamentabili* (Denzinger, no. 3059) the Holy Office condemned this fifty-ninth proposition of the modernists: "Christ did not teach a determined body of doctrine applicable to all times and all men but, rather, inaugurated a religious movement adapted or to be adapted to different times and places." Also, see the proposition that follows.

TRANSLATOR'S NOTE: The sixtieth condemned proposition reads: "Christian doctrine was originally Judaic. Through successive evolutions it became first Pauline, then Joannine, finally Hellenic and universal."

intellect] there is substituted...*adaequatio realis mentis et vitae* [the real adequation of the mind and life]."[2]

As the life in question here is human life, which changes, it was then asked how, from this perspective, one can avoid the condemned modernist proposition: "*Truth is no more immutable than man himself, since it evolved with him, in him, and through him.*"[3]

Since 1906, Blondel has moved closer to traditional metaphysics. We know that he has formally condemned the manifestly inadmissible excesses that can be found in the posthumous articles of Fr. Laberthonnière.[4] Equally, he even retracted the final chapter of *l'Action* which was most vigorously contested.[5]

However, in his latest work, *La pensée*, we still can find propositions that, taken in the obvious sense of the terms, seem quite removed from traditional doctrine. In Blondel's thought, which here is preoccupied, on the one hand, with taking into account certain results from the critique of the physical and natural sciences and, on the other, with speaking in opposition to the rationalism of this or that contemporary philosophy, these propositions do not have, we believe, the scope that they appear to have at first sight. Nevertheless, they do not seem to maintain sufficiently enough the *stability* and *ontological value* of the

2. Maurice Blondel, "Le point de depart de la recherche philosophique," *Annales de philosophie chretienne*, Vol. 152 (1906): p. 235.

3. Pius X, *Lamentabili*, no. 59 (Denzinger, no. 3459).

4. In his posthumous articles published in *Archivio di filosofia* (April and July 1933), one reads in July on p. 11: "Without a doubt, St. Thomas kept the letter of Christianity...but, by his doctrine, by his fundamental conceptions, by all the orientation of his thought, he is totally and radically outside of Christianity." "The God (whom he describes for us) is a *being of pride, nothing but pride*" (who has created all things for Himself) (April, p. 14).

    Fr. Laberthonnière forgot what is said in Prov. 16:4: "The Lord hath made all things for himself," and he has not understood that if God ceased willing everything for the sake of the Sovereign Good, which is Himself, and for the sake of the manifestation of His goodness, there would be, as it were, a mortal sin in God, that is to say, the most extreme of absurdities.

5. M. Blondel said in *l'Action*, pp. 437ff.: "*Knowledge*, which, *before one's choice* [*option*], was simply *subjective*, propulsive, becomes, afterwards, privative [*sic*] and *constitutive of being*" (depending on whether the free choice is morally bad or good). Cf. *l'Action*, pp. 426ff., 439, 463.

    TRANSLATOR'S NOTE: Fr. Garrigou-Lagrange does not cite the edition.

notions necessary for the first principles of reason (including among them that of causality), nor of those necessary for the formulas of faith.[6] When Blondel speaks of *free choice* in relation to *certitude*, one would greatly desire to see him maintain the profound distinction formulated by St. Thomas[7] concerning the influence of the will on the intellect, depending on whether there is or is not *necessitating evidence* for the object known. In the first case, the influence of the will leads the

---

6. One reads in *La pensée*, vol. 1, p. 130: "*The objects to which thought is taken and given do not find their* common denominator, *their specific stability*, their logical utilization, EXCEPT BY THE ARTIFICE OF LANGUAGE... We substantize the things that we know not to be substances." If this proposition, thus formulated, is true, how is one to maintain *the stability and real value of the notions of* nature, of substance, of person, necessary to *the enunciation of the dogmas of faith?* [TRANSLATOR'S NOTE: Fr. Garrigou-Lagrange does not cite the edition, but it appears to match the pagination of Maurice Blondel, *La pensée*, vol. 1 (Paris: Presses Universitaires de France, 1934).]

    M. Blondel also says, ibid., 131: "*The notion of an object* and the use that is ordinarily made of it is one of these divisions, one of these *illegitimate* 'overestimations' [*majorations*] which we do not cease to denounce as being *the chronic deception* and *ruinous improbity* from which many a philosophy is dying today." If one takes this proposition in its obvious sense, how can one determine *the proper object* of our intellect and affirm with the Church (cf. [First] Vatican Council, *Dei filius*, ch. 4 [Denzinger no. 3015]) that the supernatural mysteries of faith certainly *exceed* this [formal] object, which is naturally knowable for us?

    Again, one reads on the following page (p. 132): "There are, *not in an absolute fashion* (this would be an illusion), but in a relative fashion, *distinctly subsistent realities...* 'substantial forms' that, *without being stably achieved and independent*, nevertheless have...a value that is, at one and the same time, objective and subjective." Also, see ibid., vol. 1, pp. 136–37 and vol. 2, pp. 30, 57, 74, 196, and 302.

    How then is the *nature* of the human soul really and essentially distinct from grace *that is not owed to it?* How is the latter certainly above the exigencies of our nature, contrary to what Baius said?

    We read later in *La Pensée*, vol. 1, p. 179: "*Far from deducing the affirmation of the living God from a prior assertion of abstract principles*, these intellectual premises proceed in a more profound sense from the realistic conception of a divine substance."

    Is this to say that we have a firm certitude of the real and universal value of the principle of causality, necessary for the *a posteriori* proofs of God's existence only *after we believe in God*, which appears indeed to presuppose itself a *free choice*, as M. Blondel affirms in his book *l'Action* (pp. 437ff., 439, 426ff., and 463), and as voluntarist philosophy of action would require? It is this free choice that we see reappearing in the belief of which he speaks in this new work, vol. 1, pp. 390ff.; vol. 2, 65, 67, 81, 90, and 96: "*In our fashion of knowing and affirming*, there is always for the assertion and effective consent *a portion of belief* inherent to vital and intellectual certitudes all together. Not that there would be a hazard [*aléa*] for those who can see and will; but, in the most perspicuous intellect, it is necessary that to the evidence of logical reasons there be joined *the decision*, which renders to truth the primacy, the totality that is due to it."

7. *ST* I-II, q. 17, a. 6.

intellect (*quoad exercitium* [with regard to its exercise]) to *consider* this truth attentively, in a manner that is sustained long enough, likewise *considering everything that should be considered* without neglecting anything. Here, there certainly is a place for moral rectitude and intellectual probity. We likewise concede that even when there is necessitating evidence, the influence of the will can *confirm* our intellectual certitude because we daily live more in accord with the already acknowledged truth. From this perspective, a great difference separates the notion that one can form for oneself, for example, of humility after having read an excellent study upon this subject from that much more profound notion of humility which a saint has of it at the end of his life. Something similar occurs with regard to the proofs for God's existence.

All this is incontestable and should be clearly distinguished from the influence of the will on the intellect *quoad specificationem* [with regard to specification] *when necessitating evidence* from the object *does not exist*, as holds in the case of faith in the revealed mysteries. Many passages in Blondel related to the free option and to certitude would be admissible if he noted this distinction, which is common in St. Thomas and his disciples. By means of it, the role of the will in these very different forms of certitudes is easily explained, as are the certitude of science and the certitude of faith or belief.[8] It also sheds light on the character of the kinds of certitude proper to prudence,[9] hope,[10] and the gift of wisdom. In these latter, the role of the will is manifestly much greater than in the certitude born of necessitating evidence.

To remain faithful to traditional metaphysics, we absolutely must maintain that, *prior to any free option*, the human intellect can be certain of the truth of the principles of contradiction and of causality, understanding these principles in their *realist* sense.

---

8.   See *ST* II-II, q. 2, a. 1; q. 4, a. 8.

9.   See *ST* I-II, q. 57, a. 5, ad 3 (on prudential certitude, *per conformitatem ad appetitum rectum, through conformity to right appetite,* even in the case of invincible ignorance or error).
     TRANSLATOR'S NOTE: See the chapter above, entitle "Prudence's Place in the Organism of the Virtues."

10. See *ST* II-II q. 18, a. 4.
     TRANSLATOR'S NOTE: See Garrigou-Lagrange, *Sense of Mystery*, pp. 44–46.

For the nominalists and consistent [*conséquents*] idealists, the principle of contradiction is only a conditional proposition: *If something is, something is* (*si aliquid est, aliquid est*). However, according to them, perhaps nothing is. Perhaps our idea of being does not have a real value. Perhaps all things become and perhaps becoming itself is self-explanatory, a *ratio sui*. Perhaps God is only creative evolution.

For the realist, the ontological formulation of the principle of contradiction is categorical: "It is absolutely impossible that, at one and the same time, a thing be and not be." For the realist, a square circle is not only subjectively *inconceivable*. It is *really impossible, unrealizable* outside the mind, whatever Descartes may say about it. Similarly, for realism, the denial of the principle of causality leads to absurdity. To claim that *that which begins* (i.e., *the contingent*) is *uncaused* is not only an *unintelligible claim* but, moreover, is absurd and *really impossible* outside the mind. Does Blondel firmly admit, prior to every free option, the certitude of the real value of these principles and that of the principle of finality, every agent acts for an end? In certain passages, it seems like he admits these certitudes as being necessary; however, in others, he attenuates his affirmation and makes it seem like it has some sort of relativity.

Likewise, does he acknowledge, prior to every free option, the certitude of the *personal existence of the thinking subject*, and the truth that *he cannot have the experience of it* without *the existence of the experienced reality*, no sensation of resistance (distinct from hallucination) without something that resists? "Touch and see, for a spirit does not have flesh and bones" (Lk. 24:39).[11]

All these primordial questions are manifestly of a great importance for every man who seeks the truth. They are certainly no less important for the intellectual formation of priests, as the Church conceives it.[12]

What then must we think about the relationship existing between the speculative and thorough study of theology and the life of faith as

---

11. See *ST* III, q. 55, a. 6; q. 57, a. 6, ad 3; *ST* I, q. 51, a. 2.
     TRANSLATOR'S NOTE: For a more detailed account of this matter, see the chapter above, entitled "There Cannot Be Genuine Sensation Without a Real Sensed Thing," pp. 101–119.
12. Canon [1917 code] 1366, §2: "Professors should treat the studies of rational philosophy and theology and instruction of candidates in these disciplines entirely *according to the method, doctrine, and principles of the Angelic Doctor and should hold it to be sacred.*"

well as the interior life itself? In the Church, it has always been taught that the interior life owes much to theology and that the study of this science is, in turn, greatly fertilized by a profound interior life. Here, we find mutual relations whose elementary truths should be recalled, truths which turn out to be very profound when one indeed chooses to penetrate them and make them the rule of one's life with greater intensity each day.

THEOLOGY PRESERVES THE INTERIOR LIFE
FROM GRAVE DEVIATIONS

First of all, the study of theology helps the spiritual life avoid two grave, truly ruinous defects: *subjectivism* and *particularism.*

Those who approach God in prayer by allowing themselves to be led too much by the inclination of their own individual nature, temperament, imagination, sensibility, or character often fall into sentimentalist subjectivism.

In our own days, Henri Bergson thinks that the mystics are above all dominated by an emotion to which they deliver themselves, one that they then express in religious ideas or conceptions, like that of the divine mercy toward us or that of the need to offer reparation to divine justice. However, [according to him] we can make pronunciations concerning *the truth* of these religious conceptions only from the empirical and practical perspective, doing so by the welcome effect that they produce, above all if this effect is durable and has an echo in us. Therefore, one could ask oneself whether these conceptions only contain a beautiful dream arising from one's religious sentiment, a consoling reverie, though without its object exceeding the limits of probable opinion, all while becoming increasingly plausible by the increasing number of welcome results of these conceptions.

It will responded: However, to be assured of being in the truth, the fixity of faith suffices without needing recourse to theology.

Still, in order to retain the fixity of faith, one must accept the traditional definition of the *truth* and not only the pragmatist definition thereof. Otherwise, dogmas would become only a norm of action: comport yourself in relation to Jesus Christ *as though* He were God, though without affirming that He really *is* God; comport yourself in relation the Resurrection as though it really had taken place; comport yourself in relation to the Eucharist as though there really were a transubstantiation and real presence.

Moreover, to preserve oneself from subjectivism in the interior life, to truly live the great mysteries of faith, is it superfluous to meditate seriously on what the masters of theology have written concerning them? Likewise, is it superfluous to know the nature of the spiritual organism of sanctifying grace, the infused virtues and the gifts, the various forms of actual grace, and the signs of a divine inspiration along with its counterfeits?

Have not the great mystics been ever more attentive to the task of placing *truth* in their life so that they might live nothing but the truth?[13]

Of particular note, we have the case of St. Teresa of Ávila, who spoke of the esteem that she had for theology and for men of doctrine:

> In difficult matters, even if I believe I understand what I am saying and am speaking the truth, I use this phrase, "I think," because if I am mistaken, I am very ready to give credence to those who have great learning.[14] For even if they have not themselves experienced these things, men of great learning have a certain instinct to prompt them. As God uses them to give light to His Church, He reveals to them anything which is true so that it shall be accepted; and if they do not squander their talents, but are true servants of God, they will never be surprised at His greatness, for they know quite well that He is capable of working more and still more. In any case, where matters are in question for which there is no explanation, there must be others about which they can read, and they can deduce from their reading that it is possible for these first-named to have happened. Of this I have the fullest experience; and I have also experience of timid, half-learned men whose shortcomings have cost me very dear.[15]

---

13. On this point, see the beautiful study by Fr. Thomas Deman, "La théologie dans la vie de sainte Catherine de Sienne," *Vie spirituelle*, Vol. 42, Suppl. (1935): pp.[1]–[24].

14. TRANSLATOR'S NOTE: Fr. Garrigou-Lagrange has in French *les grand théologiens*.

15. Teresa of Ávila, *Interior Castle*, trans. E. Allison Peers (New York: Doubleday: 1961), pp. 100–101 (fifth mansion, ch. 1). Likewise, see the eighth chapter of the sixth mansion.

* * *

Beyond individual subjectivism, theology also preserves the interior life from particularism, which arises from the excessive influence of our environment or from that of the ideas in vogue in our era, ideas that will be outdated in thirty years' time. One can note these deviations in the ages of quietism, Americanism, and modernism. In these deviations, we have passing enthusiasms that last little longer then a fire fed upon straw, and if they are not remedied, they are followed by discouragement.

By preserving our interior life from these deviations, the attentive study of theology gives it a precious *objectivity*, a sane realism, and also, above every narrow, particular, and passing view, a *universality*, which is the mark of the great classics of spirituality, whose writings are of value for all places and all times. In a way, like something conceived above the flow of time in its continual onward course, these works do not age but, instead, retain a superior relevance.

THEOLOGY CONTRIBUTES TO PROVIDING
THE INTERIOR LIFE WITH THE PROFOUND SENSE
OF THE TRUTHS OF FAITH

The study of the great masters of theology not only preserves the interior life from the deviations of which we have spoken. It moreover helps it to know *the mind of the Church* [*le sens de l'Eglise*], which is the same *ubique et semper*. Little by little, it shows us the *profundity of the most elementary truths* of Christianity. It even habituates us to seeing that the elementary truths of Christian doctrine are the loftiest, most profound, and most vital truths we may ever know, provided that they are penetrated well, meditated upon at length, and lived upon. Thus, they ultimately become the *object of contemplation*. Such is the case for the first line of the Catechism: "Why were you created and put into the world? To know God, to love Him, to serve Him, and by these means to obtain eternal life," or, again, this expression of St. John: "God so loved the world that He gave His only Son" (Jn. 3:16).

The [First] Vatican Council admirably expresses the importance of theology for the Christian life when it says:

Nevertheless, if reason illumined by faith inquires in an earnest, pious, and sober manner, it attains by God's grace a certain understanding of the mysteries, which is most fruitful, both from the analogy with the objects of its natural knowledge and from the connection of these mysteries with one another and with man's ultimate end. But it never becomes capable of understanding them in the way it does truths that constitute its proper object.[16]

Theology enables us to arrive at a certain, very fruitful understanding of the revealed mysteries. And this is even its most precious fruit. This is why, in St. Thomas, the first questions of the great dogmatic treatises on the Trinity, the Redemptive Incarnation, the Sacraments in general, and the Eucharist, all first contain *the conceptual analysis of these revealed truths* before he is concerned with deducing from them *other truths* of less importance, truths that are theological conclusions, properly speaking, the fruit of objectively *illative* reasoning.[17] All these first questions of the great treatises contain in a general manner only *explicative* reasonings, which explain or deepen the subject and the predicate of the revealed truth, of the great mystery in question. In this way, as a result of these explications, the *consubstantiality of the Word* is not, as is sometimes said, a theological conclusion deduced from a revealed truth, but instead, is *the revealed truth* in its exact and profound sense: "*And the Word* (consubstantial to the Father) *was made flesh* (namely, man)." It is the revealed mystery itself in the light of this other expression from the Prologue of St. John: "And the Word was God." The consubstantiality of the Word [to the Father] is incomparably superior to theological conclusions.

Even were theology not to deduce *any* theological conclusions, properly so-called, but were only to explain, through a profound metaphysical analysis,[18] the subject and predicate *of revealed truths*, and even

---

16.   [First] Vatican Council, *Dei filius*, ch. 4. Denzinger, no. 3016.

17.   TRANSLATOR'S NOTE: See the chapter above, entitled "On the Search for Definitions According to Aristotle and St. Thomas," p. 26, note 9. Also, see p. 431, note 19 in this chapter.

18.   TRANSLATOR'S NOTE: By which Fr. Garrigou-Lagrange merely means something like, "a causal analysis of what something is."

were it only to show *their subordination* in order to make us be better aware of the depth, riches, and elevation of the very teaching of the Savior, even in such a case, it would have a considerable importance. And this is how theology prepares for the elaboration of increasingly explicit dogmatic formulations of one and the same dogma, that is, of one and the same assertion or revealed truth, before it is a question of deducing from it *other truths* through an *objectively illative* reasoning.[19] This deepening of the meaning of a fundamental truth sometimes takes centuries, as with the deepening of this expression: "And the Word was made flesh."

It is utterly evident that theology has contributed much to the elaboration of increasingly explicit formulations of one and the same dogma, an explication often rendered necessary for eliminating heresies.

St. Thomas, who in his Commentary on the *Posterior Analytics* of Aristotle (bk. 2, lect. 3–17) studied so profoundly how one undertakes the *venatio*, the search, for the *real* and distinct *definition* by setting out from the *nominal definition* that expresses the vague concept of the thing to be defined, was certainly not unaware of this *development [progrès] of dogmas*. The most important work of philosophy and theology is found in this methodical passage from the *vague concept* of common sense to the *distinct concept*. The latter is not *deduced* from the preceding like a conclusion. Rather, one and the same concept is given increasing precision through the *division* of the genus (or, of the most general notion) and through the inductive *comparison* of the thing to be defined with what more or less resembles it. In this way, philosophy comes to

---

19. We use the expression "*Objectively illative* reasoning" for that form of reasoning which leads *to another [objectively new] truth*. For example, from the Divine Intelligence, we can deduce the Divine Freedom through this major: every intelligent being is free. On the contrary, a reasoning is only *explicative* (or at most *subjectively illative*) when it establishes the *equivalence* of two propositions in enunciating the *same truth*. For example, there is the *equivalence* of these two propositions: "You are Peter and upon this rock I will build my Church; and the gates of hell will not prevail over it" = "The successor of Peter, when he speaks *ex cathedra* to the universal Church, in a matter of faith and morals, cannot be deceived."

See at the end of this article an *appendix* concerning the question of knowing whether theological conclusions obtained by *objectively illative* reasoning with the aid of a *natural premise* (even when the latter is the major, that is to say the more universal premise) can be *defined* as *a dogma of faith* to be acknowledged under pain of heresy properly speaking (and not only of error).

obtain precise definitions of substance, man, the soul, the intellect, the will, the different acquired virtues, etc.[20]

In theology, the same kind of conceptual analysis has contributed greatly to the *precision of notions* that are indispensable for *dogmatic formulations*: the notions of created being and uncreated being, those of unity, truth, and (ontological and moral) goodness; the notions of analogy relative to God, of the Divine Wisdom, the Divine Will, love, providence, and predestination; for the understanding of revealed truths concerning the Trinity, the notions of nature, person, and relation; the notions of grace (habitual and actual; efficacious or sufficient); the notions of free will,[21] merit, sin, infused virtue, faith, hope, charity, and justification; the notions of sacrament,[22] character, sacramental grace, transubstantiation, and contrition; the notions of beatitude and of punishment, of purgatory and hell, etc.

Even before taking up the task of deducing theological conclusions (that is, the task of arriving at new truths distinct from *revealed truths*) an immense labor must be undertaken in the *conceptual analysis* of these revealed truths so as to pass from the *vague notion* (expressed by the current nominal definition or by the terms of Scripture and of Tradition) to *the same distinct and precise notion* in view of eliminating heresy, which deforms revelation itself.

---

20. TRANSLATOR'S NOTE: See the chapter above, entitled "On the Search for Definitions According to Aristotle and St. Thomas," pp. 21–34.

21. The passage from the nominal definition to the real definition is sometimes quite lengthy; thus is it that the Thomists and the Molinists still do not agree concerning the real (exact or distinct) definition of free will inasmuch as it adds a precision to the nominal definition. Nevertheless, it is a question of the *same concept* which is at first vague and then is distinct.

22. For *the defined doctrine concerning the sacraments*, dogmatic progress is considerable, for the revealed truths relative to the sacraments had been revealed less in an abstract manner than in a *concrete and practical* manner, by the very administration of the sacraments. And thus what is necessary for a sacrament, like baptism, can be considered either from the perspective of being a *sign* (sensible thing and words), or from the perspective of the *subject* who receives it, or from the perspective of the *effects* produced, or from the perspective of the ordinary or exceptional *minister*. Thus, one and the same thing practiced in Church, in accord with the will of Christ, since her beginnings, can be expressed in *multiple propositions* in order to eliminate this or that heresy. And these propositions are not theological conclusions; they are the abstract expression of the concretely *revealed truth*.

To arrive at this penetration, it is not useless to have studied many times the Treatises on God and on the Incarnation in the work of a master like St. Thomas.

Even those who teach them come to have a command of the subject only after many years; then, little by little, they grasp the profound sense of the principles, as well as their elevation and their radiance. Thus, one arrives at the "fruitful understanding of the mysteries" spoken of by the [First] Vatican Council.

Theology aids in deepening faith so that we may live by it, and below the level of faith, it is gradually constituted as an explanatory *science* of the revealed truths and as a deduction of certain theological conclusions which are nearly universally admitted, with that which contradicts them often having been condemned not as "heresies" but as "errors."

Indeed, it is of great important not to confuse *theological science* with *theological opinions*. Classics like Bossuet draw upon this science with open hands, generally setting aside consideration of the particular opinions of theologians. They are not unaware of these various opinions. However, what they seek in faith and in the science of faith is what rises above such opinions.

To realize the importance of *the acquisition of theological science*, let us suppose for a moment that St. Thomas's *Summa theologiae* had not yet been written and that the only treatises on God, the Incarnation, grace, and faith that we had were the questions of the Master of the Sentences.[23] How much more difficult we find it to render an account of the *mutual relationships which exist among revealed truths* in the body of Christian doctrine, and how much more impoverished would we be for making a sound judgment concerning dangerous doctrinal novelties, which are sometimes born of a very slight error in a first principle: "*Parvus error in principio magnus est in fine.*" If one distorts in an almost imperceptible manner certain Thomist principles in the question of predestination and reprobation, one can fall into Calvinism (for example, if one does not

---

23. TRANSLATOR'S NOTE: I.e., Peter Lombard (c. 1100–c. 1164), whose *Sentences* played a central role in academic theological formation and commentary well into the sixteenth century.

distinguish clearly enough the divine permission which precedes sin and the subtraction of divine grace which follows at the same instant).

It is of great importance that we know the value of commonly received *theological science*. By having misunderstood it, the nominalists of the fourteenth and fifteenth century fell into grave errors that paved the way for the errors of Luther, who was formed by them. Thus, they conceived of sanctifying grace as being a *quality of the natural order*, which would nevertheless give a moral right to eternal life as a result of a divine institution, like a bank note, which gives us the right to receive a hundred dollars [*francs*], even though it all the while remains nothing other than a piece of paper. Luther came to say that grace and justification are only an *extrinsic denomination* by the imputation of the merits of the Savior unto us.

Finally, as Fr. Gardeil has noted,[24] among the various *theological systems*, we must carefully heed the importance of universal syntheses that make their master idea the very idea of God, the Author of nature and of grace or of salvation, and not some particular idea which is obviously subordinate to the preceding (for example, the idea of man's free will). A given system thus dominated by a particular idea cannot be a universal synthesis, which must be dominated by the idea of God, the proper object of theology.

In its superior simplicity, faith is like an utterly simple circle. The teachings of the greatest theologians, seeking to explain the dogmas of faith, are like a polygon inscribed within this circle, so as to elaborate its content and riches. The nominalists draw their polygon in their own particular manner; it is quite different from that which had been sketched by St. Augustine and drawn out by St. Thomas.

All this shows what the life of faith receives and can receive from the study of theology when the latter is indeed undertaken with intelligence, penetration, and docility to the great doctors whom the Church proposes to us as Masters.

* * *

---

24. Ambroise Gardeil, *Le donné révélé et la théologie* (Paris: Librarie Victor Lecoffre, J. Gabalda et cie., 1910), pp. 252–85.

TRANSLATOR'S NOTE: Fr. Garrigou-Lagrange lists only the title and pp. 252–85. It appears that he means the third chapter of the second part as cited here, pp. 252–84.

THE INFLUENCE OF THE INTERIOR LIFE ON THEOLOGY

But if the interior life receives much from the study of theology, it can, in its own turn, greatly perfect such study as well. This fact is not noted frequently enough. Nevertheless, the great doctors of the Church have spoken of it often, indeed, in a much truer manner than the current partisans of the philosophy of action.

Too often, the study of theology remains lifeless, either in its positive part or in its abstract and speculative part. It does not truly make felt the superior inspiration existing in it, the breath of the theological virtues and of the gifts of the Holy Spirit, the gifts of understanding and of wisdom. Thus we do not sufficiently find in it this *sapida scientia* spoken of by St. Thomas in the first question of the *Summa theologiae*.

Like a child who studies the piano and cannot yet fathom what gives the works of the masters their value, one comes too a halt too readily at the *formulas* without seeking to pass through in order to thereby reach the Divine Reality signified, in order to penetrate and taste the revealed mysteries.

Here we should recall that saints like St. Francis of Assisi, St. Catherine of Siena, St. Benedict-Joseph Labre, and so many others, who never undertook the conceptual analysis of the dogmas of the Redemptive Incarnation and of the Eucharist and who never studied the theological conclusions that one deduces from them, profoundly lived upon these mysteries precisely by passing through the formula so as to go on to the Divine and Living Reality that they signify.

And without calling to mind these great saints who received special graces of contemplation, how many simple but profound Christian souls live upon these mysteries more, perhaps, than many theologians! With a sound and saintly realism, they enter into these heights of God because they are humble, having pure hearts and lively faith, both of which inspire all their conduct from morning to night. As St. Thomas says: "The act of the believer is not terminated at the *enunciable statement*[25] but *at the thing*, at the revealed mystery itself."[26]

---

25. TRANSLATOR'S NOTE: I.e., at the complex of subject and predicate upon which judgment will be borne by the intellect in its second kind of act in its speculative use.

26. *ST* II-II, q. 1, a. 2, ad 2.

Now, if this is true of these souls, for how much greater a reason should it be true of a priest who has truly understood the grandeur of his vocation, he who should celebrate the Holy Sacrifice with an ever-livelier faith each day, a purer and stronger love of God, and each day make a communion substantially more fervent than the day before, given that we must not only preserve but must augment the charity that is in us, thus disposing ourselves (if some negligence does not take place) to receive our Lord the next day with a fervor of will that is not only equal to the previous day's but, rather, one that is greater still.[27]

When the interior life of a priest thus grows every day, it greatly vivifies his study of theology. These two forms of his activity have the most welcome influence upon one another: *Causae ad invicem sunt causae, in diverso genere* [Causes are mutually causes for each other, though in diverse genera of causality].

THE FRUITS OF THIS MUTUAL INFLUENCE

When the priest has a great and solid piety, if he also applies himself to study, theology becomes ever-livelier for him. Like the pianist coming to master the necessary techniques of piano playing and to understand the works of the masters, one here comes to perceive the harmonies at play in the works of someone like St. Augustine or St. Thomas.

Then, after *descending* from faith to theology to know its details in its various treatises, the theologian will experience the need to *ascend from theology to faith*, to ascend to the divine source of this science. He resembles a man who would have passed his childhood upon a mountain, like Monte Cassino,[28] then descending into the valley to traverse it in all directions. This man would feel the need to return to

---

27. St. Thomas wrote in his Commentary *In Epist. ad Hebr.*, 10:25: "The more a natural motion approaches its terminus, the *more is it inclined thereunto*. The contrary is the case for violent motion (e.g., of a stone thrown upward and ascending upward). Now, grace inclines in the manner of nature. Therefore (as the natural motion of the stone falling ever is faster), *the more those who are in grace approach the end, the more they ought to grow* [*in grace*]." The more they approach God, the more they are attracted by Him, and more rapidly do they bear themselves toward Him, as the final years of the lives of the saints show.

28. TRANSLATOR'S NOTE: The implied parallel is almost certainly to the life of St. Thomas, who was a child oblate at the Benedictine abbey of Monte Cassino and who died at the Cistercian abbey of Fossanova after his well-known late-life mystical experience.

the mountain so as to embrace all the valley in a single glance. The theologian likewise needs to embrace his science in a single glance by finding it virtually contained in the *Credo* or at the end of the Mass in the Prologue of St. John's Gospel.

When the priestly soul has become, as it must, a soul of prayer, the interior life then emphasizes what is most vital and most fertile in dogmatic and moral theology. The gifts of understanding and wisdom render infused faith penetrating and enable it to savor the truths that it knows… And let us remember, infused faith is the root of theology.

One thus discovers increasingly captivating *chiaroscuros* in the doctrines of Christianity,[29] *chiaroscuros* which are the object of the infused contemplation of the saints and of truly interior souls.

Little by little, all the great questions on grace are summarized in the following two principles. On the one hand, "*God never commands the impossible*, but in commanding, He admonishes us to do what we can and to ask [for the grace] to do what we cannot," as St. Augustine says,[30] and as cited by the Council of Trent against the Protestants.[31] On the other hand, against the Pelagians and Semi-Pelagians, "For who sees anything different in you? What have you that you did not receive?" (1 Cor. 4:7, RSV); or, according of the terms used by St. Thomas: "As the uncreated love of God is the cause of all good, nothing would be *better* than something else if it were not more loved by God."[32]

Just as each of these two principles is clear and certain when considered in isolation, so too is their intimate reconciliation obscure on account of the superior obscurity that comes from too-great a light for our weak eyes. To see this intimate reconciliation, we would need to see how infinite justice, infinite mercy, and sovereign freedom are reconciled in the Deity (or, the intimate life of God).

Let us take another example. With the progress of the interior life, one sees more and more fully the loftiness of the treatise on the Redemptive Incarnation and the motive of the Incarnation of the Son

---

29. TRANSLATOR'S NOTE: A lengthy treatment of this theme can be found in Garrigou-Lagrange, *Sense of Mystery*.

30. See Augustine, *De natura et gratia*, ch. 43, no. 50.

31. See Council of Trent, *Decree on Justification*, ch. 11 (Denzinger, no. 1536).

32. See *ST* 1, q. 20, aa. 3 and 4.

of God, *"qui propter nos homines et propter nostrum salutem descendit de caelis et homo factus est* [who for us men and for our salvation descended from heaven and was made man]."

Similarly, again, under the influence of the life of prayer, one gradually discovers what life is hidden in the Eucharist and, in a domain elevated above all the theories on the sacrifice of the Mass, the sense and scope of these words of the Council of Trent becomes increasingly clear: "For the victim is one and the same: THE SAME NOW OFFERS Himself through the ministry of priests who then offered Himself on the Cross; only the manner of the offering is different."[33] With ever better clarity, the Savior appears as the *Principal Priest* "always living to intercede for us" (Heb. 7:25) and His interior oblation, ever current, not renewed, but continued, measured, like His beatific vision, by participated eternity, appears like the soul of the sacrifice of the Mass and of all the Masses that do not cease to be celebrated on the earth's surface.

Thus, little by little, one discovers, in Scripture and the Councils, the most precious stones of the doctrinal edifice. Likewise, in the *Summa theologiae*, one comes to have increasing discernment concerning the *summa capita*, the greatest articles, which are like the most elevated and most characteristic peaks in a lengthy mountain range.

If one truly applies oneself to the study of theology in a spirit of faith and prayer, it becomes living, and then are these words of St. Thomas realized: "Doctrine and preaching (of the divine word) ought to be derived from the fullness of contemplation,"[34] as one sees after Pentecost in the preaching of the Apostles.

* * *

Understood in this manner, theology is of a great importance in preparing oneself for the ministry of souls. It *profoundly forms the mind* to judge in accord with the Gospel and to exhort souls to true Christian perfection. It shows all the elevation of the ultimate precept: "Love your God with all your heart…" It makes one see that this precept does not

---

33. Council of Trent, sess. 22, Doctrine and Canons on the Sacrifice of the Mass (Denzinger, no. 1743).

34. *ST* II-II, q. 188, a. 6.

have limits and that all Christians *must tend* to the perfection of char-ity,[35] each according to his condition, one in marriage, another in the religious state, another in the priestly life.

Now, we cannot arrive at the full perfection of the Christian life if we do not profoundly live the mysteries of the Redemptive Incarnation and of the Eucharist, if we do not penetrate and taste them by a living faith, illuminated by the gifts of understanding and of wisdom. In a subordinate but truly useful way, the study of theology contributes to this, provided that it is inspired not by natural curiosity but by the love of God and desire for the salvation of souls.

In this way, we have an ever-more powerful verification for these beautiful words enunciated by the [First] Vatican Council which were cited at the beginning of this article, and which are a definition and an encomium for theology:

> Nevertheless, if *reason illumined by faith* inquires in an earnest, pious, and sober manner, it attains by God's grace a certain understanding of the mysteries, which is most fruitful, both from the analogy with the objects of its natural knowledge and from the connection of these mysteries with one another and with man's ultimate end.[36]

The study of theology, which sometimes is difficult and arduous, is thus truly fruitful. It disposes, in a certain way, the faithful and gener-ous priestly soul to receive the light of life, the grace of contemplation and of union, which is, as St. Thomas says, "a kind of beginning of eternal life."[37]

NOTE

With regard to the *definability of theological conclusions*, in the body of this chapter, we distinguished *objectively illative* reasoning, which leads to ANOTHER TRUTH [from that which is expressed in its premises], from *explicative* reasoning, namely, that which is, at most, *subjectively*

---

35. See *ST* II-II, q. 184, a. 3.

36. [First] Vatican Council, *Dei filius*, ch. 4 (Denzinger, no. 3016).

37. *ST* I-II, q. 69, a. 2; II-II, q. 24, a. 3, ad 2; *De veritate*, q. 14, a. 2.

illative, which establishes the equivalence of two propositions that enunciate, the one vaguely, the other distinctly, THE SAME TRUTH (for example, the infallibility of Peter and of his successors).

This leads to the following question: can theological conclusions obtained by *objectively illative* reasoning using a *natural premise* (even when the latter is the major, i.e., the more universal premise) be defined as *a dogma of faith* that one must admit not only under pain of error but, indeed, under that of heresy properly speaking? For example, supposing that the Divine Freedom were not formally revealed, even in a vague manner, could it be defined as a dogma? It would be the conclusion of a process of reasoning whose natural major would be: "Every intelligent being is free." Following with the minor premise, "Now, it is revealed that God is an intelligent being," we would then conclude, "Therefore, God is free, and this is virtually revealed."

We do not think that a theological conclusion, properly speaking, as deduced from that which is revealed by means of *objectively inferential* reasoning could be defined under pain of heresy properly so called as being a dogma of the faith (although the contradictory proposition could be infallibly condemned as erroneous). The reason for this is (and the great commentators on St. Thomas generally admit the point) that it is not *simpliciter* a *revealed* truth, but instead, is a *truth deduced from a revealed proposition* using a natural premise (which even here is the major and not the minor).

Even if this conclusion enunciates a judgment concerning God, no matter how rigorous it may be, it cannot be defined as a dogma (unless it is contained elsewhere in some place within the deposit of revelation).

To defend the idea that such statements could be defined, Fr. Marín-Sola[38] said in 1924 in his *Homogeneous Evolution of Catholic*

---

38. TRANSLATOR'S NOTE: Most germane to this topic is his *Homogeneous Evolution of Catholic Dogma*. A translation of his work concerning controversies pertaining to grace and predestination has been published as Francisco Marín-Sola, *Do Not Resist the Spirit's Call: Francisco Marín-Sola on Sufficient Grace*, trans. Michael D. Torre (Washington, DC: The Catholic University of America Press, 2013). In what follows, I will include citations from the French edition cited by Fr. Garrigou-Lagrange. At the time of this volume's publication, the English edition of Fr. Marín-Sola's work is quite difficult to obtain. See Francisco Marín-Sola, *L'évolution homogene du dogme catholique*, 2nd ed. (Fribourg: Imprimerie et librairie de l'oeuvre de Saint-paul, 1924).

Dogma[39]: The truth deduced enunciates a judgment *concerning the same Divine Reality.* For example, if one deduced the *Divine Freedom* (presupposing that it would not be formally and vaguely revealed) from the *Divine Intelligence,* it is the same Divine Reality that is known.

It is easy to respond to this. The deduced truth enunciates a judgment concerning the same Divine Reality, *ut res est, concedo; ut obiectum est, nego* [as He is a reality *as such,* I concede the point; as He is an object of knowledge, I deny it],[40] according to the classic distinction explained well by Cajetan in his Commentary on *ST* I, q. 1, a. 3, no. 5.

One and the same Divine Reality is an *object* of many specifically distinct *habitus:* the light of glory, faith, theology, and metaphysics. For all the more reason, *one and the same Divine Reality* corresponds to *many truths.* Some of these truths are *revealed,* while others are *deduced* from the preceding. (*Verum est formaliter in mente, ut conformitas iudicii cum re.* [Truth is formally in the mind, as the conformity of its judgment with reality.]) And for a human intellect, inasmuch as it does not see God, there are *many truths* relative *to the same Divine Reality.* Only God forms one single truth concerning Himself.

Still, one adds: "Two propositions concerning the same subject and *really identical predicates* have a *really identical sense.*" For example: the soul is spiritual and the soul is immortal. Or again: God is intelligent and God is free, for there is not a real distinction between the divine attributes.[41]

This would mean that, precisely because they are not *really distinct,* the *divine attributes* have THE SAME SENSE, OR, IN OTHER WORDS, ARE SYNONYMS. Now, this is a nominalist thesis refuted by St. Thomas in *ST* I, q. 13, a. 4. It would follow, as the nominalists say, that one could say, "God punishes through mercy and pardons through justice." One would thus arrive at agnosticism.

It sometimes happens, as in the present case, that while believing oneself to combat the nominalist position, and by insisting upon the

---

39. Marín-Sola, *L'évolution homogene du dogme catholique,* vol. 2, pp. 332ff.
40. **TRANSLATOR'S NOTE:** On this distinction, one should consult Garrigou-Lagrange, *Sense of Mystery,* pp. 126–27, n. 9, pp. 135–39.
41. Thus speaks Fr. Marín-Sola, *Evolution homogène du dogme catholique,* vol. 2, p. 333.

divine reality in which the divine attributes are identified, one ends up in this form of nominalism, holding that *all the divine names are synonyms*, being only verbally distinct. From this perspective, divine justice and mercy would be no more distinct than *Tullius* and *Cicero*, and just as everywhere that the term *Tullius* is written, one could just as well write *Cicero*, so too everywhere that the term *justice* is written, one could just as well write *mercy*. In-depth investigation into these question of speculative theology is manifestly of great importance in all these problems.

However, it is further insisted[42]: In order for an assertion to be defined as a dogma, it suffices that it be revealed *actu implicite*. Now, each divine attribute is contained *actu implicite* in the divine nature conceived as Subsistent Being, as well as in each of the other attributes. Therefore [every divine attribute is revealed and thus can be defined as a dogma.]

In accord with what we have said, we must respond by making a distinction in the claim that in order for an assertion to be defined as a dogma, it suffices that it be revealed *actu implicite*. *I concede* that this is true, on the condition that the truth in question is *the same truth* as the one which is revealed. However, *I deny* that this holds even if it is a *new truth that has been deduced.*[43] Now, *I deny* that each divine attribute is contained *actu implicite* in the divine nature and in every other attribute, as *the same truth*. However, *I concede* that they are there as *another, deduced truth.*

Indeed, I concede that a given divine attribute is contained in the divine nature *actu implicite* by reason of the divine reality *ut res est*. However, I make a sub-distinction regarding the claim that there would be *the same truth* as an object of knowledge [*ratione obiecti*]. I concede the point for the case of the divine intellect and that of the intellects of the blessed. However, I deny that it would be the same truth for our intellect [in our current wayfaring state].[44]

---

42.   Ibid., pp. 342ff.

43.   Fr. Marín-Sola himself recognizes this, in ibid., p. 333.

44.   **TRANSLATOR'S NOTE:** Although I have kept some of the scholastic form above, including *nego* and *concedo*, this text required translation, for Fr. Garrigou-Lagrange slipped into Latin after beginning of the first French sentence.

Otherwise, all the divine names would be synonyms, and we would need to say: The two statements, "God is just," and "God is merciful," both enunciate the same truth. They enunciate *two truths concerning the same divine reality.*[45] Indeed, truth is formally in the mind. It is the conformity of its judgment with reality. Now, we are here not concerned with the divine mind, nor that of the blessed, but rather with our intellect, in relation to which one speaks of *revealed truths* and *other truths deduced* from the preceding. This is contrary to theologism, which would give, in a way that is similar to philosophism, too much importance to an acquired science[46]; however, this shows, along with the superiority of infused faith, the immense value of *revealed truth.*

---

45. When one says, "In God, justice is mercy," it is true as a *material*, not a *formal*, *attribution or predication.*

46. Between infused faith and acquired theology, there is homogeneity that is not specific but quasi-generic; these are two *habitus* that are specifically distinct by their double formal object (*quod* and *quo*), the *theological habitus* has its root in infused faith, even though it is itself acquired, "acquiritur studio humano."

INDEX

CLUNY MEDIA

Designed by Fiona Cecile Clarke, the CLUNY MEDIA *logo
depicts a monk at work in the scriptorium,
with a cat sitting at his feet.*

*The monk represents our mission to emulate
the invaluable contributions of the monks
of Cluny in preserving the libraries of the West,
our strivings to know and love the truth.*

*The cat at the monk's feet is Pangur Bán, from the
eponymous Irish poem of the 9th century.
The anonymous poet compares his scholarly
pursuit of truth with the cat's happy hunting of mice.
The depiction of Pangur Bán is an homage to the work
of the monks of Irish monasteries and a sign
of the joy we at Cluny take in our trade.*

"Messe ocus Pangur Bán,
cechtar nathar fria saindan:
bíth a menmasam fri seilgg,
mu memna céin im saincheirdd."

Printed in Great Britain
by Amazon

76427157R00271